WITHDRAWN

# Soviet Foreign Policy
## Since World War II:.
## Imperial and Global

**ALVIN Z. RUBINSTEIN**

*Department of Political Science*
*University of Pennsylvania*

**WINTHROP PUBLISHERS, INC.**

*Cambridge, Massachusetts*

*Library of Congress Cataloging in Publication Data*

Rubinstein, Alvin Z.
    Soviet foreign policy since World War II.

    Includes bibliographies and index.
    1. Russia—Foreign relations—1945–
I. Title.
DK267.R76        327.47        80-23072
ISBN 0-87626-809-2 (paperback)
ISBN 0-87626-810-6 (case)

*This book is dedicated to*
RUDA FRANKIE

© 1981 by Winthrop Publishers, Inc.
    17 Dunster Street, Cambridge, Massachusetts 02138

10  9  8  7  6  5  4  3  2  1

# Contents

# Preface

Soviet foreign policy has weathered crises and catastrophes, persisted, and flourished. Lenin, Stalin, and Khrushchev are long since dead, their roles in developing the Soviet system and Soviet foreign policy only dimly known by a Western generation now coming to political maturity. As a new group of leaders prepares to assume power in the Soviet Union, Brezhnev himself is on the threshold of becoming more a historical than a political figure. Because of the power of the Soviet Union, what the future oligarchs do in the world arena will have far-reaching consequences for the stability and security of Western civilization.

This book is intended to provide a concise, comprehensive account of the evolution, aims, and impact of Soviet foreign policy, primarily in the period since 1945; to bring coherence to complexity; to identify continuity and change; and to establish a foundation for in-depth exploration of the rich specialized literature that has been published over the past generation. For those who follow the vicissitudes of Soviet policy, the past is part of the present and contributes to speculations about the future. Hopefully, this volume will give the neophyte this needed perspective. The approach is eclectic, historical, policy-oriented, and analytical. It focuses on the USSR's actual behavior and on the external consequences of its policies, and not on the possible motivations and decisional inputs that produced the behavior. It pleads no theory, no fashionable model. A work of synthesis, this study draws freely on the storehouse of knowledge created by scholars, whose major works are cited in the bibliographies at the end of each chapter, and to whom I am indebted.

Inevitably, interpretative evaluations have been made, where it is not feasible to examine in detail the domestic determinants of policy and all the possible options available to Soviet leaders at any crucial period. No doubt policy differences and conflicting perceptions of unfolding situations exist; yet, once a policy is adopted, it acquires a life of its own and is the proper unit for examination. I have tried to sift fact from conjecture and to keep the analysis or "guesstimates" as dispassionate as possible. Throughout, I have attempted to draw attention to the concrete and specific issues that faced Soviet leaders at different times, to enable the reader to formulate an evaluation of the situation and gain an understanding of international politics. The term "communist" not "socialist" is used to describe the Soviet Union and the Soviet-dominated regimes or bloc in Eastern Europe, because the ruling political organization is the "communist party," the leaders call themselves "communists," and the ideology of Marxism-Leninism is differentiated from other varieties of socialism. Also, Moscow prefers the term "socialist" in its relations with non-communist countries and individuals, because the term has universal appeal and far fewer sinister connotations.

Grateful acknowledgement is made to the following publishers for their permission to use parts of my work which appeared in their publications: Random House, Inc.; Westview Press; *The World Today,* a monthly journal issued under the auspices of the Royal Institute of International Affairs; *Optima,* a review published by the Anglo-American Corporation of Dr Beers and Charter Consolidated Groups of Companies; and *Orbis,* a quarterly journal of the Foreign Policy Research Institute. I wish also to thank the Center for Advanced Studies at the University of Virginia for handling the typing of the final manuscript.

ALVIN Z. RUBINSTEIN

*Bryn Mawr, Pennsylvania*

# 1
# The Beleaguered Soviet State, 1917–1939

When the Bolsheviks seized power in Russia on November 7, 1917, they faced challenges for which their experiences as underground revolutionaries and exiled members of an obscure political movement had not prepared them. During their early days they were absorbed with consolidating the regime and had no real understanding of the nature of foreign policy. Leon Trotsky, in his autobiography, comments on the prevailing naiveté: the expectation was, he states, that upon assuming the position of commissar of foreign affairs, "I will issue a few revolutionary proclamations to the peoples of the world and then shut up shop."

Burdened with the czarist legacy of a dispirited, disorganized army, a population weary of war, and an internal order on the brink of collapse, the Bolsheviks considered that their first task in foreign policy was to take Russia out of the "imperialist" First World War. "Peace, bread, and land" had been a compelling slogan in their mobilization of popular support. The promise of peace represented a major political commitment, one that they neither dared nor desired to break. Furthermore, since they viewed World War I as an imperialist war started by rival capitalists seeking to redivide the world, they rejected traditional norms of international law and diplomacy as alien to a proletarian state. Accordingly, on November 8, the Bolsheviks issued the Decree of Peace, proposing "to all warring peoples and their Governments to begin immediately negotiations for a just and democratic peace," which they defined as "an immediate peace without annexations and without indemnities," They proclaimed the abolition of secret diplomacy and the firm intention "to carry on all negotiations absolutely openly before all the people" and to publish in full the secret treaties of the preceding czarist government.

1

An appeal directed as much to the peoples and governments of Western Europe as to the people of Russia, the decree was the first use by the Bolsheviks of what was later to be known as "demonstrative diplomacy," which George F. Kennan described as "diplomacy designed not to promote freely accepted and mutually profitable agreement as between governments, but rather to embarrass other governments and stir up opposition among their own peoples."[1]

The first step toward taking Russia out of the imperialist war was the preliminary armistice agreement signed with the Central Powers at Brest-Litovsk on December 15, 1917. At the time, some of the Bolsheviks balked at the Germans' insistence upon detaching those parts of the Russian empire then under German control, notably parts of Lithuania, Poland, and the Ukraine. They procrastinated in expectation of the coming revolution in Germany. Remember: these revolutionaries, who had emerged so suddenly from obscurity, lacked any experience in foreign affairs and shared an outlook that believed that world revolution was imminent, that the success of the revolution in Russia depended upon the spread of the revolution to highly industrialized Germany, and that all capitalist states were committed to the destruction of the newborn socialist state.

The Bolsheviks' unorthodox delaying tactics at the Brest-Litovsk negotiations irritated the Germans, who were eager for a speedy conclusion of peace. Only then could they transfer the bulk of their formidable army from the eastern front to the West and hope to knock out the Allies before significant American reinforcements arrived. The impatient German military commander, Major-General Max von Hoffmann, presented Trotsky with alternatives: sign a peace treaty on German terms or face an immediate resumption of the German offensive.

Trotsky, the chief Russian negotiator and the commissar for foreign affairs, returned to Petrograd (later renamed Leningrad) on January 19, 1918, to consult with party leaders. He found that the recently elected and convened Constituent Assembly had been dissolved and that the Bolsheviks had assumed absolute power. Russia's brief flirtation with democracy, epitomized by the free elections held at the end of November 1917, had ended.

## Lenin's First Foreign Policy Crisis

Now began the first momentous debate on foreign policy. The Bolsheviks had to face up to the realities of an international system of which they were inextricably a part. They had hitherto assumed that after appropriate agitation and propaganda, the German troops would revolt against their imperialist masters, thereby sparking a revolution that would spread to the rest of Europe. As committed (and still doctrinaire) Marxists, they believed that the loyalty of the proletariat of all countries was to class, not country. Despite this, and despite Lenin's espousal in the years before he came to power of the principle of national self-determination, their own nationalistic sentiments impelled them to oppose a peace with Germany that would require the dismantling of the Russian empire and the granting of independence to non-Russian peoples. At heart, most Bolsheviks remained attached to their czarist patrimony. The onrushing German advance confronted them with serious dilemmas and stark options.

Ever the realist and tactician, Lenin argued that a revolutionary outlook was not incompatible with realpolitik. He insisted that the preservation of the revolution (that is, the Bolshevik retention of political power) must outweigh all other considerations; that for the immediate future, at least, the interests of world revolution and the international proletariat must be subordinated to the task of consolidating the new Soviet state; and indeed, that the best way to ensure the eventual success of world revolution was first to safeguard and strengthen the socialist state in Russia. This had to take precedence over all else, including the waging of a revolutionary war which, in any event, the Russian army was absolutely in no condition to undertake. Therefore, Lenin called for an immediate end to hostilities in his brilliant exposition, "Theses on the Question of the Immediate Conclusion of a Separate and Annexationist Peace" (January 20, 1918).

Long-held and deeply felt beliefs were, however, difficult to shed. Those in the Central Committee who opposed Lenin's harsh decision hoped to prolong the negotiations and give time for the revolution to spread. They adopted Trotsky's formula of "no war, no peace," but agreed that should the Germans resume their advance, a peace treaty would be signed. Lenin felt that delay would be costly, but reluctantly concurred, adding facetiously that "for the sake of a good peace with Trotsky, Latvia and Estonia are worth losing."

On January 30, 1918, Trotsky returned to Brest-Litovsk. He found the Germans in a far less patient mood and in the process of recognizing as spokesman for the Ukraine a splinter anti-Bolshevik group, with whom they signed a separate peace treaty on February 9, thereby obtaining badly needed grain and raw materials.

On February 18, the Central Powers launched a general offensive and advanced rapidly against virtually nonexistent Russian resistance. In Petrograd the Central Committee hurriedly convened and, after some heated discussion, voted to sue for peace, as the Germans rolled onward. (In March the Bolsheviks moved the capital to Moscow and renamed themselves the Communist party.) Lacking any alternative, the Bolsheviks quit the war. On March 15, 1918, Soviet leaders ratified the "Carthaginian" peace with the Central Powers and agreed to the loss of a third of Russia's population, cultivated land, and industry.

The Brest-Litovsk crisis served as a crucible from which emerged the outlines of a foreign policy. First, Soviet leaders recognized that military weakness left them prey to foreign attack and increased the likelihood of their deposition. Second, the absence of expected revolutions in Germany and Western Europe meant that they could not depend on world revolution to strengthen the socialist revolution in Russia; therefore, though continuing to anticipate world revolution as the only ultimate security, they undertook the creation of a Red Army to provide for their short-term safety. Finally, the policies both of the Central Powers and of the Entente buttressed their conviction (held to this day) that the capitalist world, irrespective of its internal rivalries, was basically hostile and would undermine the Communist regime if it could. Only world revolution could guarantee the success of the socialist revolution in Russia; yet the success of socialism in the new Soviet state was deemed a prerequisite for the advancement of world revolution. Thus Soviet leaders identified their own political survival with the good of the international proletariat. This dualism — the furthering of revolution abroad and the quest for national security — has remained a salient feature of Soviet foreign policy.

## War Communism

The assumption concerning capitalist hostility was ominously confirmed by the Allied intervention, which started with the landing of Japanese troops at Vladivostok on April 5, 1918. Before it ended, British, French, American, and Japanese troops would be involved, a bitter all-out civil war would run its course, and communism would be entrenched in Russia. Confused and contradictory motives prompted the halfhearted, inept intervention in Russia's internal turmoil: the Japanese sought to carve out a sphere of influence from Russia's Far Eastern territories; the Americans wanted to check Japanese ambitions; the British landed at Murmansk to prevent the Germans from capturing stores of arms. The Western powers sought to use Czech and Slovak troops, who had originally been part of the Austro-Hungarian armies that were taken prisoner and then, when the Bolsheviks left the war, were freed and transported across Siberia for shipment to the Western front. These troops became pawns in Western efforts to weaken the Bolsheviks and encourage anti-Bolshevik forces. Allied strategists hoped in unspecified fashion to re-create an eastern front against the Germans.

Whatever military rationale the intervention originally had was no longer valid when World War I ended on November 11, 1918, but growing British and French commitments to anti-Bolshevik forces, American inertia, and Japanese persistence precluded any immediate disengagement. Fear of bolshevism's spread to the rest of Europe, French resentment over the Bolshevik repudiation of the prewar czarist debts, and the influence of émigré and pro-White groups in Western capitals all hardened the hostility of the interventionists, who sought, in Winston S. Churchill's words, "to strangle the infant bolshevism in its cradle."

On November 13, 1918, the Soviet government abrogated the Brest-Litovsk treaty, declaring its provisions null and void. During the autumn and winter, a Red Army was conscripted, trained, and toughened for battle. Under Trotsky's driving leadership, it proved superior to the smorgasbord of armies and leaders that comprised the opposition, the White Guard counterrevolutionaries. A centralized military command, a compact geographical base and internal lines of communication, effective appeals to patriotism against foreign armies, and the inability of the Whites to coordinate their military activities or agree on a common political program worked to the Bolsheviks' benefit. In addition, the Bolshevik promise of national self-determination, including the right of secession, induced nationalists in Armenia, Georgia, and central Asia to resist attempts by the White armies to reimpose Russian domination. However, once the civil war was won, the Communists proceeded to reincorporate the non-Russian nationalities in the Caucasus and central Asia into the Soviet state and suppress all separatist movements.

The year 1919 was crucial. At Versailles, a treaty was summarily handed to the Germans, and with it were sown the seeds of the next war in a Europe that did not realize the extent to which it had been weakened. In Germany, revolution met defeat at the hands of the military, and the fledgling Weimar Republic started its tragic, short life. In America, Wilson's dream of a League of Nations was defeated in the Senate and soon gave way to a "return to normalcy" — a phrase symbolizing America's abdication of international responsibility for two decades. The "Balkanized" area of central and southeastern Europe (the consequence of the collapse of the Austro-Hungarian empire) had not yet been linked with France in the unstable network of military alliances that was to give the French an illusion of security; in Paris fear of bolshevism dominated French policy, and émigré Russians pushed for all-out war against the Bolsheviks. And in Russia, after the excesses and suffering of "war communism," as the period is called in the Soviet Union, bolshevism emerged victorious. The Allies, forced to compromise by the unwillingness of their armies to fight in Russia in a struggle they did not understand, reluctantly abandoned their interventionist adventures.

In his military weakness Lenin relied heavily on the power of ideas and propaganda to defeat his enemies. Indeed, he was the first revolutionary in the twentieth century to sense the political potency of the mass media. In March 1919, at an ebb in Soviet fortunes, he established the Communist International (Comintern), nominally to further world revolution but actually to serve the interests of the Soviet state. Specifically, through a network of foreign Communist parties, the Comintern agitated against the Allied intervention and anti-Soviet activity by capitalist governments. The weapons it used to defend the weak Soviet state were revolutionary propaganda, labor strife, protest movements, and subversion. Soviet leaders probed the antagonisms within the capitalist world, not only between the great and lesser powers but also within the individual countries themselves; and they capitalized on the conciliatory, frequently sympathetic attitudes of bourgeois intellectuals toward the Soviet Union. In Lenin's words, "Our policy is to use the differences of the imperialist powers in order to make agreement [between them] difficult or to make such agreement temporarily impossible."* This was done with increasing skill through the pen and the podium.

At the second congress of the Comintern in August 1920, a high degree of centralization and discipline was introduced. The Comintern adapted its structure and operating procedures to that of the Communist party of the Soviet Union (CPSU). The twenty-one conditions for membership made certain that the Comintern would, in fact, be "a single Communist party having branches in different countries." Moscow laid down the fundamentals of policy on all significant questions and disseminated them through the worldwide system of pro-Soviet Communist parties, whose subservience to the Soviet Union became total in the Stalin period. Unconventional diplomacy, epitomized by the Comintern, was adopted as a characteristic feature of Soviet foreign policy; it included the establishment and manipulation of political front organizations in order to weaken the anti-Soviet policies of capitalist governments, the support for revolutionary movements abroad, the use of mass media and propaganda, the recruitment of disaffected foreigners to serve the Soviet state, the use of cultural and commercial organizations for espionage, the formenting of social and political unrest, and the concomitant promotion of normal government-to-government relations at one level and subversion at another. Developed as an arm of Soviet diplomacy in a period of military weakness, these techniques have been perfected, richly financed, and often skillfully utilized through the decades of growing Soviet power.

---

* V. I. Lenin, *Sochinenia,* 2nd ed. (Moscow: State Publishing House, 1930), Vol. XXVI, pp. 8–14, excerpts. From a report presented by Lenin to the Eighth Congress of Soviets of the RSFSR on December 21, 1920.

By the fall of 1920 the Soviet leadership had surmounted the foreign intervention and triumphed in the civil war. They had proven equal to the trials of war communism. Their belief in the continuing hostility of the capitalist world led to expectation of another intervention and stimulated efforts to exploit the existing international system in the quest for security.

## Adaptation and Accommodation

The pariah Soviet state also utilized conventional diplomacy to coexist with the capitalist states. While insisting upon the need for military preparedness in the expectation of a future military intervention, Lenin pioneered coexistence with the capitalists "to utilize the differences between them in order to make it difficult for them to unite" against the Soviet Union. He needed time to consolidate Communist rule. The economy was in shambles, unrest was growing in the countryside, food shortages and industrial bottlenecks were endemic, and a revolt at Kronstadt in March 1921 by naval cadres (who had been stalwarts of the revolution) all militated for a breathing spell. Moreover, by 1921 the revolutionary mood in Europe had subsided and capitalism had entered a period of stabilization. The Allied powers, too, needed to tend to domestic matters and lifted the blockade of Russia, after reaching agreements on the repatriation of prisoners of war and on trade.

To promote Russia's economic recovery, Lenin instituted the New Economic Policy (NEP). This gave the peasants monetary incentives to produce, allowed a revival of free enterprise for small firms, and relaxed governmental controls on the economy; it also welcomed foreign capital and encouraged trade with capitalist countries, as much for political as for economic reasons. Lenin sought to strengthen the Soviet state and safeguard it from a feared coalition of capitalist powers bent on its overthrow. In the diplomatic field, the end of isolation was a key objective. This was accomplished first in Europe, then in Asia.

The Anglo-Soviet trade agreement of March 16, 1921, was an important step toward the Soviets' gaining acceptance internationally, as was Moscow's acceptance of the country's new frontiers (see map) which involved the loss of Finland, Estonia, Latvia, Lithuania, eastern Poland, Bessarabia, and Kars and Ardahan (to Turkey). But the momentous development was the agreement with Germany in April 1922, ending the isolation of the two outcasts of Europe. Russia and Germany had been invited to the Genoa economic conference called by British Prime Minister Lloyd George in an effort to stimulate Europe's economic recovery. On Easter Sunday, April 16, 1922, the Soviet and German foreign ministers — Georgii V. Chicherin (1918–1929) and Walther Rathenau — met at

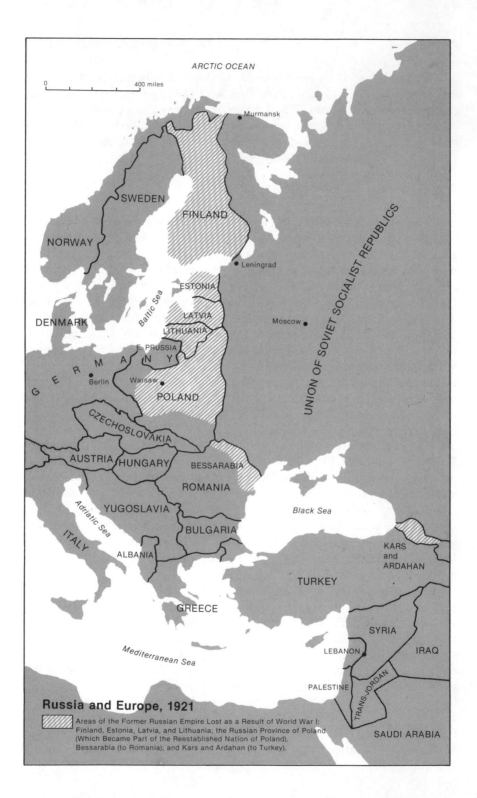

ARCTIC OCEAN

0        400 miles

Murmansk

SWEDEN

NORWAY

FINLAND

Leningrad

ESTONIA

Baltic Sea

LATVIA

DENMARK

LITHUANIA

Moscow

E. PRUSSIA

G E R M A N Y

Berlin

Warsaw

POLAND

UNION OF SOVIET SOCIALIST REPUBLICS

CZECHOSLOVAKIA

AUSTRIA  HUNGARY

BESSARABIA

ROMANIA

YUGOSLAVIA

Adriatic Sea

Black Sea

ITALY

BULGARIA

KARS
and
ARDAHAN

ALBANIA

TURKEY

GREECE

SYRIA

Mediterranean Sea

LEBANON

IRAQ

PALESTINE

TRANS-JORDAN

SAUDI ARABIA

**Russia and Europe, 1921**

Areas of the Former Russian Empire Lost as a Result of World War I:
Finland, Estonia, Latvia, and Lithuania; the Russian Province of Poland
(Which Became Part of the Reestablished Nation of Poland),
Bessarabia (to Romania); and Kars and Ardahan (to Turkey).

Rapallo, near Genoa, and signed an agreement. The rapprochement was the first significant diplomatic triumph achieved by the Soviets through traditional norms of bourgeois diplomacy and power politics. It immeasurably enhanced the bargaining position of each country. For Britain and France, though they were not then aware of it, it signified the end of political preeminence on the continent of Europe.

The Treaty of Rapallo brought the Soviet Union de jure recognition from Germany — the first major country to grant it. There was a mutual cancellation of existing financial claims, an expansion of trade, and the extension of German credits. Rapallo also promoted important secret cooperation between the Soviet and German high commands. By permitting the Germans (who were forbidden by the Versailles treaty to develop a strong army) to conduct tank and air maneuvers on Soviet soil, the Soviets learned a great deal about modern warfare and benefited from the construction of advanced armaments factories. Until the rise of Hitler in 1933, the German connection was preeminent to Moscow. It enabled the Soviet Union to end its isolation, forestall the feared coalition of capitalist countries, and maintain close contact with Europe's most important proletariat.

The essentials of Soviet foreign policy emerged clearly in Lenin's time: the primacy of the preservation of the Soviet state over revolutionary aspirations; the courtship of Germany; the normalization of relations with all capitalist countries and promotion of "peaceful coexistence" as a norm for Soviet behavior; the establishment of correct relations and nonaggression pacts with the bordering Baltic and East European countries that had previously been wholly or partially subdivisions of the czarist empire; the quest for close ties with China to counter Japanese expansion against the USSR and its client state, Mongolia; and finally, the use of the Comintern and other nongovernmental organizations to manipulate public opinion in support of Soviet policies and foment trouble in capitalist and colonial countries.

In the succession struggle that followed Lenin's death on January 21, 1924, and brought Stalin absolute power, differences over foreign policy played a decidedly minor role. In the ensuing years, foreign policy was primarily a function of domestic politics. Intent on consolidating his power, Stalin courted the new elites — who were weary of war and eager to benefit from their status and position — by disclaiming interest in world revolution and stressing the construction of "socialism in one country." National, not international, priorities predominated.

The two major foreign-policy setbacks that Moscow experienced in the 1924-to-1930 period were in its relations with Britain and China and were the result of developments in the internal affairs of these countries. In Britain, the Labour party — which had established full diplomatic relations with the Soviet Union in January 1924 — fell in elections in late October, on the heels of a "Red scare" that was triggered by publication of a letter allegedly signed by Grigorii Zinoviev, the head of the Comintern, but which has since been proven to be a forgery concocted by a group of anti-Soviet émigrés. The Zinoviev letter called on the British Communist party to intensify its revolutionary activity and infiltration of British army units. The Conservative government severed diplomatic relations, and not until 1930 did British-Soviet relations again move onto a normal track.

In China, too, Moscow's position was abruptly shaken as a consequence of domestic turnabouts that were not directly attributable to Soviet policy, though in both the British and Chinese cases, the Comintern's espousal of world revolution and undoubted intrigues created a climate of suspicion that undercut Moscow's efforts to promote better relations on a government-to-government level. The result was cynical disbelief in Moscow's policy of peace, which included signing, on August 27, 1928, the Kellogg-Briand Pact which outlawed war as an instrument of national policy, supporting the League of Nations' efforts to promote disarmament, and concluding treaties of nonaggression with Poland, Romania, and Estonia. These measures were inadequate to overcome the widespread antipathy that was felt everywhere in official circles in Europe. As a consequence, the great powers ignored Russia's traditional interests in Eastern Europe, and all major steps affecting the area in the interwar period were taken without Soviet participation. Stalin was to reverse this exclusionist policy in 1939, with far-reaching results for all of Europe.

In the 1920s no immediate threat to Soviet security was posed by any neighboring state in Europe, but the Soviet Union did have reason to fear a powerful and expansionist Japan. Japanese intervention in the Russian civil war and their attempt to detach the Maritime Province (containing the vital port of Vladivostok) had failed, largely because of Western pressure. Japan was induced to withdraw its troops at the Washington naval disarmament conference (November 12, 1921, to February 6, 1922). In a twist of irony — for which history is often noted — the Soviet Union, though not invited despite its protest that as a Far Eastern power it should have a voice in matters affecting regional security, was the principal beneficiary. Thanks to the Japanese withdrawal, in November 1922 Moscow greatly improved its military position vis-à-vis the Japanese by reincorporating Vladivostok and the puppet Far Eastern Republic, which it had created in eastern Siberia in April 1920 to serve as a buffer separating the weak Soviet state from the expansionist Japanese.

To the south, China loomed large in Soviet thinking. The ripening revolutionary situation, a desire to see Japan exhaust herself in expansion against China, and harassment from anti-Soviet forces operating in adjacent Manchuria, Outer Mongolia, and Xinjiang (Sinkiang) — areas nominally part of China but long vulnerable to Russian influence — heightened Soviet interest. In the early years when its military weakness was most evident, the Soviet state had disclaimed any desire for special privileges in China. For example, the Karakhan Declaration of 1919 renounced all former czarist spheres of influence in Manchuria and the Chinese Eastern Railroad (CER), the trunk line across northern Manchuria that connected with the Trans-Siberian line to Vladivostok and extended down to Port Arthur at the tip of the Liaotung Peninsula. But as the USSR's military position improved, such idealistic manifestos were superseded by a quest for the very same kind of concrete privileges enjoyed by the preceding czarist regime.

From the first Moscow wanted diplomatic recognition from the internationally recognized but weak government in Beijing (Peking); every revolutionary regime seeks legitimacy as much to cripple counterrevolutionary elements as to entrench its own power. But the Beijing regime was pro-Japanese and until 1924 refused to deal with the Soviet Union. Elsewhere in China, the absence of a strong central government magnified the regional power of local warlords, who were generally hostile to Moscow and therefore poor prospects for Soviet infiltration. Particularly worrying was the anti-Soviet activity in Manchuria, which was ruled by Marshal Chang Tso-lin, who followed a pro-Japanese policy until 1928.

Frustrated in these directions, Moscow in 1921 made contact through the Comintern with Dr. Sun Yat-sen, the founder of the revolutionary Kuomintang (KMT) party, who had established a political base in Canton, in the south of China. It was through the Comintern that Moscow supported Sun's aim of overthrowing the very same government in Beijing from which the Soviet government was seeking diplomatic recognition. In this way conventional Soviet diplomacy and unconventional Comintern activity pursued common goals by different routes.

By supporting the KMT, Moscow aligned itself with an emerging revolutionary movement and hoped to weaken the Japanese position in China. For the first time it began cooperating with a bourgeois nationalist leadership, in accordance with a policy laid down by Lenin at the 1920 Comintern congress. Under this approach, when "imperialism" (in this instance, Japan) was the main threat, cooperation with a progressive stratum (defined by its readiness to work with the Soviet Union and local Communists) of capitalism was justifiable. Under the agreement entered into by Sun Yat-sen and Comintern representative A. A. Joffe in January 1923, both signatories acknowledged that China was not ripe for communism, that its "most pressing problems are the completion of national unification and the attainment of full national independence," and that final disposition of the Chinese Eastern Railroad (the key to control of Manchuria) and Outer Mongolia would be postponed.[2]

The Sun-Joffe agreement was the centerpiece of Soviet policy in China until 1927. Comintern advisers flocked to aid the Kuomintang: General Vasily K. Blucher helped found the Whampoa Military Academy outside Canton, and Michael Borodin, the most important of all the Comintern agents in China, reorganized the KMT along the lines of the CPSU. (Both men were executed by Stalin during the purges of 1937–1938.) The agreement was also instrumental in persuading the Chinese Communist party (CCP), which was created with Comintern support in 1921, to subordinate immediate prospects for power by joining the KMT in 1923, albeit under conditions that permitted the CCP to retain its identity as a party within a party.

In May 1924, three months after London had granted the USSR diplomatic recognition, Beijing followed suit. The weak Chinese government, desperate for any help it could get, made far-reaching concessions to the Soviet Union. Not only did Moscow keep ownership of the Chinese Eastern Railroad and retain its special position in Manchuria, but it also secured Beijing's recognition of autonomy for Outer Mongolia, whose actual status since 1921 had been that of Soviet satellite. The consolidation of control over Mongolia (and Xinjiang province) and reaffirmation of privileges in Manchuria were another example of Moscow's familiar amalgam of security considerations and imperialist ambitions.

Three years later Soviet policy and prospects in China suffered a series of sharp setbacks. Sun Yat-sen died in March 1925 and was succeeded by Chiang Kai-shek, who felt strong enough by March 1926, because of Comintern assistance in training his troops, to launch his northern expedition to unify China under the KMT. Within a year, sweeping all before him, Chiang turned on the Communists and improved relations with the Western powers, seeing in them a more lucrative source of assistance against Japan and for China's economic development. Stalin finally broke off relations with Chiang in late 1927, but Soviet policy was not without some lasting benefit: though Chiang was ideologically hostile to Moscow, he was a nationalist whose anti-Japanese position came to be a basis for Sino-Soviet cooperation after Japan invaded Manchuria in September 1931.

Strained relations with Great Britain and the disappointments in China and elsewhere in Asia (that is, in Indonesia, India, Japan, and French Indochina) made the Soviets more insecure than ever. Internally they intensified the drive to develop "socialism in one country," introducing five-year plans for accelerated industrial growth. International events continued to be interpreted within the Marxist-Leninist mode of analysis, but Moscow's behavior generally accorded with more traditional norms of balance-of-power considerations and alignments against the main enemies of the moment; its policy was primarily reactive.

At the diplomatic level, in 1928 Stalin followed a cautious foreign policy, but at the same time he set the Comintern on an ultrarevolutionary tack. At its sixth congress in September, the Comintern enunciated guiding principles for foreign Communist parties; specifically, it held that (1) the Soviet Union was the citadel of world revolution — "She is the international driving force of proletarian revolution that impels the proletariat of all countries to seize power. . . she is the prototype of the fraternity of nationalities in all lands . . . that the world proletariat must establish when it has captured political power";* (2) the preservation of the Soviet Union must be the primary concern of the international proletariat — ""In the event of the imperialist states declaring war upon and attacking the USSR, the international proletariat must retaliate by organizing bold and determined mass action and struggle for the overthrow of the imperialist governments"; and (3) all Communist parties owed exclusive allegiance to Moscow. These principles were to be at the heart of the cleavages that beset the Communist world in the period after World War II when national communism and Eurocommunism became prominent political phenomena.

In the 1930s, Moscow faced serious threats to its security in Europe and the Far East. It maneuvered as best it could in an international system in which the significant decisions were made in Berlin, London, Paris, and Tokyo. Not until the spring of 1939 did Moscow become an important actor.

Like Lenin, Stalin preferred alignment with Germany, rather than Britain or France. Rapallo was insurance against the gnawing fear of a capitalist coalition's mounting another intervention; it provided much-needed economic and military assistance, and it forestalled isolation. The renewal of the Berlin treaty in 1931 signified continuation of the special Soviet-German relationship. Stalin saw no reason to heed the warnings of his exiled archopponent, Trotsky, about the rising danger from fascism (he had Trotsky murdered in Mexico in 1940). In keeping with the hard line that he had imposed on the Comintern in 1928, Stalin identified the social democrats, not the Nazis, as the main enemy of international communism, and actually contributed to Hitler's rise to power in early 1933 and to the consequent destruction of the German Communist party. Despite Hitler's public diatribes against the Communist menace, Stalin hoped that Germany and the USSR could do business. Machiavelli, not Marx, inspired Stalin's foreign policy.

---

* The Comintern's 1928 Program, as quoted in the U.S. Congress, House Committee on Foreign Affairs, *The Strategy and Tactics of World Communism,* 80th Cong., 2nd sess. (1948) H. Doc. 619, pp. 121–40, excerpts.

## The Quest For Security

By late 1933, Foreign Minister Maxim Litvinov (1929–1939) hinted at Moscow's disenchantment with Hitler and interest in closer ties with the West. If Germany was hostile, then Moscow would court France. At all costs, Stalin worked to prevent any German-French understanding that would neutralize France and give Germany the green light to expand to the east. Faced with growing Nazi hostility and rejection of Rapallo, Moscow accepted the French-sponsored invitation and on September 18, 1934, joined the League of Nations, where it became the leading exponent of collective security. Time and again the USSR called upon the League of Nations to resist aggression in Ethiopia, in Spain, in China, in Austria, in Czechoslovakia — to no avail.

Moscow's bilateral relationship with France foundered on a profound mutual suspicion of each other's motives and an ideological antipathy that blinded each to the common danger they faced. The two countries signed a treaty of mutual assistance on May 2, 1935, and the USSR signed a similar treaty with Czechoslovakia two weeks later. The purpose was to create an interlocking alliance system; the actual result was to give Stalin flexibility in responding to the German threat. Stalin effectively prevented any Franco-German agreement and avoided isolation in Europe. Under the Soviet-Czechoslovak treaty, the Soviet Union was committed to aiding Czechoslovakia, but only if France first took action in fulfillment of its treaty obligations. France's failure to live up to its commitment to Prague in September 1938 led to the dismemberment of Czechoslovakia, and it freed the USSR from any obligation to act on Czechoslovakia's behalf. However, that time of testing was still in the future.

In 1935, to stiffen the resolve of the Western countries to resist Hitler, Stalin ordered the Comintern to press for a popular front and to cooperate with all bourgeois parties, regardless of past differences, in the creation of this anti-Fascist front. But throughout 1935, 1936, 1937, and 1938, the Western powers gave way before Nazi Germany's relentless pressure, fearful of precipitating a showdown they were ill-prepared for; hoping, ostrichlike, that each concession would be the last, and uneasy over stumbling into a situation that would entail really meaningful cooperation with a Soviet Union they detested and mistrusted. In this sense, ideologically derived perceptions shaped the behavior of Western leaders to a greater extent than they did Soviet policy.

For his part, Stalin continued in secret to put out feelers to Berlin for a new Rapallo-type agreement. He secretly admired Hitler and "appreciated" warnings in early 1937 from the German secret service suggesting that his former chief of staff, Marshal Mikhail Tukhachevsky, was part of a plot to seize power. Stalin was especially appreciative since the allegations against Tukhachevsky had been planted abroad by the NKVD (that is, the KGB) on his orders, "in the hope — perhaps even the knowledge — that they would return to Moscow in a form which could be used to frame" Tukhachevsky and other revolutionary heroes whom Stalin was determined to destroy in order to consolidate his absolute power.[3] A speculation that has less to commend it is that Stalin's purpose was to get rid of all possible opposition to a deal with Hitler, and Tukhachevsky's fear of Nazi Germany and interest in recultivating close links with France were not shared by Stalin. What was paramount for Stalin in 1935 and 1936 was carrying through his revolution from above: he wanted to eliminate all the old Bolsheviks who might oppose the new totalitarian socioeconomic order he was intent on creating. In this he owed more to Peter the Great than to Marx or even Lenin. The purges of the 1930s were intended to leave Stalin undisputed master of the Soviet Union. However, the external threats, which were manipulated as symbols, soon became realities Stalin could not ignore.

By 1938 Nazi Germany was a power to be reckoned with. After a lightning annexation of Austria on March 12, 1938, Hitler turned on Czechoslovakia. His ostensible objective was integration of the predominantly German-speaking Sudetenland region with Germany. Litvinov's repeated calls for "collective actions" to check "the further development of aggression," which now reflected Stalin's growing perception of danger, were ignored. Hitler's threat of war prompted a hurried British-French intercession that led to an agreement with Germany for the dismemberment of Czechoslovakia. The Munich Agreement of September 15 was signed without the participation of the victim or the USSR. The British and French dismissed Soviet expressions of a readiness to act in concert with them as meaningless: the fact that the Red Army had been weakened by purges, the absence of a common border between the USSR and Czechoslovakia, and the unwillingness of either Poland or Romania to grant permission to Soviet troops to pass through its country convinced Paris and London that Moscow was not a credible partner. The fact of the matter was that Britain and France were not ready for war and suspected that Moscow hoped to see them embroiled in a conflict that it would avoid. Suspicion of Moscow ran too deep in the West for political cooperation.

Stalin watched Hitler's success, the West's surrender, and the Soviet Union's growing isolation. Whatever hope he might have had for collective action to stymie Nazi aggression disappeared at Munich. In early March 1939, a few days before Hitler occupied all of Czechoslovakia (contrary to his solemn declaration at Munich that he had no further territorial demands), Stalin delivered a major address to the CPSU's eighteenth party congress. He derided France and Britain for their pusillanimity and Germany and Japan for their aggressive acts, and conveyed his belief that war was inevitable, that the nonaggressive states "draw back and retreat, making concession after concession to the aggressors," and that a new situation was being created which the USSR could not ignore. He did not elaborate on his plans for the future, other than to say that the Soviet Union must be cautious and not allow itself "to be drawn into conflicts by warmongers who are accustomed to have others pull the chestnuts out of the fire for them." The general tenor of his speech was anti-Nazi, but the price for Soviet agreement with either coalition was left open for negotiation. For the first time in its young history, the Soviet leadership was in a strong bargaining position: it could come to terms with Hitler or join with a Britain and France now thoroughly alarmed by Germany's expansionist appetite. Stalin was waiting for the best offer.

Unimpressed by the British government's belated diplomatic activity (essentially a unilateral guarantee to Poland in March 1939), knowing Poland's anti-Soviet attitude and unwillingness to allow any Soviet troops on Polish soil even against the Nazi threat, eager to keep the USSR out of the new "imperialist" war that he sensed was imminent, and very much occupied with containing the Japanese in the Far East, Stalin let Hitler know that he was prepared for a deal. His clearest signal was the replacement on May 3, 1939, of Foreign Minister Litvinov, a Jew, by Vyacheslav M. Molotov (1939–1949, 1953–1956), one of Stalin's closest aides. This move signified the abandonment of efforts to work with the Western powers and the League of Nations — a policy Hitler associated with Litvinov — and the start of active talks with Germany.

The infamous Soviet agreement with Nazi Germany was signed on August 23, 1939. The ten-year nonaggression treaty obligated each party to neutrality in the event that the other became involved in a war with a third power. Actually, it was the green light Hitler needed to make sure that Germany could go to war without worrying about conflict on two fronts. Stalin knew of Hitler's plan to invade Poland, and the last article of the treaty stated that it was to "enter into force as soon as it is signed," an unusual diplomatic provision. Moreover, in a secret protocol (which is never mentioned in Soviet writings on the period), Stalin and Hitler agreed to a division of the spoils: Stalin's booty for signing the pact was eastern Poland, "bounded approximately by the line of the rivers Narew, Vistula, and San," Estonia, Latvia, Finland, and Bessarabia; the rest of Poland and all of Lithuania were allotted to Germany. Stalin's delight at the turn of events may be inferred from the toast he made with the German foreign minister: "I know how much the German people loves its Führer. I should therefore like to drink his health."

One eminent scholar has described the importance of the Nazi-Soviet pact for Stalin as follows:

August 1939 represented the fruition of Stalin's whole complex conception of the means of Soviet survival in a hostile world and emergence into a commanding international position. It embraced the presumption of the inevitability of a great new war: the idea that, through divisive diplomacy in the Lenin tradition, Russia could both help to precipitate the conflict and preserve neutrality during its earlier stages, allowing the combatants to exhaust themselves whilst she grew stronger and stronger; and the notion that at some point Russia would be able to take over territories to which she had historical claim and contiguous countries whose ensuing Soviet-guided revolutions would advance the world-revolutionary cause while creating the 'socialist encirclement' that would give Russia's revolution the still missing guaranteed security.[4]

Stalin looked to the coming war in Western Europe with equanimity. As he viewed the situation, the Soviet Union could sit out the European war, wait for a further weakening of the capitalist world, and prepare for the inevitable revolutionary situation that would offer new opportunities for the spread of Soviet power and the proletarian revolution.

The Nazi-Soviet pact also contributed to Soviet security in the Far East. For Soviet leaders, more than for their czarist counterparts, there has always been a discernible relationship between security in Europe and security in Asia. Fear of attack from both directions had been a Soviet nightmare ever since the Allied intervention of 1918–1920. The threat from Japan in the 1930s, coming as it did at a time when relations with Germany were deteriorating, heightened Moscow's fear of involvement in a two-front war and greatly influenced Stalin's decisions in 1939, a consideration generally given too little attention in Western writings.

After Japan's invasion and occupation of Manchuria in 1931, the main Soviet problem in Asia was determining whether Japan would strike south into China and eventually toward the raw materials of Southeast Asia, or north against Siberia. The ineffectiveness of the League of Nations and the unwillingness of the great powers to do more than protest Japanese aggression exacerbated Moscow's sense of isolation and danger. The threat from Japan brought the Soviet Union and China together again, and relations with Beijing were restored on December 12, 1932, to the detriment of ties with the Chinese Communist party, then experiencing harassment from the KMT.

Moscow's diplomacy was to encourage Chiang Kai-shek to resist Japan and simultaneously to appease Japan and encourage it to expand at China's expense. In this, it practiced the same kind of above-the-counter and below-the-counter diplomacy in the Far East that it did in Europe. On numerous occasions Litvinov proposed a nonaggression pact to Japan; he was repeatedly rebuffed. Japan was interested, however, in purchasing the northern trunk lines of the Manchurian railroad, which were still controlled by the Soviet Union. Negotiations began in Tokyo in June 1933 and continued intermittently for almost two years until, in March 1935, Moscow finally agreed — over bitter Chinese protests — to sell its interests in the railroad and grant fishing concessions in Soviet Far Eastern waters. This appeasement was due in part to concern over secret Japanese-German military talks and to a desire to remove all possible pretexts for a Japanese attack, which the USSR was not then in condition to repel.

The Japanese, satisfied in Manchuria, restlessly probed Soviet determination and defenses farther to the east. In an attempt to discourage Japanese expansion into the Chinese provinces of Jehol and Chabar in Inner Mongolia, Moscow revealed that a mutual defense treaty with the Mongolian People's Republic (MPR) had been signed in March 1936, despite Beijing's claim that the MPR was juridically part of China. Since 1924, Moscow's control over the MPR had been such that it could have annexed the area, but it chose to encourage Mongol separatism from China and use the MPR as a buffer state. By contrast, further to the east, in Xinjiang, where Soviet influence was also preeminent, the USSR did not detach Chinese territory but chose to deal with compliant warlords, possibly because it feared that an independent Turkic-speaking Muslim people's republic in Central Asia might act as a catalyst for separatism in the USSR's own Turkic-speaking subdivisions — the Kazakh, Uzbek, and Kirgiz SSR's.

As for the Chinese, their protests against these extensions of Soviet influence gave way to their urgent need for Soviet help following the full-scale Japanese invasion of July 1937. Concerned over the implications of the anti-Comintern pact between Germany, Italy, and Japan, Moscow had pushed for a popular front in China during the previous year. In December 1936, Chiang Kai-shek was dramatically kidnapped. His captors insisted that he stop the enervating punitive expeditions against the Communists and devote himself to leading the struggle against Japan. Reluctantly, he consented. The cooperation (for the most part halfhearted) between the KMT and the CCP strengthened the resistance to Japan and thus helped promote Soviet security; and Moscow provided China with important, though limited, quantities of military supplies, particularly during the period before Hitler's invasion of the Soviet Union.

From 1931 on Moscow had striven to counter the Japanese threat. Its army east of the Urals was expanded from 100,000 in 1931 to about 600,000 in 1939; thousands of tanks and hundreds of planes were deployed. Between 1934 and 1936 there were many small but sharp military clashes along the Manchurian-Mongolian-Soviet border. Japanese probes, often in great strength, were repulsed: in July-August 1938, in the Lake Khasan (Changkufeng) area of the Manchurian-Korean-Soviet border; in 1939, along the Amur River; and in the spring and summer of 1939, in the Khalkingol (Nomonhan) steppe region along the Halka River that generally delineated the Manchurian-Mongolian border.

The latter was a full-fledged war that sharpened Stalin's interest in a nonaggression pact with Nazi Germany which would insulate Moscow from involvement in a European war. Buttressed by intelligence information on Japanese military intentions from Richard Sorge, the USSR's master spy in Tokyo, the Soviets' superior generalship and weaponry bloodied the Japanese Kwangtung Army and deflected the war party in Tokyo from pushing a major war against the Soviet Union. (Purges in the forces in the Far East were nowhere near as extensive as those that wracked the Red Army's combat effectiveness in Europe. In 1941, when Western experts assessed the USSR's ability to resist the Nazi onslaught, they used as their standard the poor performance of the Red Army in the 1939–1940 Winter War against Finland — in which more than one million troops were required to overcome a Finnish army one-fifth that size — and ignored the impressive Soviet showing against Japan in the 1938–1939 battles). After the signing of the Nazi-Soviet pact, which apparently caught the Japanese by surprise, an uneasy quiet settled along the entire border, and the USSR concentrated on affairs in Europe. Soviet victories on the battlefield set the stage for the Soviet-Japanese neutrality pact of April 1941.

Stalin's diplomacy and military power in the Far East showed a sure sense of balance-of-power realities. Ideology and revolutionary agitation took a back seat to the pursuit of tactical objectives whose aim was to dissuade Japan from striking the Soviet Union and induce it to move south for satisfaction of its imperialist ambitions.

On August 31, 1939, Molotov defended the decision to conclude a pact with Nazi Germany in a major speech to the Soviet parliament. Criticizing Britain and France for the "howling contradictions" in their professed interest in cooperating with the Soviet Union, he emphasized the willingness of Germany to reach concrete and immediate agreements that were in the national interest of the Soviet Union, irrespective of the differences in the internal systems of the countries: "The art of politics in the sphere of foreign relations does not consist in increasing the number of enemies for one's country. . . It is our duty to think of the interests of the Soviet people, the interests of the Union of Soviet Socialist Republics." He stressed the importance of good relations with Germany and never alluded to the secret protocol.

Is it really difficult for these [British and French] gentlemen to understand the purpose of the Soviet-German Nonaggression Pact, on the strength of which the USSR is not obligated to involve itself in war either on the side of Great Britain against Germany or on the side of Germany against Great Britain? Is it really difficult to understand that the USSR is pursuing and will continue to pursue its own independent policy, based on the interests of the peoples of the USSR and only their interests? If these gentlemen have such an uncontrollable desire to fight, let them do their own fighting without the Soviet Union. We will see what fighting stuff they are made of . . . .*

The next day German troops invaded Poland. As the curtain rose on World War II, the Soviet Union was on the sidelines.

Stalin had become master of the Soviet Union, surmounting the enormous resistance from the peasantry to his revolution from above in the 1930s, the debilitation and reconstitution of key institutions of Soviet society, the political isolation that foreign powers had sought to impose on a distrusted Soviet Union, and the vulnerability resulting from military weakness during most of the interwar period. None of his past foreign-policy blunders seemed to have been costly: not the exaggerated fear that Britain and France were plotting another intervention to topple the Soviet regime; not the misjudgment of nazism's inherent dynamism and expansionist threat to the Soviet Union; not the detrimental effects that the Comintern, as an instrument of Kremlin diplomacy, had on cooperation with the Western powers. On the eve of World War II, it appeared that Stalin's duplicity in handling the Western powers publicly and Germany privately had been practiced with great skill. The pact with Hitler had yielded fruits — a return of former czarist lands that added strategic depth to the USSR's western defenses, and a neutrality that seemed to guarantee the nation against involvement in a two-front war or in the European war that was to change the political complexion of the continent forever.

## Notes

1. George F. Kennan, *Russia Leaves the War* (Princeton: Princeton University Press, 1956), 75-76.

2. When Russia expanded in the Far East in the late nineteenth century, it constructed the Chinese Eastern Railroad, which entrenched Russian influence in Manchuria at the expense of a weak China and a jealous but as yet militarily inferior Japan.

3. Malcolm MacKintosh, *Juggernaut: A History of the Soviet Forces* (New York: Macmillan, 1967), 92.

4. Robert C. Tucker, "The Emergence of Stalin's Foreign Policy," *Slavic Review,* vol. 36, no. 4 (December 1977), 588-589.

---

* As quoted in Alvin Z. Rubinstein, *The Foreign Policy of the Soviet Union,* 3rd ed. (New York: Random House, 1972), p. 143.

## Selected Bibliography

BELOFF, MAX. *The Foreign Policy of Soviet Russia, 1929–1936.* Vol. 1. New York: Oxford University Press, 1947.

BORKENAU, FRANZ. *World Communism.* Ann Arbor: University of Michigan Press, 1962.

BRADLEY, JOHN. *Allied Intervention in Russia, 1917–1920.* New York: Basic Books, 1968.

BRANDT, CONRAD. *Stalin's Failure in China, 1924–1927.* Cambridge: Harvard University Press, 1958.

BROOK-SHEPARD, GORDON. *The Storm Petrels.* New York: Harcourt Brace Jovanovich, 1978.

BROWDER, ROBERT P. *The Origins of Soviet-American Diplomacy.* Princeton: Princeton University Press, 1953.

CARR, EDWARD HALLETT. *The Bolshevik Revolution, 1917–1923.* 4 vols. New York: Macmillan, 1950, 1952, 1953, 1954.

———. *German-Soviet Relations Between the World Wars, 1919–1939.* Baltimore: Johns Hopkins Press, 1951.

———. *Socialism in One Country 1924–1926.* Part 3, Vol. 2. New York: Macmillan, 1964.

———. *Foundations of a Planned Economy, 1926–1929.* Vol. 3, Parts 1 and 2. New York: Macmillan, 1976.

CHAMBERLIN, WILLIAM HENRY. *The Russian Revolution, 1917–1921.* 2 vols. New York: Macmillan, 1935.

DALLIN, DAVID J. *The Rise of Russia in Asia.* New Haven: Yale University Press, 1949.

DEBO, RICHARD K. *Revolution and Survival: The Foreign Policy of Soviet Russia, 1917–1918.* Toronto: University of Toronto Press, 1979.

DEUTSCHER, ISAAC. *Stalin: A Political Biography.* New York: Oxford University Press, 1949.

———. *The Prophet Armed: Trotsky, 1879–1921.* New York: Oxford University Press, 1954.

DYCK, HARVEY L. *Weimar Germany and Soviet Russia 1926–1933: A Study in Diplomatic Instability.* New York: Columbia University Press, 1966.

EUDIN, XENIA, and HAROLD H. FISHER (EDS.). *Soviet Russia and the West, 1920–1927.* Stanford: Stanford University Press, 1957.

———. and ROBERT C. NORTH (EDS.). *Soviet Russia and the East, 1920–1927.* Stanford: Stanford University Press, 1957.

————. and ROBERT M. SLUSSER (EDS.). *Soviet Foreign Policy 1928–1934.* 2 vols. University Park: Pennsylvania State University Press, 1967.

FISCHER, LOUIS. *The Soviets in World Affairs,* 2 vols. New York: Vintage, 1960.

————. *Russia's Road from Peace to War 1917–1941.* New York: Harper & Row, 1969.

FREUND, GERALD. *Unholy Alliance: Russian-German Relations from the Treaty of Brest-Litovsk to the Treaty of Berlin.* New York: Harcourt Brace Jovanovich, 1957.

GANKIN, OLGA H., and HAROLD H. FISHER. *The Bolsheviks and the World War: The Origin of the Third International.* Stanford: Stanford University Press, 1940.

GORODETSKY, GABRIEL. *The Precarious Truce: Anglo-Soviet Relations 1924–27.* London: Cambridge University Press, 1977.

HILGER, GUSTAV, and ALFRED G. MEYER. *The Incompatible Allies.* New York: Macmillan, 1953.

HULSE, JAMES W. *The Forming of the Communist International.* Stanford: Stanford University Press, 1964.

KENNAN, GEORGE F. *Russia Leaves the War.* Princeton: Princeton University Press, 1956.

————. *The Decision to Intervene.* Princeton: Princeton University Press, 1958.

————. *Russia and the West Under Lenin and Stalin.* Boston: Little, Brown, 1960.

LEE, CHONG-SIK. *Revolutionary Struggle in Manchuria.* Berkeley: University of California Press (forthcoming).

LENSEN, GEORGE A. *Japanese Recognition of the USSR: Soviet-Japanese Relations, 1921–1930.* Tallahassee: Diplomatic Press, 1970.

————. *The Damned Inheritance: The Soviet Union and the Manchurian Crisis, 1924–1935.* Tallahassee: Diplomatic Press, 1974.

LEONG, SOW-THENG. *Sino-Soviet Diplomatic Relations, 1917–1926.* Honolulu: University of Hawaii Press, 1976.

LERNER, WARREN. *Karl Radek: The Last Internationalist.* Stanford: Stanford University Press, 1970.

MCKENZIE, KERMIT E. *Comintern and World Revolution, 1928–1943.* New York: Columbia University Press, 1964.

NORTH, ROBERT C. *Moscow and Chinese Communists.* Stanford: Stanford University Press, 1953.

PAGE, STANLEY W. *The Formation of the Baltic States: A Study of the Effects of Great Power Politics Upon the Emergence of Lithuania, Latvia, and Estonia.* Cambridge: Harvard University Press, 1959.

PIPES, RICHARD. *The Formation of the Soviet Union: Communism and Nationalism, 1917–1923.* 2nd ed. Cambridge: Harvard University Press, 1964.

ROSENBAUM, KURT. *Community of Fate: German-Soviet Diplomatic Relations, 1922–1923.* Syracuse, N.Y.: Syracuse University Press, 1965.

SCHWARTZ, BENJAMIN. *Chinese Communism and the Rise of Mao.* Cambridge: Harvard University Press, 1951.

SCOTT, WILLIAM EVANS. *Alliance Against Hitler: The Origins of the Franco-Soviet Pact.* Durham, N.C.: Duke University Press, 1962.

SMITH, CANFIELD F. *Vladivostok Under Red and White Rule: Revolution and Counterrevolution in the Russian Far East, 1920–1922.* Seattle: University of Washington Press, 1976.

SMITH, C. JAY, JR. *Finland and the Russian Revolution, 1917–1922.* Athens: University of Georgia Press, 1958.

THOMPSON, JOHN M. *Russia, Bolshevism, and the Versailles Peace.* Princeton: Princeton University Press, 1967.

THORNTON, RICHARD C. *The Comintern and the Chinese Communists,1928–1931.* Seattle: University of Washington Press, 1969.

ULAM, ADAM B. *Expansion and Coexistence: Soviet Foreign Policy, 1917–1973.* 2nd ed. New York: Praeger, 1974.

ULLMAN, RICHARD H. *Anglo-Soviet Relations 1917–1921.* 2 vols. Princeton: Princeton University Press, 1961, 1968.

WANDYCZ, PIOTR S. *Soviet-Polish Relations 1917–1921.* Cambridge: Harvard University Press, 1970.

WARTH, ROBERT D. *The Allies and the Russian Revolution.* Durham, N.C.: Duke University Press, 1954.

WHEELER-BENNETT, JOHN W. *The Forgotten Peace: Brest-Litovsk, March 1918.* New York: Morrow, 1939.

WHITING, ALLEN S. *Soviet Policies in China, 1917–1924.* New York: Columbia University Press, 1954.

# 2

# Soviet Expansion and the Coming of the Cold War, 1939–1946

At dawn on September 1, 1939, German legions rolled into Poland. Two days later, Britain and France declared war on Germany. World War II was a reality. Moscow expected the new "imperialist" war to be a replica of the first one, only this time the Soviet Union would be a spectator positioned to profit from the mutual exhaustion of the competing capitalist coalitions.

With the outbreak of war, the Soviet Union abandoned its professed policy of nonaggression for a course of territorial expansion. Exploiting the preoccupation of the other European powers elsewhere, it rationalized its actions in terms of national security. By whatever name and however legitimized, Soviet expansion was, with the subsequent defeat of Germany, to move Soviet power into the heart of Europe and thus give rise to the Cold War.

Stalin wasted little time in claiming his booty. On September 17 the Red Army occupied eastern Poland; soon thereafter Stalin pressured the Baltic states into permitting Soviet troops to be stationed on their territory, a prelude to their formal incorporation into the Soviet Union in August 1940, and he tried to intimidate Finland into surrendering territory that would strengthen the defensive position of Leningrad (concessions the Soviets had been seeking since April 1938). Upon the Finns' refusal, the Soviet Union unilaterally abrogated its treaty of nonaggression on November 28, 1939, and attacked the next day. Though resisting brilliantly, the Finns found themselves without help from the West and finally capitulated, signing a peace treaty on March 12, 1940. Thus ended the first wave of Soviet expansion.

Hardly had the Soviets begun to digest these territorial chunks than the Nazi blitzkrieg in April and May 1940 overran Norway, the Netherlands, Denmark, Belgium, and France. Britain stood alone and virtually defenseless. Stalin again availed himself of Hitler's absorption elsewhere, this time to wrench Bessarabia from Romania and make demands on Bulgaria and Turkey that would have resulted in the Black Sea's becoming a Soviet lake and Moscow's having control of the straits. With evident reluctance, Germany accepted the Soviet annexation of Bessarabia, at the same time taking measures to consolidate its own influence in the rest of Romania. The expansionist appetites of Germany and the Soviet Union sharpened their rivalry in the Balkans and in Finland. Stalin's covetousness was a match for Hitler's, and convinced Hitler that the USSR would have to be subjugated if his conquest of Europe was to be safeguarded.

Though officially neutral as far as the war in the West was concerned, the Soviet Union had a pro-German tilt: German naval vessels were outfitted in Murmansk (though after the German occupation of Norway, the Soviet port was not needed); crucial raw materials were supplied as part of overall Soviet-German economic agreements; foreign Communist parties opposed the war on orders from Moscow, thus weakening the home front in the Western countries and helping the Germans; and British ships were detained in Soviet ports because of the British blockade of Germany. Soviet deference to German needs in the prosecution of the war against the West did not, however, extend to the areas of overlapping Soviet and German ambitions.

By the fall of 1940, Germany's military power had assumed awesome proportions. Hitler negotiated a tripartite pact among Germany, Italy, and Japan on September 27, 1940. His efforts to link the Soviet Union to it failed, partly because of Soviet demands for concessions from Japan. In an effort to resolve some of the strains that were cropping up in German-Soviet relations, the two nations held talks in Berlin on November 12 and 13. The Germans asked "whether in the long run the most advantageous access to the sea for Russia could not be found in the direction of the Persian Gulf and the Arabian Sea, and whether at the same time certain other aspirations of Russia in this part of Asia — in which Germany was completely disinterested — could not also be realized."* They also indicated that they would support revision of the Montreux convention (governing access through the Dardanelles and the Bosporus) to make it more favorable to the Soviet Union. A secret protocol was drafted (but never signed) under which the USSR was to obtain recognition of its recent territorial acquisitions, a promise of peace with Japan, and a sphere of influence in the area "south of the national territory of the Soviet Union

---

* Raymond James Sontag and James Stuart Beddie (eds.), *Nazi-Soviet Relations, 1939–1941.* Documents from the archives of the German Foreign Office (Washington, D.C.: Department of State, 1948), p. 222.

in the direction of the Indian Ocean." However, Molotov kept pressing for settlement of tensions arising from German troops in Finland, the German role in Romania and Bulgaria, and the disagreement on the straits. It is interesting to note that Molotov's demands were set forth in non-Marxist–Leninist, openly power-political terms and coincided with traditional czarist imperial objectives.

The limits of compatibility had been exceeded. On December 18, 1940, Hitler issued the order to prepare for the invasion of the USSR (Operation Barbarossa), with preparations to be completed by May 15, 1941. For the next six months Berlin fell ominously quiet.

For all his shrewdness, Stalin displayed a certain political obtuseness where Germany's military priorities were concerned. For example, on April 4, 1941, Molotov informed the German government of Moscow's intention to conclude a nonaggression pact with Yugoslavia the next day, even though German troops had outflanked Yugoslavia — occupying Romania in February and Bulgaria in March — and were preparing at that very moment to attack in order to extricate Mussolini, whose invasion of Greece had turned into a disaster for the Italian army. Instead of evincing imperial interest in areas that Germany had clearly staked out for itself, Stalin would have done better to digest what he had and bide his time.

In the Far East, Stalin secured his rear against attack by signing a five-year treaty of neutrality with Japan on April 13, 1941. He obtained Japan's recognition of the USSR's preeminence in the Mongolian People's Republic, its pledge to settle all outstanding Japanese claims for concessions in the northern part of Sakhalin Island, and an end to border clashes. The treaty was also intended to encourage Japan to strike south toward Southeast Asia rather than against the Soviet Union.

Thus, from September 1939 to June 1941, Stalin took advantage of a world at war to expand at the expense of weak neighbors. In the next four years, the Soviet Union was to pay a crushing price for his greed. But despite the enormous suffering of the Soviet people in that 1941-to-1945 period, Stalin's imperialism in 1939–1941 and 1945–1946 is no more to be condoned than is the crime of the man who murders his parents and then asks the court to excuse him because he is an orphan. In 1939 and 1940, Stalin deported and killed thousands of people from eastern Poland and the Baltic states for political and ideological reasons. This bloodletting was a prologue to what he was to do in Eastern Europe after 1945, and it contributed to the fear in the West and created the environment in which the Cold War was to develop. But this was still in the future.

On May 6, 1941, Stalin tightened his grip on party and government and assumed the post of chairman of the Council of People's Commissars (equivalent to premier). This, his first formal *government* position since his rise to undisputed leadership in the USSR, revealed the Kremlin's growing uneasiness over German intentions. Outwardly, German-Soviet relations remained unchanged as the Soviet Union tried in every way to mollify Hitler. Time, however, had run out on the unholy alliance.

## The Wartime Alliance

Stalin's sense of accomplishment and security was short-lived. On June 22, 1941, the Nazi-Soviet honeymoon ended as German troops swept into the Soviet Union on an eighteen-hundred-mile front. So confident had Stalin been of Hitler's friendship that he refused to believe his own intelligence reports and Western warnings of an impending attack; he shied away from provocation, convinced that a German ultimatum would precede any attack. Not until eight hours after the Germans had crossed the frontier did Stalin accept the reality of the onslaught.

Twice within a generation Soviet leaders were engaged in a struggle for survival. This time, however, they were to have allies. A common cause — the destruction of nazism — submerged ideological antipathies and political antagonisms. Winston Churchill, long an avowed opponent of communism, offered the Soviets friendship and alliance. On July 12, the British and Soviet governments signed a protocol in which both agreed not "to negotiate nor conclude an armistice or treaty of peace except by mutual agreement" and "to render each other assistance and support of all kinds in the present war against Hitlerite Germany." Thus began the forging of the Grand Alliance against Hitler.

On July 3, Stalin overcame his shock at what had happened and spoke to the Soviet people. With rare candor, no doubt dictated by the extreme gravity of the situation, he admitted that the country was in mortal peril, that there was no time for comforting words. Sensing a need to justify his pro-Nazi policy orientation of 1939–1941, he said that it had given the Soviet Union time to strengthen its defenses. He made no mention of the territorial acquisitions of that period, emphasizing instead the initial German advantage from the treacherous attack and appealing to the people to unite to defeat the invader as their ancestors before them had triumphed over Napoleon and Kaiser Wilhelm II, both of whom had enjoyed a reputation for invincibility.*

---

* Stalin did not tell the Soviet people that he had ignored repeated warnings of the impending German invasion; nor did he assume responsibility for the nation's unpreparedness. According to Khrushchev's revelations about Stalin's shortcomings at the twentieth congress of the CPSU in February 1956, it was Stalin's refusal to heed well-founded and persistent

As the Nazis penetrated deeper into Russia, even to the outskirts of Leningrad and Moscow, the Soviets relied on their traditional scourges for any would-be conqueror — the vastness of their country and the severity of its winters. They also adopted a "scorched-earth" policy, leaving nothing of use to the invader. The Germans were at first greeted as liberators in many non-Russian areas of the Soviet Union, such as the Ukraine — an illuminating comment on a generation of Communist rule. But the Nazis, themselves captives of their racist ideology, came as self-proclaimed conquerors intent upon colonizing the country and brutally exploiting its people and resources. They thus wasted, politically and psychologically, the strong vein of anti-Communist sentiment and by this blunder contributed greatly to their eventual defeat.

While the Nazis continued to advance into the Soviet Union, anticipating the victory that would make them masters of the Eurasian land mass, the newly formed Allied coalition sought to establish a firm basis for military cooperation. Churchill had promised to render all possible aid, but obviously only the United States could meet the enormous needs of the Soviet Union. In America, as in Great Britain, all hostility toward the Soviet Union was overshadowed by the determination to work together in the common interest. President Franklin D. Roosevelt moved to extend lend-lease aid. This aspect of cooperation with the Soviets proved successful, though not without frequent difficulties. Harry Hopkins, President Roosevelt's trusted adviser and troubleshooter, flew to Moscow in July 1941 to assess the Soviet capacity and will to resist Hitler. His favorable report convinced Roosevelt, and shipments to the USSR began almost immediately under an interim lend-lease agreement. In 1942, though eager to take the offensive against the Japanese after their attack on Pearl Harbor

---

reports of imminent German invasion that cost the Soviets so much and facilitated the rapidity and extent of the initial Nazi advances. Khrushchev noted:

> Despite these particularly grave warnings, the necessary steps were not taken to prepare the country properly for defense and to prevent it from being caught unawares.
>
> Did we have time and the capabilities for such preparations? Yes, we had the time and capabilities. . . .
>
> Had our industry been mobilized properly and in time to supply the Army with the necessary material, our wartime losses would have been decidedly smaller. Such mobilization had not been, however, started in time. . . .
>
> When the fascist armies had actually invaded Soviet territory and military operations began, Moscow issued the order that the German fire was not to be returned. Why? It was because Stalin, despite evident facts, thought that the war had not yet started, that this was only a provocative action on the part of several undisciplined sections of the German Army, and that our reaction might serve as a reason for the Germans to begin the war. . . .
>
> As you see, everything was ignored: warnings of certain Army commanders, declarations of deserters from the enemy army, and even the open hostility of the enemy. Is this an example of the alertness of the Chief of the Party and of the State at this particularly significant historical moment?

on December 7, 1941, the United States undertook to deliver more than $1 billion's worth of war material and supplies to the Soviet Union. Subsequently, other lend-lease agreements were concluded. (The USSR's contact with its allies was effected via Murmansk, Iran, and Vladivostok, particularly the first two.) America eventually supplied the USSR with approximately $11 billion in vitally needed goods of every description, from tanks and trucks to shoes and food. So grave was the danger that Stalin, according to a memoir published in 1978 by former Politburo member Anastas Mikoyan, at one time requested the presence of Western troops on Soviet soil.

British-Soviet cooperation first developed in Iran, where events impelled the two nations to act to forestall an imminent pro-Nazi coup in Tehran. They jointly occupied the country. In its note of August 25, 1941, the Soviet government justified the Allied action on the basis of the pertinent provision of its 1921 treaty with Iran, which held that

> if a third party should attempt to carry out a policy of usurpation by means of armed intervention in Persia, or if such power should desire to use Persian territory as a base for operations against the Russian Socialist Federal Soviet Republic, or those of its allies, and if the Persian government should not be able to put a stop to such a menace after having been once called upon to do so by the Russian Socialist Federal Soviet Republic, the Russian Socialist Federal Soviet Republic shall have the right to advance its troops into the Persian interior for the purpose of carrying out the military operations necessary for its defense. The Soviet Government undertakes, however, to withdraw its troops from Persian territory as soon as the danger has been removed.*

By mid-September 1941, the shah had capitulated and abdicated in favor of his son (who ruled until January 1979, when a revolution forced him to leave the country). The joint Allied occupation was followed by a treaty of alliance with Iran, signed on January 29, 1942, and Iran soon became a main Allied artery of supplies for the Soviet war effort. In addition to outlining Allied prerogatives, including the right to "maintain in Iranian territory land, sea, and air forces in such numbers as they consider necessary," the treaty assured Iran that the Allies would withdraw their forces "from Iranian territory not later than six months after all hostilities between the Allied powers and Germany and her associates have been suspended by the conclusion of an armistice or armistices, or on the conclusion of peace between them, whichever date is the earlier." Soviet failure to abide by the terms of this provision precipitated one of the early

---

* Alvin Z. Rubinstein, *The Foreign Policy of the Soviet Union* (New York: Random House, 1972), p. 152.

crises of the postwar period — one involving Iran, the great powers, and the United Nations.

Meanwhile, the German advance overran the Soviet economic and industrial heartland. It failed, however, to attain its principal strategic objective: the destruction of the Red Army. Moscow and Leningrad held firm, and by the beginning of December it was apparent that Hitler would not winter in the Kremlin. As in 1812, winter providently came early. Furthermore, the Japanese surprise attack on Pearl Harbor meant that the Soviets no longer had to fear a two-front war. Nonetheless, the danger to the Allied cause was never greater than during the bleak winter of 1941–1942 — a winter of successive defeats and disasters — and the summer of 1942. But when the Nazis and the Japanese had failed to attain victory by late 1942, their ultimate defeat was assured. Time and resources favored the Allies.

In November 1942, the British and Americans landed in North Africa while the Soviets engaged the Germans in the epic struggle for Stalingrad. The battle to the death for this vital industrial center on the lower Volga was a symbol of Soviet determination to retreat no further. The grim struggle for the city continued for weeks, fought street by street, house by house. On February 2, 1943, the Nazi forces surrendered. Stalingrad was saved. The defeat was one from which the Nazis never recovered, and the Allied cause received an incalculable boost of morale.

On all fronts, 1943 marked the turning of the tide. Now political differences within the strange alliance between the Soviet Union and the Western democracies assumed added dimensions. All had shared the resolve to defeat the Axis powers, subordinating other war aims to this overriding objective. However, as *military* victory approached, the *political* dilemmas and disagreements over the postwar settlement sharpened. The post-1945 Cold War was rooted in the incompatible objectives of the wartime Allies. Each sought security against a possible German revival, but this meant different and conflicting things to each. Subsequent Soviet maneuvering for power, position, and economic advantage and insistence on ideological conformity from the elites under its military control increased Washington's suspicion and rendered the task of shaping a congenial postwar settlement impossible. Throughout the war, even during the darkest days of the Nazi advance, Stalin was more concerned with political issues than was Roosevelt or Churchill. Certainly he had a clearer idea of what he wanted as a victor, though for the time being military necessities superseded political differences.

From the first forging of the coalition, the Soviet Union pressed for the launching of a second front in Europe that would draw forty to sixty German divisions away from the east. Stalin broached the issue in his first direct communication to Churchill on July 18, 1941, and the oft-repeated demand was a constant source of discord. Stalin's xenophobia and memory of two trying decades of Soviet-Western relations were reflected in his complaints of Allied unwillingness to make military efforts comparable to those being made by the Red Army. More than any other single issue, this signified the uneasiness that existed within the alliance. The British tried to overcome such attitudes by signing a twenty-year treaty of alliance with the USSR on May 26, 1942. A vague promise by Churchill to expect a second front in France in 1942 was seized on by Molotov, who stated it as a promised certainty rather than an eventual intention, in his speech of June 18, 1942, which called upon the Supreme Soviet to ratify the Soviet-British treaty. (Churchill had compelling reason to promise all possible assistance to the Soviet Union, fearing that Stalin might make a separate peace with Hitler.)

Of the many political problems besetting Soviet-Western wartime relations, none assumed more dramatic proportions or proved more elusive of accord than that of the future of Poland. Since the Nazi-Soviet partition of 1939, there had been no diplomatic relations between the Soviet Union and Poland. As far as the Soviet government was concerned, Poland no longer existed. With the advent of the Nazi attack, however, Stalin adopted a conciliatory position with respect to the Polish question — a gesture designed to strengthen the newly formed bonds of friendship with the West. On July 30, 1941, an agreement was reached in London between the Soviet and Polish governments that was supposed to serve as a basis for future amicable relations. In a fundamental reversal of policy, the Soviets conceded that the territorial changes of 1939 were no longer valid. Diplomatic relations between Poland and the USSR were reestablished, and plans were made for training and equipping a Polish army on Soviet soil from among the thousands of Poles imprisoned after the 1939 partition.

Several days later, a portentous article appeared in *Pravda*. Though applauding the Soviet-Polish pact, it justified Soviet action in the 1939 partition on the grounds that Moscow was "duty-bound to give a helping hand to the Ukrainians and Byelorussians who made up most of the population in the Eastern regions of Poland."[1] *Pravda* also asserted that although the time was not suitable for discussion of final frontier lines, there was nothing "immutable" in the Polish-Soviet frontier as established by the 1921 Treaty of Riga: "The question of future Soviet-Polish borders is a matter for the future." Thus did the Soviets dilute the sense of their signed word even as the ink dried on the agreement. Similar occurrences were to mar future Allied unity.

During British Foreign Minister Anthony Eden's visit to Moscow in December 1941, Stalin insisted on recognition for the Soviet frontiers as they existed in June 1941, which would sanction all Soviet territorial acquisitions since September 1939. Though evaded at the time, this frequently repeated demand became, with the change in Allied fortunes, another source of discord. The Allies opposed Soviet claims to eastern Poland, as well as any prospective incorporation of the Baltic states into the Soviet Union.

Tension between the Polish government-in-exile and the Soviet government reached the breaking point over the Katyn Forest controversy. After the partition of Poland, the Soviets had interned, among others, some 15,000 Polish officers and men, the elite of the defeated Polish army. By the spring of 1940 the whereabouts of these men was a mystery. With the resumption of Polish-Soviet diplomatic relations in July 1941, the Polish government-in-exile repeatedly requested information concerning their fate. Soviet officialdom maintained an ominous silence. On April 13, 1943, the Nazis reported the "discovery" of the mass grave of the Polish officers in the Katyn Forest and blamed the Soviet Union for the atrocity. The Polish government-in-exile in London proposed an impartial investigation of this allegation. Stalin's reply was quick and harsh: he severed diplomatic relations with the Polish government, holding that Polish belief in the Nazi accusations indicated a lack of faith in the integrity of the Soviet government.

Though the ostensible cause of the breach was the Polish request for an investigation of the German charges, in the background was the continued insistence of the Poles upon a restoration of their 1939 frontier with the Soviet Union. The Poles refused to settle for territorial compensation at the expense of Germany. The Katyn incident was most convenient for Stalin. Eager to ensure a pro-Soviet (Communist) regime in postwar Poland, he announced the establishment of an organization known as the Union of Polish Patriots a few days later. This group subsequently served as the basis for the Soviet puppet Lublin government.

As a postscript to the Katyn Forest controversy, it may be noted that upon reconquering the area, the Soviets conducted their own investigation and "conclusively" placed the blame on the Nazis. The issue was again raised at the Nuremberg war-crimes trials, but the Soviet representatives chose neither to refute the German accusation of 1943 nor to take advantage of the opportunity to clear themselves in an open forum. Subsequent evidence proved that the Soviets had been responsible for the massacre.[2]

The Soviet-Polish rupture seriously tried Allied unity. The Allies — ever fearful of jeopardizing the alliance and pushing Stalin to conclude a sudden and separate agreement with Hitler, as in 1939; beset by continual Soviet demands for a second front; and increasingly indignant at Soviet disparagement of their own efforts on the battlefield — did not wish to make too much of the Polish issue. The tension eased noticeably when Moscow announced the dissolution of the Comintern on May 22, 1943.

In a reply to a question from a British correspondent, Stalin expressed the hope that this action would end all fears that the Soviet Union "intends to intervene in the life of other nations and to 'Bolshevize' them" and would demonstrate the USSR's interest in promoting the unity of all groups fighting Hitler. A psychologically dramatic gesture aimed at allaying Western suspicions and obscuring the Polish question, the announced dissolution of the Comintern purportedly meant that the Kremlin was disbanding its global apparatus for influencing and subverting foreign governments and promoting Soviet interests. We now know that Stalin did not have the slightest intention of shedding this multifaceted weapon of unconventional diplomacy. The Comintern was never dissolved; it merely relocated its headquarters in an undisclosed part of Moscow and functioned in secret.

The growing complex of political problems convinced the heads of state that a meeting was essential. Accordingly, at a preliminary conference of foreign ministers — Cordell Hull, Anthony Eden, V. M. Molotov — in Moscow from October 15 to 30, 1943, an agenda was prepared; and on November 28, 1943, Stalin, Churchill, and Roosevelt met at Tehran. A broad range of topics was discussed, but no final decisions were made, though Roosevelt did imply to Stalin that the United States would not challenge the Soviet position in Poland and the Baltic states.

Meanwhile, the military picture progressively brightened. Soviet offensives drained Nazi strength and drove the Germans from Soviet soil. By January 1944, the Red Army had crossed the former Polish frontier. On January 10, the Soviet news agency TASS contradicted Polish claims to the 1939 boundary and accused the Polish government-in-exile of deliberately aggravating the frontier question. No longer was Stalin prepared to accept only minor changes in the Soviet-Polish boundary, as he had implied in 1941; now he called for the existence of a strong, independent, friendly Polish state whose western frontier should be extended "through incorporation with Poland of ancient Polish lands previously wrested by Germany."

The irreconcilability of Stalin and the Polish leaders, who rejected Churchill's suggestion that they accept territorial compensation at the expense of Germany, and the unwillingness of the Western powers to jeopardize postwar cooperation with the Soviets prevented an acceptable settlement. At the urging of Churchill and Roosevelt, Polish Prime Minister Mikolajczyk journeyed to Moscow in a desperate effort to reach an agreement. He arrived on July 30, 1944, the eve of the tragic attempt by the Polish underground army to expel the Germans and liberate Warsaw before the entrance of the Red Army (then on the outskirts of the city) and thereby to gain control of the capital and force Soviet recognition of the Polish government in London, beneath whose banner the underground fought.[3] But four days before Mikolajczyk's arrival, the Soviet government had signed an agreement with its puppet creation, the Committee of National Liberation, which became the core of the postwar Communist Polish regime. Moscow declared that it had no desire to alter existing institutions and no territorial ambitions — by which it meant beyond the 1941 lines. Molotov had made a similar statement on April 2, 1944, as the Red Army approached the Soviet-Romanian frontier, and then, too, he had meant specifically the Soviet-Romanian frontier as it existed in 1941, thus making it clear that the 1940 Soviet annexation of Bessarabia was not open for negotiation.

A particularly embarrassing source of dissension among the Allies in the early days of the war was Finland. Finland had long had Western sympathy, and its joining the Nazi attack on the USSR placed American policymakers in a quandary. The Finns attempted to rationalize their behavior on the grounds that they only wanted to regain their lost land, but once America entered the war, it had to treat Finland as a belligerent. Efforts to induce Finland to disengage from Germany failed, and by the summer of 1944, Finland stood alone with no prospects of help from Germany. On September 19, 1944, it signed an armistice with the Soviet Union and was out of the war. (The terms of the peace treaty signed in 1947 were harsh, but they did ensure that Finland's independence would be preserved. They provided that Finland would withdraw to the Soviet-Finnish frontier line of March 12, 1940; this would continue as the boundary, except that in the far north Finland ceded the port of Petsamo to the Soviets and granted them a naval base at Porkkala-Udd, while in return the USSR agreed to relinquish its previously held lease on the peninsula of Hangoe; Finland would pay a $300 million indemnity in kind in six years; and Soviet forces would not occupy Finland.)

The year 1944 was one of Allied victories. On June 6, Anglo-American-Canadian forces landed in France, the long-awaited second front was a reality. By the end of the year, France had been liberated and the final preparations for the invasion of Germany itself were under way. On the eastern front, Soviet armies crossed the border into Germany. With the approach of victory, the unresolved political problems could no longer be evaded. Agreements had to be reached on the future of Poland and of all Eastern Europe, the division of Germany, the role of the Soviet Union in the war against Japan, the coordination of the final assault on Germany, and the preparations for the establishment of the United Nations.

Stalin thought in terms of spheres of influence. Security through expansion was a principle that had motivated the Kremlin for centuries; expansion entailed control, and control meant regimes that would unquestioningly toe Moscow's line. However rational and understandable Stalin's search for security was — after all, the Soviet Union had been devastated and lost more than twenty million people — what he did in the name of security in time triggered Western reactions that decreased his security and that of the West as well.

Stalin knew what he wanted and was open to a deal. In Moscow on October 9, 1944, Stalin and Churchill reached a secret understanding allocating spheres of influence. Under their so-called percentages agreement, Soviet influence in Bulgaria and Romania would be 90 percent as against 10 percent for Britain; in Hungary, 80/20; in Greece, 10/90; and Yugoslavia was to be divided on a 50/50 basis. This was Churchill's attempt to obtain the best possible deal for the West in an Eastern Europe that was already falling mainly to Soviet forces: Sofia, Bucharest, and Belgrade were then in Soviet hands. Because of the agreement, Stalin said nothing when the British suppressed an attempted takeover in Athens by the Greek Communists in December 1944. (But in a letter to Stalin on April 28, 1945, Churchill was to express dissatisfaction: "I must say that the way things have worked out in Yugoslavia certainly does not give me the feeling of a 50/50 interest as between our countries. Marshal Tito has become a complete dictator. He has proclaimed that his prime loyalties are to the Soviet Union."[4]) However, the United States was unwilling, for moral and domestic political reasons, to countenance politically what it was not prepared to resist militarily, namely, a cynical division of Europe into spheres of influence. This disagreement between Churchill and Roosevelt confused Stalin, who was eager for such an arrangement, and it was to be a source of future American-Soviet discord.

To reach agreement on plans for the final defeat of Germany and Japan and to establish a framework for a postwar settlement, the Big Three met in the Crimean resort of Yalta. The conference was held in the former czarist palace of Livadia from February 4 to 10, 1945.

Much has been written about the Yalta conference. Some insist that Eastern Europe and China were here "sold out" to the Soviets; others argue that the agreements reached were the best possible given the military situation and political alternatives at the time. Any appraisal must consider that differences in the relative weights accorded the same "facts" will result in strikingly different final judgments. On the eve of the conference, most Western leaders firmly believed and hoped that it would be possible to extend the unity forged in wartime to the postwar period. Suspicion of Soviet intentions did exist among some professional diplomats, but popular sentiment in the West favored continued cooperation with the Soviet Union. Admiration for the courage displayed by the Soviet people and sympathy for their suffering and sacrifice were widespread.

Briefly, the military and political picture was this: Western troops were at the Rhine; Soviet forces were prepared to cross the Oder and launch the final attack on Berlin, some forty miles away. The Red Army already controlled most of Eastern Europe; Tito's pro-Moscow Communists dominated Yugoslavia. In the Far East, despite major victories over the Japanese at Iwo Jima and Okinawa, American military leaders expected a difficult fight before Japan's final surrender and urged that the USSR be brought into the final assault. In November 1944, the Joint Chiefs of Staff had weighed the pros and cons of Soviet participation and concluded that:

> (a) We desire Russian entry at the earliest possible date consistent with her ability to engage in offensive operations and are prepared to offer the maximum support possible without prejudice to our main effort against Japan.
> (b) We consider that the mission of Russian Far Eastern Forces should be to conduct an all-out offensive against Manchuria to force the commitment of Japanese forces and resources in North China and Manchuria that might otherwise be employed in the defense of Japan, to conduct intensive air operations against Japan proper, and to interdict lines of communication between Japan and the mainland of Asia.[5]

The discussions between Western and Soviet military staffs went smoothly in their planning for the final drive on Germany. However, the political issues affecting the fate of postwar Europe did not fare so well. The most important political discussions at Yalta focused on the Polish and German questions, the conditions under which the Soviet Union would later enter the war against Japan, and the voting procedures to be used in the United Nations Security Council. The Polish question figured in seven out of the eight plenary meetings. Attention centered on four key aspects of this, perhaps the most vexing of all pending questions: (1) a formula for establishing a single provisional government for Poland; (2) how and when to hold free elections; (3) possible solutions to the future of Poland's frontiers, both in the east and the west; and (4) steps designed to safeguard the security of the Soviet rear. The final communiqué issued on February 12, 1945, took note of these and other problems and sketched solutions that, if applied with fidelity and good faith, might have served the interests of all. But it was evident even before the war was won that Stalin intended to interpret the Yalta accords in a manner most apt to maximize Soviet security and power. A prime catalyst in the disintegration of the wartime alliance, the Polish question represented in a larger sense a barometer recording the perilous points of two incompatible conceptions of security.

Agreement on Germany's immediate future came more readily. All parties agreed that Germany must surrender unconditionally. Upon the termination of hostilities, an Allied Control Council was to serve as the top coordinating and policy organ of the occupying powers; three zones of occupation were established, a fourth later being allocated to France from the American and British zones; the Soviets agreed that the Western powers were to have free and unhampered access to Berlin, which was situated deep inside the Soviet zone of occupation; and the basic principles guiding reparations arrangements were reached. Accord was also achieved on the proposed organization of the United Nations and on the broad approaches determining future political actions in Eastern Europe and the Balkans. The stage was well set at Yalta to finish off Germany and manage its surrender.

The Far East played no part in the published formal deliberations at Yalta; it was the subject of a secret protocol. No mention of it, therefore, appeared in the public statement or the grandiloquent Declaration on Liberated Europe issued at the end of the conference. Throughout the war the Soviet Union had maintained formal relations with Japan in accordance with the 1941 neutrality pact. However, despite its official posture of neutrality, it associated itself with the Chinese government and signed the Four-Power Declaration of November 1, 1943, under which the United States, Great Britain, China, and the Soviet Union pledged themselves to cooperate against all their common enemies. More significant, as early as August 1942, Stalin privately assured U. S. Ambassador Averell Harriman of Soviet help in the war against Japan at the appropriate time, and he had specifically repeated this assurance in November 1943 and in September and October 1944. There had been some informal discussion at the Tehran conference of Soviet territorial objectives in the Far East, with Stalin expressing interest in a warm-water port and the return of southern Sakhalin and the Kuril Islands, but nothing definite was settled at the time. In October 1944, at the Moscow conference, Stalin reaffirmed to Churchill his willingness to enter the war against Japan three months after the defeat of Germany, subject to certain conditions, which were presented to the American government in December and served as the basis for the secret agreement on the Far East concluded at Yalta.

The agreement provided for the preservation of the status quo in the Mongolian People's Republic; the restoration of "former rights of Russia violated by the treacherous attack of Japan in 1904," namely, the return of southern Sakhalin, the internationalization of the commercial port of Dairen — "the permanent interests of the Soviet Union in the port being safeguarded and the lease of Port Arthur as a naval base of the USSR restored" (these were territories of China that were being disposed of) — and the restoration of former Russian economic privileges in Manchuria; and the annexation of the Kuril Islands, which Russia had granted to Japan by the Treaty of St. Petersburg (May 7, 1875) in return for renunciation of Japanese claims to Sakhalin Island. These stipulations, made without Chiang Kai-shek's approval, were later accepted by China and incorporated into the Sino-Soviet Treaty of Friendship and Alliance, signed on August 14, 1945, which contained a Soviet promise "to render to China moral support and aid in military supplies and other material resources, such support and aid to be entirely given to the national government as the central government of China."

Was the price paid for Soviet participation excessive, considering the dividends expected? Would the United States government have accepted Stalin's conditions had it realized the imminence of Japan's surrender? Could it have prevented Stalin from seizing these territories on his own? Indeed, in view of traditional Russian Far Eastern objectives, would Stalin not have entered the war even without the Yalta concessions? Ironically, it was the American military — including Generals George C. Marshall and Douglas MacArthur and Admirals Ernest King and Chester Nimitz — with their estimates of another eighteen months of war after the defeat of Germany and anticipated heavy casualties in any invasion of the Japanese home islands, who convinced Roosevelt to grant Soviet demands. Three months later, the strategic position of the United States in the Pacific was so vastly improved that the Joint Chiefs of Staff felt less need for Soviet participation, but the die had been cast. The concessions gave Moscow a commanding position on the Asian mainland, far greater than that which it had held in 1904, on the eve of the Russo-Japanese war.

The intricate story of all the controversies, discussions, and compromises that marked the Yalta deliberations, and their implications for the postwar period, will long be debated. We who examine the record in retrospect would do well to ponder the afterthoughts on Yalta so eloquently expressed by Sir Winston Churchill:

> It is not permitted to those charged with dealing with events in times of war or crisis to confine themselves purely to the statement of broad general principles on which good people agree. They have to take definite decisions from day to day. They have to adopt postures which must be solidly maintained, otherwise how can any combinations for action be maintained? It is easy, after the Germans are beaten, to condemn those who did their best to hearten the Russian military effort and to keep in harmonious contact with our great Ally, who had suffered so frightfully. What would have happened if we had quarrelled with Russia while the Germans still had three or four hundred divisions on the fighting front? Our hopeful assumptions were soon to be falsified. Still, they were the only ones possible at the time.[6]

On May 8, 1945, Germany surrendered unconditionally. Japan collapsed quickly thereafter. The dropping of the atomic bomb on Hiroshima on August 6 and the entry of the USSR into the war two days later — as Stalin had promised, though only by breaking his neutrality pact with Japan — sealed Japan's fate. It capitulated on August 14; the formal signing was aboard the battleship *Missouri* in Tokyo Bay on September 2.

The war was over. The challenge of the peace remained.

## Cold War

The inability of the victors to maintain their wartime cooperation — and the consequent division of the world into two hostile camps — overshadowed all else in the immediate postwar period. Within months after the defeat of the Axis powers, this tragedy was revealed in the fundamental disagreements over Eastern Europe, Germany, Turkey, Iran, and the Far East. An investigation into the causes of the Cold War would take us far afield, and besides, an enormous literature on the subject does exist. However, to understand Soviet policy, we need to keep in mind a few relevant considerations.

First, there are these constants: the survival of Soviet-Western suspicion, only partially mitigated by wartime collaboration; the Soviet search for security, which involved not only an extension of military power westward into the center of Europe but also a radical transformation of the existing social, economic, and political order; the paranoia that led Stalin to regard the West as an enemy again; and, above all, territorial expansion, which went far beyond the demonstrable needs of national security and was manifest in czarist as well as in Stalinist foreign policy.

Second, we must consider the unpredictable chance actions and perceptions that shape historical events. Stalin viewed power in military terms: witness his depreciation of the Vatican's role in world affairs with the query, "How many divisions does the Pope have?" Considering remarks of American officials at Yalta, he may have expected a rapid American military withdrawal from Europe and felt free to use the Red Army with impunity to bring about desired political outcomes in Eastern Europe. One may also muse on the Kremlin's view of the precipitate American decision, prompted by domestic politics, to end all lend-lease aid in May 1945, and on its view of Washington's silence regarding its request in January 1945 for a long-term reconstruction loan. The effect may have been to dispel any fleeting hopes Stalin had of basing Soviet recovery on continued American assistance. This in turn may have diminished his interest in a more conciliatory line toward the West and the problems it faced. Moreover, America's development of the atom bomb intensified Stalin's attention to military expenditures and modernization and to the urgency of overcoming the USSR's technological inferiority.

Finally, the inexorable drift in the 1945–1946 period toward the Cold War can also be discerned in the xenophobia, brutal domestic tyranny, and Great Russian chauvinism of Iosif V. Stalin and in his absolutist conception of security, which entailed total hegemony over all of Europe east of the Stettin-Trieste line. For example, the Soviet Union was of course entitled to firm guarantees against another attack through Poland. But Stalin treated Poland more as an accomplice of nazism than as its victim. He was no

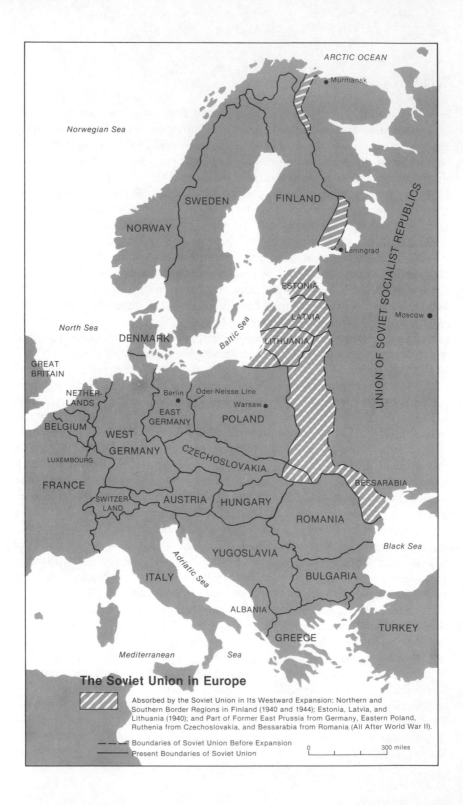

ARCTIC OCEAN

Murmansk ●

Norwegian Sea

SWEDEN

FINLAND

NORWAY

Leningrad ●

UNION OF SOVIET SOCIALIST REPUBLICS

ESTONIA

Moscow ●

North Sea

LATVIA

DENMARK

Baltic Sea

LITHUANIA

GREAT
BRITAIN

NETHER-
LANDS

Berlin ●

Oder-Neisse Line

BELGIUM

EAST
GERMANY

Warsaw ●

POLAND

WEST

LUXEMBOURG

GERMANY

CZECHOSLOVAKIA

FRANCE

BESSARABIA

SWITZER-
LAND

AUSTRIA

HUNGARY

ROMANIA

YUGOSLAVIA

Black Sea

Adriatic Sea

ITALY

BULGARIA

ALBANIA

TURKEY

GREECE

Mediterranean          Sea

## The Soviet Union in Europe

Absorbed by the Soviet Union in Its Westward Expansion: Northern and
Southern Border Regions in Finland (1940 and 1944); Estonia, Latvia, and
Lithuania (1940); and Part of Former East Prussia from Germany, Eastern Poland,
Ruthenia from Czechoslovakia, and Bessarabia from Romania (All After World War II).

- - - - Boundaries of Soviet Union Before Expansion
———— Present Boundaries of Soviet Union

0                    300 miles

more considerate or generous toward Poland than he was toward the ex-enemy states of Bulgaria, Hungary, and Romania. Certainly, the expansion of Soviet power into the heart of Europe in 1945 exceeded the wildest dreams of the most imperialistic czar. For the first time in European history, one great power dominated the entire area between the USSR's western border and Western Europe, an area extending from the Arctic Ocean to the Black Sea (see map). This expansion of Soviet military power was seen by the Western nations as a permanent threat to their security. The roots of the Cold War lay in this fundamental conflict between incompatible conceptions of security and in the worst-case assessments that each side made of the other's moves and intentions.

Even before the war was over, Stalin showed signs of the implacable enmity that was to occasion a countervailing response of domestic anticommunism in the West. As soon as Stalin judged the defeat of Germany inevitable, he ordered Communist parties abroad to purge those who advocated continued "peaceful coexistence and collaboration in the framework of one and the same world." To convey the new line, he had published an article in April 1945 in a French Communist journal, *Cahiers du Communisme.* The Duclos Letter, so dubbed because the article was signed by the French Communist leader, Jacques Duclos, was the signal for party organizations to purge as unreliable those members who were not prepared to follow Moscow's twisting political line and wage political war against the policies of the Western governments. The "defunct" Comintern was soon to experience a public revival under a new imprimatur.

Why Stalin chose this moment to call attention to Moscow's control over foreign Communist parties, thereby inevitably raising Western suspicions of international communism again, is unknown. There are a number of possible explanations, none mutually exclusive. It could have been the counterpart of the move toward ending the relative relaxation of the war-time period and reimposing repressive measures at home. Perhaps it was deemed necessary in order to justify autocratic discipline over the Communist parties coming to power in Eastern Europe. Then again, Stalin may not have believed that the West would acquiesce to his conquests in Eastern Europe and wanted the extra margin of leverage over Western policies that indigenous Communist and Communist-front organizations provided. Or perhaps it was merely a reflection of his normal mode of political operation, one that he could comfortably revert to once the war was over.

Stalin's demands on Turkey were nothing but a blatant land grab, encouraged by the belief that Turkey could be pressured and that the West would not make an issue of the matter in the interest of agreement in Central Europe and the Far East. On March 19, 1945, the Soviet government informed Turkey, which had remained neutral throughout most of the war, that it would not renew the 1925 treaty of neutrality and nonaggression when it expired on November 7, 1945. As the price for a new treaty, Moscow insisted on the return of the northeastern districts of Kars and Ardahan, originally taken by Russia from the Ottoman Empire in 1877 but given up by the Bolsheviks in 1918 by the Treaty of Brest-Litovsk, a loss they accepted in the Soviet-Turkish treaty of 1921; and on military bases in the straits and on the Aegean Sea (at the port of Dedegeatch, which is in the European part of Turkey near the Greek port of Alexandroupolis). There was no Turkish provocation, no threat to the USSR, no insecurity to overcome. This territorial outreach of Stalin's heightened fears in Western circles that his aims in Central and Eastern Europe were not limited to the territory already under Soviet control.

The postwar difficulties may conveniently be dated from the Potsdam conference of July 1945. Relations between the USSR and its Western allies had deteriorated noticeably since Yalta. Discord centered on the Polish issue, the heavy-handedness of Soviet rule in Bulgaria and Romania, the disposition of Trieste, the reparations question, and Allied administration of Germany. Stalin saw no reason to compromise. Behind his inscrutability and gruffness lay a disdain for discussions about principles and confidence that whatever his artillery could reach was his to keep. In a conversation in the spring of 1945 with Milovan Djilas, an intimate of Tito's, Stalin put this attitude in this way: "This war is not as in the past; whoever occupies a territory also imposes on it his own social system. Everyone imposes his own system as far as his army can reach. It cannot be otherwise."[7]

The West accepted the Oder-Neisse boundary between Poland and Germany, failed to insist on guaranteed land access to Berlin, and accepted Stalin's puppet creation in Poland. The conference reinforced the disenchantment that had followed Moscow's installation of coalition governments in which the Communists were assured control of the all-important ministries of interior and of the courts. In a moment of candor, Stalin admitted that a freely elected government in any of the East European countries "would be anti-Soviet, and that we cannot allow." While conflicting interpretations of what constituted "democratic" government aggravated relations, America's rapid demobilization encouraged Stalin to act without fear of effective countermeasures.

The foreign ministers of the big four powers met in the fall, primarily to draft treaties with Finland, Italy, and the Balkan countries. Old problems remained unsolved, and new ones appeared, such as Soviet demands for a trusteeship over one of the former Italian colonies and for the establishment of an Allied control council in Japan comparable to the one operating in Germany, which would have given Moscow a veto over U. S. occupation policy.

Against the background of these protracted, stalemated negotiations, Stalin delivered a preelection speech on February 9, 1946, that signified repression at home and ideological and political conflict on the international level. He reaffirmed the fundamental postulates of Marxist-Leninist theory on the causes and nature of capitalist wars and blamed the West for World War II. He insisted that the defeat of Germany did not necessarily eliminate the danger of war and, lauding the superiority of the Soviet system, called for a "new mighty upsurge in the national economy" that would treble prewar production and guarantee the Soviet Union against another invasion.

The call for improving the standard of living could not disguise the implicit stress on developing the industrial strength on which military power was based. Stalin's gloomy outlook on relations with the capitalist world paralleled Moscow's toughness on the diplomatic front, and was interpreted in the West as an indication of Soviet hostility. The world was sliding toward bipolarity. One month later, on March 5, at Fulton, Missouri, Churchill called for a strengthening of Anglo-American ties in the face of growing Soviet expansion. Though no longer in power, Churchill was still a leader who commanded attention: "From Stettin in the Baltic to Trieste in the Adriatic an iron curtain has descended across the Continent. All these famous cities and the populations around them lie in the Soviet sphere and are subject, in one form or another, not only to Soviet influence but to a very high and increasing degree of control from Moscow." The Iranian crisis lent immediacy to his warning.

## The Iranian Crisis

Iran was occupied by the USSR and Britain during the war in order to safeguard the flow of supplies to the Soviet Union. In early 1946 it could not obtain the promised evacuation of Soviet troops. During their occupation of northern Iran, Soviet authorities had denied the central government in Tehran access to the area and at the same time strengthened the local Communist (Tudeh) party. In September 1945, the Tudeh party sought increased autonomy for Azerbaijan, the Iranian province bordering on the Soviet Union. The central government refused Tudeh demands for fear of augmenting Communist influence elsewhere in Iran. In December 1945 the Communists announced the creation of a new government in Tabriz, capital of Iranian Azerbaijan, under Ja'far Pishevari, a veteran Communist and Comintern agent; they proclaimed a Kurdish People's Republic, with its capital in Mahabad, in western Azerbaijan, and they intensified their efforts to kindle an irredentist movement among the Kurdish tribes of northern Iraq and eastern Turkey, which further heightened Ankara's apprehensiveness. Meanwhile, Iranian troops seeking to reenter Azerbaijan were turned back by the Red Army.

Despite Stalin's assurance that the Soviet Union had no designs, territorial or otherwise, on Iran, Soviet troops continued to occupy the northern provinces. Iran appealed to the United Nations on January 19, 1946, charging the Soviet Union with interference in its internal affairs and with endangering the peace. American efforts to effect a withdrawal of all foreign troops by January 1, 1946, were rejected by the Soviet government, which maintained that under the Iranian-Soviet-British treaty of 1942, it was entitled to remain in Iran until March 2, 1946. During the often acrimonious negotiations in the UN Security Council, a cabinet crisis in Tehran led the shah to appoint Qavam Saltaneh, generally regarded by Western officials as pro-Tudeh, as premier. Qavam began direct talks with Soviet leaders and spent almost a month in Moscow attempting to negotiate a settlement. In the United Nations, Soviet tactics thwarted every effort at a solution — a portent of future Soviet behavior in the world organization. As the date for the departure of Soviet troops under the 1942 agreement came and went with no visible change in Soviet attitude, Western leaders grew profoundly disturbed, particularly in light of Stalin's February speech.

On April 4, the Soviet government agreed to evacuate Iran in return for Iranian concessions, including the formation of a joint-stock Soviet-Iranian oil company and a degree of autonomy for Azerbaijan. Westerners viewed this as a Soviet triumph and glumly awaited Iran's early disappearance behind the Iron Curtain. Though the final decision by the Soviet government to withdraw from Iran by May 9 is usually attributed primarily to President Harry S Truman's tough talk, pressure by the UN Security Council, and world public opinion, the credit, according to Richard N. Frye, should go mainly to the shrewdness of Premier Qavam.

> The Soviet evacuation of northern Iran was the result of a number of factors; probably the most important was the belief on the part of the Russians that Qavam had been won over to their side. He had suppressed the anti-Soviet elements and had agreed to a joint oil company, subject to ratification of parliament. The rebel government in Azerbaijan was growing in strength and there was every reason to suppose that it would maintain its position and even gain at the expense of the Teheran government. The pressure of world opinion and the debates in the United Nations, although they may have been responsible in influencing the Soviet government to evacuate Iran earlier than had been planned, were probably of much less significance than the factors mentioned above. When the Soviet government did announce that it had evacuated all its troops on May 9, 1946, it seemed as though Iran had fallen on the Soviet side of the curtain.[8]

Late that year, the Iranian parliament rejected the proposed economic treaty with the USSR. Qavam had outfoxed Moscow, and by the end of 1946, the danger of a Communist coup had passed. Azerbaijan was once again under the control of the central government. Shortly after, in an ironic twist, Qavam was dismissed and all but exiled because of palace intrigue.

## The Iron Curtain Descends

Preparations for the conference to conclude peace treaties with the East European countries dragged on through the spring of 1946. Not until the end of July did representatives of twenty-one nations meet in Paris. Though no agreement was reached on Germany or Austria — both occupied by the four powers — the Soviet Union agreed to treaties with Italy, Finland, Hungary, and Romania in February 1947. The West had the treaties it so coveted, but time quickly revealed how irrelevant they were. The Soviet government ignored the provisions guaranteeing democratic safeguards and entrenched its domination of Eastern Europe. Stalin pursued his principal political and strategic objectives in Eastern Europe with a singleness of purpose that became only too clear to the Western powers by early 1947. He sought to eliminate all Western influence from the area and concomitantly to establish Soviet hegemony.

The 1947 treaties legalized most of Stalin's territorial acquisitions in Eastern Europe: from Finland, the ice-free port of Petsamo and territory extending the Soviet frontier to Norway; seventy thousand square miles of eastern Poland, including the Vilno area which was ceded to Lithuania; the province of Ruthenia from Czechoslovakia; northern Bukovina and Bessarabia (and control of the Carpathian mountain passes into Central Europe and the Danubian plain) from Romania; and a common border with Hungary (see map, p. 40). The USSR advanced westward territorially by annexing land from each of the countries on its western border; indeed, its policy of expansion and annexation was designed specifically to give the Soviet Union a common border with every country in Eastern Europe, the easier to manage military and political control.[9] Moscow's annexation of Estonia, Latvia, and Lithuania (still not recognized by the United States) gave it control of the eastern shore of the Baltic Sea, and the incorporation of East Prussia from Germany was not recognized by the West until the Helsinki conference in 1975.

Of all the postwar problems, none contributed more to East-West hostility than that of the future of Germany. In a sense, the German problem is *the* European problem. Economic, political, strategic, and technological considerations all coalesce in the struggle over Germany; and the present unchallenged position of the Soviet Union in Eastern Europe cannot be permanently assured as long as Germany, with its reservoir of skilled manpower, scientific expertise, and industrial strength, remains a potential opponent.

The Soviets at first favored an exploitative policy to weaken Germany industrially. However, the Kremlin soon realized the folly of this course and shifted to a more conciliatory policy. This was first expressed by Molotov at the July 1946 Paris meeting of foreign ministers. Asserting that the spirit of revenge could not underlie negotiations with Germany, he acknowledged that it would be foolish to seek to destroy Germany as a state or to agrarianize her and deprive her of major industries. Molotov suggested instead that Germany be permitted to become "a democratic and peace-loving state . . . but [one] which would be deprived of the economic and military potentiality to rise again as an aggressive force." He proposed that the Ruhr, the key to German industrial power, be placed under inter-Allied control and that a single German government willing to fulfill all its obligations, particularly those concerning reparations to the USSR, be set up.

Secretary of State James F. Byrnes responded to this bid for German favor by making similar conciliatory comments in his Stuttgart speech of September 6, 1946. He also, significantly, threw American support behind Germany in the question of a return of the eastern territories. Before the Potsdam conference, the Soviet Union had unilaterally transferred all German territory east of the Neisse River to Poland, thus strengthening Poland's claim to the area that served to compensate it for the seventy thousand square miles of eastern Poland annexed by the USSR, and not unintentionally making Poland dependent on continued Soviet goodwill for preservation of its new territorial configuration. Byrnes's strategy forced the Soviets to side with the Poles against the Germans, thus deflating Soviet prestige in West Germany. Less than eighteen months after the defeat of Germany, the victors had fallen out among themselves and were courting public opinion in the former foe.

The chill of Cold War, already perceptible in the middle of 1945, penetrated to the core of East-West relations by late 1946. The steel in Stalin's policy may be gleaned from a generally overlooked interview given to CBS correspondent Richard C. Hottelet in June 1946 by Maxim Litvinov, then a sidetracked, isolated, pessimistic deputy foreign minister, a holdover from the days when Moscow pushed collective security with the Western powers and he was its prime spokesman. When asked how he viewed prospects for East-West cooperation, Litvinov replied, "The outlook is bad. It seems as though the differences between East and West have gone too far to be reconciled . . . ." He gave two reasons: first, "there has been a return in Russia to the outmoded concept of security in terms of territory — the more you've got, the safer you are"; and second, "the root cause is the ideological conception prevailing [in Moscow] that conflict between the Communist and capitalist worlds is inevitable."[10]

By the beginning of 1947, Stalin's policy of imperial expansion had crested; he had what he wanted in the Baltic area, Eastern Europe, and the Far East. But his reach had exceeded his grasp in Iran and Turkey; his tyranny at home and exploitation of tensions abroad through foreign Communist parties had aroused a countervailing anti-Communist and anti-Soviet sentiment and policy; his obstructionism in the United Nations was interpreted as hostility to cooperation with non-Communist countries; and he faced the whirlwind of Western fears for the outcomes of the ongoing civil wars in China and Greece (though in neither instance was Soviet assistance of any importance). The net result of all of this was a major transformation in the USSR's relations with the West.

# Notes

1. *Pravda,* August 4, 1941.

2. J. K. Zawodny, *Death in the Forest: The Story of the Katyn Forest Massacre* (Notre Dame, Ind: University of Notre Dame Press, 1962).

3. Samuel L. Sharp, *Poland: White Eagle on a Red Field* (Cambridge: Harvard University Press, 1953), 168–170.

4. *Sunday Times* (London), November 24, 1968.

5. U. S. Department of Defense, *The Entry of the Soviet Union Into the War Against Japan: Military Plans, 1941–1945* (Washington, D.C.: Government Printing Office, 1955).

6. Winston S. Churchill, *Triumph and Tragedy* (Boston: Houghton Mifflin, 1953), 402.

7. Milovan Djilas, *Conversations With Stalin* (New York: Harcourt, Brace & World, 1962), 114.

8. Lewis V. Thomas and Richard N. Frye, *The United States and Turkey and Iran* (Cambridge: Harvard University Press, 1951), 239–240.

9. Huey Louis Kostanick, "The Significance of Geopolitical Changes in Eastern Europe," *Education,* vol. 72 (February 1952), 381–387.

10. Quoted in Robert G. Kaiser, *Cold Winter, Cold War* (New York: Stein and Day, 1974), 12–13. For an overall evaluation of Litvinov's series of revealing discussions with Western journalists between May 1943 and February 1947, see Vojtech Mastny, "The Cassandra in the Foreign Commissariat: Maxim Litvinov and the Cold War," *Foreign Affairs,* vol. 54, no. 2 (January 1976), 366–376.

## Selected Bibliography

ALPEROVITZ, GAR. *Atomic Diplomacy: Hiroshima and Potsdam.* New York: Simon and Schuster, 1965.

BEITZELL, ROBERT. *The Uneasy Alliance: America, Britain and Russia, 1941–1943.* New York: Knopf, 1973.

BETTS, R. R. (ED.). *Central and South East Europe, 1945–1948.* London: Royal Institute of International Affairs, 1950.

BUTOW, ROBERT J. C. *Japan's Decision to Surrender.* Stanford: Stanford University Press, 1954.

CHURCHILL, WINSTON S. *The Second World War.* 6 vols. Boston: Houghton Mifflin, 1948–1953.

CLARK, ALAN. *Barbarossa: The Russian-German Conflict, 1941–1945.* New York: Morrow, 1964.

CLEMENS, DIANE SHAVER. *Yalta.* New York: Oxford University Press, 1970.

DALLIN, ALEXANDER. *German Rule in Russia, 1941–1945: A Study of Occupation Policies.* New York: St. Martin's, 1957.

DAWSON, RAYMOND H. *The Decision to Aid Russia, 1941.* Chapel Hill: University of North Carolina Press, 1959.

DEANE, JOHN R. *The Strange Alliance: The Story of Our Efforts at Wartime Cooperation with Russia.* New York: Viking, 1947.

DJILAS, MILOVAN. *Conversations with Stalin.* New York: Harcourt Brace and World, 1962.

ERICKSON, JOHN. *The Road to Stalingrad: Stalin's War With Germany.* Vol. 1. New York: Harper and Row, 1975.

FEIS, HERBERT. *Churchill-Roosevelt-Stalin.* Princeton: Princeton University Press, 1957.

———. *Between War and Peace: The Potsdam Conference.* Princeton: Princeton University Press, 1960.

FISCHER, LOUIS. *The Road to Yalta: Soviet Foreign Relations, 1941–1945.* New York: Harper and Row, 1972.

FLEMING, D. F. *The Cold War and Its Origins, 1917–1960.* 2 vols. Garden City, N.Y.: Doubleday, 1961.

GADDIS, JOHN LEWIS. *The United States and the Origins of the Cold War, 1941–1947.* New York: Columbia University Press, 1972.

HERRING, GEORGE C., JR. *Aid to Russia 1941–1946: Strategy, Diplomacy, the Origins of the Cold War.* New York: Columbia University Press, 1973.

HERZ, MARTIN F. *Beginnings of the Cold War*. Bloomington: Indiana University Press, 1966.

IATRIDES, JOHN O. *Revolt in Athens: The Greek Communist "Second Round," 1944–1945*. Princeton: Princeton University Press, 1972.

INGRAM, KENNETH. *History of the Cold War*. New York: Philosophical Library, 1955.

KACEWICZ, GEORGE. *Great Britain, the Soviet Union and the Polish Government in Exile (1939–1945)*. The Hague: Nijhoff, 1979.

KENNAN, GEORGE F. *Memoirs 1925–1950*. Boston: Atlantic–Little, Brown, 1967.

KIRK, GEORGE E. *Survey of International Affairs: The Middle East in the War*. New York: Oxford University Press, 1953.

KOT, STANISLAW (ED.). *Conversations with the Kremlin and Dispatches from Russia*. New York: Oxford University Press, 1963.

LENSEN, GEORGE ALEXANDER. *The Strange Neutrality: Soviet-Japanese Relations During the Second World War, 1941–1945*. Tallahassee, Fl.: Diplomatic Press, 1972.

LUKACS, JOHN. *The Great Powers and Eastern Europe*. New York: American Book, 1953.

———. *A New History of the Cold War*. 3rd ed. Garden City, N.Y.: Doubleday, 1966.

———. *1945: Year Zero*. New York: Doubleday, 1978.

MARTEL, LEON C. *Lend-Lease, Loans, and the Coming of the Cold War*. Boulder, Col.: Westview Press, 1979.

MASTNY, VOJTECH. *Russia's Road to the Cold War*. New York: Columbia University Press, 1979.

MCCAGG, WILLIAM O., JR. *Stalin Embattled, 1943–1948*. Detroit: Wayne State University Press, 1978.

MCCAULEY, MARTIN (ED.). *Communist Power in Europe, 1944–49*. New York: Barnes and Noble, 1977.

MCNEILL, WILLIAM H. *America, Britain, and Russia: Their Cooperation and Conflict, 1941–1946*. New York: Oxford University Press, 1954.

MOSELY, PHILIP E. *The Kremlin and World Politics*. New York: Vintage, 1960.

NAGAI, YONOSUKE, and AKIRA IRIYE (EDS.). *The Origins of the Cold War in Asia*. New York: Columbia University Press, 1977.

PATERSON, THOMAS G. *Soviet-American Confrontation: Postwar Reconstruction and the Origins of the Cold War*. Baltimore: Johns Hopkins University Press, 1973.

PETROV, VLADIMIR. *June 22, 1941: Soviet Historians and the German Invasion.* Columbia: University of South Carolina Press, 1968.

RIEBER, ALFRED J. *Stalin and the French Communist Party, 1941–1947.* New York: Columbia University Press, 1962.

ROZEK, EDWARD J. *Allied Wartime Diplomacy: A Pattern in Poland.* New York: Wiley, 1958.

SEATON, ALBERT. *The Russo-German War, 1941–1945.* New York: Praeger, 1971.

SETON-WATSON, HUGH. *The East European Revolution.* New York: Praeger, 1956.

SHARP, SAMUEL. *Poland, White Eagle on a Red Field.* Cambridge: Harvard University Press, 1953.

STEPHAN, JOHN J. *The Kuril Islands: Russo-Japanese Frontiers in the Pacific.* New York: Oxford University Press, 1974.

STRIK-STRIKFELDT, WILFRED. *Against Stalin and Hitler, 1941–1945.* London: Macmillan, 1970.

WHALEY, BARTON. *Codeword Barbarossa.* Cambridge: MIT Press, 1973.

XYDIS, STEPHEN G. *Greece and the Great Powers, 1944–1947: Prelude to the "Truman Doctrine."* Thessaloniki, Greece: Institute for Balkan Studies, 1963.

YERGIN, DANIEL. *The Shattered Peace.* Boston: Houghton Mifflin, 1977.

# 3
# Stalinization and Imperial Consolidation, 1947–1953

Stalin's policies gave rise to two developments — one American, the other Soviet — that institutionalized the Cold War and the division of East and West into mutually antagonistic blocs. The Truman Doctrine and the Zhdanov line were the formal expressions of the superpower impetus toward a bipolar world. The former led to an economic recovery program and military buildup and the latter to a closed ideological and political system, the consequences of which were to reinforce the trend toward bloc exclusivity.

On March 12, 1947, President Truman announced the decision to extend economic and military assistance to Greece and Turkey, and "to support peoples who are resisting attempted subjugation by armed minorities or by outside pressure," i.e., international communism. The announcement was prompted by the inability of Great Britain to continue to bear the responsibility for the defense of the eastern Mediterranean, and British power in the area was gradually replaced by that of the United States. Moscow branded the Truman Doctrine "a smokescreen for expansion." It described the policy as an example of America's postwar imperialism and circumvention of the UN and dismissed the U.S. contention that the USSR threatened the Turkish straits or the provinces of Kars and Ardahan, insisting that "no one and nothing actually threatens Turkey's integrity. This 'assistance' is evidently aimed at putting [Turkey] also under U. S. control."

The Truman Doctrine was a watershed in U. S. postwar policy. Once committed to the proposition that no other European countries should be allowed to fall under the heel of international communism, the United States went beyond the Truman Doctrine with a more permanent and far-reaching program of economic assistance. On June 5, 1947, Secretary of

State George C. Marshall, speaking at Harvard University, expressed America's willingness to help rebuild Europe and invited the European nations to draw up a list of their needs. Under the leadership of British Foreign Secretary Ernest Bevin and French Foreign Minister Georges Bidault, a conference of all European nations, including the Soviet Union, was convened in Paris on June 27. Discussions were at first secret. Then, on June 29, Moscow unexpectedly issued a statement denouncing the conference and the proposals. The thrust of the attack was to begin with largely economic, with Moscow alleging that the proposals entailed an integration of the various national economies that would require it to abandon its own plans for Eastern Europe's industrialization and incorporation into the Soviet five-year plans. It also intimated that the Marshall Plan, which provided economic assistance to promote Europe's recovery from World War II's destruction and dislocation, was intended to advance the economic, and hence political, expansion of American influence.

By July 2, Moscow had withdrawn from the conference and forced all the East European countries to follow suit. It is unlikely that the U.S. Congress would have appropriated any funds for the program had the USSR remained one of the possible recipients, and continued Soviet participation in the talks might well have sounded the death knell for the Marshall Plan and for European recovery, but Stalin was not prepared to run any risks where Soviet control of Eastern Europe was concerned.

The Soviet refusal to participate in the Marshall Plan program was a logical outcome of the East-West estrangement. First, many Soviet leaders believed in an impending severe economic crisis in the United States; certainly most periodicals stressed this theme. Accordingly, the Soviets could scarcely be expected, given their ideology and objectives, to join any plan specifically designed to stabilize the capitalist world. Of particular pertinence was the denunciation in May 1947 of Eugene Varga, a prominent Soviet economist, for arguing that a capitalist crisis was not imminent and that capitalism was entering an era of stabilization and growth.

Second, Stalin's interest in "Sovietizing" Eastern Europe made him doubly suspicious of any Western proposal that could interfere with this overriding strategic objective. To have permitted the East Europeans extensive economic access to the West would have politically strengthened the pro-Western elements still hanging on in the Moscow-managed coalition governments and complicated the process of full Sovietization.

Third, Stalin was not interested in all-European recovery unless there was immediate and significant advantage to the USSR. This was understandable economically, given the Soviet Union's need to tend its own wounds. It was also sound politically, since an unstable Western Europe decreased the likelihood of interference with Soviet policies in Eastern Europe. Indeed, instability might further strengthen Communist parties, particularly in Italy and France, where the Communists had emerged from the war with enhanced prestige and broad electoral support. Thus, impeding Western Europe's recovery would not only keep the West from challenging Soviet hegemony in Eastern Europe, but might even help the spread of communism.

Fourth, Stalin mistrusted American motives. He assumed that the United States had imperial ambitions that mirrored his own and that the flag would follow the funds, with U.S. influence and military control accompanying its aid.

Finally, Soviet participation would have required Moscow to divulge statistical data revealing its economic weaknesses. A xenophobic and secretive Kremlin would hardly be receptive to such a requirement.

Whatever the compelling reasons, during the summer and fall of 1947, East-West relations sharply deteriorated as Soviet attacks on the Marshall Plan intensified. On September 18, 1947, Andrei Y. Vyshinsky, the Soviet delegate to the United Nations, set the general tenor for official policy in a speech before the General Assembly:

> As is now clear, the Marshall Plan constitutes in essence merely a variant of the Truman Doctrine adapted to the conditions of postwar Europe. In bringing forward this plan, the United States Government apparently counted on the cooperation of the Governments of the United Kingdom and France to confront the European countries in need of relief with the necessity of renouncing their inalienable right to dispose of their economic resources and to plan their national economy in their own way. The United States also counted on making all these countries directly dependent on the interests of American monopolies, which are striving to avert the approaching depression by an accelerated export of commodities and capital to Europe. . . .
>
> Moreover, this Plan is an attempt to split Europe into two camps and, with the help of the United Kingdom and France, to complete the formation of a *bloc* of several European countries hostile to the interests of the democratic countries of Eastern Europe and most particularly to the interests of the Soviet Union.

## Institutionalizing Sovietization

Stalin completed the breach by organizing his satellites into a formal grouping of states subservient to the Soviet Union. The Comintern was resurrected as the Cominform (Communist Information Bureau) at a special conference of Communist parties in Polish Silesia on September 22–23, 1947. Only nine parties — from Bulgaria, Czechoslovakia, France, Hungary, Italy, Poland, Romania, Yugoslavia, and the USSR — were invited because Stalin's primary aim was to consolidate Eastern Europe, not promote international communism or the parliamentary prospects of Communist parties elsewhere in Europe.

By ending the policy that had encouraged West European Communist parties in the 1944-to-1947 period to enter into coalitions with bourgeois governments and by ordering them to oppose Marshall Plan programs, Stalin sought to intensify Western uneasiness over the revolutionary potential of their own Communist parties and thereby to divert the West's attention away from Soviet policy in Eastern Europe.[1] Besides, Stalin turned his regional need into an international advantage: Seeing that Communist movements in China, Vietnam, the Philippines, and Greece had already implicitly rejected Moscow's leadership by not waiting for the Red Army to "liberate" their countries, and by choosing the revolutionary rather than the evolutionary road to power, he used his about-face in Europe to reassert Soviet militancy and again place the USSR in the vanguard of world revolutionary activity.

To justify the establishment of the Cominform ideologically, the Kremlin formally revived the thesis of the capitalist menace and emphasized the enduring and irreconcilable antagonisms between the capitalist and Communist systems. Andrei A. Zhdanov's speech at the founding conference must be regarded as the most significant effort since the Comintern program of 1928 to formulate the position of international communism in the world and to integrate it into a unified whole. The importance of the speech lay not only in its ambitious scope, but in the powerful position of the man charged with its presentation. Zhdanov, who died the following year, was regarded as second only to Stalin.

Zhdanov began by announcing that the war had altered world power relationships:

> The fundamental changes caused by the war on the international scene and in the position of individual countries have entirely changed the political landscape of the world. A new alignment of political forces has arisen. The more the war recedes into the past, the more distinct become two major trends in postwar international policy, corresponding to the division of the political forces operating on the international arena into two major camps; the imperialist and antidemocratic camp, on the one hand, and the anti-imperialist and democratic camp, on the other. The principal driving force of the imperialist camp is the USA. Allied with it are Great Britain and France. . . . The cardinal purpose of the imperialist camp is to strengthen imperialism, to hatch a new imperialist war, to combat socialism and democracy, and to support reactionary and antidemocratic profascist regimes and movements everywhere.*

---

* Andrei Zhdanov, *The International Situation* (Moscow: Foreign Languages Publishing House, 1947), excerpts.

Clearly, he identified the United States as the principal antagonist and castigated the economic, ideological, and military bases of its foreign policy, claiming that its underlying motif was expansionism. Justifying Moscow's opposition to the Marshall Plan and its determination to control Eastern Europe, he at the same time dropped an olive twig along the way: "Soviet foreign policy proceeds from the fact of the coexistence for a long period of the two systems — capitalism and socialism. From this it follows that cooperation between the USSR and the countries with other systems is possible, provided that the principle of reciprocity is observed and that obligations once assumed are honored." But this hint that the Kremlin was open to a deal formalizing the division of Europe into spheres of influence was lost in the hostility that flowed from the rest of the speech and that characterized the behavior of the Soviet Union and its Communist agents in the months that followed. Zhdanov's call for all Communist parties to act in concerted opposition to the Marshall Plan was interpreted in the West as a declaration of permanent Cold War. The tactical consequences of this militant policy soon emerged in France and Italy, where in November 1947 general strikes accompanied by labor violence were instigated in an attempt to paralyze the nascent Marshall Plan program, and in Southern Asia, where Communist parties split with bourgeois nationalist movements and attempted to subvert the newly independent governments in India, Burma, Indonesia, and the Philippines by direct revolutionary means.

In addition to mobilizing Communist parties against the Marshall Plan and Western policy in Europe, the Cominform had other, longer-term, Soviet-bloc oriented purposes. Ideologically, it promulgated the line from Moscow and provided political guidance for foreign Communists. Organizationally, it facilitated the consolidation of Soviet power, ensuring Moscow's control over the various East European Communist parties. Politically, as a focal point for international communism, it not only crystallized opposition to the West, but symbolized Communist unity and Soviet leadership of the international Communist movement. The establishment of the Cominform was a turning point for Stalin. Henceforth, accommodation and cooperation with the non-Communist world — the official line during the 1941-to-1947 period — was dropped, and the focus was on antagonism between blocs.

Soviet belligerency sharpened in the UN, in Germany, and in Austria, but it was in Czechoslovakia in February 1948 that Stalin showed his hegemonic absolutism and dropped the last fig leaf of democracy in Eastern Europe. The Communist takeover that ordained Czechoslovakia's disappearance behind the Iron Curtain shocked the West. After all, the Communists had been in control of most of the country's institutions since 1945; the first postwar elections in May 1946 had given them 38 percent of the vote (the largest percentage), and Czechoslovakia had pulled out of the Marshall Plan discussions on Stalin's orders. Moscow's preeminent influence was accepted as a fact of East European reality. But that was not enough for Stalin, who would settle for nothing less than total domination. Perhaps more than any other single Soviet-inspired move, the fall of Prague dispelled remaining Western illusions concerning Soviet intentions, heightened fears of new Soviet thrusts, hastened Western rearmament, and froze the division of Europe. The disappearance of Czechoslovkia as a middle ground in which democratic socialist and Communist groups could coexist symbolized the end of possible cooperation between East and West.

Next, Stalin took steps to end the last vestiges of coalition government in Eastern Europe and to consolidate his empire — a process noticeably accelerated after the split with Tito. Through an intricate network of alliances, trade and economic agreements, joint-stock companies, and Communist party and secret police connections, Soviet hegemony was entrenched throughout the region. Cultural and political ties with the West were eliminated, and economic transactions were reduced to insignificant levels. By June 1948, the Soviet Union had created a cowed empire from the Baltic to the Black Sea. To the West it seemed that only America's monopoly on atomic weapons barred Soviet domination of all Europe and prevented the Red Army from marching to the English Channel.

Two dramatic developments occurred in that month: the Berlin blockade and the expulsion of Tito from the Cominform. Each had an effect far beyond its immediate frame of reference. In retrospect, these were two of Stalin's major postwar miscalculations (the aggression in Korea might be considered a third), setting in motion a chain of events unfavorable to the consolidation of the Soviet empire and to the perpetuation of Stalinism as the modus operandi of Muscovite rule over Eastern Europe.

## The Berlin Blockade  χ

On June 24, 1948, the Soviet Union imposed a blockade on the Western sectors of Berlin, which lies 110 miles inside the Soviet zone of Germany, saying that the Western powers were carrying out a separate currency reform in their sectors of the city without Soviet agreement. In the previous months, Soviet authorities had periodically interfered with Western access to Berlin, but had hesitated to impose a full blockade. Several considerations motivated their behavior. First, by forcing the Western powers out of Berlin and bringing the entire city under their control, the Soviets expected to gain added prestige that would improve their prospects of controlling Germany. Second, they hoped to undermine the efforts that were being made to establish West Germany as an independent country within the Western camp. Third, an Allied retreat in Berlin would

have strengthened Communist party prestige elsewhere in Western Europe, further improving its electoral chances.

However, once the Berlin airlift started, the Soviets' decision in favor of a lengthy test of strength brought results that were almost diametrically opposite to their original expectations. The stakes were high, particularly for the United States. American willingness to pay the price of the airlift eventually convinced Stalin of the danger of his gambit, and a settlement was reached in May 1949, after months of trying negotiation. The Kremlin had suffered its first postwar setback in Europe. The blockade failed to drive the Western powers out of Berlin and also to prevent the establishment of the Federal Republic of Germany (FRG) on May 23, 1949.

Moscow responded in kind by setting up the German Democratic Republic (GDR) in October 1949. This formalized partition of Germany is an ever-present reminder of the division between West and East and of the deep-rooted rivalry between them. As long as the West lacks guaranteed land access to West Berlin, it is captive to Soviet and East German squeezes. Berlin is a local sore in East-West relations, easily irritated and quickly swollen to international proportions.

## Titoism: The End of the Muscovite Monolith   X

The world first learned of the deep fissure within the supposedly solid edifice of international communism on June 28, 1948, when the Cominform announced the expulsion of the Yugoslav Communist party for "anti-Party and anti-Soviet views, incompatible with Marxism-Leninism." The Yugoslavs were accused of having deviated from "the united socialist front against imperialism" and "taken up a position of nationalism." In a word, they were unwilling to turn their country into a colony of the Soviet Union.

Stalin would not accept Tito, his most faithful and "Stalinist" disciple in Eastern Europe, as an equal. He insisted upon unchallenged political and economic control by the Kremlin and a privileged position for Soviet diplomats and advisers stationed in Yugoslavia. Irritated by his inability to dominate the Yugoslav Communist party — to infiltrate it and the Yugoslav governmental apparatus with agents loyal to the Kremlin — or to reduce Yugoslavs were accused of having deviated from "the united socialist front countries, Stalin invoked the ultimate weapon, excommunication, against his former protégé. He expected to overthrow Tito by waging an intensive propaganda campaign through the Cominform and by utilizing Soviet prestige to wean Yugoslav party members away from Tito, and he used every means at his disposal, short of military intervention. The result, Stalin assumed, would be to bring to power a pro-Soviet leadership prepared to do Moscow's bidding.

However, in positing that the highest loyalty of all good Communists must be to the Soviet Union as the "socialist motherland," Stalin underestimated the countervailing pull of nationalism (as had Karl Marx). He did not realize the broad basis of Tito's support or the force of Yugoslav nationalism. Aided by the fortunate circumstance of not sharing a common border with the Soviet Union, by the loyalty of party and military cadres whose bonds had been forged in the common struggle against Nazi overlordship and not in the bureaucratic intrigues of Kremlin-prescribed compounds, and by the undoubted popularity of Tito as a national hero, the Yugoslav leadership held firm. Stalin was to rue his boast that "I will shake my little finger, and there will be no more Tito. He will fall."

One may glean something of the way in which Stalin dealt with the East European and Baltic satellites from an account that the Yugoslav government, fearful of a Soviet attack and eager for international support, published in 1951:

> From the very moment inter-State relations were established, the Soviet Government began organizing espionage against the existing socialist order in Yugoslavia and against the independence of the Yugoslav peoples. The primary aim of these actions was to create a network of secret agents which would be a tool of the Soviet Government for undermining the Yugoslav Government. By a whole series of steps and acts which it undertook even before the Cominform Resolution of June, 1948, the Soviet Government attempted to impose unequal relations on Yugoslavia and to interfere in its internal affairs. . . .

The Yugoslav white paper noted that "the Soviet Government considers that its diplomatic and other representatives [secret police agents] in a friendly country should have a special privileged status and that they have the right of prying into all State and Party affairs without the knowledge of the Government of that country." The Soviet government considered itself "a super-Government in another socialist country" and Soviet officials "did not hesitate to inveigle the citizens of that country into their intelligence service, taking as a point of departure the concept that Communists owe allegiance to the Soviet Goverment first and then to the leadership of their own socialist State." The Yugoslavs denounced the Cominform resolution of June 1948 as an open provocation to civil war:

> The Cominform Resolution was in effect a signal for the launching of the unprecedented campaign against Yugoslavia, aimed at forcing the Yugoslav Government and peoples, by way of political, diplomatic, economic, propagandistic, military and other kinds of pressure and threats, to renounce their rights to sovereignty and independence, their right to be the master in their own home. . . .

The principle of economic cooperation with all countries, regardless of their internal systems, which the Governments of the USSR and the Eastern European countries support in words, has actually been transformed into an economic war which the Governments of those countries are waging against Yugoslavia in the most varied forms, including cancellation of regularly concluded contracts; the circumvention, violation and breach of trade agreements; the complete cessation and breaking off of all economic exchanges; the stoppage of reparations payments, issuing from the Peace Treaty, by Hungary; the obstruction and cessation even of transport and postal connections; the impeding of free navigation on the Danube, etc., etc.[2]

Yugoslavia's resistance to Soviet domination was to have profound consequences for Soviet foreign policy after Stalin's death. Titoism, polycentrism, or national communism (as the phenomenon is most commonly called) is more than a reaction against Soviet domination; it represents a fusion of nationalism and communism into a doctrine and a movement having a variety of forms and signifying a measure of independence from Soviet control, varying from complete opposition to significant autonomy in domestic matters. It represents the primacy of nationalism over communism and poses permanent dilemmas for Soviet leaders: Under what circumstances should the Kremlin use diplomacy and accommodation as opposed to compulsion and pressure in order to eliminate or moderate challenges to its established position and vital interests? How far dare Moscow go in acceding to demands for local autonomy in return for allegiance to the USSR, without jeopardizing its preeminent strategic and political position?

After 1948, Stalin initiated a series of purges of possible Titos and intensified the pace of Sovietization and Stalinization. He insisted on total subservience; leading Communists — Gomulka in Poland, Rajk in Hungary, Kostov in Bulgaria, Slansky in Czechoslovakia — were swept from power. The Stalinist pattern of organization was imposed upon Eastern Europe. Industry, foreign trade, and transportation were nationalized; centralized economic control and planning were introduced, and all economies were geared to servicing Soviet needs. Party organizations were purged and secret police ties with the Soviet KGB were expanded. To ensure the permanence and stability of his empire, Stalin sought to remake the economic, social, and political fabric of Eastern European societies.

This process, though piecemeal and wasteful, when combined with the Soviet pressure on Berlin and the rising threat from Communist revolutions in Asia, heightened Western feelings of insecurity and prompted the creation of a more formalized system of military alliance. On April 4, 1949, the North Atlantic Treaty Organization (NATO) was established. This Western response was intended to serve as a trip wire, a reminder to the Soviet Union that any military move farther westward on its part would meet with an American nuclear response, which, at the time, was the West's only deterrent to a possible military attack. By its founders, NATO was regarded as a legitimate exercise of the "inherent right of individual or collective self-defense" granted under Articles 51 and 52 of the UN Charter. But Moscow saw the treaty as a manifestation of groundless anti-Sovietism directed against the Soviet Union and the countries of Eastern Europe. Denying that its own treaties with the Eastern European countries could be interpreted "as treaties which are in any degree aimed against the allies of the USSR in the late war," it declared that Western rearmament and establishment of NATO could "in no way be justified by the interests of self-defense." Rather, "the North Atlantic Pact is designed to intimidate the states which do not agree to obey the dictates of the Anglo-American grouping of Powers that lay claim to world domination."* NATO was seen as the newest expression of aggressive capitalism that could perpetuate itself only by embarking on imperialist ventures.

NATO and the unexpectedly rapid revival of Japan and Germany confirmed Stalin's perception of an evolving bipolar world. To supplement its political opposition to NATO, Moscow stepped up anti-Western propaganda. Operating through numerous front organizations, the most important being the Partisans of Peace, it attempted to preempt the theme of peace, encourage resistance to rearmament in the West, and undermine Western influence in Asia and the Middle East. Regarding military matters, by late 1949 two events had enhanced Moscow's prestige and overall strategic military position: the detonation of the USSR's first atom bomb, and the triumph of the Communists on the mainland of China, which meant that domination of the Eurasian land mass had passed to the Communist world. As the lines of hostility and military wariness froze in Europe, events in the Far East attracted increasing attention.

## A New Relationship with China  ☓

Soviet aims in the Far East had been realized at Yalta. Western agreement to restore the sphere of influence controlled by Russia in 1904, at the time of the Russo-Japanese war, fulfilled Stalin's ambitious territorial objectives; he had even improved on czarist Russia's patrimony in Asia.

Quite remarkably, Nationalist China quickly accepted the accords on Asia reached at the Yalta conference, to which it had not been invited. Like Sun Yat-sen in 1923, Chiang Kai-shek in 1945 was prepared to acquiesce to Soviet demands for hegemony over portions of imperial China that he then was unable to control in return for support against a domestic

---

* Memorandum of the USSR Government of March 31, 1949, excerpts.

rival — in Chiang's case, Mao Zedong (Mao Tse-tung) and the CCP. Such was Chiang Kai-shek's eagerness that Washington on several occasions cautioned the Chinese against granting too many concessions, as, for example, agreeing to the unsupervised plebiscite in Mongolia in October 1945. Chiang recognized the "independence" of the Mongolian People's Republic and agreed to Soviet participation in the operation of the Chinese Eastern Railway (and the consequent privileged Soviet economic position), to joint Sino-Soviet use of the naval base of Port Arthur, and to the internationalization of Dairen. These Soviet gains were formally acknowledged in the Sino-Soviet Treaty of Friendship and Alliance, signed on August 14, 1945 (one day before the Japanese surrender). In return, the Soviet government recognized the government of Chiang Kai-shek as the legitimate government of China and pledged itself "to render to China moral support and aid in military supplies and other material resources, such support and aid to be entirely given to the Nationalist Government as the central government of China." But Mao's successful revolution was to change all of this.

After the Soviet and Chinese Communist debacle in 1927, Soviet control over the reorganized CCP had diminished, and Moscow's contact with it was rather limited in the 1935-to-1945 period, notwithstanding a common commitment to Marxism-Leninism. It is true that in the wake of the Japanese surrender, the Chinese Communists' takeover of major portions of Manchuria was aided by Soviet military authorities still occupying the area, who obstructed the easy deployment of advance elements of Chiang's army and who stacked quantities of captured Japanese weapons in places convenient for Mao's troops to collect them. Moscow had no interest in seeing a unified and strong China emerge too quickly. By covertly encouraging the rebel CCP, Stalin expected to acquire some added leverage on a Kuomintang (KMT) already dependent on Soviet goodwill and to obtain more time to consolidate Soviet acquisitions.

Stalin did not expect Mao to emerge the victor from the Chinese civil war, certainly not as quickly as he did. In late 1945, shortly before the CCP guerillas moved in, Soviet authorities stripped Manchuria of all usable industrial equipment, rolling stock, and valuables; they evidently did not foresee that within four years they would need to establish formal state-to-state relations with a fellow Communist and "fraternal" regime. Moscow was committed to Chiang's government; three times it agreed to his requests that Soviet troops remain in Manchuria until such time as the KMT could be present in sufficient force to forestall a Chinese Communist takeover of the area. (Soviet forces finally withdrew in May 1946.) Stalin may have been as surprised as the West at the shocking disintegration of the well-equipped, well-supplied Kuomintang forces and at the dramatic Communist military advances in 1947 and 1948, and perhaps he feared

U.S. intervention to prevent a CCP victory. According to a Yugoslav official, Stalin had recommended to Mao that he reach an agreement with Chiang and enter into a coalition government. Supposedly Mao agreed, but on returning home went his own way and won. Stalin is also alleged to have had doubts about the extent to which the Chinese Communists were genuine Communists, more than once referring to them as "radish Communists — red on the outside but white on the inside."

The outcome of the Chinese civil war was not determined in Moscow. At best, Soviet leaders contributed only marginally to Mao's victory. The CCP's reputation for reform and efficiency, the purposefulness and honesty of Mao and his associates, and the appeal that a strong and united China had for all strata of Chinese society contrasted vividly with the Kuomintang's failure to cope with China's inflation, poverty, and socioeconomic collapse, the venality of KMT officials, and Chiang Kai-shek's insensitivity to the peasants' profound desire for an end to war.

American efforts to mediate the civil war proved futile. It is doubtful that they ever enjoyed the faintest prospect of success. Moscow pursued a policy of outwardly correct diplomatic relations with the KMT while taking tentative steps to strengthen the position of what it considered to be the most pro-Soviet factions in the CCP. For example, without consulting Mao, Stalin invited Kao Kang, who was the Communist in charge of Manchuria, to Moscow in July 1949 to sign a trade agreement.[3]

On October 1, 1949, the People's Republic of China (PRC) was proclaimed in Beijing. An era of Far Eastern history had come to an end. China's destiny was no longer decided in Europe or Japan. For the first time in more than a century, all of mainland China was ruled by one Chinese elite. The century of weak central authority, civil wars, unequal treaties, economic subordination to foreign powers, and military helplessness was now past. Out of this crucible emerged a ruthless, dedicated, disciplined leadership — the Calvinists of Asia — intent on creating a powerful, industrialized, independent China. This development inevitably affected Soviet foreign policy and great-power relationships in Asia, relationships already greatly altered as a consequence of World War II and the unstable 1945–1949 interregnum.

For Moscow, a replacement for the Sino-Soviet treaty of 1945 was necessary. In December 1949 Mao went to Moscow and for two months negotiated a new political and military relationship between China and the Soviet Union. Though distrustful of Stalin on the basis of their previous dealings, Mao decided against a Titoist alternative, which might well have created problems for him in the CCP, and succeeded in exacting significant concessions from the Soviet leadership. After tough bargaining, three agreements were signed on February 14, 1950. First, a thirty-year treaty of alliance directed against the United States (though formally it was directed against "Japan or any other State which should unite with Japan, directly or indirectly. . .") was concluded. Second, an agreement was reached on Manchuria, whereby the Chinese Changchun Railway and the naval base at Port Arthur were to be returned to China "immediately upon the conclusion of a peace treaty with Japan, but not later than the end of 1952," and the commercial port of Dalny (Dairen) was recognized as China's though its dispositon was left in abeyance pending a peace treaty with Japan. (In case of war, Port Arthur was to be jointly operated, so because of the Korean War its final transfer to China was postponed until 1955.) Third, the Soviets agreed to a $300 million credit, a niggardly amount that sealed Mao's coolness toward Moscow and prompted Khrushchev's observation in 1956 that "Stalin treated Mao Tse-tung like a beggar."

These agreements were modified in 1954 to the further advantage of China, but even in 1950 they reflected the Kremlin's awareness that Mao, like Tito, had come to power under circumstances completely different from those that had led to Soviet hegemony over Eastern Europe. Historically, Russian policy had dealt with a weak, divided China, but Stalin recognized that new conditions necessitated concessions. He decided to pursue a "correct," if hardheaded, policy toward Beijing. He did force Mao to accept the independence of Mongolia and joint exploitation of Xinjiang's mineral resources, but he was careful not to overreach himself. Mao, commanding his own army and controlling a vast land mass, was accorded a basic equality vis-à-vis the Soviet Union. Stalin had learned the lesson of Tito well. Once burnt, twice shy.

Within a few months, the Sino-Soviet alliance was tested by conflict in Korea. The Korean War, like the Berlin blockade and the excommunication of Tito from the Cominform, was to have far-reaching significance for Soviet relations with the Western world and profoundly to affect its dealings with other Communist countries, though not until after the tyrant's death did the seeds that he had sown yield bitter fruit.

## The Korean Adventure ⋊

Stalin's interest in neighboring Korea was strategic. Like "Russian policymakers in the late nineteenth and early twentieth centuries," he recognized the importance of Korea, "with its warm-water ports in the southern part of the peninsula and its strategic location vis-à-vis both China and Japan."[4] Moreover, he aimed to undo the 1911 Japanese annexation of Korea, thereby reversing one result of Russia's defeat in 1904–1905 and ending the Japanese threat to the USSR.

During the Allied conferences in World War II, Stalin maintained a strategic silence on his aims in Korea, shrewdly permitting the absence of concrete arrangements to allow him maximum military and diplomatic flexibility. It was to his advantage that neither at Yalta, in the secret agreement on the USSR's entry into the war against Japan, nor at Potsdam in July 1945 were specific dispositions made for Korea. The Soviet Union entered the war against Japan on August 8, 1945, "contrary to what Stalin and other Soviet spokesmen had been consistently saying about the need to conclude an agreement with China before Soviet entry into the Pacific War."[5] But Stalin was not one to be hobbled by consistency.

Soviet troops could have occupied all of Korea, because U.S. forces were nowhere in the vicinity and in no position to establish a foothold. However, Stalin was not looking for a quarrel with the United States. Therefore, on August 15, when in General Order Number 1 the United States proposed a temporary U.S.-Soviet occupation of Korea divided along the 38th parallel, Stalin acquiesced. He did so in part to avoid a confrontation with the United States; in part because he hoped Washington would agree to his request for a Soviet zone of occupation in Japan (in cabling his acceptance on August 16, Stalin asked that Soviet troops also be permitted to occupy the northern half of Hokkaido Island); and in part because he assumed that an early withdrawal of U.S. and Soviet forces would leave political control of the Korean peninsula in the hands of well-organized Soviet-trained Korean Communists. Under the pro-Moscow faction of the Korean Communist party (renamed the Korean Workers' party in August 1946), headed by Kim Il-sung, North Korea was quickly built up militarily and industrially. In contrast to what occurred under Soviet occupation of Manchuria, North Korea was not ravaged economically, since it was in Communist hands from the very beginning;[6] and in contrast to U.S. policy toward South Korea, Soviet policy in North Korea was a model of clarity, determination, and rationality.

With the onset of the Cold War in Europe, Moscow blocked UN efforts to effect a peaceful reunification, and the division of Korea took on an appearance of permanence. American and Soviet troops withdrew, leaving the country divided at the 38th parallel "between two rival authorities, each bent on the elimination of the other and on unification of Korea after its own pattern."[7] All prospects for a peaceful reunification vanished on June 25, 1950, when North Korean Communist troops invaded South Korea in a calculated attempt to settle the issue by force. Well equipped, having the advantage of surprise, and encouraged by the evident U.S. lack of interest and the widespread discontent with the Syngman Rhee regime that had appeared in the May elections, they came very close to victory.

The UN Security Council convened in emergency session on the very day of the invasion in response to a request by the United States government. The Soviet Union was not represented at this or any of the subsequent meetings of the council, having undertaken a boycott of the United Nations in January 1950 in protest against its failure to recognize the PRC as the legitimate government of China. The Soviet delegate did not return until August 1. With the USSR absent, the Security Council passed a resolution calling for the immediate cessation of hostilities and the withdrawal of the North Korean forces to their side of the border. It also requested all UN members to help in implementing this resolution. President Truman immediately committed U.S. forces, abruptly reversing his previous view that Korea was indefensible and beyond the area strategically necessary for America's own defense.

Soon afterward, the Soviet government set its vast propaganda apparatus in motion and, relying heavily on foreign Communist front organizations, condemned the United States for allegedly intervening in a civil war, carrying on an aggressive war, practicing bacteriological warfare, and perpetrating assorted atrocities. By October 1950, U.S. forces (fighting under the UN banner) counterattacked, crossed the 38th parallel, and advanced northward toward the Yalu River — and the Manchurian border. Once across the 38th parallel, they were no longer merely repelling aggression; they were seeking to unify all Korea by force of arms. This decision by General Douglas MacArthur was never explicitly sanctioned by the UN. The Chinese, apprehensive over the approach of a hostile army and insecure enough to fear invasion of the mainland by Kuomintang troops who had fled to the island of Taiwan, sent in "volunteers" in early November. The war took on a new dimension. After much bitter fighting, a stalemate developed, roughly along the 38th parallel. Truce negotiations and hard fighting dragged on for almost two years. An armistice agreement was finally signed in July 1953, and today an uneasy truce prevails in a divided Korea.

What were Stalin's motives in approving the invasion of South Korea? In the absence of archival materials, all explanations must be tentative. The impending return of Port Arthur and Dairen to the PRC, agreed on in the 1950 Sino-Soviet treaty, must have lent added importance to the warm-water ports in South Korea and prompted Stalin to gamble on what seemed like a reasonably sure thing. Two persistently argued hypotheses have generally been discredited: first, the revisionist New Left contention that South Korea started the war (an aggressor always has the advantage initially, and it was North Korean forces that swept rapidly into South Korean territory in the early weeks of the war), and second, the conspiracy theory, that the attack was planned by Stalin and Mao in early 1950. Both are overly simplistic and based on distorted data, derived more from partisan bias than solid evidence. Most observers no longer assume that Moscow imperiously ordered the invasion. Soviet leaders knew what was in the offing and approved — witness the elaborate preparations that were required for the attack and the Kremlin's undeniable influence at the time in Pyongyang.

A more intricate variant, suggested by Khrushchev's memoirs and linked to political rivalries within the North Korean Communist movement, holds that Kim Il-sung convinced Stalin that the fighting would be an internal affair involving only the Koreans themselves, that the South Koreans would turn against Syngman Rhee's dictatorship once the invasion began, and that the civil war would end quickly, precluding any outside intervention.[8] Seeing an opportunity for seizing prime real estate at little risk, Stalin gave the go-ahead. After all, he had good reason to believe that the United States would accept a *fait accompli* and do nothing to save Korea. America's apparent lack of interest in South Korea had been dramatically highlighted by Secretary of State Dean Acheson's failure to include it in the U.S. "defense perimeter" in a major speech on January 12, 1950, and Kim Il-sung's persuasive assurance that the forcible reunification of Korea could be accomplished swiftly and by North Korean forces alone whetted Stalin's strategic appetite. Nor did Stalin expect that the UN would do anything other than pass some resolutions of admonition, as the League of Nations had done in similar circumstances in the 1930s; hence the continued Soviet absence from Security Council deliberations. Even though he expected a quick victory, Stalin took elaborate precautions to keep Soviet advisers away from the fighting, so as not to give the United States an excuse for intervening. Ultimately, he was betrayed by Washington's unpredictability — by Truman's decision to fight for what Washington had previously declared not to be a vital interest for the United States.

Though thwarted militarily, Stalin benefited politically in two important ways. First, the United States was required to commit a large part of its limited existing strength to a remote area, thereby rendering it impotent in frustrating the establishment of the Soviet imperium in Eastern Europe. Second, the Korean War made Mao more dependent on Soviet weaponry and assistance, and thereby widened the split between the PRC and the United States. For the next fifteen years or so, the existence of a common enemy — the United States — induced the PRC to stay (roughly until the mid-1960s) on reasonably close terms with the Soviet Union and enabled Moscow to strengthen its position in Europe and expand in the Third World.

## Stalin's Policies in Retrospect

Stalin pursued the Sovietization of Eastern Europe and its economic subordination to Soviet interests, operating through the Council for Mutual

Economic Assistance (Comecon) — the Soviet counterpart of the Marshall Plan — and through an elaborate network of interlocking bilateral military treaties. Whereas in the Far East he could count on disciplined revolutionary proxies to advance communism and Soviet interests, in Europe he had to rely primarily on the Red Army and the KGB. He even went so far as to place a Soviet marshal in command of the Polish army in order to ensure its reliability.

Soviet military domination, the extensive purges, and the concomitant Soviet-type restructuring of the sociopolitical systems in Eastern Europe greatly vitiated Stalin's campaign to promote a relaxation of tensions between the two Europes. Following the failure of his policies in Berlin and Korea, Stalin sought to ease tensions in Europe sufficiently to "check the adverse trend in the world power position of the Soviet Union by removing the stimulus to Western cohesion and mobilization, and by encouraging divergent trends within the Western alliance."[9] Specifically, he groped for a policy that would stabilize the situation in Europe at a time of military engagement and volatility in Asia. In order to check the Western military buildup that had begun in earnest in 1950, he played on French-German animosities and deep-rooted uneasiness over West German rearmament, and he exploited "the peace issue, neutralism, trade, and other forms of collaboration with elements of the bourgeoisie."[10] Above all, he wanted to forestall the effective integration of the Federal Republic of Germany into NATO and its attendant remilitarization.

In retrospect, we can discern Stalin's innate conservatism in foreign policy. His policies were expansionist but pragmatic and geared to the avoidance of war with the United States. He sought not to overwhelm the West by force, but to undermine its power and prestige and correspondingly to enhance the strength and stability of the imperial system he had created in Eastern Europe. Under this system, each country in Eastern Europe was permitted to retain its form as a sovereign nation-state (in contrast to the fate of Estonia, Latvia, and Lithuania, which in 1940 were incorporated into the USSR itself); but each was communist in character, its institutions and developmental pattern an imitation of the USSR's. Stalin sought to ensure Soviet security by a permanent military presence, unquestioned political control, ideological conformity, and economic exploitation; his aim was strategic control, not absorption, of the East European rimland. His imperial system (the "socialist camp") was an uninterrupted land mass extending from the Baltic to the Black Seas. Though Europe was the scene of greatest Soviet expansion, Stalin appreciated the importance of Asia and did well in advancing Soviet interest there. His approach was to exploit revolutionary situations where feasible and to avoid the direct use of Soviet forces.

Stalin understood the realities of the postwar international system and used ideology to serve his ends. Ideology is by its very nature ambiguous and malleable. The Bolsheviks had come to power believing that the capitalist world was uniformly hostile, that "imperialism" was dedicated to the destruction of "socialism." However, they quickly learned to differentiate among the imperialists, some being more threatening than others, though all being targets for exploitation, one against the other. After the Bolsheviks were in power and had established the first Communist state, Leninist scripture referred to the irreconcilability of capitalism and socialism (that is, communism) and the inevitability of "frightful collisions"; but it was Stalin in the late 1920s and 1930s who developed the theory of "capitalist encirclement," partially out of a genuine sense of insecurity, but primarily to justify the suffering and sacrifice demanded of the Soviet people by his decisions to industrialize, collectivize, and radically transform Soviet institutions and society.

In doctrinal terms, this theory reflected the pervasive fear of an imperialist attack against the Soviet Union and implied a type of war quite distinct from Lenin's "inevitable" *intercapitalist* wars, which would stem from the nature and contradictions of capitalism, impelled to expand abroad in search of markets and raw materials (that is, imperialism). No systematic attempt was ever made to link Lenin's theory of these inevitable competitive intercapitalist wars with the subsequent Stalinist corollary of the "inevitable" capitalist war against the Soviet Union. Thus there were, in fact, two distinct Communist doctrines on war, though the impression that they were one and the same was encouraged. First came the Leninist theory of imperialism, with its focus on wars and rivalries between capitalist countries, and second was the theory of capitalist encirclement, with its focus on the inevitability of war between the capitalist and Communist camps.

Shortly before the nineteenth congress of the CPSU in October 1952, Stalin published his *Economic Problems of Socialism in the USSR*, which contained an astute diagnosis of the international scene and of Soviet relations with the non-Communist world. He held that as an aftermath of World War II, capitalism had suffered grievous wounds and no longer ruled the world. Economically, the world had split into two parallel and self-contained trading systems. Politically, the capitalist countries had lost much of their former awesome power and therefore were not likely to attack the Soviet Union, although the contradictions and antagonisms between the two systems would continue to exist. A capitalist attack on the Soviet Union was unlikely because "war with the USSR . . . is more dangerous to capitalism than war between capitalist countries; for whereas war between capitalist countries puts in question only the supremacy of certain capitalist countries over others, war with the USSR must certainly put in question the existence of capitalism itself." He perceptively foresaw the reemergence of Germany and Japan as powerful nations and their competition with the United States for shrinking world markets. (Remember, this was said at a time when the United States was preeminent in the world, and both its allies and its former enemies Germany and Japan were weak and very much under its influence.) Finally, while emphasizing the continued and fundamental ideological and political hostility between the Communist and capitalist systems, Stalin carefully implied that *armed* conflict between them was not probable. In this way he kept alive the quest for a measured relaxation of tensions, though it remained for his successors to give substance as well as form to the policy of peaceful coexistence.

The year 1953 was a fateful one. Stalin had ruled the Soviet Union for a generation. One of history's most ruthless tyrants, he was, in the words of France's General Charles de Gaulle, "possessed by the will to power. Accustomed by a life of machination to disguise his features as well as his inmost soul, to dispense with illusions, pity, sincerity, to see in each man an obstacle or a threat, he was all strategy, suspicion and stubbornness. His fortune was to have found a people so vital and so patient that the worst servitudes did not paralyze them, a soil full of such resources that the most terrible destruction and waste could not exhaust it." Undistinguished as a theorist, Stalin was seldom deluded by the orthodoxy that he imposed in ideological and party affairs. He placed no store in the imminence of world revolution, but was quite willing to use revolutions abroad to improve the international position of the Soviet Union. He understood the nature of power and used it to advantage to expand the Soviet empire, in the process fusing the needs of national security with his imperialist ambitions. He modernized the country's economy and institutions and transformed a backward nation into one of the world's greatest industrial-military powers. Stalin ruled in the autocratic tradition of the harshest and most expansionist of the czars.

On March 5, 1953, Moscow announced the death of Stalin. An era had come to an end.

## Notes

1. William O. McCagg, Jr., *Stalin Embattled 1943–1948* (Detroit: Wayne State University Press, 1978), 261–284. This is a revealing investigation of the links between Stalin's domestic intrigues and Soviet foreign policy and between Soviet interests in Europe and in other regions.

2. Ministry of Foreign Affairs of the Federal People's Republic of Yugoslavia, *White Book on Aggressive Activities by the Governments of the USSR, Poland, Czechoslovakia, Hungary, Romania, Bulgaria, and Albania Towards Yugoslavia* (Belgrade, 1951), 14–37, excerpts.

3. Nakajima Mineo, "The Sino-Soviet Confrontation in Historical Perspective," in Yonosuke Nagai and Akira Iriya (eds.), *The Origins of the Cold War in Asia* (New York: Columbia University Press, 1977), 210.

4. Robert M. Slusser, "Soviet Far Eastern Policy, 1945–50: Stalin's Goals in Korea," in Nagai and Iriya (eds.), *The Origins of the Cold War in Asia,* 127.

5. Ibid., 136

6. Joungwon Alexander Kim, "Soviet Policy in North Korea," *World Politics,* vol. 22, no. 2 (January 1970), 237–254.

7. Peter Calvocoressi, *Survey of International Affairs, 1949–1950* (London: Oxford University Press, 1953), 466.

8. Edward Crankshaw (commentary), Strobe Talbott (trans, and ed.), *Khrushchev Remembers* (New York: Bantam, 1970), 400–402.

9. Marshall D. Shulman, "Some Implications of Changes in Soviet Policy Towards the West: 1949–1952," *Slavic Review,* vol. 20 no. 4 (December 1961), 630.

10. Ibid., 631.

## Selected Bibliography

ADLER-KARLSON, GUNNAR. *Western Economic Warfare 1947–1967: A Case in Foreign Policy.* Stockholm: Almquist & Wiksell, 1968.

ARMSTRONG, HAMILTON F. *Tito and Goliath.* New York: Macmillan, 1951.

BADER, WILLIAM B. *Austria Between East and West, 1945–1955.* Stanford: Stanford University Press, 1966.

BELOFF, MAX. *Soviet Policy in the Far East, 1944–1951.* New York: Oxford University Press, 1953.

BOORMAN, H., A. ECKSTEIN, P. MOSELY, and B. SCHWARTZ. *Moscow-Peiping Axis.* New York: Harper & Row, 1957.

DAVISON, W. PHILLIPS. *The Berlin Blockade: A Study in Cold War Politics.* Princeton: Princeton University Press, 1958.

DEDIJER, VLADIMIR. *The Battle Stalin Lost: Memoirs of Yugoslavia, 1948–1953.* New York: Viking, 1971.

FEIS, HERBERT. *Contest Over Japan.* New York: Norton, 1967.

HALLE, LOUIS J. *The Cold War as History.* New York: Harper & Row, 1967.

HELLMANN, DONALD C. *Japanese Foreign Policy and Domestic Politics: The Peace Agreement with the Soviet Union.* Berkeley: University of California Press, 1969.

KAPLAN, MORTON. *The Life and Death of the Cold War.* Chicago: Nelson-Hall, 1977.

KENNEDY, MALCOLM. *A History of Communism in East Asia.* New York: Praeger, 1957.

KORBEL, JOSEF. *The Communist Subversion of Czechoslovakia.* Princeton, N.J.: Princeton University Press, 1959.

LATTIMORE, OWEN. *Pivot of Asia: Sinkiang and the Inner Asian Frontiers of China and Russia.* Boston: Little, Brown, 1950.

MACVICKER, CHARLES P. *Titoism: Pattern for International Communism.* New York: St. Martins's, 1957.

MELBY, JOHN F. *The Mandate of Heaven, Record of a Civil War, China 1945–1949.* Toronto: University of Toronto Press, 1968.

NAGAI, YONOSUKE, AND AKIRA IRIYA (EDS.). *The Origins of the Cold War in Asia.* New York: Columbia University Press, 1977.

NETTL, J. P. *Eastern Zone and Soviet Policy in Germany.* New York: Oxford University Press, 1951.

SETON-WATSON, HUGH. *The East European Revolution.* New York: Praeger, 1956.

SHEPHERD, GORDON. *Russia's Danubian Empire.* London: Heinemann, 1954.

SHULMAN, MARSHALL D. *Stalin's Foreign Policy Reappraised.* Cambridge: Harvard University Press, 1963.

SIMMONS, ROBERT R. *The Strained Alliance: Peking, P'yongyang, Moscow and the Politics of the Korean Civil War.* New York: Free Press, 1975.

ULAM, ADAM B. *Titoism and the Cominform.* Cambridge: Harvard University Press, 1952.

WHITING, ALLEN S. *China Crosses the Yalu: The Decision to Enter the Korean War.* New York: Macmillan, 1960.

———, and GENERAL SHEN SHIH-TS'AI. *Sinkiang: Pawn or Pivot?* East Lansing: Michigan State University Press, 1958.

WOLFE, ROBERT LEE. *The Balkans in Our Times.* Cambridge: Harvard University Press, 1956.

# 4

# The Soviet Union
## and Eastern Europe

Since 1945, the lodestar of the Soviet Union's European policy has been strategic control of Eastern Europe in order to prevent that territory from ever again serving as a springboard for an invasion of the Soviet Union. Stalin's postwar objectives were relatively clear-cut: to eliminate Western influence from Eastern Europe and concomitantly to establish Moscow's hegemony, and to develop a belt of submissive Communist regimes whose leaders governed at Moscow's discretion and depended for their survival on Soviet troops. From 1945 to 1953, the Soviet Union's Draconian policy toward Eastern Europe was unmistakably Stalin's handiwork.

His successors, however, were faced with more subtle challenges; to preserve yet decentralize their empire; to obtain Western acceptance of the permanence of Soviet domination over Eastern Europe; and to expand Soviet power without jeopardizing the security of the USSR or its imperial system. They soon discovered that preserving an empire is more difficult than acquiring one. Not only do the techniques of rule differ from those of revolution, but the price of empire may prove so high that it weakens the structure of power within the metropolitan country itself. Over the years, Stalin's successors alternated reform and repression in a never-ending search for a mix that extended the range of permissible autonomy within a framework that ensured loyalty, stability, and strategic control.

The Soviet leaders, eager to establish the legitimacy of their rule and effect an orderly transition of power, revived the principle of collective leadership. Except for the purge and execution in the summer of 1953 of Lavrenti Beria, the head of the secret police, who posed a physical threat to their survival, shifts at the top were managed without recourse to the terror of the Stalin period; and the struggle for power has remained bloodless, a reflection of the changing, more sophisticated nature of Soviet autocracy. In addition to reassuring the various privileged groups (such as the party, the military, and the technocracy) whose support is essential for the maintenance of the regime, the leadership — impelled by a series of unfavorable economic, demographic, social, and political trends — has divested itself of the more oppressive and inefficient aspects of the Stalinist legacy.

During the period from 1953 to 1956, decompression in the Soviet Union produced a ripple effect in Eastern Europe that resulted in three major upheavals — in East Germany, Hungary, and Poland. The first satellite eruption broke out in June 1953, four months after Stalin's death. A wave of strikes and riots swept East Berlin and parts of Soviet-occupied Germany in protest against increased production quotas and police repression. The Soviet army quickly and brutally suppressed the outbreaks. Though the West had stayed out of the crisis, the danger of the situation, and of inadvertent escalation, was not lost on Soviet leaders. They understood that in the GDR, as elsewhere in Eastern Europe, the task was to chart a course between the Scylla of Stalinism and the Charybdis of runaway relaxation of controls.

Throughout most of 1953 and 1954 the Kremlin was occupied with intra-Communist–world problems, in Eastern Europe, in China, and within the Soviet Union itself. To decrease the likelihood of intrusive pressure from the West, Soviet leaders held out prospects of an easing of Cold War tensions, most immediately by accepting an armistice agreement in Korea on July 27, 1953. Thus began the effort to liquidate the liabilities bequeathed by Stalin. The armistice enabled the Soviet government to reduce the military drain on its economy, return the East-West conflict to the political and diplomatic arenas, and provide the Chinese Communists with time to consolidate their hold on the mainland; and it gave them more leeway in tackling the succession problem and in meeting the expectations of the Soviet people for a better life.

## De-Stalinizing the Empire

On August 9, 1953, Premier G. M. Malenkov spoke of the government's intention to allocate more resources to satisfy consumer needs. He alluded to a departure from the previous hostility toward the West, though simultaneously he used the occasion to inform the world that the United States was "not the only possessor of the hydrogen bomb."

The "de-Stalinization" process that reached its apogee at the CPSU's twentieth congress in February 1956 developed slowly, varying in degree and scope from country to country but following a common pattern. Amnesties were proclaimed, forced collectivization was halted, price cuts on consumer staples were instituted, the more oppressive features of the labor and criminal codes were changed, and the arbitrary power of the secret police was curbed. The aim was to "return to Leninism." In Eastern Europe, those who were too closely identified as Stalinists were gradually replaced by national Communists, that is, those Communists who were popularly regarded as defenders of the country's interests against unreasonable exploitation by and abject subservience to the Soviet Union. Party and government apparatuses were separated, and economic reforms were introduced.

In another major policy reversal, Moscow decided on a reconciliation with Tito. The USSR and Yugoslavia concluded a barter agreement in September 1954, ending the Cominform's economic blockade. In May 1955, party leader Nikita S. Khrushchev and other top Politburo members went to Belgrade and did penance for Stalin's sins against Yugoslavia. They signed a joint government declaration endorsing the principle of nonintervention in domestic affairs and tacitly recognizing Yugoslavia as a socialist state, although it is significant that a comparable accord on party-to-party reconciliation was not agreed upon until Tito's visit to the USSR in June 1956. At that time Moscow formally acknowledged the principle of "many roads to socialism," which was to serve as the doctrinal basis for granting greater measures of autonomy to the members of the Soviet bloc.

The errant Tito's return to the fold was a necessary step in the reconstitution of the formal unity of the Communist world. Moscow hoped it would stem the appeal of Titoism, that is, full independence and equality for all Communist states, and reconcile loyalty to the Soviet Union with acceptance of the national autonomy allowed by Moscow. Moscow also hoped that the rapprochement would weaken Yugoslavia's ties with the West and diminish the value of the Balkan pact which Belgrade had signed in 1954 with Greece and Turkey. Improved Soviet-Yugoslav relations "harmonized with the then current Soviet policy of attaining cooperation with the respectable socialist parties of the West, demonstrating to the world Moscow's reasonableness and flexibility, and of encouraging neutralist tendencies in the free world by demonstrating that the USSR was not a threat against which an unaligned country needed to seek protection by joining the other bloc."[1] The Soviet-Yugoslav second honeymoon, however, lasted only until late 1956, when, in the aftermath of the Hungarian revolution, Moscow's temporary turn from diversity to bloc unity and neo-Stalinism alienated Belgrade. But this time, unlike in 1948, the quarrel did not result in a rupture.

Khrushchev's determination to carry out far-ranging reforms at home and to place Soviet-East European relations on a more truly fraternal basis required improved relations with the Western countries. Accordingly, in the spring of 1955, over the objections of Molotov and others, Khrushchev agreed to a peace treaty with Austria, thus reversing Moscow's previous insistence on linking the treaty with a settlement of the German problem. The treaty, signed on May 15, ended the four-power occupation and committed Austria to a policy of permanent nonalignment with either bloc. It was significant because it marked the first voluntary Soviet withdrawal from an entrenched position in the center of Europe (in May, the USSR also officially returned Port Arthur to the CPR, and in September, it withdrew from the military base that it had been granted in 1947 at Porkkala-Udd, only twelve miles from Helsinki in Finland). Moscow's surprising amiability extended to other areas as well. For example, in 1953 the Soviet Union renounced all claims against Turkey, made overtures for closer relations with Greece and Iran, and began to participate actively in the economic development and technical assistance programs of the various UN organizations.

Moscow's previously unchallenged authority in the Communist world was seriously shaken as a consequence of what was perhaps the most spectacular event in Soviet politics of the post-Stalin period: Khrushchev's secret speech at the CPSU's twentieth congress in February 1956, denouncing Stalin's crimes and self-deification. An outgrowth of the struggle for power among the Kremlin oligarchs, the speech had a powerful effect on the course of developments in Eastern Europe, China, and the world Communist movement. It immediately set in motion in Eastern Europe additional pressures for changes that gathered momentum and threatened to unhinge the Soviet empire.

The twentieth congress would have been important even without Khrushchev's speech against Stalin because of the significant doctrinal shifts that affected the Kremlin's approach to world affairs. Khrushchev affirmed the Leninist thesis of the irreconcilability of capitalism and communism, but stated that war between the two systems "is not fatalistically inevitable." The emergence of the "world camp of socialism" (and by implication its possession of nuclear weapons) enabled the forces for peace in the world to find a champion and to rebuff would-be aggressors; the USSR's possession of nuclear weapons would deter any would-be capitalist aggressor, and if "all anti-war forces" cooperated with the Soviet camp, "the greater the guarantees that there will be no new war." Khrushchev also formally embraced the Titoist thesis that there are many roads to socialism, thereby providing doctrinal approval for diversity or polycentrism in the Communist world and a theoretical basis for closer cooperation not only with Yugoslavia but also with the socialist parties of Western Europe. Moscow hoped that this position would also lead to better relations with the new nations and nationalist movements of the Third World. Third, Communists in capitalist countries were encouraged to seek power, where and when possible, through parliamentary means.

In bringing Soviet foreign-policy perceptions and guidelines into line with emerging international realities, Khrushchev greatly disturbed the Chinese, who saw in his stress on peaceful coexistence and efforts to effect a limited détente with the United States a downgrading of the Sino-Soviet alliance, a shift in Soviet foreign-policy priorities and methods, and a possible shelving of Beijing's quest for international recognition and for the overthrow of the Kuomintang regime on Taiwan. But the disruptive effects of de-Stalinization were most apparent in Eastern Europe. An unwary Kremlin had unwittingly released turbulent anti-Russian, anti-Communist, and nationalist currents. The result was the most substantial uprising against Soviet rule ever witnessed. Shaking the very foundations of the Soviet empire, it led to a Stalinist revival and to serious reconsiderations of ways in which to ensure the permanence of Soviet strategic gains in Eastern Europe and avoid the perils of liberalization.

Riots broke out in Poznan, Poland, in June 1956. Sparked by Khrushchev's revelations, smoldering resentment of a decade of economic exploitation and Soviet domination flared into open denunciations of the Moscow-controlled government. The Poles' traditional hatred of Russia made for a volatile political situation. The Kremlin, realizing the gravity of the situation, grudgingly made concessions. It permitted the ouster of many known pro-Moscow Communists from the Central Committee of the Polish United Workers' (Communist) party and in October 1956 accepted the elevation of Wladyslaw Gomulka, who had spent several years in prison for supposed Titoist tendencies, to the post of party secretary. Moscow also publicly reaffirmed Poland's sovereignty and independence, agreed not to interfere in its domestic affairs, and withdrew Soviet Marshal Rokossovsky as head of Poland's armed forces. Trade and financial relations were adjusted to Poland's advantage, and the number of Soviet troops permitted by special agreement to remain in Poland pending a settlement of the German question was sharply reduced. (Notwithstanding its greater independence in internal affairs, Poland remains inevitably influenced in important foreign-policy decisions by its powerful Communist neighbor, if only because friendship with the USSR is Poland's ultimate guarantee against the possibility of another Soviet-German "understanding" at its expense, as in 1939. Soviet troops in East Germany and in Poland, as well as Poland's deep-rooted fear of the claims of a revived, united, expansionist Germany to the territories east of the Oder-Neisse line that are now incorporated into Poland, are Moscow's levers to assure that nation's continued adherence to the Soviet bloc.)

Events in Hungary took a violent and tragic turn. Matyas Rakosi, a confirmed Stalinist and longtime party boss of Hungary, was deposed in June 1956, and his successor, Ernö Gero, was not up to the challenge of mounting popular pressure for change. On October 23, revolution erupted in Budapest. Anti-Communist and anti-Soviet, it threatened the entire Soviet position in Central Europe. Moscow could not find a political solution as it had in Poland because the Hungarians wanted full independence and their party leadership had lost control of the situation. The rebels wanted to disband the Communist party, leave the Warsaw Pact organization, and liquidate all vestiges of Soviet rule. Confronted with the imminent loss of Hungary and possible disintegration elsewhere in Eastern Europe, Moscow hurled 250,000 troops and 5000 tanks against the Hungarians on November 4, after it violated a truce that betrayed key Hungarian military leaders and delivered them into Soviet hands. Where negotiation had failed, brute force and deceit succeeded.

The UN General Assembly called upon the Soviet government "to desist from its intervention in the internal affairs of Hungary, to withdraw its forces from Hungary, and to cease its repression of the Hungarian people." Aided by the coincidence of the Suez and Hungarian crises, the Soviets ignored UN and Western protests. Whereas through the temporary coalescence of Soviet and American policy on Suez the UN was able to end the Middle Eastern hostilities, no similar congruence of power could be marshaled on behalf of Hungary. As the Soviet steamroller crushed the Hungarians, the West watched, helpless to intervene for fear of precipitating World War III. This moment of truth for the West tragically confirmed what Raymond Aron has described as "the unwritten law of the atomic age": that the Soviet Union can do as it pleases within its sphere of influence without fear of retaliation. And Hungary is part of that sphere.

But the Kremlin learned several bitter lessons. First, Soviet control in Eastern Europe can be preserved *only* if backed by the Red Army. Military force, not ideology, is the effective cement for cohesion. Second, nationalism remains strong, even among avowed Communists, and in Eastern Europe it is permeated with an anti-Russian tinge. Third, authority once weakened cannot easily be reimposed. Fourth, a prerequisite for the continued political and military adherence of East European countries to the Soviet-dominated Warsaw Pact military alliance is Soviet acceptance of a substantial measure of economic, cultural, and political autonomy in those countries.

Strategically, control of Eastern Europe plays a key role in Soviet military thinking about the defense of the USSR; and Moscow will undoubtedly resist any attempt, either by the West or by the region's members, to dislodge its military influence and control. Khrushchev implied as much when he castigated "some comrades" for opposing the decision to intervene and noted that "the saliva of the imperialists was running in their mouths at the prospect of Hungary's leaving the Socialist camp. They thought that one by one they could sever the Socialist countries from their united base." [2] His successors have been no less decisive and are always on guard lest diversity lead to disaster.

On the other hand, Eastern Europe can no longer be considered an unquestioned asset to the Kremlin. The area represents a material drain on Soviet resources; the reliability of East European troops remains a continual question; and East European nationalism, a force too often slighted in the West, greatly complicates the process of Soviet rule. The intervention in Hungary cost Moscow heavily among influential West European intellectuals and in the consequent agonizing reappraisals that occurred in Western Communist parties. African and Asian leaders expressed varying degrees of disappointment, but the remoteness of Hungary to them blunted their concern and indignation. They were far more outraged over the British, French, and Israeli attack on Egypt, a country only recently emerged from colonialism and one with which they felt intimate emotional ties. Moreover, Soviet leaders, unlike their Western counterparts, who must contend with an influential public opinion, could simply ignore the protests. What the 1956 crises in Eastern Europe (and the 1968 crisis in Czechoslovakia) have shown is that the Soviet Union regards Eastern Europe as vital to its national security and that it is prepared to use force if necessary to preserve its hegemony there.

In November 1957, on the occasion of the fortieth anniversary of the Bolshevik Revolution, the leaders of international communism met in Moscow to repair the damage of 1956. They issued a "declaration of unity" reaffirming the solidarity of the Communist camp "headed by the Soviet Union." This declaration implicitly acknowledged the disruptive consequences of national communism, emphasized the unity of the Communist world, and attacked "revisionism" (sin of going further than Moscow in doctrinal, internal, or international innovation). The Chinese gave lip service to Moscow's leadership for the last time and tried to nudge the Soviet Union back to Stalinism, especially as it related to Moscow's policy toward the United States and Western Europe. Throughout the meeting, Moscow groped for a way of replacing the Cominform, which had been disbanded in the heady days of de-Stalinization in 1956, and of reimposing bloc unity, particularly in Eastern Europe. But like Humpty-Dumpty, the Cominform could not be put back together again, largely because of Yugoslav and West European Communist oppositon to Chinese efforts on behalf of a forceful reassertion of Soviet political and ideological authority within the bloc.

## Courting Belgrade

Tito, who absented himself from the gala get-together, refused to sign the Moscow declaration — an indication of the brittleness of the 1955–1956 Soviet-Yugoslav reconciliation. He had supported Khrushchev's intervention in Hungary out of fear that the "counterrevolutionary fever" might spread elsewhere in Eastern Europe, even to Yugoslavia, out of a desire to bolster Khrushchev in curbing the Stalinists in the Kremlin, and in order to retain a degree of influence on Soviet policy in Eastern Europe. But the declaration made him uneasy. Soon after the conference, the Soviet press launched an intensive antirevisionist campaign. The Yugoslavs bore the brunt of direct criticism when, in April 1958, they published their new party program, which read like a codification of revisionism that "contradicted point by point the programmatic directive for the bloc and the world Communist movement" issued the previous November.[3]

During the years 1958 to 1961, the Soviet-Yugoslav controversy centered on four main points. First, the Yugoslavs maintained that the USSR as well as NATO was responsible for the Cold War and the division of the world into rival blocs. Second, they insisted on the unqualified right of each Communist state to determine its own course toward socialism. Third, they accused Moscow of continuing Stalinist practices and of having developed into a bureaucratic state that kept "strengthening in all fields of social life" instead of withering away in accordance with Marxist-Leninist theory. And fourth, the League of Yugoslav Communists' party program claimed for Yugoslavia a democratic and socialist evolution that Moscow could not accept or allow to go ideologically unchallenged. The Soviet leadership denounced the Yugoslavs for "assisting imperialism" and deviating from the position taken by the Communist parties of other socialist countries, applied economic and political pressure, but stopped far short of military threats or another break.

In November 1960, at another international Communist conference in Moscow, Khrushchev failed to heal the growing disunity in the Communist world, most prominently the Soviet problems with Beijing. The continuing deterioration of Soviet relations with China in the 1960s gave impetus to better relations with Yugoslavia. However, the Soviet invasion of Czechoslovakia in August 1968 triggered Yugoslavia's deepest anxieties over Soviet intentions in Eastern Europe, and the Soviet-Yugoslav relationship has fluctuated ever since. Moscow has found the Yugoslav position congenial on many issues, such as the convening of the Conference on Security and Cooperation in Europe (CSCE), the establishment of a nuclear-free zone in the Balkans, the admission of the two Germanies to the

United Nations, the condemnation of U.S. policy in Southeast Asia and the Middle East, and the need for disarmament. However, on other issues of core concern to each, for example, on the issue of Soviet authority in Eastern Europe and the world Communist movement, on the policy of nonalignment, and on nonintervention in the internal affairs of socialist countries, their disagreement persists.

Throughout the 1970s, Soviet-Yugoslav relations were generally good: Tito and Brezhnev exchanged visits, disagreed without rancor on bloc politics, Eurocommunism, and China, and encouraged expanded economic ties. Moscow carefully avoided overt threats, though after the 1968 Czechoslovak crisis Belgrade took firm steps to improve its defenses against attack from the east. However, with the death of Tito in May 1980, Soviet-Yugoslav relations enter a period of new uncertainty. A Soviet invasion is always a possibility that cannot be dismissed, since the Kremlin covets permanent military access to the Mediterranean and an end to Yugoslavia's irritating type of national communism, but Moscow is unlikely to bite on such a tough nut. Facing its own succession problem, Moscow is apt to practice patience and await promising opportunities for affecting Yugoslav developments. Through a combination of pressure and accommodation, it will prod the Yugoslav leadership in an attempt to nudge Belgrade closer to the Soviet position on bloc and world issues. Soviet temptation will be a function of Yugoslavia's internal cohesion: the more the post-Tito republic party oligarchs satisfactorily negotiate their differences and sustain national unity, the less the Kremlin will be tempted to intervene, and vice versa.

After the tumultuous events of 1956, Moscow's policy toward Eastern Europe underwent a number of important changes that have dominated its approach since then. First, Moscow accommodated to East European nationalism by granting substantial domestic autonomy to indigenous Communist elites. In Hungary, Janos Kadar, who came to power under the worst possible circumstances (he was installed by the Red Army in 1956), was still able to implement far-reaching economic reforms and political liberalization and in the process gain general acceptance, even popularity, in the country. In Poland, Gomulka defused Polish rebelliousness and de-Stalinized the economy and social life. He got along well with the USSR until he was forced by labor unrest and inflation to resign in December 1970, but his successors have continued to accord highest priority to good relations with Moscow, for economic as well as political reasons. There have been no serious problems with Bulgaria, the most pro-Soviet of the East European countries, or with East Germany, which is a bulwark of orthodoxy. However, in Romania and Czechoslavakia, Moscow has encountered difficulties with national Communist leaders and has sought a workable policy.

Second, the USSR readjusted its economic relations with Eastern Europe. It gave the East Europeans concessionary rates on imports of some Soviet raw materials and extended long-term credits without visible political strings. Third, it accepted expanded economic and cultural links between Eastern Europe and the West, though it did caution bloc members against using "their relations with capitalist countries at the expense of other fraternal countries."

By the time Khrushchev was deposed in October 1964, Soviet policy toward Eastern Europe had changed considerably. From the one-sided and callous exploitation of the Stalin era, it had moved to a more businesslike and sophisticated economic give-and-take. From day-to-day control by pro-Moscow satraps and resident KGB procurators, it had changed to allow considerable autonomy to national Communists in managing their internal affairs, as long as there was no threat to the Communist character of the regime or its loyalty to the USSR. And from imposed conformity to Soviet norms in all things Soviet policy had grown to tolerate diversity in most areas. From a classic type of colonial system, the Soviet–East European bloc has evolved into an imperial system, in which the center places greatest importance on strategic and military control rather than on economic exploitation or cultural conformity.

The duumvirate of Leonid Brezhnev and Alexei Kosygin altered the style — the ebullience of Khrushchev was replaced by the deliberateness of Brezhnev — but not the substance of Khrushchev's policy. They have followed the trail he marked to preserve Soviet hegemony in Eastern Europe. Confronted with intensifying nationalism in Eastern Europe, worsening relations with China, and the end of the myth of international Communist solidarity, the Soviet leaders have tried to improve relations with the West and find a formula for asserting their authority within the bloc.

In April 1967, at a meeting of European Communist parties convened at Karlovy Vary, Czechoslovakia, Brezhnev dwelt on the problems of East-West relations and intrabloc relationships, but failed noticeably to reconcile the differences between Moscow and the national Communist parties on how much East European autonomy was consonant with Soviet security and the bloc's unity. At the celebrations in Moscow of the fiftieth anniversary of the Bolshevik Revolution, Soviet leaders persuaded eighteen Communist parties to cosponsor a consultative meeting in Budapest in late February 1968 for the purpose of planning a world conference of Communist parties, the first since November 1960. In its effort to restore Soviet centralizing authority, Moscow got its staunchest support from the

East Germans. This struggle against revisionism came at a time when events in Czechoslovakia were moving the Kremlin toward another decisive intervention.

## Intervention in Czechslovakia

In January 1968 a combination of disgruntled Stalinists and reformers ousted Antonin Novotny, Moscow's man in Prague, as general secretary of the Czechoslovak Communist party, and brought in Alexander Dubcek. Long a loyal party bureaucrat, Dubcek became the rallying figure for all factions and groups seeking to liberalize Czechoslovak society and to assert a greater autonomy in domestic affairs. By mid-February, liberalization was occurring so rapidly that the skepticism among the population at large changed to hopeful anticipation. By late spring, the air of freedom intoxicated the country. Dubcek and the reformers spoke of a parliament free from party control; they rehabilitated the victims of the Stalinist past, began to rid the party and trade unions of the front men for Moscow, and eliminated censorship. Ludvik Svoboda replaced Novotny as president. In the Central Committee, the Dubcek group was in control. Democratization flowered. From early February to August 1968, Czechoslovakia experienced a rebirth of political, cultural, and social freedom. The secret police were stripped of their arbitrary powers; links to the Soviet KGB apparatus were exposed; criticisms of the past and proposals for the future were aired with a candor and passion that disturbed the oligarchs of Byzantine communism in Moscow.

The "Prague spring" lasted until August 21. In the early hours of that day, Soviet troops invaded Czechoslovakia. As in Hungary in 1956, Moscow responded with overwhelming force to a perceived threat to its strategic military position in Central Europe. Joined by Polish, East German, Hungarian, and Bulgarian (but not Romanian) troops in order to give the intervention a Warsaw Pact imprimatur, the Red Army quickly occupied the country.

From the very beginning, Moscow was exposed and discredited by its own lies. It said that Soviet troops were sent at the request of party and government officials, but Svoboda, Dubcek, and other leaders denied this allegation. It claimed to have acted to forestall an insidious effort at counterrevolution, but the collapse in late August of its initial efforts to install pro-Soviet puppets showed that what was in jeopardy in Czechoslovakia was Soviet domination, not socialism. It resorted to anit-Semitism to tarnish all Czech reformers, a few of whom were Jewish, but abandoned this ploy when it became counterproductive.

The Soviet justification for the invasion of Czechoslovakia appeared in *Pravda* on September 26, 1968. Quickly dubbed the Brezhnev Doctrine, it proclaimed the inherent right of the Soviet Union to intervene anywhere in the socialist world to preserve socialism. While reaffirming the principle of many roads to socialism, it insisted that no action "should do harm either to socialism" in the country or party involved "or to the fundamental interests of other socialist countries and of the entire working-class movement which is striving for socialism. This means that each Communist party is responsible not only to its own people but also to all the socialist countries and to the entire Communist movement." Moreover, the article warned, though every Communist party is free "to apply the basic principles of Marxism-Leninism," it is not free to depart from those principles or to adopt a "nonaffiliated" attitude toward the rest of the socialist community; and though self-determination is each nation's right, it cannot be applied in a way that would weaken the socialist community. World socialism "is indivisible and its defense is the common cause of all Communists." In defending socialism, Moscow proclaimed that it would be the sole judge and jury of when the limits of permissible autonomy had been exceeded, and that it would act accordingly.

In proceeding as they did, Soviet leaders demonstrated the paramountcy of Eastern Europe in their thinking about the defense of the Soviet Union. They used force even at the risk of jeopardizing many of their policy goals — for example, détente with the United States, including prospects for an agreement limiting strategic delivery systems; the weakening of NATO; and the support of foreign Communists, many of whom publicly condemned the Soviet aggression against an ally and fellow-Communist country. The reasons for the invasion may help us project probable Soviet policy in the future.

What may have been the most important single catalyst was the domestic situation in the Soviet Union. The ethnic and racial diversity of the USSR has a profound effect on Soviet politics and policymaking, though given the secrecy shrouding Soviet foreign-policy decision-making, it is often difficult to adduce this in specific instances. The Russians, who constitute no more than 52 percent of the approximately 260 million Soviet people, have had trouble for more than three-hundred years with the 42 million Ukrainians, the second largest nationality group. Of all the peoples in Eastern Europe, the Czechs and Slovaks are regarded by Ukrainians as the nearest to them in tradition and culture. The Kremlin may well have been afraid that the virus of Czechoslovak liberalization would find a congenial breeding ground in the national consciousness of the Ukrainians and stimulate demands in the Ukrainian SSR for extensive reform. After all, if the Slavs and fraternal Communists of Czechoslavakia were permitted democratization, why not those of the Soviet Union?

Ethnic nationalism is a perennial and intensifying nightmare for Moscow. Soviet leaders proclaim abroad the notion of "proletarian internationalism" (that is, unswerving acceptance by all Communists of the primacy of defending the homeland of socialism — the Soviet Union) to justify Soviet claims to leadership of the world Communist movement; but they may be even more concerned with its acceptance *internally* as ideological justification for Great Russian domination over the non-Russian nationalities of the Soviet Union. Reinforcing this hypothesis of the salience of nationality considerations in Kremlin thinking is the trend under Brezhnev and Kosygin toward a general tightening of party control and a defensiveness about dissidence. The present oligarchs are anxious authoritarians, suspicious of arguments for decentralization of the economy and greater encouragement of innovation, preferring to retain familiar institutions and procedures rather than experiment with new ones.

A second major consideration in the Soviet decision to invade Czechoslovakia was the pressure of the military to safeguard the Soviet position in Central Europe against possible erosion; strategic imperatives transcended political risks. The Czech suggestion in July 1968 that the Warsaw Pact be revised raised the specter of another Hungarian crisis. The military argued that Czechoslovakia was too centrally placed geographically for Moscow to let it go neutralist or succumb to instability. As it was, Warsaw Pact maneuvers in 1966 had exposed glaring weaknesses along the Czechoslovak–West German border; and Prague's unwillingness to agree to the permanent stationing of Soviet troops on Czech soil was an objection the Soviet high command wished to override. East German leaders strongly supported the Soviet military, arguing that if Czechoslovakia continued to liberalize, to open her economy to Western investment, and to follow her own way in dealing with the Federal Republic of Germany, as Romania had, the net result would be a severe weakening of the GDR, Moscow's ally in orthodoxy and most important economic partner. Finally, it is also possible that Soviet intelligence had assured the Politburo that the Czechs would not fight and that the affair could be handled swiftly and satisfactorily if massive power were applied.

Thus for both domestic and strategic reasons, Moscow acted in Czechoslovakia as it had in Hungary twelve years earlier. The USSR showed that control over East European real estate is nonnegotiable — that its policy is based on the axiom "What's mine is mine; what's yours is negotiable." It will use force to preserve its imperial system intact. Though seeking better relations with Western Europe, it will not tolerate any erosion of its strategic hold over a contiguous Communist country; nor will considerations of prestige among foreign Communist parties deter it from expeditiously suppressing national Communists who exceed Moscow's guidelines for autonomy.

In Moscow's behavior we see again the dominance of Russian national and imperial interests over the needs and wishes of Communist parties abroad. Different political constellations in control in the Kremlin at any given time may be prepared to accept lesser or greater parameters of autonomy, but the ultimate determination of what is permissible is Moscow's prerogative. Eastern Europe cannot divest itself completely of Soviet influence; geography, the reliance of the "new class" in Eastern Europe on the protective power of the Red Army, growing dependency on imports of Soviet energy, and the realities of international relations preclude such a situation. By keeping fears of a West German revanche alive, particularly among the Poles and East Germans, Moscow ensures their military dependence. Should any of the East European regimes show signs of assuming an anti-Soviet, anti-Communist stance, Moscow would presumably feel impelled to act militarily once again to preserve its perceived vital interests. Its velvet glove contains an iron fist. To paraphrase what the Mexican dictator Porfirio Diaz once said of Mexico and the United States: "Poor Eastern Europe, so far from God, so close to the Soviet Union."

Moscow's toleration of polycentrism in Eastern Europe also received an assist in the 1960s and 1970s from the deepening Sino-Soviet rift. In addition to the rapprochment with Yugoslavia, the quest for a rationalization of economic relationships, and the spillover from its own internal decompression, Moscow sought Eastern Europe's support for its position in the quarrel with Beijing. Especially after the rupture with Albania in 1961, it permitted larger doses of autonomy in return for adherence to the Soviet line against China. Thus desatellitization has accompanied the end of monolithism in the bloc. The degree of polycentrism has varied from country to country, but each member of the bloc has benefited, with Romania's assertiveness in foreign policy perhaps representing the most dramatic example of the utility of the Sino-Soviet rift to the emergence of nationalism and political assertiveness. Notwithstanding the Soviet invasion of Czechoslovakia and the enunciation of the "Brezhnev Doctrine," Moscow has preferred to try to restore its authority by a time-consuming and formalized system of bargaining and consensus-building that is particularly evident in its approach to military and economic integration within the bloc.

## Institutionalizing Soviet Hegemony

To stabilize its imperial position in Eastern Europe and promote bloc cohesion and integration, the Soviet Union increasingly relies on a number of multilateral institutions, most notably the Warsaw Treaty Organization (WTO), more commonly referred to as the Warsaw Pact, and the Council for Mutual Economic Assistance (Comecon). The Warsaw Pact was created on May 14, 1955, the day before the signing of the Austrian state treaty. Moscow decided that it needed a formal alliance binding the bloc together. In shifting from an exclusive reliance on bilateralism to a heavy emphasis on multilateralism, it was motivated by several aims. The first and most immediate, given the imminence of the treaty with Austria, was to find a way to legitimize the continued presence in Hungary and Romania of the Soviet troops that had been justified until then on the basis of assuring lines of communication for Soviet occupation forces in Austria. The second, after Moscow had failed to prevent the FRG's rearmament and formal entry into NATO on May 9, 1955, was to carry through on its previously announced intention to have Soviet-bloc countries "take common measures for the organization of armed forces and their commands," and to create a counterpart to NATO. Third, Moscow wanted an effective instrument for safeguarding its interests in the area.

From the beginning, political objectives were paramount — witness that the first joint military exercises were not held until late 1961. The WTO's Political Consultative Committee, responsible for coordinating all but purely military matters, was inactive in the early years, but took on added importance after the 1968 Czech crisis. In November 1976, it established a Committee of Foreign Ministers and a Unified Secretariat in order to improve "the mechanism of political collaboration."

Though formally a military alliance protecting the bloc against external threats, the Warsaw Pact mainly serves an intrabloc policing function. This has been acknowledged by Soviet General Sergei Shtemenko, who shortly before his death in April 1976 wrote in an article commemorating the WTO's twenty-first anniversary that alliance plays an important role in suppressing counterrevolutionary activity against members of the "socialist community"; he mentioned Czechoslovakia as a case in point. The pact is also used by Moscow to pressure a reluctant member to go along with the consensus view, to persuade bloc members to join with it in isolating a dissident member (for instance, excluding Albania from participation because of its pro-Beijing policies from 1961 to 1978), to rebut Chinese accusations that the USSR is a disintegrating rather than integrating influence within the Communist world, and to encourage a sense of common interest among the members.

The military objectives of the Warsaw Pact, though subordinate, are substantial. They include organizing Eastern Europe as a defensive buffer zone against a possible invasion from the West, extending the Soviet air defense system as far west of the Soviet homeland as possible, serving as an offensive prod against NATO in the event of a war in Europe, creating military forces loyal to the Communist regimes, and promoting bloc unity through standardization of weaponry, tactical coordination, and interlocking command structures.

Overall, "the Warsaw Pact is evolving into a conventional alliance."[4] Moscow's very success in transforming the alliance and in permitting diversity within it, however, has given rise to serious problems.[5] In recent years, for example, though the Soviet Union has urged greater financial commitments, Romania and Poland have resisted, pleading pressing domestic priorities and economic difficulties due to rising costs of energy and raw materials imports. Nicolae Ceausescu, the Romanian leader and a thorn in Moscow's side since the mid-1960s, cites Soviet statements on the shift in the correlation of world forces in favor of the socialist camp to bolster his opposition to larger military spending and to argue that it would adversely affect Romania's socioeconomic development.

In its quest for improved military effectiveness and integration, the Soviet Union finds Romania a persistently troublesome stumbling block. Since 1966, when he proposed that the position of commander-in-chief of Warsaw Pact forces be rotated and that the East European members be consulted on decisions affecting the use of nuclear weapons, Ceausescu has moved steadily to reduce Romania's participation. Not only did he refuse to join the invasion of Czechoslovakia and publicly condemn the action as a "flagrant transgression" and contradiction "to the fundamental standards concerning relations that must reign among socialist countries and among Communist parties and of generally recognized principles of international law," but since 1972 he has withdrawn from joint military maneuvers and has had Romanian representatives at WTO meetings maintain a relatively inactive role. There have not been any major Warsaw Pact maneuvers on Romanian territory for a number of years; Soviet troops wishing to cross the country must be granted permission by Romania's parliament, and "on the few occasions that Soviet troops were allowed to cross Romania to take part in maneuvers in Bulgaria — the only land route from Russia — they were required to travel unarmed, their weapons carried separately on freight trains."[6]

Moscow has so far acted with remarkable restraint. It permits Romania to prevent full military integration because there is no serious NATO force on the "southern tier" Balkan flank and also because it has no fear of liberalization occurring in Romania, where Ceausescu runs a Stalinist-type society. For the moment, imposing a greater degree of military cohesion would only jeopardize the long-term viability of the alliance. So Moscow continues to be patient.

The Soviet leadership has also been unsuccessful in its periodic efforts to persuade members to amend the Warsaw treaty to include non-European states, for example Mongolia. All these complications raise the ultimate question concerning the Warsaw Pact: How reliable would the East European forces be in the event of a war in Europe? A great deal would depend on the kind of war and the circumstances under which it begins. However, judging by the USSR's difficulties in fashioning agreement on basic issues, the thin crust on which the legitimacy of Communist regimes stands, the pervasive suspicion of Moscow that permeates public perceptions in Eastern Europe, and the unwillingness of Soviet leaders to decrease their force levels significantly in the area, the pact's future must be a matter of continuing concern in the Kremlin. One is reminded of Winston Churchill's prophetic comment to de Gaulle in November 1944: "At present, Russia is a great beast which has been starved for a long time. It is not possible to keep her from eating, especially since she now lies in the middle of the herd of her victims. But after the meal comes the digestion period. When it is time to digest, the Russians will have their difficult moments . . . ."[7]

Moscow has used Comecon to promote economic integration, and thereby political stability, in the Soviet bloc. Originally established in January 1949 as a symbolic facade to parallel the Marshall Plan, the Council for Mutual Economic Assistance was for many years a moribund organization. Under Stalin, there was no necessity for a regional organization; the USSR was in physical control and preferred to maximize its exploitation on a bilateral basis. It felt no need to legitimize the Soviet–East European economic relationship.

Starting under Khrushchev in 1955, Comecon went through a period of gradual upgrading: information was pooled, economic agreements were placed on a five-year instead of a one-year basis, and an atmosphere of bargaining replaced that of acquiescence. On December 14, 1959, Comecon adopted a charter (heavily amended in December 1962 and June 1974) defining its purposes and organizational structure. Standing commissions deal with a wide range of subjects, from electric power and nuclear energy to financial problems and transportation. In institutional terms, Comecon came of age in the 1960s, but actual integration has proceeded very slowly.

At Khrushchev's behest, in June 1962 a programmatic document, "The Basic Principles of the International Socialist Division of Labor," was adopted. In November Khrushchev pushed for a supranational entity capable of rationalizing and transforming the economies of the bloc:

> We must move more boldly toward establishing a single planning agency for all countries in common; this agency should include representatives of all the countries that belong to the Council for Mutual Economic Assistance. This planning agency should be empowered to draw up joint plans and settle

organizational questions so as to coordinate the development of the countries of the socialist system.*

But his optimism and drive were not enough to overcome the legacy of autarky-oriented economies that Stalin had imposed on the East European countries, or the opposition of the Romanians, who did not want to abandon major industrial projects. The technological backwardness that made most East Europeans feel that the plan for division of labor was intended to keep them in an inferior position to the Soviet Union was also a stumbling block. The kind of cooperation that Khrushchev envisaged implied a sense of genuine community, which did not exist.

There were many other reasons for Khrushchev's failure. First, the idea of a supranational organization was perceived in Eastern Europe as entailing a surrender of newly regained national prerogatives to the USSR. The countries of the area were still in the early stages of their existence as nation-states, and for them, nationalism was (and is) a positive force. Second, bureaucratic vested interests resisted the retooling and dismantling of national economic institutions. Further, they lacked the sense of shared trust and commitment to rely on their counterparts for fulfillment of national economic targets. The East Europeans mistrusted not only the Soviet Union, but each other. There is no love of neighbors in the area, which remains a cauldron of ethnic animosities. (The West's common suspicion of the USSR tends to make them overlook this aspect of East European reality.) Finally, the heterogeneity of Eastern Europe, with its different levels of economic, industrial, technological, and educational development, heightened protectionist attitudes and militated against meaningful multilateralism.

After several years of drift, Moscow's determination to promote economic interdependence in the "socialist commonwealth" (a concept popularized by Khrushchev) was renewed. Comecon has had some successes — the Druzhba (Friendship) oil pipeline, an electrical power grid system, and a pool of rolling stock — but basic planning, investment, production, and pricing patterns have not easily been reshaped. In derision of integration, this Hungarian joke made the rounds: The Comecon countries, wanting a common emblem to signify their unity and fraternity, adopted a flag with a red field in which there were seven lean cows milking one another.

In July 1971 Comecon adopted a twenty-year blueprint for integration, albeit within the existing sovereign nation-state system. Moscow is serious about the comprehensive program and insists that it be accorded the status

---

* *Pravda,* November 20, 1962.

of a multilateral treaty. The program postulates cooperation in drafting five-year economic plans, joint planning, a convertible ruble for making commercial transactions in the bloc easier, pooling of research and productive capacities, cost-sharing for the development of energy resources, and raising the standard of living of less-developed members. However, fundamental problems continue, such as the absence of a supranational authority, the reliance on consensus-building, and the indefiniteness in the statutes about implementing recommendations.[8] The Long-Term Target Programme for Cooperation in the fields of energy, machine construction, transportation, agriculture, and consumer-goods production over the next decade was worked out in 1976; its implementation is still in the preliminary stage. Before Soviet-bloc integration can match Western Europe's, Moscow will have to overcome Eastern Europe's suspicion that integration will weaken their national sovereignties and bring a new, disguised form of Soviet interference; regional differences in levels of economic development and each country's desire to industrialize; the desire to insulate national economies from disruptive price competition; and the persistence of political over economic factors in shaping policies toward Comecon.

How stable is Soviet rule in Eastern Europe? Notwithstanding the impressive array of military, economic, political, and ideological arrangements that Moscow uses to perpetuate its strategic control, it must remain very watchful. As one wit observed, the Soviet Union is the only Communist country surrounded by hostile Communist states. The centrifugal forces — nationalism, neorevisionist national communism, slothful economies that consume more than they produce, sociocultural alienation, demands for human rights in accordance with the provisions of the 1975 Helsinki Conference on Security and Cooperation in Europe, and the weakening ideological vigilance of increasingly nationalistic party elites — are a constant worry. On the other hand, Moscow can look with some confidence to the centripetal forces to keep Eastern Europe securely in the Soviet orbit.

First and most unequivocally, the presence of approximately thirty Soviet divisions in East Germany, Poland, Hungary, and Czechoslovakia acts as a constant reminder of the limits of Moscow's tolerance of dissidence, of its capacity to settle any crisis with dispatch. Not only has the USSR shown its readiness to use force if need be to suppress threats to "socialism", but the nations of Eastern Europe know that no help will come from the West. Militarily, Moscow has a free hand to maintain hegemony over the bloc. The constraints on its use of force are internal and bloc-derived.

Second, and of growing importance, Eastern Europe's dependence on Soviet energy and raw materials has increased enormously, and its more active participation in Comecon may well be the sine qua non for continued

Soviet assistance. Ever since the energy crisis exploded on the international scene in the mid-1970s, Eastern Europe's economic situation has worsened. Except for Romania, the area is energy poor. By contrast, the USSR is the world's largest producer of oil and natural gas. Since 1975, Moscow has begun to raise the prices of oil and raw materials; it is no longer willing to give its East European partners concessionary benefits. Moscow has told the East Europeans that if they want assured supplies in the future, they must invest in the development of Soviet resources or look elsewhere. No longer will the Soviet Union play the role of a colony to Eastern Europe. This has led the East Europeans to invest in some Soviet projects: the 1800 mile Bratstvo (Brotherhood) natural-gas line from Orenburg in the Ural Mountains to Uzhgorod on the Czech border; a huge cellulose plant in Siberia that will provide paper; an asbestos complex at Kiyembayevski; and a large nuclear power station in the Ukraine, planned to have four 1000-megawatt plants. In addition, rising energy costs mean that many East European manufactures are even less competitive than before on world markets, making sales to the USSR imperative; and Moscow is beginning to balk at the shoddy goods that it freely accepted in the past. Economic necessity may well prompt the East Europeans to reassess more favorably the definite advantages that they derive from Comecon, and the Soviet Union in particular. At a Comecon summit in June 1979, Premier Kosygin promised to increase Soviet fuel deliveries to member states by 20 percent during the 1980–1985 period, presumably in return for their greater efforts at integration and economic cooperation. An agreement with the GDR, signed on October 5, 1979, providing for Soviet oil and natural-gas deliveries over the next decade, serves as a model for other bloc countries of what Moscow can do for loyal allies.[9]

Third, the fears of the individual East European leaderships bind them to a policy of friendship with the Soviet Union. The Poles' phobia is of another Soviet-German deal at their expense; the GDR worries about a Rapallo-type accord between Moscow and Bonn; Romania dreads an imposed return of its part of Transylvania to Hungary, and so on. Discord among nationalities, a potentially explosive brew, lends credence to the Soviet Union's claim that its policy contributes to the maintenance of peace and stability in Eastern Europe.

Fourth, a generation of party–military–secret-police cadres has acquired a stake in the political status quo. They know their regimes ultimately depend on Moscow's friendship, and therefore they pay ritualistic tribute to Marxist-Leninist internationalism to mollify the Kremlin. At the same time, they try to mobilize popular support in order to obtain internal acceptance of their authoritarian regimes.

Finally, there is that least reliable unifying cohesive, ideology — or Moscow's interpretation of what it is at any given moment. It legitimizes

Soviet policies, but cannot be counted on for inoculative potency against the virus of nationalism or polycentric communism. When applied to domestic issues, ideology is in many respects nothing more than a fig leaf, a flimsy cover for pretended unity, not a guide to problem-solving or political bargaining within the bloc.

Eastern Europe is destined to remain the USSR's Achilles' heel. Soviet leaders would prefer to prevent crises and not have to suppress them. While recognizing and wishing to avoid the prohibitive costs of a return to Stalinist methods, they must at the same time minimize the contradictions of policies established by Khrushchev — decentralization, diversity, and consumerism, which contain within them the seeds of rampant nationalism, incipient anticommunism, and cynicism toward ideology. Their policy is geared toward reinforcing mutual dependencies and transmuting them into a genuine interdependency that will assure Soviet strategic interests and promote bloc cohesion. Barring serious instability in the USSR, there is no real threat on the horizon to the preeminent Soviet position in Eastern Europe.

## Notes

1. U.S. Department of State, *Soviet Affairs Notes,* no. 224 (July 28, 1958) (Washington, D. C.), 3.

2. *New York Times,* December 3, 1959.

3. Department of State, *Soviet Affairs Notes,* no. 224, 4.

4. Raymond L. Garthoff, "The Military Establishment," *East Europe*, vol. 14, no. 9 (September 1965), 15–16; see also Robin Remington, *The Warsaw Pact* (Cambridge: MIT Press, 1971).

5. For a full discussion, see Charles Andras, "A Summit with Consequences," Radio Free Europe Research, *RAD Background Report 271* (East Europe), December 14, 1978.

6. *Los Angeles Times,* June 13, 1979.

7. John Lukacs, *A History of the Cold War,* 3rd ed. (New York: Doubleday, 1966), 250.

8. See George Ginsburgs, "Unification of Law in the Socialist Commonwealth: The Implications of the 20-Year Comprehensive Programme of Economic Integration," in Donald D. Barry, et al. (eds.), *Codification in the Communist World* (Leiden: A. W. Sijthoff, 1975), 123–144.

9. *New York Times,* October 6, 1979.

## Selected Bibliography

BROMKE, ADAM and DERRY NOVAK (eds.). *The Communist States in the Era of Detente 1971–1977.* Oakville, Ontario: Mosaic Press, 1979.

BRZEZINSKI, ZBIGNIEW K. *The Soviet Bloc: Unity and Conflict.* Rev. ed. Cambridge: Harvard University Press, 1967.

COLLIER, DAVID, and KURT GLASER (eds.). *Elements of Change in Eastern Europe.* Chicago: Regnery, 1968.

DALLIN, DAVID J. *Soviet Foreign Policy After Stalin.* Philadelphia: Lippincott, 1961.

FEJTO, FRANÇOIS. *A History of the People's Democracies: Eastern Europe Since Stalin.* New York: Praeger, 1971.

GATI, CHARLES (ed.). *The International Politics of Eastern Europe.* New York: Praeger, 1976.

GRIFFITH, WILLIAM E. (ed.). *Communism in Europe.* Vol. 1. Cambridge: MIT Press, 1965.

GRZYBOWSKI, KAZIMIERZ. *The Socialist Commonwealth of Nations.* New Haven: Yale University Press, 1964.

HOLZMAN, FRANKLYN D. *International Trade Under Communism — Politics and Economics.* New York: Basic Books, 1976.

IONESCU, GHITA. *The Breakup of the Soviet Empire in Eastern Europe.* Baltimore: Penguin, 1965.

KASER, MICHAEL. *COMECON.* London: Oxford University Press, 1967.

KERTESZ, STEPHEN D. (ed.). *East Central Europe and the World: Developments in the Post-Stalin Era.* Notre Dame, Ind.: University of Notre Dame Press, 1962.

LITTELL, ROBERT (ed.). *The Czech Black Book.* New York: Praeger, 1969.

LONDON, KURT L. (ed.). *Eastern Europe in Transition.* Baltimore: Johns Hopkins University Press, 1966.

LOWENTHAL, RICHARD. *World Communism: Disintegration of a Secular Faith.* New York: Oxford University Press, 1964.

LUKACS, JOHN. *A New History of the Cold War.* 3rd ed. Garden City, N. Y.: Doubleday, 1966.

MIĆUNOVIĆ, VELJKO. *Moscow Diary.* Garden City, N. Y.: Doubleday, 1980.

NATO-DIRECTORATE OF ECONOMIC AFFAIRS. *COMECON: Progress and Prospects.* Brussels: NATO, 1977.

REMINGTON, ROBIN A. (ed.). *Winter in Prague: Documents on Czechoslovak Communism in Crisis.* Cambridge: MIT Press, 1969.

————. *The Warsaw Pact.* Cambridge: MIT Press, 1972.

SCHAEFER, HENRY WILCOX. *COMECON and the Politics of Integration.* New York: Praeger, 1972.

SUGAR, PETER F., and IVO J. LEDERER (eds.). *Nationalism in Eastern Europe.* Seattle: University of Washington Press, 1969.

SZAWLOWSKI, RICHARD. *The System of the International Organizations of the Communist Countries.* Leiden: Sijthoff, 1976.

SZAZ, ZOLTAN M. *Germany's Eastern Frontiers: The Problem of the Oder-Neisse Line.* Chicago: Regnery, 1960.

TATU, MICHEL. *Power in the Kremlin: From Khrushchev to Kosygin.* New York: Viking, 1969.

VALENTA, JIRI. *Soviet Intervention in Czechoslovakia, 1968.* Baltimore: Johns Hopkins University Press, 1979.

VALI, FERENC A. *Rift and Revolt in Hungary.* Cambridge: Harvard University Press, 1961.

WETTIG, GERHARD. *Community and Conflict in the Socialist Camp: The Soviet Union, East Germany and the German Problem 1965–1972.* New York: St. Martin's, 1975.

WHELAN, JOSEPH G. *World Communism, 1967–1969: Soviet Efforts to Re-establish Control.* Wayhington, D. C.: U. S. Government Printing Office, 1970.

WOLFE, THOMAS. *Soviet Power and Europe, 1945–1970.* Baltimore: Johns Hopkins University Press, 1970.

ZINNER, PAUL. *Revolution in Hungary.* New York: Columbia University Press, 1962.

# 5

# Soviet Policy
## Toward Western Europe

For generations, Russian leaders have seen Europe as "the most important peninsula in the Eurasian continent" and believed that it is their continent and "that they have the right to be politically predominant in the European area."[1] The expansion of Soviet military power into the center of Europe after 1945 gave rise to the Cold War and a permanent threat to the nations of Western Europe. Yet despite the USSR's sustained military buildup and forward deployment of conventional forces far beyond what might be presumed necessary to assure control of Eastern Europe or to deter an attack by NATO, Moscow is not aiming at an all-out war. Its sights are on hegemony in Eastern Europe and influence in Western Europe.

In the early post–World War II years, Moscow's objectives in Western Europe were subordinated to its East European policy and the demands of internal reconstruction, even though in the process Stalin aroused a sorely weakened and vulnerable Western Europe and an America intent on a return to normalcy to undertake a collective defense that he had hoped to forestall. Stalin was especially interested in the future disposition of Germany. The Soviet Union initially favored an exploitative and Carthaginian solution to the German problem: extensive reparations; the cession of territory east of the Oder and Neisse rivers to Poland as compensation for the USSR's absorption of eastern Poland; the expulsion of twelve million Germans from Eastern Europe; and the establishment of a Moscow-controlled Communist party in the Soviet-occupied part of Germany. However, by mid-1946 it had adopted a more conciliatory position, seeking to obtain a voice in the management of the Ruhr and to disrupt the West's decision to include Germany's economy in its effort to promote overall West European recovery.

During the tense years of 1947, 1948, and 1949, Stalin's imperial strategy crystallized in the establishment of the Cominform, the Communist takeover of Czechoslovakia, the Berlin blockade, and the Sovietization of Eastern Europe. Unable to prevent the creation of NATO, Moscow played on European fears of a militaristic and revanchist Germany, hoping to forestall the Federal Republic's rearmament under U.S. auspices. In a diplomatic note to the Western powers on March 10, 1952, Stalin went so far as to propose a peace treaty and Germany's reunification as a neutral state; but this was very likely a ploy to kill West Germany's integration into the Western military alliance rather than a serious proposal for fundamentally restructuring the polarized alignments that gave Moscow a hegemony in middle Europe. The proposal implied that Moscow had "doubts about the long-term viability of the East German regime" and hoped to be "compensated for the loss of East Germany with a greater Soviet voice in the affairs of a united Germany — in short, the advantage of what later came to be called 'Finlandization'"; Moscow hoped to ease tensions, but within a framework that would at the same time assure Soviet military preeminence on the continent.[2] Even in retrospect it is difficult to take Stalin's proposal seriously: a unified — possibly Communist — Germany could only be a Soviet planner's nightmare, a threat not only to the imperium in Eastern Europe but also to the USSR itself.

Under Khrushchev the Soviet leadership ushered in an era notable for its flexible and differentiated approach to Western Europe. A mixture of blandishment, pressure, need, and growing military power, Soviet policy has shown remarkable persistence and continuity as well as a skillful pursuit of priorities. This emerges clearly from an examination of the key issues that have absorbed Soviet attention under Khrushchev and Brezhnev.

## Moscow and the FRG

For more than a century, Moscow has alternated between fascination with and fear of German discipline, drive, efficiency, and technology. The revival of German military power is a cause of constant Soviet concern. In 1954, an article in *Kommunist*, the journal of the CPSU, charged that to realize its "aggressive plans," the United States needed "a powerful, well-trained land army in Europe equipped with the latest weapons" and therefore had initiated German rearmament in order to make West Germany "into an obedient instrument of its aggressive policy, into a mailed fist that would be directed against the Soviet Union and the People's Democracies and at the same time be used to subject NATO to United States control."* This Soviet interpretation has not changed fundamentally.

From 1955 on, the Soviet Union sought Western acceptance of the territorial status quo in Europe, recognition of the division of Germany and the legitimacy of the GDR, a weakening of ties between West Berlin and the FRG, and a minimal level of rearmament by the Federal Republic. To prod the West on these issues, Khrushchev decided to aggravate the Berlin problem. On November 27, 1958, he provoked a minicrisis, insisting that West Berlin be set up as a "free" city, guaranteed by the four occupying powers and the two existing German states, and that the Western powers withdraw from the city. Khrushchev's pseudoultimatum was extended for almost three years, as the Soviet government avoided any precipitous action; there was petty harassment of traffic from the Federal Republic to West Berlin, but no repeat of the 1948 blockade as the West held firm. Frustrated and in need of some visible sign of achievement to still his critics in the Kremlin — and to help East Germany party boss Walter Ulbricht, whose regime was hemorrhaging from the flight of refugees, most of whom were skilled workers essential to economic development — he agreed to a politically humiliating but extremely effective move. On August 13, 1961, without warning, workers put up the Berlin wall, physically sealing off the two sectors of the city. A monument to Communist weakness, it helped Ulbricht and permitted Khrushchev to save face. The crisis petered out, especially after the upturn in Soviet-American relations that followed the Cuban missile crisis of October 1962, and ended on June 12, 1964, when the Soviet Union and the GDR signed a twenty-year treaty of friendship. The treaty was reassurance for Ulbricht, who had feared a Soviet deal with Bonn at his expense. But more important, by ending the Berlin crisis, Moscow was able to proceed on a new tack toward Western Europe.

Within hours after Ulbricht had signed the treaty and left Moscow, Khrushchev held a talk with the ambassador from the Federal Republic to discuss a new Soviet policy and a proposed visit to Bonn. Aware of the advantages of improved bilateral relationships with key Western countries, Khrushchev aimed for greater influence on FRG politics, particularly for arms limitation and nuclear abnegation. He believed that a major Soviet initiative could aggravate intra-NATO tensions and prevent the FRG from acquiring control of or developing nuclear weapons, and he hoped to use the specter of Rapallo to extract concessions from the FRG's allies, particularly France. His son-in-law, Alexei Adzhubei, traveled to Bonn in July,

---

* I. Yevgenov, "Reestablishment of Militarism in West Germany — A Threat to European Security," *Kommunist,* No. 11 (July 1954), pp. 104–105.

and in the following month Khrushchev announced his intention to visit. However, two months later he was deposed by his closest associates — some speculate because of his German policy, though more likely it was because of domestic issues.

By 1966, after having assessed the situation themselves, Khrushchev's successors adopted his line and explored ways of improving Soviet-FRG relations. They dropped the "demand" for a German peace treaty, kept Berlin quiet, stressed the need for a European security treaty without offering details, and permitted the repatriation of many Soviet citizens of German origin (a decision that had been made by Khrushchev). At the twenty-third congress of the CPSU in March and April 1966, Foreign Minister Andrei Gromyko declared that "the normalization and improvement of relations with the Federal Republic of Germany" depended, in effect, on the Bonn government's renouncing nuclear weapons and accepting the existing frontiers of all states in Europe. He also called for a European security conference. The matter dragged on inconclusively until after the Soviet occupation of Czechoslovakia in August 1968, when polemics in the Soviet media against the Federal Republic dropped sharply as Moscow hinted at a desire to continue the talks. The discussions were given new impetus in March 1969, when the Soviet ambassador in Bonn pointedly briefed the government about the Chinese "aggression" on the Ussuri River; faced with tension in the East, Moscow again signaled that it desired normalization in the West. A few days later, the Political Consultative Committee of the Warsaw Pact, meeting in Budapest, repeated the oft-made Soviet proposal for "the holding of a general European conference on questions of security and cooperation in Europe." Soviet overtures received a welcome reception in Bonn with the coming to power of the Social Democratic party (SPD) in October 1969.

SPD Chancellor Willy Brandt's *Ostpolitik* meshed with Brezhnev's *Westpolitik*. Convinced that reunification was unlikely in the foreseeable future and desirous of easing the situation of West Berliners, reducing the hostility between the FRG and the GDR, and opening the way for better relations with Eastern Europe, Brandt abandoned Bonn's previous insistence on reunification and expressed a willingness to recognize the territorial and political status quo in Europe. On November 28, 1969, the Federal Republic signed the nonproliferation treaty, renouncing any right to acquire, develop, or use nuclear weapons. On December 7, 1969, at Brandt's initiative, talks opened in Moscow on renouncing the use or threat of force between the two counties; and on February 1, 1970, the FRG and the Soviet Union reached a major economic agreement under which the FRG agreed to provide 1.2 million tons of large-diameter pipes on favorable terms financed by a consortium of German banks, in return for which the

Soviet Union was to deliver natural gas over a twenty-year period starting in 1973. Key Soviet military, political, and economic objectives were within reach.

The capstone of the Soviet diplomatic strategy was the treaty signed in Moscow on August 12, 1970, in which the USSR and the FRG agreed to settle their disputes by peaceful means. The treaty further stipulated that the two parties(1) "undertake to respect without restriction the territorial integrity of all States in Europe within their present frontiers"; (2) "declare that they have no territorial claims against anybody nor will assert such claims in the future"; (3) "regard today and shall in future regard the frontiers of all States in Europe as inviolable such as they are on the date of signature of the present Treaty, including the Oder-Neisse line which forms the western frontier of the People's Republic of Poland and the frontier between the Federal Republic of Germany and the German Democratic Republic." For Moscow, the treaty meant that the Federal Republic accepted the division of Germany, the reality of the GDR, and the renunciation of nuclear weapons; it was the augury — and essential precursor — of what Moscow was to achieve at Helsinki five years later, namely, Western recognition of Soviet hegemony in Central and Eastern Europe; and it accelerated the acquisition of advanced technology and extensive credits from the FRG — an objective that was increasingly important for Moscow.

Brandt's only condition for satisfying Soviet desires was an acceptable arrangement for West Berlin. After very difficult negotiations lasting from March 1970 to August 1971, the four powers — the Soviet Union, the United States, France, and Britain — signed an agreement that went a long way toward improving the condition of the West Berliners. Unimpeded civilian transit traffic to West Berlin, which is situated 110 miles inside the GDR, from the Federal Republic by road, rail, and waterways was assured; West Berlin could maintain its special relationship with, but not be part of, the FRG; and the West Berliners were to be granted easier access to visit family in the GDR. The 1970 treaty was ratified by the German parliament in May 1972, but by a very narrow majority, because Brandt's opponents felt that he had given away too much for too little.

That Moscow was keen on Brandt's *Ostpolitik* was evident: in May 1971, it forced the old-guard and antiaccommodationist Walter Ulbricht to resign from the party secretaryship (he died on August 1, 1973) and replaced him with the more compliant Erich Honecker, who was prepared to subordinate the GDR's long-term aims and make concessions to Bonn's demands on the West Berlin issue. By implication, the USSR eschewed the use of the city's vulnerability as a lever against the FRG. However, between treaties and practices there is many a slip. In miniviolations of the 1971 four-power agreement, East Germany has made frequent demonstrations of military power in East Berlin, with Soviet approval. It has elected representatives from East Berlin to the GDR parliament, and it has periodically interfered with transit traffic between the FRG and West Berlin. The Cold War rivalry over Germany has not ended; it has merely become more subtle. For the moment, Moscow has deemed it appropriate to downgrade the GDR's political goals in order to achieve influence in Bonn and to exploit intra-NATO conflicts.

Economic cooperation with the Federal Republic is also important to the Soviet Union (as well as to the GDR, which received more than $3 billion from Bonn during the 1971–1978 period for the upkeep of transit routes and other projects linked with West Berlin). By 1978, the FRG had become the USSR's leading non-Communist trading partner and source of high-technology imports. Soviet imports include a vast iron and steel complex, turbines for the natural-gas pipeline to Eastern Europe and the FRG, electronic equipment for petrochemical plants, trucks, and heavy machinery. Most of this has been financed by long-term German credits, estimated at upwards of $10 billion. During Brezhnev's visits to the Federal Republic in 1973 and 1978, discussions of economic relations loomed large, as did Soviet attempts to curtail the arms buildup and persuade the Germans to agree to renounce the use or deployment of the neutron bomb.

It is important to differentiate between maximalist and minimalist (hence more realizable) goals in the Soviet Union's courtship of the FRG. A maximalist aim may well "envisage a neutralized West Germany, detached from both NATO and the EEC":

> If the FRG were neutralized, Western Europe's cohesion and strength would be severely diminished, since the FRG is by far the strongest link in the European Community. If West Europe were weakened, the USSR could expand its influence there and determine what happened on the whole European continent, although there is no reason to anticipate any physical Soviet takeover. A neutral Germany would eradicate any possible threat to the USSR from a resurgent FRG with expansionist aims.[3]

A Rapallo-type rapprochment, in which the USSR and the two Germanies (or a reunified Germany) enjoyed a special relationship reminiscent of the 1920s, is a "somewhat more realistic, but still unattainable Soviet goal."[4] For the foreseeable future, however, the minimalist goal of encouraging mutually advantageous political and economic ties within the framework of the existing European balance-of-power system seems likely to guide Soviet leaders.

# The Courtship of France

After assuming power, the Brezhnev-Kosygin leadership continued Khrushchev's "opening to the West" with its attention to France. The Soviet media had long castigated French colonialism in Southeast Asia and North Africa, and when Charles de Gaulle returned to power in 1958, Moscow attacked him for seeking to establish a military dictatorship and for refusing to grant independence to Algeria. But this changed as Khrushchev saw opportunities to exploit French differences with Bonn, London, and Washington. He did not permit the Soviet interest in penetrating the Third World to interfere with his European policy.

Perhaps nowhere is the complexity and often indeterminate character of Soviet policy toward Western Europe more apparent than in Moscow's attempt to court the Federal Republic and France simultaneously. When it tries to attract the one, it often dismays the other. With the FRG, the USSR suggests the mutual benefit of a relationship reminiscent of Rapallo, leaving vague the issues of unification and the military power that such a German state would require to pursue an independent policy, all of which is anathema to Paris. With France, Moscow stresses the Franco-Russian alliance in two world wars and the dangers of German militarism. Its effectiveness in dealing with both is limited because the French and Germans compare notes on what Soviet officials say, and act accordingly.

De Gaulle's grant of independence to Algeria was welcomed in Moscow, but his dissatisfaction with NATO, his rejection of the U. S. proposal for a multilateral nuclear force, his opposition to Western European economic and political intergration, his quest for a reduced American role in Europe, his acceptance of the Oder-Neisse boundary, and his readiness to improve relations with Moscow unilaterally accounted for the Kremlin's interest in the French connection. It saw France as the odd-member-out of NATO and was pleased with the Gaullist preference for a Europe of cooperating but nationalistic and independent sovereignties, which conflicted starkly with the "Atlanticist" formulations so favored by American and British officials. As one Soviet writer noted, "A powerful France holds no menace for the Soviet Union or its interests. On the contrary, the more France asserts her great-power independence, the easier it will be for us to work in common for solution of the pressing problems of Europe and the world." De Gaulle's distinctive blend of unsentimental realism and striking purposiveness (for example, his veto in January 1963 of the British application for membership in the Common Market) intrigued Moscow, so much that it was not deterred from pressing for closer bilateral relations by his *force de frappe* (independent nuclear force), refusal to sign the nuclear test ban treaty or discuss arms control, tenacious opposition to Soviet pressure during the Berlin and Cuban crises, and cultivation of a special relationship with Bonn.

President de Gaulle visited the Soviet Union during the halcyon stage of the Soviet courtship, in June 1966, scarcely three months after he had informed NATO of his intention to withdraw France's participation in the integrated military commands and indicated the desirability of a shift of venue for NATO's headquarters from Paris to Brussels. Soviet leaders sought to encourage de Gaulle's weakening of NATO and urged more intimate Franco-Soviet ties. The Moscow declaration of June 30, 1966, announced the plan of the two governments "to continue regular consulations." Moscow persisted in its efforts to strengthen the relationship, but after the Soviet invasion of Czechoslovakia, which coincided with the twilight of de Gaulle's political career, a certain disenchantment and constraint developed in Paris. Succeeding French Presidents Georges Pompidou and Valery Giscard D'Estaing have continued high-level visits, however, and Soviet leaders have regularly returned them. Though the mood has not been the same as it was in de Gaulle's time, Soviet and French leaders met ten times in the 1966-to-1979 period, a frequency no other Western leadership can match.

By the early 1970s, France edged back toward military cooperation with NATO and noticeably muffled the acid exchanges with its allies that were so characteristic of the de Gaulle era. Moscow is under no illusions that France can disengage itself from the Atlantic alliance and play a completely independent role in Europe, but it finds enough promise in the neo-Gaullist propensities that shape the outlook of French leaders and the tenor of French domestic politics to seek agreement with France on the convergent strands of the two countries' foreign policy. Moscow, like Paris, supports the preservation of the territorial status quo in Europe, a non-nuclear FRG, a diminished role for the United States in Europe, a NATO of modest size, and expanded East-West economic cooperation. Both retain vestigial uneasiness over the danger of a resurgent German nationalism and militarism. Overall, France is useful to the Soviet Union in the ongoing process of détente, which is favored by each country. France's demands are few, and its contributions are important to the advancement of Soviet aims.

In the economic and technological realm, France has led the way to the Soviet market. In October 1964, it extended the USSR a seven-year credit for $356 million, which was used to finance chemical plants and equipment; this action made France the first member of the European Economic Community (EEC) to break with the community's previous five-year limit on credits to the Soviet Union. A ten-year Franco-Soviet trade agreement was concluded in October 1971, during the first of Brezhnev's visits to France; and during his visit in December 1974, he signed a far-reaching accord under which the USSR will deliver natural gas over a twenty-year period and France will construct several major industrial plants in the USSR, including a massive complex for the production of aluminum. By the late 1970s, France had become the USSR's second most important Western trading partner — a distant second to the Federal Republic.

The Soviet state-to-state "privileged" relationship (a term stressed by Gromyko during his visit to Paris in October 1978) with France has continued, despite Moscow's unhappiness with French plans to sell arms to China, military interventions against Soviet-subsidized insurgents in Zaire, Chad, and Mauritania, and resistance to inclusion of nuclear weapons in talks on European arms control. The USSR seems determined that friendly relations with France will serve as a model of what it seeks to establish with other West European countries. It appreciates the French attitude toward détente and its disdain of the American penchant toward human rights and regulation of great-power relationships by recourse to principled declarations instead of reliance on the solid basis of military power and delineated spheres of influence. For Moscow, good relations with France take precedence over encouragement to the French Communist party at election time. There is little to suggest that Moscow would jeopardize the former to benefit the latter.

In Moscow's policy toward the key European members of NATO (West Germany, France, and Britain), it is evident that the Soviet theme is peaceful coexistence and détente, a term added since the early 1970s because of its felicitious connotation to many Western leaders. Whatever the term, the attitude Moscow seeks to convey is one of reasonableness, accommodation, and limited goals, certainly for the immediate future. What Moscow seldom mentions, though it is crucial to the political reality that it seeks to fashion, is the role of military power in shaping policy responses and public perceptions. The Soviet military buildup along NATO's central front causes considerable uneasiness and is widely discussed in Western Europe because a Soviet strike across the North German plain would threaten the nerve centers of the alliance; but what is less known is the awesome power and diplomatic pressure that Moscow directs along the northern tier of Western Europe.

## The Nordic Sector

Short on population but long on strategically prime real estate, Scandinavia comprises about one-third of non-Communist Western Europe. Its political and military roles are of crucial importance to the Soviet Union. On the Baltic side, Scandinavia controls the approaches to Leningrad and the Baltic republics of the USSR; on the Atlantic side, Norway sits astride the approaches to the Kola peninsula, where the Soviet network of military installations is considered by Western intelligence analysts to be the most heavily concentrated system of air, naval, and missile bases in the world. The Kola Peninsula offers the Soviet Union the shortest trajectory route over the top of the world to targets in the United States and safeguards the sea and air lanes to key military and industrial sites in the Soviet north; it is also the base for two-thirds of the Soviet submarine fleet.

The Soviet Union desires the neutralization of the Nordic area: Finland, Sweden, Norway, and Denmark. Finland's neutrality and policy of deferring to Soviet wishes on most foreign-policy issues was introduced in 1944 by former Prime Minister J. K. Paasikivi, and has been the centerpiece of Finnish statecraft ever since. For eight hundred years a dukedom of Sweden and then part of the Russian Empire for more than a century, Finland acquired independence only after World War I. After 1945, having sided with Germany, it was forced to cede eastern Karelia, including the ice-free port of Petsamo (Pechenga), to the USSR. Under the 1948 Soviet-Finnish treaty of friendship, cooperation, and mutual assistance, the Finns agreed to consult with the Soviet government if Moscow should feel threatened by Germany or any country that is allied with it, that is, any member of NATO. These consultations severely limit but do not eliminate Finland's possible initiatives in foreign affairs. For most of the post-1955 period, Moscow has pursued a moderate policy toward Finland, a reward for that nation's favoring the USSR's position in foreign affairs.

Sweden followed a policy of neutrality in the two world wars, but it is well armed and would presumably resist any invasion. It has never seriously considered joining NATO and argues for keeping the Nordic area nuclear-free, a policy that sits well with Moscow and reassures it on the security of its Baltic flank.

Moscow's awareness of Norway's strategic importance was an outgrowth of World War II, when German submarines operated out of occupied Norway to interdict the American lend-lease aid that was shipped to Murmansk. After the war, a slice of territory taken from Finland made the Soviet Union Norway's neighbor in the far north, along 110 miles of bleak, frozen wasteland that Norwegians say is land the strategist remembered but God forgot. To the east of Norway's northernmost district of Finnmark, the Soviet Union has the three ice-free ports of Petsamo, Severomorsk (a new naval base), and Murmansk, located fifteen, sixty, and one hundred miles, respectively, from the Norwegian frontier. Their security is a prime Soviet concern.

Norway is a staunch member of NATO, but it has no desire to fuel Soviet apprehensions or precipitate trouble through any misperception of its behavior. Therefore, Norway (and Denmark) announced in 1961 that no nuclear weapons would be introduced on its territory, that no NATO bases would be housed, and that no large-scale NATO exercises would be permitted near the Soviet border. Nor, it announced in early 1978, would large numbers of West Germany forces participate in NATO exercises on Norwegian soil. Norway has also kept force levels in Finnmark at a low threshold and has been slow to develop radar facilities and military bases there to avoid arousing undue Soviet alarm over its defensive and missile capabilities. Moscow would prefer that the Nordic countries officially agree to the establishment of a nuclear-free zone in the area, but neither Norway or Sweden is prepared to foreclose the possible option of acquiring nuclear weapons should they ever deem that necessary.

While suspicious of Norway's membership in NATO and the silent war of electronic eavesdropping and intelligence surveillance that continually goes on, Moscow has accepted Norway's self-imposed limitations as evidence of a desire not to threaten Soviet security, and in all likelihood will continue to do so as long as no power other than Norway controls the approaches to the Kola Peninsula. But since all Soviet ships and submarines must pass through the Norwegian Sea en route to the Atlantic Ocean, Moscow cannot be happy at the monitoring of Soviet naval deployments. Control of Finnmark would, of course, seal this gap in Soviet military secrecy.

Though Soviet policy toward Norway is overwhelmingly strategic, economic considerations in the Svalbard archipelago that commands the approaches to the Kola Peninsula foreshadow future tensions. In 1920, Norwegian sovereignty over Svalbard (which includes the island of Spitzbergen) was internationally recognized, but the archipelago was demilitarized and the forty signatories to the treaty — including the Soviet Union — were granted most-favored-nation status, allowing them the same rights as the Norwegians for fishing, mining, and other commercial ventures. In addition to Norway, only the Soviet Union has so far been active in the region, maintaining a coal-mining concession. (The approximately 2000 Soviet miners do not produce as much as the 1000 Norwegians, but that may be due to the inclusion of a large component of intelligence agents in the Soviet community.) The discovery of offshore oil has greatly enhanced the area's importance, some estimates holding that 40 percent of the world's reserves of oil may exist in the Arctic region. The prospect of having international oil companies drilling in their backyard makes the Soviets very nervous, and Moscow may decide to press for an exclusive Soviet-Norwegian sovereignty in the area. Moreover, the Barents Sea is a rich fishing area. Negotiations between Norway and the Soviet Union for delineating national jurisdictions over the seabed and the seas surrounding the Svalbard-Spitzbergen archipelago are under way.

The Norwegians are under no illusions about Moscow's ultimate strategic objectives on Svalbard; they remember Molotov's ham-handed approach with members of Norway's government-in-exile in Moscow in late 1944, during the German occupation. "The Soviets then demanded a rewriting of the Svalbard treaty of 1920, claiming that the new Soviet government has signed it because it was politically and militarily weak at the time, but that it did not correspond to Soviet interests. Molotov wanted removal of the clause that expressly prohibits military installations and military forces on Svalbard."[5] The Norwegians resist Soviet pressure for revision of the treaty, but they go out of their way to permit the Russians to operate easily under its present terms. Soviet long-term intentions toward Norway should emerge from the lengthy legal discussions now underway.

Moscow believes in continually testing an adversary's determination, in probing its political will. Therefore, the growing Soviet military boldness in the area has to be of concern: "Naval and air exercises move westward into the Norwegian Sea. The number of reconnaissance flights over Finnmark and adjacent districts increases. Unidentified submarines are deteected in the fjords."[6] In August 1978, the Soviets on Spitzbergen built a radar station at their helicopter landing strip near the Soviet-run town of Barentsburg, without informing Norwegian authorities. Soviet ships frequently violate Norwegian territorial waters, testing alertness and gathering intelligence on the Allied radio navigational stations used by Polaris submarines and on electronic capabilities, expeically the cable at Gamvik on the Nordkinn Peninsula, which links submarine-listening equipment on the seabed between Norway proper and the island of Spitzbergen. The USSR also test-fires ICBMs into the contested area of the Barents Sea.

By exposing Norway's vulnerability, Moscow serves notice of its opposition to any Norwegian-NATO buildup that might alter Soviet military superiority in this strategic sector, and it may expect to obtain additional concessions in the bargaining over the boundaries of the continental shelf. But by increasing its military pressure, Moscow is risking a boomerang effect: the more the Soviet Union probes, the less credible become the arguments of Norwegian neutralists and the more Norway seeks security in closer ties with NATO.

## Iberia

In contrast to Scandinavia, the Iberian Peninsula has only recently attracted Soviet attention, as a result of the revolution in Portugal in April 1974 and the death of Francisco Franco in Spain in November 1975, which ended decades of right-wing dictatorships. Both countries are classic Marxist examples of societies ripe for Communist revolutions. They have strong, well-organized Communist parties, tempered by decades of survival underground and led by able, experienced Communists (Alvaro Cunhal in Portugal and Santiago Carrillo in Spain) and weak bourgeois parties; they have troubled economies beset by intensifying "contradictions"; they have a politicized working class; they have archaic, rigid social structures in need of modernization and rising mass expectations; and Spain has discord among nationality groups.

The Communists, and the diverse coalition of peasants and workers they tried to manipulate, came very close to seizing power in Portugal in the 1974–1975 period, but they overplayed a strong hand. Two aspects of Soviet policy require consideration. First, the Soviet Union could do very little to affect the outcome of Cunhal's bid for power directly beyond helping the Portuguese Communist party (PCP) by covertly channeling funds for organizational and electoral activities. Other than that, it maintained a correct attitude at the government-to-government level to avoid straining Soviet-U.S. relations, then in difficulty because of competitive policies in the Middle East and Vietnam. Second, Moscow's policy of détente in no way impelled it to restrain Cunhal, the most pro-Soviet and unregenerate Stalinist among the West European Communists and presumably highly responsive to Kremlin "advice." Had Cunhal succeeded in his strategy of infiltrating and polarizing the armed forces movement, in which pro-Communists and pro-Marxists held key positions, Portugal would most likely have drifted toward a neutralist stand in NATO and would have terminated U. S. military bases. It might even have withdrawn from NATO and provided basing privileges for Soviet ships. Soviet foreign policy stood only to gain, and Moscow would have denied playing any role and credited the development to the Portuguese people. A Communist success without avowed Soviet participation would have left the United States upset but paralyzed. Despite an inevitable increase in tensions between the Soviet Union and the United States, the strategic setback to NATO would have been a significant gain for Soviet policy in Europe. As it was, even Cunhal's failure benefited Moscow, allowing it to parade its adherence to the principle of nonintervention in the domestic affairs of West European countries and its concern for détente.

In June 1974, the USSR and Portugal established diplomatic relations and agreed to an exchange of ambassadors for the first time since 1917. In October 1975, Soviet leaders received the Portuguese president, and the two governments negotiated an expansion of commercial and cultural ties. Normalization has been the objective.

Relations with Spain have proceeded more slowly. Commercial ties resumed in 1971, but not until February 1977 did the two governments establish diplomatic relations, ending a hiatus of thirty eight years. Gromyko's visit to Spain on November 19, 1979, was the first ever by a Soviet foreign minister. All in all, Moscow views the breakthrough in the mid-1970s as a prelude to greater interaction in the 1980s.

## Opposition to European Unity

A major hurdle for Moscow's promotion of détente and normalization of relations in Europe has been its opposition to West European integration and unity. Ideologically, Moscow is hostile to the idea, in accordance with the canons of Marxist-Leninist scripture, which hold that the drastic and desperate measures of "monopoly capital" may temporarily stave off the inevitable collapse of capitalism but will ultimately lead to increased international tensions and a further deterioration in the condition of the working class. At the operational level, "the Europe of Trusts" (as the edifice of supranational institutions is called) politically limits the Soviet Union's freedom of diplomatic maneuver, ability to play one capitalist country against another for maximum commercial benefit, and economic penetration of that part of the Third World that fashioned a special relationship with the EEC. Though preferring bilateral diplomacy, Moscow could not indefinitely ignore the EEC, which came into being with the Treaty of Rome in March 1957.

The subject of considerable discussion in Moscow, the EEC was acknowledged to have brought an accelerated rate of economic growth and unexpected stability to member countries. Khrushchev publicly denounced it in May 1962, but this capitalist creation forced him to offer proposals for strengthening the economic structure of Comecon. Paradoxically, in order for his "socialist commonwealth" to compete and deal with its capitalist counterpart, he had to allow the nations of Eastern Europe greater measures of autonomy, thus further complicating Soviet hegemonic ambitions.

When de Gaulle vetoed Britain's application for membership in the EEC in January 1963, Moscow was elated, seeing this as vindication of Leninist expectations. However, propaganda aside, the Kremlin could not ignore the Common Market's vitality. The Soviet policy of détente in Europe; the eagerness of the Soviet bloc for expanded economic relations with Western Europe; the pressure from West European Communist parties, who sensed the general support that the EEC enjoyed in their respective countries; the interest of the East Europeans in more economic, technical, and cultural "windows to the West"; and the desire for a status quo *cordiale* with Western Europe to offset the widening rift with Beijing wrought a subtle change in Soviet perceptions and attitudes and posed a dilemma for Kremlin policymakers.

In March 1972, in a speech marking the subtle evolution in Soviet policy from unrelenting hostility to incipient accommodation, Brezhnev implicitly recognized the EEC:

> The USSR is far from ignoring the actual situation in Western Europe, including the existence of such an economic group of capitalist countries as the 'Common Market.' We attentively follow its evolution and its activities. Our relations with its members, naturally, will depend on the extent to which they, on their part, recognize the realities existing in the socialist part of Europe, in particular the interests of Comecon countries. We are for equality in economic relations and against discrimination.[7]

After an unproductive eighteen-month period, the EEC accepted an invitation in September 1974 from the secretary-general of Comecon to send a delegation to Moscow. The talks in early 1975 yielded little beyond establishing the first official contacts. In 1977, when the EEC imposed a two-hundred mile limit on North Sea fishing, Moscow sent an official delegation to Brussels. For the first time it opened actual negotiations with the EEC, in order to obtain fishing privileges in the territorial waters of member states, thereby according de facto recognition to the community; but it steadfastly refuses to accredit an official ambassador to EEC's Brussels headquarters.

Despite having taken the initiative in proposing that official relations be established between Comecon and the EEC, the Soviet Union is a reluctant suitor. Its dialogue is halfhearted: in early 1980, it was still an exaggeration to describe the sporadic and vague exchanges on the form of agreement each community wants as serious negotiations. Basically, Comecon (that is, the USSR) wants an agreement on trade and commercial cooperation, conducted on a bilateral basis between individual member states; the Common Market insists that negotiations be carried out by each community as a unit. Obviously, the process of working out a satisfactory agreement between the EEC and Comecon has been difficult. Romania, Hungary, and Poland took the lead in trying to adjust to the community's requirements, but they were limited by Soviet restraints, which may be eased by improved East-West relations. Soviet reluctance to proceed may be a function of Comecon's failure to evolve as a viable economic community and of the strained condition of East–West relations. Politics is still in command in the Kremlin, but in the 1980s, economics may force Moscow to allow the East Europeans to make the best deal possible with the West Europeans. More than that, it may require Moscow to swallow its ideological and political antipathies and pioneer a working relationship between Europe's two economic communities, with consequences for Soviet policy toward Eastern and Western Europe that can only heighten the anxieties of the autocrats in the Kremlin.

## CSCE

The central political objective permeating almost all Soviet diplomatic moves after 1945 was Western recognition of the post–World War II territorial and political status quo in Europe. To this end, and to forestall the European Defense Community and West German rearmament, Moscow started to lobby for a European security conference as early as 1954. It raised the idea often in the 1960s, but the Western powers gave it a cool reception.

By 1970, the mood had changed in the West; interest in an accommodation with the Soviet Union and improved East-West relations was strong. The USSR was now acknowledged to be a superpower in every military sense of the term: it enjoyed essential equivalence with the United States in nuclear weapons and delivery systems and a numerically commanding advantage in conventional forces. Moreover, though the Soviet Union remained solidly entrenched in Eastern Europe, it was allowing increasing measures of autonomy and its own sociopolitical system had relaxed since the Stalinist period. Washington's interest was evident in the unseemly haste with which it swept the Soviet invasion of Czechoslovakia and the Brezhnev Doctrine under the rug and urged the Strategic Arms Limitation Talks (SALT), no doubt also hoping that Moscow's interest in a limitation on strategic weapons would have a salutary effect on U.S. efforts to reach an agreement with Hanoi for an end to the American involvement in Vietnam. With the 1970 Soviet-FRG treaty, the 1971 quadripartite agreement on Berlin, and the Soviet acceptance of American and Canadian participation, Western opposition to the Conference on Security and Cooperation in Europe (CSCE) weakened. Moscow overcame what was perhaps the last hurdle when in May 1971, Brezhnev challenged the West to judge the Soviet Union's peaceful intention by "tasting" the wine of negotiations, offering to meet NATO's demand for parallel but interrelated talks on the reduction of forces in Central Europe.

Deliberations on CSCE started in Helsinki on November 22, 1972. When the final act was signed by the heads of state of thirty-five countries on August 1, 1975, the Soviet Union realized a thirty-year ambition. Though officially only a political statement of intent and not a treaty or a legally binding document, the final act in effect ratified the existing frontiers in Europe. It was a political settlement of World War II and recognized

Soviet hegemony over the Communist half of Europe. Still, the Soviet triumph was not unmixed. The Helsinki conference may have given the East Europeans ammunition to use against Moscow in their struggle for greater autonomy and expanded contacts with the West, though more time must elapse before the validity of this proposition can be assessed. The final act reiterated those general principles that are the staples of international summitry: sovereign equality of states, inviolability of frontiers, territorial integrity of states, nonintervention in the internal affairs of other countries, renunciation of force or the threat of force to change existing frontiers, and so on. The lengthy follow-up meeting in Belgrade from October 1977 to March 1978 left unresolved the degree to which these principles will be realized.

Basket 1, as the set of principles on security, confidence-building measures (CBMs), and disarmament is called, was of most interest to Moscow. By noting that "the participating states regard as inviolable all one another's frontiers as well as the frontiers of all states in Europe, and therefore they will refrain now and in the future from assaulting these frontiers," it filled Soviet needs. The Western powers contented themselves with CBMs such as prior notification of major military maneuvers, notification of smaller military exercises, and the exchange of observers at maneuvers. While voluntary in nature, the CBMs were working through late 1979 and held out some prospect for preventing sudden eruptions of military tensions. Basket 2 deals with economic and technological cooperation, issues also of interest to Moscow. However, Basket 3, which constitutes a potpourri of political principles on the freer flow of people, ideas, and information, was included at the dogged insistence of the West Europeans and contains the fly in the CSCE ointment Moscow so readily bought. The importance the Carter administration gave to human rights willy-nilly marred the process of Soviet-American détente. Moscow believes that the lapse of SALT I in October 1977, the brouhaha over Soviet intervention in Africa and Afghanistan, and the checkered course of Soviet-American economic relations are the political and military consequences of President Carter's ideologically motivated concern with human rights.

## Deranging NATO

Of far greater potential importance for Soviet policy than CSCE are the talks that began officially in Vienna on October 30, 1973 (preparatory meetings were held from January 31 to June 28, 1973). Originally termed Mutual and Balanced Force Reduction (MBFR), the official title is the Conference on Mutual Reduction of Forces and Armaments and Associated Measures in Central Europe, commonly referred to as MFR. MFR was the price Moscow paid to obtain CSCE. Its outcome will determine the military component of détente in Europe. Ironically, just as Moscow's harvest from Helsinki may prove to be smaller than Moscow originally anticipated, so NATO may find MFR more of a problem for the Atlantic alliance than for the Soviet Union.

MFR reveals the multiple and adaptive nature of Soviet policy. Though not at all enthusiastic in the beginning, Moscow has used MFR to stabilize its present favorable military advantage in Europe. It seeks to weaken NATO through MFR, not merely militarily, but politically as well. Though Moscow considers NATO to be dominated by the United States, it recognizes the existing differences in national positions and exploits them, playing off one member or faction against another. NATO's failure to resolve essential policy questions on strategy, interoperability and standardization of weapons, and new weapons, such as the neutron (enhanced radiation) bomb and cruise missiles, is therefore grist for the Soviet mill. These conflicts strengthen the Soviet belief in the divisive propensities inherent in relations among capitalist countries and lead Moscow to wait for the right time and circumstance to capitalize on the disagreements. Thus ideological predilections and perceptions are reinforced by political phenomena, in this case the MFR negotiations.

Perpetuation of a favorable military balance depends on checking the growth of the Bundeswehr; through arms reduction and limitation, Moscow hopes to place ceilings on the military forces of the Federal Republic. One wedge in this drive was the Warsaw Pact proposal submitted on June 8, 1978, in which the Russians agreed for the first time that both sides should have an equal number of troops in Central Europe and that no country would be permitted to increase its forces above present levels. The joker in this game is the number of Soviet troops in Central Europe, the Kremlin's figures being significantly lower than NATO's. This data issue has anesthetized MFR talks.

Other issues that Moscow has raised are the limitation of NATO forward-based systems (FBS), a treaty on the renunciation of the first use of nuclear weapons, and a limit on the size of military maneuvers. Disengagement as a way of encouraging a withdrawal of U.S. forces crops up repeatedly; for example, in the late 1950s, Moscow proposed a demilitarized zone of four hundred kilometers on either side of the Elbe. Among other Soviet proposals has been one for the establishment of a nuclear-free zone that would include Poland, Czechoslavakia, and the two Germanies. And in 1978, the Soviet Union convinced the West Europeans that deployment of the neutron bomb would harm the negotiations aiming at a reduction of forces in Central Europe, as well as the promotion of détente.

Soviet political strategy in Europe rests on a strong military base. Despite anticipated major economic difficulties in the 1980s, the Soviet

Union shows no disposition to stabilize, much less reduce, military expenditures or the modernization of its strategic and conventional forces. The buildup of strategic forces begun by Khrushchev and accelerated by Brezhnev in the mid-1960s gives no sign of tapering off. No longer do Western experts talk of NATO's military superiority. The discussion now centers on the nature and extent of Moscow's military superiority, nuclear weapons aside.

The characteristics of Soviet military policy in Europe are important to any consideration of the range of Moscow's probable and possible political objectives. Briefly, these characteristics are high conventional force levels and their strong forward deployment; a commitment in military doctrine "to wage and to win a campaign" with *all* available weapons, including nuclear arms; an impressive buildup of mobile battlefield cover for moving combat forces; a substantial numerical advantage over NATO forces in tanks, motor-rifle divisions, armored personnel carriers (half of which have an amphibious capability), and artillery; improved and highly effective logistical support; and the buildup of what Richard Burt has called Eurostrategic weapons, that is, aircraft and missiles capable of carrying nuclear weapons with great accuracy against targets in Europe but not included under SALT II because they lack an intercontinental capability.[8] Soviet forces maintain a high level of combat readiness, and they are consistently modernized and given deeper penetration capability. The Soviet Union is deploying a new generation of tactical or theater nuclear surface-to-surface missiles: the SS-21, which replaces the very short-range Frog; the SS-22, with a 500-mile range, which replaces the SCUD that had a 180-mile range; and, most threatening of all the Eurostrategic weapons, the mobile SS-20s, which can hit targets anywhere in Western Europe from movable platforms in the Soviet Union.

That a major Soviet military buildup is under way in Central Europe is undisputed. Soviet forces are being equipped and trained to fight a blitzkrieg war. Nonetheless, NATO officials do not believe Moscow intends an all-out aggression against Western Europe. Several explanations may help illumine the Kremlin's military purposes.

First, massive military power is perceived as the best defense, not only against any NATO attack or attempt to intervene in Eastern Europe, but also against attempted national Communist defections or uprisings.

Second, the Soviet leadership, like its czarist predecessor, values redundancy. As the saying goes, "Russians feel more comfortable with three armies too many than with three divisions too few." Overinsurance is axiomatic in Soviet military doctrine.

Third, if war comes, Moscow wants an overwhelming retaliatory capability. In recent years, it seems to have shifted from the expectation that the next European war would be nuclear to predicate a war-winning strategy on the forward deployment of massive conventional forces, which are expected to neutralize the nuclear option. Some British analysts contend that Soviet troops are being trained to live off the land, carry sufficient ammunition with them during rapid forward thrusts, and achieve a decisive victory before NATO can react. The ability to strike suddenly, with minimal reinforcements, is expected to provide the clout either to deter or to demolish, as need requires.

Fourth, by forward deployment, the Soviet Union seeks a critical edge over NATO and the eventual acquiescence to Soviet military superiority in Central Europe. Expecting that in the short run NATO may react with intensification of its military buildup and modernization (and this is a matter of concern to Moscow), the Soviets think that the West has a short memory and will in time accept the forward Soviet deployment as the norm for a tolerable balance of power in Europe.

Finally, since the mid-1970s, Soviet commentators have called attention to the downturn in détente and NATO's growing modernization program. When they "quantify the NATO threat, normally they use a method similar to Western worst-case analysis. Seldom does one see qualitative distinctions made among various NATO members' weapons or divisions."9 They fear the trend in NATO is toward increased defense budgets and weapons modernization; hence their own sustained programs.

Politically, the Soviet Union prefers an orderly and stable environment in Western Europe. It does not like changes that might complicate the realization of its specific objectives: a nonnuclear Federal Republic of Germany and a modest U.S. presence, both of which are keys to keeping NATO minimally potent; a Western Europe of nation-states at a low level of integration; worsening West European–U.S., and especially FRG-U.S., relations; assured access to West European technology and markets; and better leverage over West European Communist parties, whose ideological assertiveness and prospects for sharing power are beginning to complicate Soviet hegemony in Eastern Europe and leadership of the world Communist movement. Moscow aspires to be security manager of Europe and assumes that the position can best be attained in an atmosphere of détente and through expanded bilateral relations with the existing capitalist governments.

Soviet diplomacy is active and resourceful. On October 6, 1979, during a speech in East Berlin, Brezhnev unexpectedly announced the unilateral withdrawal in the coming year of up to 20,000 Soviet troops, 1000 tanks, and other equipment from East Germany. He also offered to reduce the number of medium-range "theatre" missiles based in the European part of the USSR, if no new missiles were added to NATO's arsenal. Moscow's main aim is to forestall the deployment of 572 new medium-range missiles that will be capable of reaching targets in the west-

ern part of the USSR, though not as far as Moscow (of the total, 108 are
to be improved Pershing II missiles with a range of 1000 miles; and 464
will be ground-launched cruise missiles with a 1500 mile range, still not
enough to reach Moscow, given the circuitous flight pattern of GLCMs);
by contrast, the Soviet SS-20, now deployed, can hit any target in Western
Europe. Brezhnev has also made propaganda capital out of a military
liability, since the tanks to be withdrawn from the GDR are obsolete.
Despite NATO's decision in December 1979 to proceed with the upgrading of its theatre nuclear missiles, he hopes intra-NATO dissension will
intensify over how to respond to his offer and save the arms control talks,
and that it will eventually defer the deployment in much the same way it
affected President Carter's decision not to deploy the neutron bomb. However, a veiled threat in Brezhnev's offer may drive NATO to proceed,
irrespective of the consequences. Whatever the outcome, the nexus between military and political considerations is continually present in Soviet
attempts to limit Western Europe's military buildup and political unity.

If Moscow does indeed have a long term political strategy for an ideal
relationship with the countries of Western Europe, it could be that commonly referred to as "Finlandization."[10] With due apologies to the Finns,
this term is used to signify a process whereby the Soviet Union influences
the domestic and foreign policy behavior of non-communist countries in
a way that leads them voluntarily to follow policies congenial to or approved
by the Soviet Union. It is a policy of special constraints where Soviet
interests and preferences are involved, in which governments are overly
careful beforehand in dealing with the Soviet Union and in acting on issues
of special interest to Moscow.

Reality is more complex than the theories or conceptual formulations
that we use to explain it. The NATO countries may disagree on many
issues, but they are far from fatalistic acceptance of Soviet military superiority. They do not manifest the telltale signs of Finlandized states, unlike
neutral Austria and Finland, who are sensitive to the wishes of Moscow.
If the Finlandization of the West should come to pass, it would be a
consequence not just of Soviet strength but also, perhaps mainly, of Western weakness — debilitating domestic politics, intra-alliance bickering, a
contraction of power under the guise of advancing détente, and a lack of
commitment to professed ideals and institutions. Naturally Moscow will
try to exploit the disarray in the West and induce a lowering of its guard.
For the moment, at least, the Kremlin seems committed to the same
general policy in the 1980s that brought it such handsome benefits in the
1970s. Although it is heir to constraints, dilemmas, and problems that
frustrate and divert its diplomacy from desired paths, Moscow seems, in
recent decades to have always been attentive to longer-range schemes for
the attainment of key objectives and the ordering and management of

European affairs. Soviet pragmatism should not obscure Moscow's outlook and ambitions. At a time of troubles on its eastern flank, Moscow has reason for satisfaction with its European policy.

## Notes

1. Malcolm MacKintosh, "Future Soviet Policy Toward Western Europe," in John C. Garnett (ed.), *The Defence of Western Europe* (London: Macmillan, 1974), 39.

2. Victor Baras, "Stalin's German Policy After Stalin," *Slavic Review,* vol. 37, no. 2 (June 1978), 262–263.

3. Angela Stent Yergin, "Soviet–West German Relations: Finlandization or Normalization?" in George Ginsburgs and Alvin Z. Rubinstein (eds.), *Soviet Foreign Policy Toward Western Europe* (New York: Praeger, 1978), 127.

4. Ibid.

5. Per Egil Hegge, "The Soviet View of the Nordic Balance," *The Washington Quarterly,* vol. 2, no. 3 (Summer 1979), 66.

6. *New York Times,* June 20, 1977.

7. *Pravda,* March 21, 1972.

8. John Erickson, "The European Military Balance," *Proceedings of the Academy of Political Science,* vol. 33, no. 1 (1978), 111–113, 121.

9. Keith A. Dunn, "Soviet Perceptions of NATO," *Parameters,* vol. 8, no. 3 (September 1978), 59–60.

10. For a discussion of this concept as it applies to Soviet relationships with West European countries, see George Ginsburgs and Alvin Z. Rubinstein (eds.), *Soviet Foreign Policy Toward Western Europe* (New York: Praeger, 1978).

## Selected Bibliography

ANDREN, NILS, ET AL. *The Future of the Nordic Balance.* Stockholm: Ministry of Defense, 1977.

BIRNBAUM, KARL E. *The Soviet Union and the Two German States: East-West Negotiations in Europe, 1970–1972.* Lexington, Mass.: Lexington Books, 1973.

BRZEZINSKI, ZBIGNIEW K. *Alternative to Partition.* New York: McGraw-Hill, 1965.

CATUDAL, HONORÉ M., JR. *The Diplomacy of the Quadripartite Agreement on Berlin.* Berlin: Berlin Verlag, 1977.

DePORTE, ANTON W. *Europe Between the Superpowers: The Enduring Balance.* New Haven: Yale University Press, 1979.

GILBERG, TROND. *The Soviet Communist Party and Scandinavian Communism: The Norwegian Case.* Oslo: Universitatsforlaget, 1970.

GINSBURGS, GEORGE B., and ALVIN Z. RUBINSTEIN (eds.). *Soviet Foreign Policy Toward Western Europe.* New York: Praeger, 1978.

KING, ROBERT R., and ROBERT W. DEAN (eds.). *East European Perspectives on European Security and Cooperation.* New York: Praeger, 1974.

KORBEL, JOSEF. *Detente in Europe, Real or Imaginary?* Princeton: Princeton University Press, 1972.

LAQUEUR, WALTER Z. *Russia and Germany.* Boston: Little, Brown, 1965.

MAUDE, GEORGE. *The Finnish Dilemma: Neutrality in the Shadow of Power.* New York: Oxford University Press, 1976.

MENSONIDES, LOUIS J., and JAMES A. KUHLMAN (eds.). *The Future of Inter-Bloc Relations in Europe.* New York: Praeger, 1974.

MOSELY, PHILIP E. *The Kremlin and World Politics.* New York: Vintage, 1960.

MYAGKOV, ALEKSEI. *Inside the KGB.* London: Foreign Affairs Publishing Company, 1977. (Provides an account of KGB operations to take France out of NATO.)

PIPES, RICHARD (ed.). *Soviet Strategy in Europe.* New York: Crane, Russak, 1976.

PISAR, SAMUEL. *Coexistence and Commerce: Guidelines for Transactions Between East and West.* New York: McGraw-Hill, 1970.

PRENDERGAST, WILLIAM B. *Mutual and Balanced Force Reduction: Issues and Prospects.* Washington, D. C.: American Enterprise Institute, 1978.

SHLAIM, AVI, and G. N. YANNOPOULAS (eds.). *The EEC and Eastern Europe.* Cambridge: Cambridge University Press, 1978.

SLUSSER, ROBERT M. *The Berlin Crisis of 1961: Soviet-American Relations and the Struggle for Power in the Kremlin.* Baltimore: Johns Hopkins University Press, 1973.

TIERSKY, RONALD. *French Communism, 1920–1972.* New York: Columbia University Press, 1974.

VALI, FERENC A. *The Quest for a United Germany.* Baltimore: Johns Hopkins University Press, 1967.

VINCENT, R. J. *Military Power and Political Influence: The Soviet Union and Western Europe.* Adelphi Paper no. 119. London: International Institute for Strategic Studies, Autumn 1975.

VLOYANTES, JOHN P. *Silk Glove Hegemony: Finnish-Soviet Relations, 1944–1974.* Kent, Ohio: Kent State University Press, 1975.

WETTIG, GERHARD. *Community and Conflict in the Socialist Camp: The Soviet Union, East Germany and the German Problem 1965–1972.* New York: St. Martin's, 1975.

WHETTEN, LAWRENCE L. *Germany's Ostpolitik: Relations Between the Federal Republic and the Warsaw Pact Countries.* New York: Oxford University Press, 1971.

WOLFE, THOMAS. *Soviet Power and Europe, 1945–1970.* Baltimore: Johns Hopkins University Press, 1970.

# 6
# Moscow's Cold War in the Far East

Security considerations transcend expansionist ambitions in Soviet Far Eastern policy. The relative stability and continuity of the Soviet Union's European policy contrast with the major accommodations to unforeseen difficulties that have been required of its policy in the Far East (China, Japan, Mongolia, the two Koreas) during the past few decades. In retrospect, the Stalin era looms as the apogee of Sino-Soviet accord. Stalin found dealing with Chiang Kai-shek easy and advantageous, and when the Communists took power in China, Mao Zedong was prepared to accept a junior partnership and follow the Soviet lead in world affairs. All of this changed rapidly in the post-Stalin period.

In October 1954 Nikita Khrushchev led a Soviet delegation to Beijing to negotiate a series of political and economic agreements that would more accurately reflect China's independence and growing stature within the Communist world. Under the agreement of October 11, 1954, Moscow made a number of concessions, indicative of its desire to eliminate obvious past inequities and possible sources of future friction. The naval base of Port Arthur was returned (formally in May 1955), in accordance with the 1950 treaty; the Soviet share in the four joint-stock companies that had been set up in 1950 and 1951 (to mine nonferrous and rare metals, to extract and refine petroleum, to build and repair ships, and to develop civil aviation) was transferred to the CPR, with appropriate compensation to be paid in goods over a number of years; and the USSR provided an additional long-term credit of $230 million and agreed to help build fifteen additional industrial projects and participate in the construction of a railway line from Lanchow through Urumchi (in Xinjiang) to Alma Ata, on Soviet territory, and of another line between Tinmin in Chinese Inner Mongolia and Ulan Bator in the MPR to the USSR's Trans-Siberian Railroad. Moscow would not, however, return Tanu-Tuva, which had been detached from Chinese Turkestan during a time of maximum Kuomintang weakness and incorporated into the Soviet Union in 1944; nor would it agree to any questioning of Mongolia's independence or weakening of Soviet-MPR ties. Finally, it resisted Beijing's effort to convert North Korea into a Chinese satellite, but agreed to a compromise whereby the Yenan (Chinese) faction of the Korean Workers' (Communist) party was assured of suitable minority representation.

This was the high-water mark of Sino-Soviet amity and cooperation in the post-Stalin period. From 1955 on tensions mounted and relations deteriorated, as national interests overshadowed Communist ecumenism.

## The Sino-Soviet Conflict: Origins

The catalysts for Sino-Soviet disagreements came from Europe. Khrushchev's reconciliation with Tito, his acceptance of the principle of many roads to socialism, and his interest in better relations with the United States, Beijing's main enemy, alienated the Chinese. His attack on Stalin at the twentieth party congress and subsequent de-Stalinization policy was the final shock to Mao. An implicit criticism of his own rule in China, this policy forced Mao to launch his own equivalent of de-Stalinization — the very short-lived policy in 1956–1957 of "let a hundred flowers bloom, let a hundred schools contend." Mao used this bogus liberalization to draw opponents into the open, destroy them, and reassert his authority against leading rivals (Marshal Peng Teh-huai, purged in 1959, and Liu Shao-chi, purged in 1966). Mao's perceived need to respond to Khrushchev's disruptive policy initiatives may have forced him on to ideological and economic paths that hastened the separation from Moscow. The animus between Khrushchev and Mao was profound, as Khrushchev suggests in his memoirs and as their acrimonious exchanges confirm.

There was a lull in the gathering storm in late 1956, when, in the wake of the Soviet repression in Hungary, Khrushchev assured the Chinese that "We are all Stalinists. . ."; and at the November 1957 Moscow conference of Communist parties, when Mao backed Khrushchev's anitrevisionist line, which was directed against Tito and other national Communists. (The supreme irony was that Mao himself had been communism's first "Titoist" in departing from reliance on Moscow in the 1930s and fashioning his own strategy for making a revolution.) But as Soviet policy explored the path of detente with the United States, Moscow's relations with Beijing took a turn for the worse. The adhesive of Marxism-Leninism (and the sharing of a common enemy) that had bound the Soviets and the Chinese in the Stalin period loosened under the strain of divergent national interests.

Khrushchev's ideological innovations and his stress on peaceful coexistence with the West contrasted with Mao's preference for doctrinal orthodoxy and monolithism, and the polarizing strategy epitomized by the 1947 Zhdanov line.

The tensions increased with Moscow's criticism of the ideological pretensions that underlay Mao's "Great Leap Forward" campaign in 1958 to bypass socialism and move directly to communism through a system of communes, mass mobilization, and do-it-yourself backyard industrialization. At the 1956 party congress, Khrushchev superseded Stalin's "two-camp" thesis with his "zone of peace" concept, which gave ideological sanction to the USSR's courtship of bourgeois Third World governments and movements (and this at a time of serious Chinese tensions with India and Indonesia). He maintained that as a result of the emergence of the Communist camp and the weakening of colonialism, "a vast 'peace zone,' including both socialist and nonsocialist peace-loving states in Europe and Asia, has emerged in the world arena" and that these new nations could play a "progressive" role in weakening "imperialism" (that is, the United States) and strengthening the Communist world.

The resulting clash with Mao's revolutionary line took place on the Third World stage. Mao saw Khrushchev's formulation that war was no longer "fatalistically inevitable" as the ideological rationale for Moscow's reluctance to use its putative missile superiority, represented by the launching of Sputnik in October 1957, on China's behalf. In August and September 1958, during the crisis between China and the United States that had been triggered by the Communists' bombardment of the Kuomintang-held offshore islands of Quemoy and Matsu, Moscow's restraint emphasized that it would not risk nuclear war with the United States in order to help Beijing liberate Taiwan. The Quemoy crisis demonstrated that neither the Sino-Soviet alliance nor the shared commitment to Marxism-Leninism was sufficient to overcome diametrically opposed national interests in a concrete situation.[1]

Whatever chances there were for a reconciliation probably vanished with Mao's mastery over his rivals, many of whom favored better relations with Moscow (and a more pragmatic approach to domestic problems) because they wanted to modernize the Chinese army with Soviet assistance or develop China's nuclear capability with Soviet expertise and have a common front in Asia against the United States.[2] Khrushchev's unwillingness to provide more substantial economic assistance and his refusal in 1959 to help China acquire a nuclear capability undermined the anti-Mao faction in the CCP. Adding insult to injury, Khrushchev expanded his relations with the United States, and his visit there in 1959 showed that he had no intention of helping China regain Taiwan. Nor was he going to play nuclear brinkmanship to please Mao. In response to Mao's derisory

description of the United States as a paper tiger, Khrushchev retorted, "The United States may be a paper tiger, but [it is] a paper tiger with nuclear teeth."

At a meeting of ruling Communist parties in Bucharest in June 1960, Moscow made a number of concessions in an effort to find a formula for bridging the rift. In return for Beijing's acceptance of Khrushchev's 1956 doctrinal innovations — the possibility of many roads to socialism and the noninevitability of war — Moscow agreed that armed revolutions as a way of bringing about change should be accorded ideological equality with the thesis that the working class could come to power through parliamentary means. In November 1960, at the Moscow conference of eighty-one Communist parties, Khrushchev again looked for a course through the troubled sea of differences with Mao over revisionism and dogmatism (the latter being the charge leveled by the Yugoslavs against the Chinese position that war was inevitable and cooperation with capitalism impossible). However, no amount of ideological circumlocution could resolve the concrete policy differences that divided the two colossi of communism. Khrushchev's peremptory withdrawal in the summer of 1960 of all Soviet technicians (and their blueprints) from China, leaving dozens of incomplete Soviet-assisted projects, intensified Beijing's hostility. If Khrushchev's purpose was to pressure Mao into submission, he failed dismally.

By 1961, the seriousness of the rift had become a matter of public record, as Moscow and Beijing hurled charges and countercharges at one another. The kid gloves came off at the CPSU's twenty-second congress in October of that year. Khrushchev declared that the line established in 1956 was correct and would not be altered to suit the "Albanian leaders," who were not invited to the congress and were regarded by Moscow as Chinese clients, or "anyone else." The Chinese, who had sent a delegation headed by a moderate, Premier Zhou Enlai, were surprised by Khrushchev's open attack on Albania. To the indirect but evident castigation of Beijing, Zhou responded, "If there are quarrels in the socialist camp, we consider that they should be settled through bilateral contacts and that a public denunciation does not contribute to the cohesion of the socialist camp," and then he walked out of the meeting.

The condemnatory attacks crescendoed throughout the remaining years of the Khrushchev period. Moscow called Mao "a megalomaniac warmonger," "an irresponsible scribbler," and "a dogmatist" of whom it could truly be said, "Blessed is he who chatters about war and does not understand what he is chattering about." It assailed the Chinese, "who have learned by heart the general formula about imperialism and stubbornly turn their eyes away from life," and labeled them "imitators of Trotsky" (the most serious charge that can be leveled by one Communist against

another). Beijing responded with comparable venom and vigor, referring to Khrushchev as "a Bible-reading and psalm-singing buffoon."

A high-level meeting of Soviet and Chinese party officials was held in Moscow from July 5 to 20, 1963, in an effort to mediate the dispute, but like previous attempts it failed. On July 14, *Pravda* published a major statement, an open letter from the Central Committee of the CPSU to all party organizations and members in which it presented the main lines of the Soviet position: that the CPSU favored a diametrically opposite approach from that of the CCP to such vital problems as "the possibility of averting thermonuclear war" and "peaceful coexistence between states with different social systems"; that the Soviet Union had not been guilty of "adventurism" in introducing missiles into Cuba in the fall of 1962, as the Chinese alleged, but rather had taken effective steps to prevent "aggression on the part of American imperialism"; and that indiscriminate revolution was no way to advance the cause of socialism or national liberation movements.

Each side printed lengthy charges and rebuttals. In March 1964, for example, *Kommunist,* the journal of the CPSU's Central Committee whose articles are intended primarily for Soviet party cadres, printed a lengthy assessment and indictment of Chinese behavior.[3] It accused the "Chinese deviationists," whose "nationalistic vanity" had forestalled all Soviet attempts at reconciliation, of disrupting the unity of the socialist camp and instilling in the Chinese people a feeling of hostility toward the USSR. Behind Chinese slander is the desire to pose as "supreme arbiter" of socialist ideology. Beijing calls disarmament an illusion, deliberately distorting the Soviet position and denouncing nuclear nonproliferation and efforts to improve relations with the West while "trying feverishly to set right" its own relations with Britain, France, Japan; it obviously would improve relations with the United States, too, if only it could find the opportunity. The Chinese think that the central question in revolution is whether socialist countries will lead it, but this is secondary to the problem of choosing the correct path leading to revolution and power for the working class. All good Communists today should know that a country may become socialist irrespective of its economic development. The Chinese attack the creature comforts of the USSR, but we must fulfill our obligations to our own people. Trotsky had factionalism in his soul, plus willfulness and bourgeois attitudes. The Chinese have stolen many of their ideas from his baggage. They echo him, in both his "no war, no peace" and "permanent revolution" formulations. Despite the concluding call for reconciliation, the tenor of the article and Khrushchev's attempt to convene an international Communist meeting evinced the depths of the chasm separating Moscow and Beijing.

In July 1964 the CPSU sent an invitation to twenty-five Communist parties to attend a conference in Moscow on December 15. Moscow and Beijing seemed on the brink of a formal and irrevocable rupture when Khrushchev was deposed on October 14, 1964. By that time, the specific reasons for the rift had been well documented.

## Issues

Though the Sino-Soviet dispute is often cast within a ideological framework, it is fundamentally a rivalry over power and mirrors the divergent strategies, interests, and objectives of the two countries. Briefly, the main sources of discord were five broad issues.

First, Moscow believed that as the senior and most powerful member of the international Communist community, it should be accorded the authority to interpret Marxist-Leninist doctrine and establish basic strategy for the bloc, in particular to decide on the best way to deal with the capitalist world. It resented Chinese pretensions to leadership and felt that the Chinese, as newcomers, were not familiar with global realities and did not appreciate the extent to which imperialism could be weakened by nonmilitary means.

Second, the two nations disagreed over priorities: the areas and issues that were most important to Moscow were least important to Beijing, and vice versa. For example, if for no other reason than that the main military threat to the USSR came from the West, Moscow's primary political interest was drawn to European developments, to centrifugal tendencies in Eastern Europe, to the resurgence of West Germany, and to the impact of the Common Market. A satisfied power territorially, the Soviet Union was not prepared to go to war against the United States over the Taiwan question, an issue that was paramount in Chinese thinking. Thus did geography, history, and economics shape national priorities.

Third, Moscow and Beijing differed in their approach to developing countries. While their differences were not as clear-cut as many in the West sometimes imagined, they did connote China's readiness to advocate militant policies that would have interfered with Moscow's courtship of key Third World countries and exacerbated relations between the Soviet Union and the United States. The Chinese sought to profit politically from the failure of Khrushchev's Cuban gamble, but they themselves did not, in practice, precipitate any such dramatic showdowns with the "paper tiger," the United States. A major source of discord between Moscow and Beijing was Soviet assistance to India, particularly the military help given after the Sino-Indian war of 1962. Another was Moscow's program of extending extensive economic and military assistance to non-Communist non-aligned countries, whereas aid to China was brusquely terminated in 1960. By emphasizing the revolutionary path to power and opposing (more in principle than in practice) cooperation between local Communist parties and bourgeois-nationalist parties, China directly challenged the Soviet strategy for spreading Communist influence in the Third World.

Fourth, Moscow's unwillingness after 1959 to help China to develop a nuclear capability and its signing of the limited nuclear test ban treaty in 1963 signified to China a Soviet desire to keep its Communist ally a second-rate military power dependent on Moscow's nuclear shield. Ironically, the Chinese detonated their first nuclear explosion literally within hours of Khrushchev's fall from power.

Fifth, China had long-standing border grievances against the USSR. Under treaties imposed on imperial China by czarist Russia in 1858, 1860, and 1881, China was forced to cede almost one million square miles of territory in central Asia and the maritime provinces of Siberia. Beijing argued that these "unequal treaties" should be renegotiated, a demand rejected by Moscow.

After Khrushchev was toppled, Brezhnev acted quickly to suspend the vituperative exchanges with the Chinese, a priority second only to the reintegration of the Communist party, which Khrushchev had divided in two in 1962. In the hope of encouraging exploratory discussions with the Chinese, the conference scheduled for December 1964 (which Khrushchev had organized) was postponed until March 1, 1965. Though the new Soviet leadership stressed the consultative character of the meeting and disclaimed any intention of excommunicating any Communist party from the international movement, the Chinese Communists and their adherents boycotted it. The March meeting did little more than highlight the depth of the Sino-Soviet rift and reaffirm the desirability of holding a world conference of Communist parties. For a time the Soviets shelved their polemics and refrained from responding to Chinese gibes that they were practicing "Khrushchevism without Khrushchev." However, within the world Communist movement, Moscow strengthened its ties. For example, it concluded a new treaty of alliance with the Mongolian People's Republic, which had long depended on Moscow and feared Beijing's ambitions; it supported the establishment of a rival Communist party in Japan to compete with the entrenched pro-Chinese one; and in February 1965, Premier Kosygin visited North Korea and North Vietnam, which generally followed China's lead in intrabloc politics for geostrategic reasons but which were noncommittal in the dispute itself.

By late 1966 the grievances between the Soviet Union and China were unchanged. In October, Moscow ordered all Chinese students to return home, in retaliation for expulsion of Soviet students from China. In November, it resumed open attacks on Beijing, charging that "experience

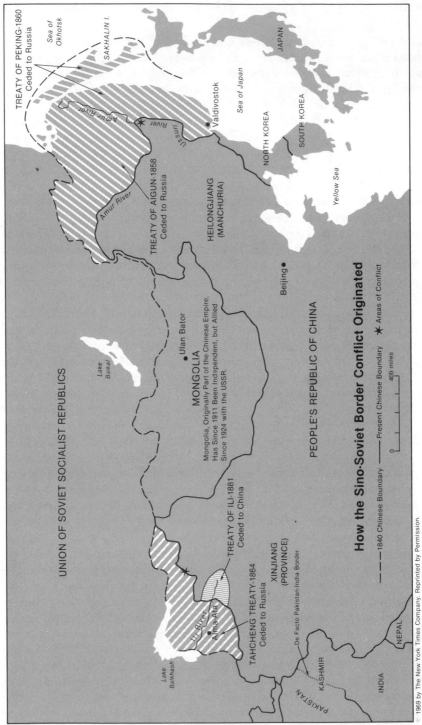

UNION OF SOVIET SOCIALIST REPUBLICS

TREATY OF PEKING-1860
Ceded to Russia

Sea of Okhotsk

SAKHALIN I.

Amur River

TREATY OF AIGUN-1858
Ceded to Russia

Amur River

Ussuri

Ussuri River

Valdivostok

Sea of Japan

NORTH KOREA

SOUTH KOREA

JAPAN

Yellow Sea

HEILONGJIANG
(MANCHURIA)

Lake Baikal

Beijing

MONGOLIA

Ulan Bator

Mongolia, Originally Part of the Chinese Empire,
Has Since 1911 Been Independent, but Allied
Since 1924 with the USSR.

PEOPLE'S REPUBLIC OF CHINA

TREATY OF ILI-1881
Ceded to China

XINJIANG
(PROVINCE)

TAHCHENG TREATY-1864
Ceded to Russia

Lake Balkhash

Ili River

Alma-Ata

De Facto Pakistan-India Border

KASHMIR

PAKISTAN

NEPAL

INDIA

**How the Sino-Soviet Border Conflict Originated**

------- 1840 Chinese Boundary    ——— Present Chinese Boundary    ✶ Areas of Conflict

0    400 miles

shows that success is achieved by Communist parties that guide themselves unswervingly by Marxism-Leninism, while those espousing pseudorevolutionary phraseology and dogmas inevitably suffer a fiasco." In March 1967, *Kommunist* accused Mao Zedong of following a policy of "splittism" that "undermined the unity of world revolutionary forces, greatly damaged the national liberation movement, and is playing into the hands of the imperialists, primarily the U.S. imperialists."

Events in Eastern Europe and the Middle East, the restiveness of many nonruling Communist parties over Moscow's centralist aims, the jubilee celebration in Moscow in November 1967, and the turmoil in China arising out of the Cultural Revolution (which was neither cultural nor a revolution, but a struggle for power) diverted Moscow's attention for a while. At a consultative meeting in Budapest in late February 1968, again boycotted by the Chinese, Moscow engineered enough support to convene an international conference of Communist parties (originally scheduled for November 1968, but postponed until June 1969 because of the Soviet invasion of Czechoslovakia).

On March 2, 14, and 15, 1969, border clashes erupted at the confluence of the Amur and Ussuri rivers below the Soviet city of Khabarovsk in the vicinity of a swampy, uninhabited, vaguely delineated area known as Damansky Island. For the first time, regular military units of one Communist country fought against those of another. A common adherence to Marxism-Leninism was no automatic bar to conflict. Skirmishes in this area had been going on since 1959, and each side had cited thousands of violations by the other. As the result of a Soviet initiative on May 17, 1963, discussions on a wide range of border questions had been started in Beijing in February 1964, but broke off soon thereafter. The two governments agreed to resume the talks in Moscow on October 15, 1964, but the overthrow of Khrushchev resulted in an indefinite postponement. The Damansky affair symbolized a dangerous deterioration in diplomatic relations;[4] it was followed in late spring and early summer by border clashes in Xinjiang and veiled Soviet threats of a preemptive strike against China's nuclear installation at Lop Nor. Realizing the gravity of the situation, Beijing reopened talks on October 20, 1969.

Brezhnev used the Moscow conference of world Communist parties in June 1969 to condemn and try to isolate China (which did not attend), and China was conspicuously excluded in his proposal to create a "system of collective security in Asia." (Soviet diplomacy has worked ever since to conclude friendship treaties with the countries bordering China: Afghanistan, Pakistan, India, Burma, Laos, Vietnam, Mongolia, and North Korea.) However, the blandness of the conference's final document, which made no explicit mention of China (or Czechoslovakia), indicated that Moscow was not able to censure — much less excommunicate — Beijing without risking a serious split and wider challenge to its authority within the world Communist movement.

In other spheres Moscow could proceed more forcefully against China. To make sure that the ideological militancy and economic disruptiveness of the Cultural Revolution would not tempt Mao to start new border incidents, *Pravda* issued a stern warning on August 28, 1969. Observing that "given goodwill, the necessary conditions can and must be assured to guarantee normal relations between the Soviet Union and the People's Republic of China," it called on China to cease "its absurd territorial claims on the Soviet Union" and warned that if a war broke out, "with the existing weaponry, lethal armaments, and modern means of delivery, it would not spare a single continent." This is as close as the Soviet Union has ever come to threatening the use of nuclear weapons against China. There is conjecture that Moscow was not only warning China but also trying to sound out Washington's reaction to a possible strike against the nuclear facility at Lop Nor in Xinjiang.[5]

For a time, government-to-government relations showed some improvements. In September 1969, after attending Ho Chi Minh's funeral in Hanoi, Premier Kosygin made a quick visit to Beijing where he and Zhou Enlai agreed that the two countries would start negotiating the boundary issues to improve relations, that the disagreement on principles should not interfere with the normalization of state relations, that talks would begin on the dispute along the Amur and Ussuri rivers, and that the that the negotiations would be conducted without threat and with every effort to maintain the status quo.[6] In October the border negotiations were resumed; in late 1970, after a hiatus of three years, ambassadors were exchanged and new trade agreements were signed.

Nevertheless, the Soviet leadership's growing perception of implacable Chinese hostility has prompted a major military buildup. Beginning in the mid-1960s, even before the Damansky Island crisis, Moscow increased the number of divisions in the Far East from fifteen in 1967 to twenty-one in 1969 to thirty in 1970 and forty-five in 1980 — about 25 percent of the entire Soviet army (to which should be added 200,000 well-armed KGB border guards) — an unmistakable sign that diplomatic efforts to bridge the chasm have been less than successful. The Soviet army is well-equipped, possessing commanding superiority in tanks, artillery, combat aircraft, and, of course, nuclear-capable missiles. The 4500-mile border is heavily fortified. The superior system of Soviet communications allows for rapid reinforcement; for example, in the sparsely settled Xinjiang region (Chinese Turkestan), the Soviets have a railroad line running from Alma Ata in Soviet Kazakhstan to the border at Druzhba, whereas the Chinese are poorly situated for serious fighting in this predominantly non-Chinese, Muslim area. (Moscow's advantageous position prompted speculation during the Chinese invasion of Vietnam in the spring of 1979 that the USSR might occupy part of Xinjiang, holding it hostage to a Chinese withdrawal, without necessarily escalating such an incursion to a major war.) As a result of the Soviet-Mongolian treaty (as renewed on October 19, 1976), Moscow has significantly increased its combat forces in the MPR. Militarily, the Soviet army is more than a match for the numerically larger Chinese forces, whose level of modernization and firepower is perhaps ten to twenty years behind the USSR's. Moreover, the Soviet naval buildup in the Far East in the late 1970s, though an additional source of tension with Japan serves as a constant reminder to China of its vulnerability to Soviet military power.

Sino-Soviet tensions festered on after the dramatic announcement in mid-August 1971 that Secretary of State Henry Kissinger had arrived secretly in Beijing and arranged for President Richard Nixon to visit China the following year. This completely new variable, a stunning turnabout, fueled Soviet paranoia over possible U.S.-Chinese collusion against the USSR. For Moscow there was bitter irony in Beijing's startling policy reversal, which was in its own way every bit as politically momentous as Moscow's deal with Berlin in 1939 had been.

Moscow's détente toward the West having failed to perpetuate the isolation of China, the Kremlin's policy of containing China had to be adapted to the new political situation. Soviet leaders declared that they were not in principle against the Sino-U.S. normalization of relations, provided that it was not used as a lever against other parties. Their worst fears were of secret arrangements designed against the USSR. After Nixon's visit to China in February 1972 (he was also scheduled to go to Moscow in May), Brezhnev continued to work for the containment of China through a combination of military and diplomatic means, while holding out the offer of improved ties and hoping that when Mao died his successors would prove amenable to a Sino-Soviet reconciliation. Thus, in March 1972, at the All-Union Trade Union Congress, Brezhnev expressed readiness for improved relations on any basis:

> Official Chinese representatives tell us that the relations between the USSR and the People's Republic of China must be built on the basis of the principles of peaceful coexistence. [*Note*: In the Communist lexicon, "peaceful coexistence" refers to relations between a Communist and a non-Communist country.] Well, if Beijing does not think it possible to have more than this in relations with a socialist state, then we are ready to build Soviet-Chinese relations at the present time on such a basis.[7]

For the next few years, Soviet policy in the Far East sought to offset Beijing's opening to the West with a campaign to strengthen Moscow's own ties with Mongolia, North Korea, and Japan; to undercut Chinese standing in the Third World by exposing its negligible ability to help national liberation movements or governments in need of military or economic assistance; to play on the fears of Southeast Asian countries, including Vietnam, of Chinese ambitions; and to enhance the USSR's prestige through projection of its formidable military power. Like much of the world, Moscow became the inveterate Mao-watcher.

## The Post-Mao Situation

The death of Mao in September 1976, however, brought little substantive change in Beijing's policy, though the polemics somewhat abated. Indeed, the new Chinese leadership went out of its way to downgrade Soviet overtures. For example, Brezhnev's message the following month addressing Hua Guofeng as "comrade" and congratulating him on his appointment as chairman of the CCP was returned by Chinese officials, who noted that "we have no party-to-party relations with them."[8] Even the messages of condolence on the death of Mao Zedong from Soviet-bloc party leaders were rejected, for the same reason.

Soviet criticisms of China were halted to test Beijing's receptiveness. Then, on April 22, 1977, at a celebration marking Lenin's birth, a member of the CPSU Secretariat accused Beijing of fomenting "international tensions" and of "striking alliance with the most reactionary forces"; and on May 14, *Pravda* warned that "China is today the only country in the world whose official circles advocate publicly and without any camouflage a new world slaughter" and cautioned the West and Japan against arming China or allowing themselves to be used by "the Maoists and other provokers of war."

A technical agreement in October 1977, to which both sides deliberately gave no publicity, resulted in the lifting of the ten-year Soviet blockade of Chinese shipping at the heavily trafficked junction around Bear Island (Hei Hsia-tzu, in Chinese), situated just below Khabarovsk. New navigation rules for this very limited sector of the Amur-Ussuri basin were negotiated as a matter of mutual convenience, to prevent recurring incidents that could create more difficulties than either country would like. They in no way affected the general boundary problem, which seems likely to remain unresolved as long as the USSR rejects the idea that "disputed territories" exist because the very use of the phrase implies acceptance of the legitimacy of Chinese claims to some Soviet territory. Moscow refuses also to concede Beijing's claim that the treaties of Aigun (1858), Beijing (1860), and Ili (1881) were "unequal" and should be renegotiated. Therefore, notwithstanding the Bear Island agreement, the persistence of widely divergent points of view on how to proceed with the boundary talks suggests that progress in this sector depends on an a priori improvement in overall Sino-Soviet relations, and this does not seem in the offing.

The essentials of the Sino-Soviet rift are more complex today than ever before. In the late 1950s, when the split was developing and before Westerners were even aware that there was a problem, esoteric doctrinal exegeses obscured policy differences. These emerged full-blown in the 1960s. The root cause remains nationalism, and precisely because the split derives from rival national interests and conceptions of security, each side views the other as a long-term threat, which geography has confirmed in perpetuity. In international relations, neighbors are rarely friends. Political and ideological considerations are more significant than military ones, though the USSR and China each fear that its geographic and economic vulnerabilities may tempt the other. Each seeks to enhance its prestige by denigrating the backsliding of the other. The Soviet Union sees China as a competitor for leadership in the international Communist movement and among radical groups. The two seek influence in the Third World, though for different reasons — Moscow to undermine the United States, Beijing to undermine the USSR. They have serious border problems. It is probable, too, that continuation (or termination) of the dispute has become enmeshed in the internal struggle for power in the party-military elite of each country. Finally, both the Russians and the Chinese have long historical memories, and the deeply ingrained psychological, cultural, and racial (particularly on the Russian side) antagonisms inevitably make reconciliation more difficult.

The Sino-Soviet dispute is a dynamic one, constantly changing its contours in response to international developments and new power-political and economic considerations. When Soviet leaders, seeking to contain China and promote Soviet security in the Far East, look ahead to dealing with Beijing in the 1980s and coping with its multidimensional challenges, they face a relationship that is significantly changed from what it was in, say, the beginning of the 1970s. In the changes one can see the evolving, expanding, complex, and interrelated range of issues and concerns that now confront Soviet leaders.

First, the Sino-Soviet alliance established in February 1950 is dead. On April 3, 1979, Beijing informed Moscow that the treaty would not be renewed when it expired in April 1980. Though long regarded as an anachronism, the alliance did signify a certain ideological kinship and sense of shared antagonists. To Moscow, China's renunciation of the alliance, coupled with its rapprochement with the United States and Japan, leaves no doubt that in Beijing's eyes, the Soviet Union has become the main enemy in Asia, and the Kremlin will have to act accordingly.

Second, China is more of a military threat now than it was a decade ago. The time for nuclear preemption has passed. China has an adequate number of nuclear weapons and a missile capability, limited though it is, to wreak considerable destruction on the Soviet Union. Moscow must expend an ever-increasing portion of its military budget for defense against the Chinese threat. Brezhnev's whistle-stop tour of the Soviet Far East in early 1978 was a reflection of the emergence, for the first time in Russian history, of a permanent and significant military adversary on the mainland of Asia. The shift in late 1978 of sizable naval forces to the Pacific fleet was intended to augment the USSR's overall military capability in the Far East theater.

Third, the USSR faces a China that is no longer diplomatically isolated. The normalization of Sino-American relations, the signing of the Sino-Japanese treaty of friendship and cooperation in August 1978, the seating of the CPR in the United Nations in 1971, and the ever-widening range of contacts with Western and Third World countries all mock the Soviet effort to isolate China, and give Beijing greater authority in its dealings with Moscow. China's opening to the West in particular necessitates continual Soviet reassessments of Beijing's military, economic, and political options, since the modern technology and expertise that China imports will make it a more formidable adversary and its diplomatic flexibility has in the main limited Soviet maneuverability. The Soviet-Vietnamese friendship treaty of November 1978 provided the USSR with some middle-range options for frustrating China's policies in Cambodia, Laos, and Vietnam, but at the same time it strained relations with the United States and forced Moscow to react to Chinese thrusts instead of making its own. To the extent that the USSR exercises its privileges in Vietnam or Vietnam's Spratly Islands, ostensibly to protect Vietnam against China, Moscow risks arousing U.S. and Southeast Asian fears of Soviet expansion and a consequent deterioration in relations with these countries, whose instinctive response will be to draw closer to China — a prospect Soviet leaders seek to prevent.

Fourth, every projection of Soviet power adds credence to Chinese accusations of Soviet moves toward hegemonism. Politically, Moscow is on the defensive and in the position of having to deny that it is ambitious, provocative, or covetous. It is a truism that in almost any confrontation between a stronger and a weaker power, the former has the greater difficulty in justifying its actions to interested regional and international onlookers, as China found out when it attacked Vietnam in March 1979 to punish it for having invaded Kampuchea (Cambodia) to unseat a pro-Chinese but exceptionally bloodthirsty and belligerent Communist leadership.

Fifth, the competition for authority in the world Communist movement that loomed large in the 1950s and 1960s has become far less of a factor in the determination of Soviet policy toward China. Doctrinal disquisitions are less common, if only because fewer of the faithful regard them as anything other than verbal rituals to justify what was done for other quite tangible, nonideological reasons. The acentric character of international communism is accepted, and Moscow's search for supporters relies more on demonstrating the advantages of association than on its skill at dialectical hair-splitting. In its efforts to develop a reliable grouping within the world Communist movement, Moscow tries to manifest flexibility and forebearance, in contrast with Beijing's stridency and fulminations.

Sixth, the USSR's position in the Third World is vastly superior to that of the CPR's. The appeal of the Yenan way, of Mao's strategy for waging a people's war, has palled. As the target areas of Sino-Soviet competition have spread, the Soviet Union's advantage has become pronounced. Moscow simply commands enormously greater resources for an ambitious imperial policy in the Third World and possesses a credibility in crises for prospective clients that Beijing lacks. It is increasingly evident, too, that the Chinese model of development, about which so much was written in the 1960s and early 1970s, is unsuited to most Third World countries, which lack the organization and total control necessary to exact sustained sacrifices on a mass scale; see the model being discarded in China itself as the post-Mao leadership unabashedly introduces bourgeois reforms and seeks aid from abroad; and can obtain the military assistance they need to stay in power and fight their enemies from the USSR by eschewing a Maoist line. And too, simply stated, such countries lack the cultural cohesion, drive, and discipline of the Chinese.

Moreover, whereas Moscow proclaims a principled purpose in extending support to Third World countries — that is to help them either to overthrow "reactionary" governments or to defend themselves against external threats from "aggressors" (pro-Western rivals) — Beijing no longer disguises the anti-Soviet animus that motivates its policy. This was clearly apparent when China withdrew support in 1973 from the Dhofari rebels in Oman and drew closer to the shah of Iran, when it supported anti-Communist nationalist groups in southern Africa in the 1970s because the Communists mostly looked to Moscow, and when it approved of Egyptian President Anwar Sadat's decision to sign a peace treaty with Israel in 1979. By consistently supporting Third World governments or movements that are pursuing a line that places them in opposition to the United States, Moscow has effectively undercut Beijing's diplomacy in the Third World.

Seventh, the Soviet Union has reason to be quite concerned in the 1980s about the possible formation of an anti-Soviet constellation. Beijing has normalized relations with the United States and Japan and obtained extensive credits from Britain, France, and the Federal Republic of Germany. Moscow fears that the transfer of advanced weapons and technology from the West and the know-how to accelerate industrialization from Japan will transform China into a superpower within a decade or two, and that such a transformation could tempt the United States to play the so-called China card, joining forces with China in order to challenge Soviet interests in the northwest Pacific, Southern Asia, and possibly even in Eastern Europe. Admittedly a worst-case scenario, it is one that Soviet planners do not dare to ignore.

Eighth, the Chinese factor in particular and Far East considerations in general demand a bigger chunk of Soviet military power. The permanent deployment of sizable military contingents in the Far East is costly and requires the diversion of already scarce pools of labor, capital, and materials from the civilian to the military sector and from the European to the Asian part of the Soviet Union. A decade ago, a troublesome China was relatively easy to handle militarily; a decade hence, the problem will be magnified many times over.

Ninth, Moscow can no longer look forward to the post-Mao period for a return to the halcyon days of the Sino-Soviet relationship. That period is here, and for the time being, the new Chinese leadership has chosen Maoism without Mao. Mao may have aggravated the dispute in the 1960s and early 1970s out of a measure of personal pique, but the essentials of his far-ranging hostility have been accepted by his successors, who have carried on his opening to the West and anti-Soviet line with a verve that dismays Moscow.

Finally, the Soviet leadership is unlikely to make any major concessions to the Chinese on the territorial issue, especially in the Amur-Ussuri river basin, which may contain rich coal and mineral deposits. As the global competition for raw materials intensifies, Moscow will have even less reason to relinquish control of potentially valuable pieces of real estate. The more uncompromising the Soviets are on the border issues, the less likely they will be to find the Chinese prepared for a genuine reconciliation. The diplomatic negotiations that were begun in Moscow in late September 1979, which are intended to find a set of principles for replacing the 1950 treaty of alliance that expired in April 1980, are the first major negotiations between the Soviet Union and China since 1964. They are expected to be lengthy and difficult.

All in all, the USSR's failure to maintain the alliance with China was a major diplomatic setback that inevitably colors any assessment of Soviet policy in the Far East. In the case of China, Moscow certainly fared poorly in the matter of advancing Soviet ambitions and safeguarding essential national interests. Never mind who was responsible for the turn of events — the net result was to change China from an ally to an adversary. Coping with this new relationship and the challenge it poses to Soviet interests will place great demands on Soviet diplomacy.

Apart from the absorption with China, the USSR has also conducted an active policy toward the other regional actors in northeast Asia — Japan, Mongolia, and North Korea — with which it has some accomplishments to its credit. A few comments about each are appropriate.

## Soviet-Japanese Relations

At the time of the Korean War, Moscow regarded Japan as "the main American bridgehead in the Far East." Japan was the staging area from which the United States mounted its military operations in Korea and threatened the Soviet Union and China with long-range air power. The United States used the war to accelerate the transition of Japan from occupied ex-enemy state to passive participant and incipient ally. In September 1951, at the San Francisco conference convened to sign a peace treaty with Japan, Soviet aims toward Japan emerged in the open. The Soviet delegate proposed Japan's neutralization: that Japan agree "not to enter into any coalitions or military alliances directed against any Power which participated with its armed forces in the war against Japan," and that it not permit any foreign power to have its troops or military bases on Japanese territory. There were other proposed amendments as well, including limits on Japanese rearmament, demilitarization of all straits leading into the Japan Sea, and acknowledgment of Soviet title to all the northern islands under Soviet occupation. The Soviet proposals were rejected; the peace treaty was signed, though not by the Soviet Union (or China), and Japan concluded a mutual security treaty with the United States.

After Stalin's death, Soviet leaders desired to establish diplomatic ties with Japan but were unwilling to accede to Japan's demand for the immediate return of Shikotan and the Habomai Islands off northern Hokkaido. They persuaded a weak Japanese government to agree to the Adenauer formula, which had led to the reestablishment of diplomatic ties between the USSR and West Germany, namely, "restoring diplomatic relations before the differences between the two countries were resolved"; and to accept the promise of the return of the above-mentioned island "under certain conditions" after the signing of a formal peace treaty.[9] In the declaration signed on October 19, 1956, leading to the resumption of bilateral relations, Moscow recognized the right of Japan to enter into diplomatic and military agreements with any country and disengaged itself from a common approach with Beijing to Japan. It saw normalization as essential for further Soviet influence over the Japanese and for helping the domestic effectiveness of the various Japanese organizations — cultural, political, and commercial — that favored closer ties with the USSR and that had been instrumental in pressuring their government to accept the Soviet formula for the restoration of diplomatic relations.

Over the years, there has been a remarkable continuity in Soviet objectives: to undermine the U.S.-Japanese mutual security pact; to keep Japan from acquiring nuclear weapons or rearming on a major scale (which would be contrary to a provision in the U.S.-imposed Japanese constitution limiting Japan to "self-defense" forces); to see the U.S. military presence in Japan reduced; and to expand economic relations.

A major impediment to better political relations has been Moscow's unwillingness to return what Japan calls the northern territories, which include Shikotan and a group of five islands called Habomai (all of which Moscow in 1956 agreed to return) as well as Iturup and Kunashir, both of which Moscow insists Japan renounced in 1951 at San Francisco. In a reversal of its promise of 1956, the USSR has repeatedly linked the return of Shikotan and Habomai to Japan's renunciation of the U.S.-Japanese security pact. For example, at the time of the pact's renewal in June 1960, when mass Japanese demonstrations prevented a state visit by President Eisenhower, the Soviet government attacked the treaty for permitting U.S. military bases and fostering Japan's remilitarization and stated that "the abrogation of the American-Japanese treaty would clear the way for the favorable development of Soviet-Japanese relations. The practical questions [that is, the return of the islands] between our countries, which find no solution under the present conditions . . . would be settled without difficulty."* In November 1967 Politburo member Mikhail Suslov told a visiting Japanese Socialist party delegation that the USSR would never return any former Japanese territory as long as Japan's military pact with the United States was in effect.

Throughout the 1960s Moscow saw no reason for softening its position. Skillfully exploiting the strong antimilitary, pacifist sentiment in Japan and the growing opposition to U.S. control of Okinawa (which was returned to Japanese jurisdiction in 1970), it watched the pressures of domestic Japanese politics force a diminished American military presence. The antinuclear movement also made it politically difficult for U.S. nuclear submarines to have easy access to Japanese ports.

In the early 1970s Soviet leaders found it expedient to hint at a possible compromise, without ever being really specific. This attitude was motivated by the beginnings of a Sino-Japanese rapprochement, which led China to support the Japanese claim to the northern territories as Sino-Soviet relations worsened, and by the Nixon visit to China in February 1972, which aroused Soviet fears of U.S.-Chinese-Japanese collusion against the USSR. High-level exchanges, such as Prime Minister Kakuei Tanaka's meeting with Brezhnev in Moscow in October 1973, Gromyko's visit to Tokyo in January 1976, and Japanese Foreign Minister Sunao Sonoda's visit in January 1978, all faltered on the inability to reach agree-

---

* *Soviet News,* No. 4298 (June 30, 1960), p. 270.

ment on a peace treaty, which in turn foundered on the territorial dispute. Moscow is reported to have offered, on occasion, the return of Shikotan and Habomai in exchange for a treaty, but Tokyo insisted on all four territories, a reflection of the growing inflexibility of all Japanese political parties on this issue.[10] Not only have the two northernmost, larger islands become Soviet military bases, but Moscow fears that the surrender of what it has regarded as Soviet territory since 1945 would establish a precedent that could be exploited by Beijing.

The issue was further complicated in December 1976 when the Soviet government announced the establishment of a two-hundred mile fishing zone, effective March 1, 1977, that makes the ability of Japanese fishermen to operate in Soviet waters and in the vicinity of the disputed islands hostage to Soviet goodwill.[11] Interim agreements have been reached, but the size of Japanese catches has been curtailed and the number of Japanese fishing boats seized by Soviet authorities for violation of Soviet territorial waters has jumped. The fisheries issue, long a bone of contention between the two countries, provides Moscow with a strong lever with which to pry economic and political concessions from Japan. If Moscow insisted on making the Sea of Okhotsk a closed sea, the Japanese fishing industry would be hard pressed to find alternative sources for the more than 40 percent of its annual catch that traditionally come from this area.

One of the USSR's important objectives in recent years has been to enlist Japanese industry and expertise to aid in the economic development of Siberian resources. Serious talks began in January 1966 with the establishment of the Joint Japan-Soviet Economic Committee. But not until 1974 was any significant agreement concluded. Japan invested $450 million for the purchase of equipment abroad to develop the coalfields in the South Yakutian Basin of Siberia, in return for which it will be repaid over a twenty-year period with 100 million tons of coking coal. (The coal mines are located at Neryungri, one of several sites being developed in conjunction with the new 2000 mile-long Baikal-Amur Mainline [BAM] railroad.) Another agreement, the Tyumen oil project, fell through at the last minute; the Japanese backed out because costs were prohibitive and because Japan still exports far more than it imports from the USSR.

The economic potentialities of Soviet-Japanese trade have been limited by Japan's political dissatisfaction, even though economic considerations generally play a very important role in Japanese foreign policy. Moscow courts Japanese investment to develop its rich oil, natural-gas, and mineral deposits in Siberia and to discourage Japan's keen interest in the Chinese market. It hopes that a combination of economic inducements and pressure will influence Japanese foreign policy and that an innate pragmatism on both sides will keep economics fairly separate from politics (much more than in Soviet-American relations).

Thus, the expansion of Soviet-Japanese economic relations continues despite Moscow's opposition to the Sino-Japanese peace treaty, signed on August 12, 1978. During the six years of the treaty's negotiation, Moscow repeatedly expressed displeasure and warned that it would have to reconsider its efforts to conclude a peace treaty with a state pursuing a policy hostile toward the Soviet Union. In 1975 and 1976, it proposed a Soviet-Japanese treaty of amity that would sidestep territorial issus — as did the prospective Sino-Japanese treaty that avoided any mention of the disputed Senkaku Islands — but the Japanese replied that the Soviet-Japanese territorial issue involved vital national interests. The Soviet government regards the Sino-Japanese treaty as anti-Soviet, first, because of inclusion, at Beijing's insistence, of the antihegemony clause, which states that "the contracting parties declare that neither of them should seek hegemony in the Asia-Pacific region or in any other region and each is opposed to efforts by any other country or group of countries to establish such hegemony"; and second, because it reinforces Moscow's fear of a Beijing-Tokyo-Washington military alliance being formed against the USSR. The treaty has intensified Moscow's diplomatic efforts to obtain Japan's agreement to a comparable document.

For its part, Japan has not brandished economic levers to protest the USSR's growing military buildup in areas close to Japan. Ever since the late 1970s the Soviet Union has strengthened its military installations and presence on Etorofu and Kunashir, a move the Japanese termed "a very unfriendly gesture." Whether it signifies the USSR's disapproval of the Sino-Japanese treaty, is a warning against Japan's providing China with advanced military technology (a new wrinkle in the ongoing bargaining over a Soviet-Japanese peace treaty), or is part of the general strengthening of Soviet forces levels in the Far East, the buildup has not prevented business as usual. Indeed, in late 1978, the Japanese delivered a huge floating dry dock to Vladivostok, where it will help service Soviet naval vessels, including the KIEV-class aircraft carriers.

The massive expansion of Soviet military power in the Far East is part of Moscow's policy of containment of China. Also integral to this strategy is friendship with the Mongolian People's Republic and North Korea, both of which are front-line pieces on the Sino-Soviet chessboard.

## The USSR and the MPR

An area of 604,000 square miles with a population of less than two million, Mongolia shares a 1500-mile border with the USSR and a 2500-mile border with China. Landlocked as it is between the USSR and the CPR, the MPR could not help being influenced by the wishes of its stronger neighbor, that is, the USSR. Under effective Soviet tutelage since 1921, it is solidly in Moscow's camp. China (under the Kuomintang) formally recognized Mongolia's independence on January 5, 1946, in accordance with the public preference expressed in a plebiscite held on October 20, 1945. When the Communists came to power, they too recognized the MPR's independence, in a 1950 treaty. (However, after Chiang Kai-shek was chased from the mainland, he reversed the Kuomintang's recognition of MPR independence, and for more than twenty years the U.S. government ignored Mongolia out of deference to Taiwan!)

Mongolia's pro-Moscow position on the Sino-Soviet dispute was confirmed by the Soviet-Mongolian twenty-year treaty of mutual assistance of January 15, 1966, which replaced the treaty of February 1946 and authorized the stationing of Soviet troops in the country to deter any probes from the Chinese autonomous region of Inner Mongolia. Mongolia fears absorption by the Chinese, which it sees occurring in Inner Mongolia. A thick network of fortifications has been constructued on the MPR side, and the civilian population has been largely relocated away from a sixty-mile belt along the border. In contrast to North Korean leader Kim Il-sung, Mongolia's party boss, Yumjagiin Tsedenbal, has openly taken the Soviet side in the Sino-Soviet dispute and frequently criticized Mao and other Chinese leaders. Agreements in the mid-1950s and early 1960s permitted Chinese laborers to enter the country to work on various construction projects, but these have long since expired, and Soviet economic influence predominates. Ulan Bator's economy is closely tied to the USSR, and the once discreet Sino-Soviet competition for Mongolia's allegiance has been supplanted by an obviously commanding Soviet presence. (Mongolia became a full member of Comecon in 1962.) Though its economy is enmeshed with that of the USSR, on whose power it relies for preservation as an independent state, the MPR manages to maintain its cultural distinctiveness and internal autonomy. Moscow's interest is strategic, and its policy has been to strengthen the MPR's status as a buffer state.

## The Korean Triangle

Soviet relations with the Democratic People's Republic of Korea (DPRK) are more complex. Since the end of the Korean War, Kim Il-sung has gained control of his internal affairs, skillfully playing off Moscow and Beijing.[12] The modernization of the DPRK's substantial armed forces has been accomplished primarily with Soviet assistance and weapons; and Pyongyang's assertive foreign policy, aimed at Korea's reunification under Communist rule, depends in large measure on Soviet and Chinese forebearance and implicit support.

By virtue of the United States' support for and military presence in South Korea, the Soviet Union has leverage over the DPRK, which it uses to prevent Pyongyang from slipping closer to China and to insure that it does not start a war to reunify Korea. Moscow expects the status quo to persist for the foreseeable future and wants to restrain Kim Il-sung without edging him toward Beijing, as happened in January 1968, after the crisis occasioned by the DPRK's seizure of the U.S. intelligence ship *Pueblo*. At the time, Moscow saw in Kim's action a bellicosity and unpredictability that could prove dangerous; it feared that Pyongyang might invoke the security provisions of the Soviet-DPRK military treaty if the U.S. retaliated.

On a number of occasions in the 1960s and 1970s — for example, during President Nikolai V. Podgorny's visit to Pyongyang on the eve of the 1969 conference of Communist parties in Moscow, and during Mao's meeting with Nixon in 1972 — the Soviet leadership tried to bring the DPRK more into harmony with its tune on China. In the main, however, Moscow (and Beijing) understand the nationalism that underlies the DPRK's attempt to maintain a balanced position between its two giant Communist neighbors and benefactors. With great-power relationships taking so many unexpected twists, Moscow prefers its Korean flank to remain quiet and stable. Certainly it has far fewer reasons for unleashing war on the Korean peninsula in the 1980s than it had in 1950.

## The Balance Sheet

Any assessment of the strengths and weaknesses, the accomplishments and failures, the prospects and dilemmas that have characterized Soviet policy in the Far East over the past few decades is complicated and must at best be an approximation. The unequivocal accomplishments have been remarkably few.

The USSR has become the preeminent military power on the mainland of Asia, but in the process it has aroused the fears of its neighbors. It does not face, as it did in the 1930s, a dangerous and expansionist Japan, but it has more independent-minded actors to contend with.

China is still more a nuisance than a military threat, but it is now thoroughly anti-Soviet. Moscow's deep-rooted fears of China stem from China's *potential* to develop into a genuine superpower and from Moscow's own *actual* weaknesses — shortages of labor and capital which may reduce the USSR's rate of growth; ethnic diversity, which may place in question the reliability of non-Russian military contingents; the need to import advanced technology; the enormous economic inefficiency and waste that plague the Soviet system, and so on.

Moscow can derive satisfaction from the role that it played in bringing about a thinning-out of American power in Asia. In contrast to the decade after World War II, in the 1980s the United States will not be in a position to project significant military power (conventional, not nuclear) in the Far East in a way that could threaten Soviet clients or interests. The United States may be able to deter Soviet expansion, but its capacity for generating threats to the USSR is limited.

Finally, the USSR has excellent relations with Mongolia, and its relations with Japan, which admittedly leave much to be desired, are nevertheless closer than they were in the 1950s.

Against this modest list of achievements can be set developments that call into question the wisdom and farsightedness of Soviet policymakers.

First and foremost, there is the Khrushchev-Brezhnev squandering of Stalin's legacy of close relations and alliance with China. No possible improvement of relations on the state-to-state level is likely to restore the relationship that existed at the signing of the 1950 treaty of alliance. The next generation of Soviet leaders will have to divert significant resources away from economic growth to beef up the defenses along the rimland of Sino-Soviet confrontation.

Second, Brezhnev's proposal for an Asian collective security system has been a dud in the Far East. As a device for containing China, it never worked — which means that Soviet diplomacy must continue to stress bilateralism if it is to make any headway on this aim.

Third, the Soviet courtship of Japan has stumbled badly. Moscow had hoped to secure much greater Japanese participation in the development of Siberia. Moreover, the Japanese have rejected the Soviet proposal for an Asian version of the Conference on Security and Cooperation in Europe (held in Helsinki in 1975) and have seen fit to draw closer to China, over strenuous Soviet objectives.

Looking back at the record of Soviet diplomacy in the Far East since the death of Stalin, one must conclude that, with the exception of its important contribution to the defeat of the United States in Vietnam, Moscow had little effect on the major developments and new trends that are emerging in the area. The 1980s may provide some clues to the fundamentals on which future Soviet policy is to be conducted: whether the Soviet Union will become more interested in projecting its growing military power in order to influence the course of events, or whether it will adhere to a cautious, essentially status-quo policy, reacting to opportunity rather than forcing the pace of desired change.

# Notes

1. See John R. Thomas, "Soviet Behavior in the Quemoy Crisis of 1958," *Orbis,* vol. 6, no. 1 (Spring 1962), 38–64.

2. See Donald S. Zagoria, "Mao's Role in the Sino-Soviet Conflict," *Pacific Affairs,* vol. 47, no. 2 (Summer 1974), 146–148. See also Gerald Segal, "Chinese Politics and the Soviet Connection," *The Jerusalem Journal of International Relations,* vol. 2, no. 1 (Fall 1976), 96–128.

3. "For the Unity of International Communist Activity on the Principles of Marxism-Leninism," *Kommunist,* no. 5 (March 1964), 13–52, excerpts.

4. For example, see George Ginsburgs, *The Damansky/Chenpao Island Incidents: A Case Study of Syntactic Patterns in Crisis Diplomacy,* Asian Studies Occasional Paper Series, no. 6 (Edwardsville: Southern Illinois University, 1973); and Thomas W. Robinson, "The Sino-Soviet Border Dispute: Background, Development, and the March 1969 Clashes," *American Political Science Review,* vol. 66, no. 4 (December 1972), 1175–1202.

5. Victor Louis, a foreign journalist alleged to have close ties to the KGB and Soviet officials, caused shock waves when he suggested that whether the Soviet Union attacked Lop Nor or not was only "a question of strategy," and that if the Soviet Union had intervened in Czechoslovakia to defend socialism, why should it not also apply the Brezhnev Doctrine to China? See *New York Times,* September 18, 1969. The Soviet government also circulated a note to its East European allies asking whether the USSR should launch a preemptive strike against China.

6. Zhou Enlai told this to Audrey Topping at a dinner in Beijing in May 1971. See *New York Times,* May 21, 1971.

7. *Pravda,* March 21, 1972.

8. *New York Times.* October 29, 1976.

9. James William Morley, "Soviet-Japanese Peace Declaration," *Political Science Quarterly,* vol. 72, no. 3 (September 1957), 373–374.

10. *New York Times,* January 11, 1976.

11. Robert Rand, "Sonoda's Visit to Moscow," Radio Liberty Research Paper (January 17, 1978), 2.

12. After 1956, Kim effectively purged the pro-Soviet faction in the Korean Workers (Communist) party. Since Kim's opponents "were inspired by the de-Stalinization campaign in the Soviet Union and the Soviet representative in Pyongyang was sympathetic to their cause, Kim had little choice but to denounce them. Obviously, both Kim Il-song and Mao Tse-tung had reasons to resent Khrushchev's unilateral decisions of 1956. The outcome, particularly the removal of the Russian faction men, was a consolidation of the position of Kim Il-song." Kim emerged as the undisputed leader in North Korea. "The events in 1956 also stimulated the North Korean regime to adopt a more

nationalistic line of policy and to assert independence within the international Communist camp. Having eliminated the moderating influence of the Soviet faction men, the party also veered to the left in ideology and in economic policies, paralleling the steps taken by Peking." See Chong-sik Lee and Ki-wan Oh, "The Russian Faction in North Korea," *Asian Survey,* vol. 8, no. 4 (April 1968), 287–288.

## Selected Bibliography

AN, TAI SUNG. *The Sino-Soviet Territorial Dispute.* Philadelphia: Westminster Press, 1973.

BAWDEN, C. R. *The Modern History of Mongolia.* New York: Praeger, 1968.

BORISOV, O. B., and B. T. KOLOSKOV. *Soviet-Chinese Relations 1945–1970.* Bloomington: Indiana University Press, 1975. (An introductory essay by Vladimir Petrov enhances the value of this study by two Soviet scholars.)

BRZEZINSKI, ZBIGNIEW K. *The Soviet Bloc: Unity and Conflict,* Cambridge: Harvard University Press, 1967.

CHENG, CHU-YUAN. *Economic Relations Between Peking and Moscow, 1949–1963.* New York: Praeger, 1964.

CHUNG, CHIN O. *Pyongyang Between Peking and Moscow.* University: University of Alabama Press, 1978.

CLUBB, O. EDMUND. *China and Russia: The "Great Game."* New York: Columbia University Press, 1971.

CRANKSHAW, EDWARD. *The New Cold War: Moscow and Pekin.* Baltimore: Penguin, 1963.

DALLIN, ALEXANDER, JONATHAN HARRIS, and GREY HODNETT (eds.). *Diversity in International Communism: A Documentary Record, 1961–1963.* New York: Columbia University Press, 1963.

FLOYD, DAVID. *Mao Against Khrushchev.* New York: Praeger, 1963.

GINSBURGS, GEORGE and CARL F. PINKELE. *The Sino-Soviet Territorial Dispute 1949–64.* New York: Praeger, 1978.

GITTINGS, JOHN (ed.). *Survey of the Sino-Soviet Dispute.* New York: Oxford University Press, 1968.

GRIFFITH, WILLIAM E. *Albania and the Sino-Soviet Rift.* Cambridge: MIT Press, 1963.

———. *The Sino-Soviet Rift.* Cambridge: MIT Press, 1964.

——— (ed.). *Communism in Europe: Continuity, Change, and the Sino-Soviet Dispute.* Cambridge: MIT Press, 1966.

KIM, YOUNG C. *Japanese-Soviet Relations.* Beverly Hills: Sage, 1974.

LONDON, KURT (ed.). *Unity and Contradiction: Major Aspects of Sino-Soviet Relations.* New York: Praeger, 1962.

LOW, ALFRED D. *The Sino-Soviet Dispute.* Madison, N. J.: Fairleigh Dickinson University Press, 1978.

MANCALL, MARK. *Russia and China: Their Diplomatic Relations to 1728.* Cambridge: Harvard University Press, 1971.

MEHNERT, KLAUS. *Peking and Moscow.* New York: Putnam, 1963.

NORTH, ROBERT C. *Moscow and Chinese Communists.* 2nd ed. Stanford: Stanford University Press, 1963.

ROTHENBERG, MORRIS. *Whither China: The View From the Kremlin.* Coral Gables, Fl.: Center for Advanced Studies, University of Miami, 1977.

RUPEN, ROBERT A. *Mongols in the Twentieth Century.* Paris: Mouton, 1964.

STEPHAN, JOHN J. *The Kuril Islands.* New York: Oxford University Press, 1974.

SWEARINGEN, ROBERT. *The Soviet Union and Postwar Japan: Escalating Challenge and Response.* Stanford: Hoover Institution Press, 1978.

VISHWANATHAN, SAVITRI. *Normalization of Japanese-Soviet Relations 1945–1970.* Tallahassee: Diplomatic Press, 1973.

ZAGORIA, DONALD S. *The Sino-Soviet Conflict, 1956–1961.* Princeton: Princeton University Press, 1962.

# 7
# Soviet Policy and the
## World Communist Movement

Ever since March 1919, when the Comintern was established, the Soviet Union has been considered the godfather of the world Communist movement, the term favored by Soviet writers for the collectivity of almost one hundred Communist and workers' parties. It has committed enormous resources to this instrumentality in order to advance Soviet foreign-policy interests.

Paradoxically, Moscow's manipulation of foreign Communist parties to defend Soviet state interests was never managed with more telling effect than in the period of the USSR's maximum weakness. At the time of Soviet diplomatic isolation and military vulnerability in the 1920s and 1930s, the world Communist movement was truly the handmaiden of Soviet policy. There was no questioning of Stalin's injunction that internationalism required proletarians of all countries to support the Soviet Union, since an internationalist is one who "unhesitatingly, unconditionally, without vacillation, is ready to defend the USSR because the USSR is the basis of the world revolutionary movement, and it is impossible to defend. and to advance [this movement] unless the USSR is defended." *

In the 1980s, when Soviet military power and international influence are greater than ever before in the USSR's history, the movement is split, unruly, dominated by nationalism. The CPSU leadership finds itself challenged not only by ruling parties within the Communist world (the "world socialist system," in the Soviet lexicon) but also by nonruling Communist parties that often lack much political influence in their own countries. Moscow must learn to adapt to the increasingly fragmented character of

---

* Jane Degras, *Soviet Documents on Foreign Policy* (New York: Oxford University Press, 1952), Vol. II, p. 243.

the world Communist movement, because it sees no way to stop the centrifugal tendencies that make the movement as much a source of embarrassment and disunity as of strength and prestige.

Before exploring the factors that produced the present erosion of the once unchallenged Soviet leadership over the world Communist movement and its transformation from monolithism to polycentrism, along with the effect that this has had on Soviet foreign policy, we must look briefly at the nature of Soviet authority, past and present, and the parameters within which it operates.

In general, authority may rest on one or more elements: it may be based on the charismatic personality of an outstanding figure; it may devolve upon an individual or group who is in the vanguard of a quest for a shared objective and who for the moment embodies the transcendent idea; it may be forcibly imposed by those who control the instruments of coercion; or it may come from the voluntary accession of affiliated members whose own weakness leads them to rely on the external source of authority represented by one of the preceding.[1] As we look at Soviet history since 1917, we can distinguish the periods in which one or another of these bases of authority was ascendant.

From 1919 to 1945 the world Communist movement was characterized by two fundamental considerations: the existence of the Soviet Union as the *only* Communist state, and the complete subservience, especially under Stalin, of foreign Communist parties to the will of Moscow. Those who disagreed either quit or were expelled from the movement. During this period, authority devolved upon Moscow because of the esteem in which it was held by the membership despite periodic disagreements, and not because Moscow was in a position physically to compel obedience. The early adherents to Soviet authority willingly followed Lenin, who uniquely combined "the individual prestige of a charismatic personality with the authority of the idea of World Revolution";[2] Stalin's authority came from manipulation of symbols, personalities, bureaucracy, and the use of force.

Foreign Communists accepted Moscow's policies, often at the sacrifice of their own interests and prospects for power. They did so because the Soviet Union, as the only Communist state, embodied the ideal of world revolution; because the realization of world revolution was feasible only as long as the Soviet state survived and thrived; because of the exalted feeling that comes from membership in a universalistic movement; because Moscow's approbation meant that an otherwise political nonentity would be "taken seriously not merely by his party but also by his fellow countrymen, for whom he personifies Moscow's power locally";[3] and because of the power over an organization, however small, that flowed to a leadership willing to do Moscow's bidding. Their blind obedience brought disaster to many parties in the 1920s and 1930s, including the German, Chinese (before Mao), Indonesian, and Spanish. During the honeymoon period of the Nazi-Soviet pact, West European Communists did nothing to help their countries resist German aggression; not until Hitler's attack on the Soviet Union in June 1941 did they take up arms against nazism. In all of this, Soviet state interests transcended those of world revolution, though Moscow rationalized the former in terms of the latter, and the party faithful voluntarily did as Moscow asked.

The big change in the world Communist movement came in 1945, when the Soviet Union extended its authority over Eastern Europe through the Red Army. With this coercive instrument, it created new Communist states, although at the time they were merely compliant, exploited Soviet imperial possessions. Intent on subordinating Yugoslavia to Soviet wishes, Stalin tested his authority, trying by dint of his prestige to have Tito removed, but he failed and, unwilling to use the Red Army to compel obedience, resorted to excommunication. But the heretic survived and in the process retained his credentials as a Communist and a revolutionary.

However, Tito's rejection of Soviet authority was a minor matter compared to the situation that was inherent in Mao's conquest of mainland China. At first Mao acknowledged Moscow's ideological preeminence and leadership in foreign affairs. The charisma of Stalin and the convergence of national interests ensured unity, and the nature of Soviet authority did not become an issue as long as Stalin lived. Stalin died in 1953, and the turning point in the relationship of authority between Moscow and Beijing came in February 1956. Khrushchev's denunciation of Stalin at the CPSU's twentieth congress compromised his own standing in Beijing and led Mao to stake his claim to leadership of the world Communist movement. The November 1957 attempt to paper over the policy differences between Moscow and Beijing failed, and the rift widened. It became public knowledge after 1960, and forced foreign Communist parties to take sides. The quarrel ended Moscow's pretension to speak for all parties on matters of doctrine and policy. Its authority was being challenged by a major center of power fully qualified to carry on the mission of the proletariat to bring about world revolution and communism.

At the heart of this struggle for authority is what Benjamin Schwartz has called "the myth of the Communist party," that is, the ascription to "the Communist party — conceived of as the total Communist movement" — of the "transcendental and messianic qualities attributed by conventional Marxism to the world proletariat."[4] But there is a contradiction inherent in the myth: "The infallibility and monolithic unity presupposed in the myth can be maintained only so long as there is an unquestioned ultimate instance of authority."[5] Lenin's unquestioned authority derived from his charismatic influence and unshakable conviction that he was uniquely endowed to apply the "changeless and universal truths" of Marxism to the specific situations faced by the proletariat in other countries. Stalin, lacking Lenin's powerful personality, derived his authority from a combination of bureaucratic and coercive methods. He also benefited from an international context in which defense of the socialist homeland took on a crusading zeal that subordinated all other considerations.

## De-Stalinization and Polycentrism

By Khrushchev's time the rival claimants of authority in Beijing and Belgrade were forcing Moscow to confront the challenge of reconciling unity with diversity. But Moscow lacked the instruments necessary for restoring bloc unity: it had neither the charismatic leader nor the monopoly of force. A series of irreversible developments inevitably weakened its attempts to reassert Soviet authority in the Socialist camp and in the world Communist movement: the USSR's de-Stalinization that spread to Eastern Europe and nurtured nationalistic demands for greater independence; the Sino-Soviet dispute that enabled the mice in the socialist camp to play, while the two cats fought; the Soviet leadership's surrender, implicit in its acceptance of the notion of "many roads to socialism," of the prerogative of proclaiming the universality of the Soviet model, in return for support of the Soviet position in the dispute with China and on major foreign-policy issues; Moscow's readiness to discard the former exploitative economic relationship with Eastern Europe and seek bloc cooperation; and its realization that greater independence from the center was essential to preserve the Communist character of the countries in Eastern Europe.

The monolithism that existed until 1948 is part of the "ancient" history of international communism. The Kremlin has since had to cope with three different kinds of Communist parties in order to exercise what remains of its once preeminent authority. First, there are the ruling Communist parties that are part of the Soviet bloc and that can, in extreme circumstances, be brought into line by the Red Army. Second, there are the ruling parties that lie outside of Moscow's ability to impose its authority if need be and with whom Moscow's relationships are as complex as the one with Beijing; these are to be found in Yugoslavia, Albania, North Korea, Cuba, Vietnam, Kampuchea, and Laos. Third, there are the nonruling Communist parties, which for convenience may be roughly divided into two groups: those permitted to operate openly, which possess a solid core of electoral support, have prospects for attaining a measure of parliamentary power, and are found primarily in Western Europe but also in Japan and India; and those prescribed in ways that severely limit their political possibilities, at least through legitimate channels, and which exist in the Third World. The first two categories of parties and their relationships with Moscow have already been discussed, primarily in chapters 4 and 6; here we shall predominantly treat the third category.

## Authority versus Autonomism

Moscow has used two types of forums in its efforts to reimpose a measure of authority: the international meeting, epitomized by the conferences of world Communist and workers' parties held in Moscow in 1957, 1960, and 1969 (and supplemented by frequent annual gatherings of the dozen or so leading Communist-front organizations in the fields of labor, education, science, and culture); and the regional forum, intended primarily for European Communist parties, exemplified by the meetings in 1967 in Karlovy Vary, Czechoslovakia, and 1976 in East Berlin.

In the wake of de-Stalinization, the revolutions in Eastern Europe, the shock and disillusionment that reverberated through Western nonruling Communist parties, and the call by Italian Communist party (PCI) chief Palmiro Togliatti for the independence of all Communist parties and their right to determine their own strategy for achieving socialism (he coined the term *polycentrism*), the 1957 Moscow conference sought to restore unity to the movement. In addition, a Soviet-edited journal, *Problems of Peace and Socialism,* was set up the following year to replace the Cominform's organ, *For a Lasting Peace, For a People's Democracy.* A unity of sorts was fashioned, acknowledging the leading position of the Soviet Union in the struggle against imperialism and condemning revisionism, which meant the Yugoslavs. Moscow and Beijing closed ranks, leaving Yugoslavia out and the Italian and Polish Communists uneasy. However, Sino-Soviet relations soon worsened, and at an accelerating pace.

By the 1960 Moscow conference of eighty-one Communist parties, the cracks in the Sino-Soviet relationship could no longer be puttied over. The exchanges were "frank" (a Soviet euphemism for bitter disagreement). The final document was more "a collation" of views than a compromise; its very "ambiguities and qualifications were so numerous that it could hardly serve as a guide for any of the Communist parties."[6] There was no agreement on the fundamental issue of authority within the world Communist movement, and the seeming accord hardly outlived the conference. So ended Moscow's former unquestioned sway.

Ironically, the Chinese were the ones pressing for a formulation that would recognize "the camp of Socialism headed by the Soviet Union," in order to alienate Yugoslavia and other revisionists, while Khrushchev disclaimed any interest in reestablishing Moscow's hegemonial role. In general, the Moscow declaration reflected the Soviet views in a way that "was sufficiently ambiguous so that the Chinese could (and did) interpret it in their favor: on the 'nature of the present epoch,' on the relative danger of dogmatism and revisionism, on local war (where Khrushchev after the conference recognized the justness and inevitability of 'wars of national liberation' but condemned 'interstate' wars), on the destructiveness of world war (where in general the statement took the Soviet position), on disarmament, on underdeveloped areas (where the compromise ideological concept of a 'national democracy' was outlined), on peaceful transition to Socialism, and on Communist strategy in capitalist countries (which reflected primarily the Soviet view), and on Yugoslavia."[7]

An indication of how far the Soviet Union's authority had slipped can be seen in the difficulty Moscow experienced in trying to convene an international Communist conference to condemn or excommunicate Beijing. Khrushchev determined in late 1963 to hold such an ecumenical kangaroo court, but encountered stiff opposition from the Yugoslav, Romanian, Polish, and Italian party leaders. The PCI's secretary-general, Palmiro Togliatti, told his Central Committee in April 1964: "When talk arose of a new international meeting of all Communist parties to examine and assess the attitude of the Chinese comrades . . . this . . . was likely to end in another excommunication . . .; and it appeared to us unnecessary and dangerous." Togliatti, a highly respected veteran Communist — a survivor of the Stalin period — carried his criticism of Khrushchev's course and his insistence on the independence and equality of all parties to the Kremlin itself and to the movement as a whole.

Togliatti died of a stroke while on vacation with Khrushchev in the Crimea in August 1964, but not before publishing an extraordinary memorandum on the problems of the world Communist movement. In it he opposed an international conference as untimely, and urged a continual round robin of working groups to defeat and alter the Chinese views. He called for "the unity of all socialist forces in a common action, going also beyond ideological differences, against the most reactionary imperialist groups." Deploring "the old atheist propaganda" as counterproductive to reaching the Catholic masses and coming to grips with the challenge posed by a changing Vatican, he denounced the "cult of Stalin" as well as stressed the need to study "the political errors" that gave rise to it. He cited the worrying centrifugal tendency of nationalism among the socialist countries and noted that "in this lies an evident and serious danger with which the Soviet comrades should concern themselves." For all of these reasons, he said, "we would be against any proposal to create once again a centralized international organization. We are firm supporters of the unity of our movement and of the international workers movement, but this unity must be achieved in the diversity of our concrete political positions, conforming to the situation and degree of development in each country."[8]

Khrushchev and his successors have not heeded all of Togliatti's advice, but neither have they ignored his admonitions or the impact that the memorandum had on the evolution of the world Communist movement.

At the time of Khrushchev's deposal in October 1964, Moscow could count on attendance by only forty-six parties, not the seventy Khrushchev had originally claimed. Brezhnev postponed the December conference, convening instead a "preparatory meeting" in Moscow in March 1965, which was attended by only eighteen of the twenty-six parties invited. Faced with widespread resistance to the excommunication of the Chinese and to any return to the monolithism of the Stalinist period, Soviet leaders groped through subsequent meetings in 1967 and 1968 for a way to accommodate both the diversity demanded by foreign parties and the minimal unity the Kremlin could accept and still retain the authority necessary for promotion of foreign-policy priorities.

Far from forging the movement's unity, the world conference finally held in Moscow from June 5 to 17, 1969, demonstrated conclusively that the Balkanization of world communism had taken place. The very holding of the conference was a minor feat of sorts for Moscow. Seventy-five parties attended (five did not sign the final document) — the remaining 25 percent followed China and stayed away (absentees who had been present in 1960 included the Communist parties of Vietnam, North Korea, Japan, Burma, and Indonesia). The final document, which did not mention China or the Soviet invasion of Czechoslovakia, was a bland mélange of generalities. The conference left the movement pretty much where it had been before and where it has remained ever since: polycentric, beset with divergences, wedded on paper to a common ideology that frays badly when used, and firm in rejecting any attempt to restore the CPSU's former leading position in the movement; its professions of unity reduced mainly to denunciations of U.S. imperialism (though, as opponents noted, the USSR seeks continually to reach agreements with the United States on a variety of issues).

Moscow fared no better in the regional conferences of European Communist parties, the most important of which was held in East Berlin in June 1976.[9] Moscow failed even with the timing: it had wanted the conference a year earlier, to link it to the Conference on Security and Cooperation in Europe, hoping thereby to "lessen the effect of the concessions that the East Europeans would have to make in Helsinki with regard to 'Basket 3' (the freer movement of information, ideas, and persons); at the same time, it would at least implicitly reaffirm the status of the CPSU as *primus inter pares* (or *imparies*) in the European Communist movement."[10]

The conference document signed by the twenty-nine participants was not what Moscow wanted. It stressed the voluntary cooperation of the participating parties, "strictly adhering to the principles of *equality and sovereign independence* of each party, noninterference in internal affairs and respect for their *free choice* of different roads in the struggle for social change of a progressive nature and for Socialism" (italics added). In the seven years since the 1969 international conference, Moscow had made no headway in regaining any of its former authority. Indeed, the statements of individual leaders had become even more forceful in the assertion of their independence. For example, the PCI's Enrico Berlinguer said that the solidarity of the world Communist movement "is based on recognition that each party elaborates autonomously and decides in full independence its own political line, both internal and international . . . . The truth is that . . . there is not and cannot be any leading party or leading state . . . ."

What Moscow wanted was stated on several occasions by Konstantin Zarodov (the Russian editor-in-chief of *Problems of Peace and Socialism,* the theoretical journal of pro-Moscow Communist parties) and others: acceptance of the "unchanged necessity for 'a revolutionary democratic dictatorship of the Proletariat', led 'from above' by the [Soviet] Communist party," which, by virtue of its historical experience, should in essence have the "right to impart ideological and political lessons to other CP's."[11] Moscow wanted the conference to adopt a "general line," but it did not. To ensure the participation of the Yugoslav, Romanian, Italian, Spanish, and even French party leaders, Moscow had to swallow such bitter pills as equality of parties; independence in interparty relations; no special status for the CPSU, though it could claim support for its foreign policy vis-à-vis the capitalist world; no criticism of any party; no binding requirements; and no acceptance of "proletarian internationalism," but substitution instead of the formulation "internationalist voluntary cooperation."

## Eurocommunism

The new independence shown by West European Communist parties has been termed "Eurocommunism." Many consider that Eurocommunism came of age in the statement issued by Enrico Berlinguer and Georges Marchais in mid-November 1975, all the principles of which were included in the June 1976 document issued at the East Berlin meeting. Continued agreement by the Italian and French Communist parties (PCI and PCF, respectively), the most important in Western Europe, was a development the Kremlin could not ignore.

Eurocommunism heralds the entry of West European Communist parties into the political mainstreams of their respective countries, and their professed commitment to an evolutionary quest for power and a readiness to share office in coalition with non-Communist parties. It also implies greater independence from Soviet ideological and political authority; rejection of the concept of the dictatorship of the proletariat; and formal acceptance of the principles underlying Western pluralist democratic societies, including free elections, toleration of competing parties, and respect for fundamental civil liberties and majority rule. A variegated, multifaceted adaptation of nonruling West European Communist parties to their national political environments, Eurocommunism signifies the right of party leaderships to develop their own tactics in the quest for power. Even the "Stalinist" leaders — Cunhal in Portugal and Marchais in France — toe only that part of the Soviet line that suits their own situation: thus, both dropped the phrase "dictatorship of the proletariat" from their respective party programs as a convenience, to avoid alienating groups to whom the term means "fascist" or "Stalinist." Psephological tactics mandate doctrinal flexibility. This adaptation to reality is pure Leninism, and Moscow can live with it, especially since neither Cunhal or Marchais dispute Soviet leadership of the world Communist movement or the USSR's policy in the Third World, including the invasion of Afghanistan.

The differences between the Cunhal-Marchais breed of Eurocommunist and the self-styled democratic/libertarian Berlinguer-Carrillo breed reflect different political contexts, challenges, and constituencies. A Marchais, for example, is against the Common Market and attacks the flight of the boat people from Vietnam as part of a campaign to denigrate the Vietnamese regime and communism, because to do so is popular among large segments of his country's populace; a Berlinguer defends the EEC and calls for aid to the refugees for the same reason. Neither checked with Moscow before deciding which position to adopt, and Moscow is not overly sensitive to this kind of polycentrism, which does no harm to Soviet foreign-policy aims in Europe. Carrillo and Berlinguer in particular have tried to organize closer cooperation and political initiatives to draw the Latin parties into a joint approach to "the problem of how to face up to the crisis in European society." They predict increasing economic and social tensions, a prognosis shared by many in Moscow. Whether their efforts will challenge Moscow's relations with Eastern Europe remains to be seen.

There are times, however, when Eurocommunism seriously troubles Moscow, as when it seems to be eroding the basis for the USSR's extant authority and claim to special status in the world Communist movement. The Carrillo affair is a good example. In early 1977, after decades of clandestine existence, the Communist party of Spain (PCE) emerged as a legal party in the post-Franco period and contested seats in the parliamentary elections in April. The brouhaha between Moscow and the PCE's secretary-general, Santiago Carrillo, broke out shortly after publication of his book, *Eurocommunism and the State.* Carrillo angered Moscow on a number of counts: he criticized and rejected the Soviet model of socialism;

equated the military hegemony of the USSR with that of the U.S., cautioned Eurocommunist parties to avoid the embrace of either, and suggested that Spain might join militarily with its neighbors (NATO members) to protect itself against invasion; criticized the deformation of Soviet society, the persistence of Stalinism and the "cult of personality" in the USSR, and the PCE's past blind obedience to the CPSU; called for an objective evaluation of Trotsky's role in history; referred to Khrushchev's fall as "a sort of palace coup"; and accused the Soviet leadership of trying to perpetuate dogmas and relationships that "may have some propagandistic value for the type of system that has been achieved in the USSR" but that have no relevance for the Communists in Western Europe.

The initial Soviet answer was a heavy barrage that appeared in late June 1977 in *Novoe vremya* and had the effect of raising the specters of Soviet censorship of foreign Communists and another excommunication campaign similar to that launched against Yugoslav leaders in 1948.[12] Moscow attacked Carrillo for transgressing the correct norms of proper interparty relations by denigrating Soviet achievements, society, and foreign policy and shamelessly echoing Western charges concerning Soviet human-rights violations. It may have reacted this sharply out of fear that the Eurocommunist summit that Carrillo, Berlinguer, and Marchais held in Madrid in March 1977 was the precursor of some form of anti-Soviet coalition within the Communist movement.

It is probable that Soviet leaders used Carrillo's book, which was hastily written and not always very analytical, as a pretext to criticize the Italian and French party leaders, who are far more important on the European scene and whose behavior could have serious repercussions in Eastern Europe. The very weakness of the PCE made it a good surrogate target for the bigger fry. The criticisms were delayed until after the Spanish elections (in which the PCE fared poorly), perhaps to avoid the accusation that Moscow was trying to sow factionalism or undermine a Eurocommunist party with which it was at odds. One lesson Moscow hoped other parties would learn from the Spanish case was that anti-Sovietism does not pay. The sniping, like the phenomenon, is apt to remain a feature of the European scene.[13]

The recent behavior of Marchais and the PCF, however, suggests that the heyday of the Eurocommunist challenge to Moscow has passed. In late 1979-early 1980, Marchais reverted to uncritical endorsement of Soviet policy on virtually all important issues. Faced internally with the collapse in 1977 of cooperation with the Socialist party, the erosion of electoral strength, and the withering away of prospects for coming to power by parliamentary means, he sought to restore the PCF's political fortunes through alignment with Moscow on international questions and militancy at home. His objective is to contrast the self-styled principled position of the PCF from the Eurocommunist and "Euroleft" strategy, which calls for a linking of Eurocommunists and socialists. Accordingly, at the end of April 1980, the PCF hosted a conference, boycotted by leading Eurocommunist parties like the Italian and Spanish, but attended by twenty-two European Communist parties, which endorsed the Soviet position on arms limitation in Europe, China, and Afghanistan. With Marchais' return to the fold, the PCF has become the spearhead of a major Soviet "peace offensive" in Western Europe.

## The Japanese Variant

The growing assertiveness of the non-ruling communist parties in Western Europe has absorbed but not monopolized Moscow's attention. There is in Asia a less well-known counterpart to the phenomenon of Eurocommunism. It is clearly manifested in the behavior of the Japan Communist Party (JCP). Founded in 1922, the JCP is the best-organized and strongest Communist party in non-Communist Asia, with a membership of about 300,000. It has undergone tortuous reversals; finally, in the 1970s, it succeeded in establishing an image of nonviolence, accepted the parliamentary system, and emerged as the third most important party in the Diet.

After World War II, the JCP slavishly followed the Soviet line. In 1950, the Cominform "suggested" a revolutionary tack that led the Japanese leadership to admit its mistakes and adopt a violent approach, with the result that for the next five years, the party had to go underground.[14] From the mid-1950s to the mid-1960s — from the USSR's de-Stalinization to the CPR's Cultural Revolution — the JCP drew closer to Beijing; it opposed Moscow because of the U.S.-Soviet limited nuclear test ban treaty (1963), the Soviet détente with the United States, and the lingering resentment over the humiliation that party leaders had suffered at Stalin's hands for advocating the very kind of policy that Brezhnev had come to espouse. Soviet leaders were accused of meddling in intra-JCP activities, encouraging factionalism, and seeking improved relations with the JCP's arch-foes, the socialists.[15] However, by late 1966, the JCP's pro-Beijing position on the Sino-Soviet dispute came a cropper in the revulsion against Mao's Cultural Revolution and his rejection of a common front with Moscow in support of North Vietnam's struggle against U.S. imperialism. This led the chairman of the JCP, Kenji Miyamoto (the party's secretary-general is Tetsuzo Fuwa), to pioneer a policy of independence from both Beijing and Moscow, and it gave rise to statements like the one in support of Dubcek during the Czech crisis. The JCP edged toward a reconciliation with Moscow, sending a delegation to the CPSU's twenty-fourth congress in March 1971 (it had not been present at the previous congress in 1966), but matters proceeded slowly, and it did not attend the twenty-fifth congress in February 1976.

Moscow's troubles with the JCP stem from a variety of causes. Ideologically, the JCP has over a period of years been discarding traditional formulations such as the "dictatorship of the proletariat" in favor of "the power of the laboring class," which lacks the threatening overtones associated with "dictatorship."[16] Politically, it has aligned itself with such independent-minded ruling Communist parties as those of Romania, Vietnam, and North Korea, and with Eurocommunist nonruling parties such as those of Italy and Spain. And on foreign policy, it has become a tenacious advocate of the Soviet return of all the Kuril Islands, not just the Northern territories, thus enhancing its popularity at home and eliciting denunciations from Moscow for "chauvinistic, nationalistic attitudes."[17]

The Soviet leadership persists in trying to normalize ties because it approves of the JCP's opposition to the U.S.-Japanese security pact, U.S. imperialism in Asia, Beijing's opening to the United States, and the incipient Washington-Beijing-Tokyo axis. On most international issues in Asia that matter to Moscow, the JCP is drifting away from China and toward the Soviet Union. Judging by the joint statement issued in Tokyo on December 25, 1979, by representatives of the JCP and the CPSU, condemning China's invasion of Vietnam earlier in the year, a reconciliation is probable, though the Soviet invasion of Afghanistan constitutes a new roadblock to normalization.

## The Kremlin's Dilemmas

How is Soviet foreign policy affected or apt to be affected by Eurocommunism? An obviously complex question, this needs to be differentiated from the more general considerations of the relationship between the Soviet Union and the weblike phenomenon known as the world Communist movement. If Soviet foreign-policy priorities are seen as avoidance of nuclear war, maintenance of the cohesion of the USSR and its imperial system in Eastern Europe, promotion of peaceful coexistence and détente with the West — with all that this entails for Soviet leaders in terms of trade, technological borrowing, and forestalling a stronger NATO — then it can be stated with reasonable certainty that Eurocommunism does not now affect the overall strategic balance between the Soviet Union and its prime adversary, the United States, or the USSR's military hegemony in Eastern Europe. The Soviet capability to pursue these specific objectives is not fundamentally weakened by the phenomenon of *nonruling* Communist parties playing a more assertive role in their respective polities and speaking out more frequently and forcefully in ways critical of the USSR's past and present authority within the world Communist movement. The erosion of Soviet authority in this sphere does not directly affect its capacity for conducting a multifaceted diplomacy in other spheres that touch more concretely on vital Soviet security interests.

Yet, the Kremlin realizes that Eurocommunism does pose long-term challenges for Soviet foreign policy (1) globally, within the world Communist movement; (2) regionally, within the bloc, especially in Eastern Europe; (3) diplomatically, in relations with the countries of Western Europe; and (4) internally, in intraparty debates on the proper strategy and tactics to adopt in dealing with the capitalist world.

First, at the global level, Eurocommunism further weakens Soviet authority within the world Communist movement. What Titoism began and the Sino-Soviet split aggravated, Eurocommunism chips away at still more — namely, Moscow's loss of its leading role in guiding the policies of foreign Communist parties in ways that effectively supplement Soviet diplomatic activities. The additional leverage Moscow once had through the calibrated manipulation of unconventional diplomacy has significantly waned. Diversity has superseded monolithism, complexity supplanted simplicity, and criticism replaced blind acceptance of abrupt political turnabouts. Moscow can no longer summarily issue commands to foreign Communist parties. When it acts as it did in Hungary in 1956 or Czechoslovakia in 1968, it must expect dissonance and disillusionment among foreign Communists. Thus far, the price has not been too high.

Second, in Eastern Europe, Eurocommunist formulations may encourage indigenous reformers to demand greater autonomy, thereby intensifying the danger that another "Czech spring" will break out elsewhere in the bloc. If Moscow did not trust the Czechoslovak leadership to superintend the internal liberalization in 1968, fearing that the Czech virus might spread, it must be even more anxious over the continual flow of heretical and fermenting ideas from West European Communists to their comrades in Eastern Europe, not to mention the difficulty of squelching ideas such as equality of parties, nonintervention in party affairs, and respect for the right of each party to find its own road to socialism — principles that the Soviet leadership seemingly accepted at Moscow in 1969 and East Berlin in 1976. Soviet leaders have shown little tolerance for deviations from the political and institutional forms that were grafted onto Eastern Europe after 1945. For them to tolerate the validity of the pluralist and democratic procedures formally espoused by the PCI and PCE would be to give inadvertent support and legitimacy to dissidents in Eastern Europe, and ultimately even in the Soviet Union.

In theory, at least, there is no reason why East European parties should not covet for themselves what their counterparts profess in Western Europe, but the spillover effect could prove politically dangerous. Soviet leaders know, and fear, that "Eurocommunism is a promising source of ideological justification and political leverage" for the East Europeans in their quest for greater independence from Moscow:

> It tends to reinforce the image East Europeans have always had of their historic role in Europe as a bridge between East and West and, more recently, as a kind of ideological potting shed for the introduction of Western ideas into the Soviet Union.[18]

Moscow knows enough about the unanticipated consequences of social and political forces to sense the threat to its East European imperium that lies untapped in some unforseen mixture of Eurocommunist ideas, "the potential effects of Basket III of the Helsinki Final Act, and the economic difficulties in some countries of the Eastern bloc."[19] What irony if democracy, like communism, comes to the Soviet world from the West. Yet all of this is very much in the future; the Soviet position in Eastern Europe is far from threatened. Nevertheless, the nature of the challenge is one that can only demand ever-increasing attention from a wary Kremlin.

Third, Soviet government-to-government relations with key countries in Western Europe could be adversely affected if the local Communist parties were in a position to influence their countries' foreign policy, either through participating in a coalition government or through coming to power on their own, because the closer a Communist party comes to power, the more the Western countries coalesce against the USSR and the more difficult becomes the Soviet task of exploiting divisions within the capitalist world. At this stage in its relations with Western Europe, Moscow benefits greatly from the independent opposition of Communist parties to policies that it also opposes — for example, deployment of the neutron bomb. It has traditionally tried to maintain good interparty and intrastate relations and has been careful to keep the two components of its foreign relations separate. Occasionally, as in Indonesia in the early 1960s and the Sudan in 1971, internal conflicts between the party and the state have created government-to-government tensions. But in the main, Soviet diplomacy has successfully promoted good relations with a government (for instance, France under de Gaulle) while at the same time managing good relations with the Communist party challenging the policies of that government.

If a Communist party did come to power, Moscow would make the appropriate accommodation. However, judging by past experiences with China, North Korea, Yugoslavia, and Albania, it has no reason for assuming that a Communist accession to power in Western Europe would automatically be a net gain for Soviet foreign policy. Indeed, since such a development would undoubtedly exacerbate pressures in Eastern Europe for greater independence, Moscow may well prefer that Eurocommunists remain perennially in the opposition. It knows that the more nationalistic Communist parties become, the less compliant they are apt to be to its wishes. Bolshevization is a thing of the past and Stalinism is passé. Autonomist propensities spell trouble.

Finally, Soviet leaders are divided on how to deal with Eurocommunism. We may therefore expect to see all kinds of zigs and zags in Moscow's responses, varying from polemical campaigns in the vein of the Carrillo–*Novoe vremya* affair to frequent party get-togethers to keep the lid on the more serious disputes. As far back as the early 1970s, "the ever-present duality between Soviet *raison d'état* and revolutionary commitment" was taking on particular intensity in the intra-Kremlin debate on how to respond to revolutionary situations, first in Chile, then in Portugal, with Soviet hard-liners like Mikhail Suslov and Konstantin Zarodov favoring preservation of the party's separate identity, direct action, and the use of revolutionary means to gain power, and moderates such as Leonid Brezhnev and Vadim V. Zagladin leaning toward coalition-building, electoral alliances, and a gradual transition toward socialism.[20] Soviet writings acknowledge that Soviet leaders differ on the approach that should be adopted toward Western Europe and on the implications of Eurocommunism for Soviet foreign policy.

Moscow distrusts Eurocommunism. Its criticisms, forcefully stated in the campaign against Carrillo, have been expressed even more astringently by East European surrogates. Thus, the Bulgarian party leader, Todor Zhivkov, labeled the "so-called Eurocommunism" an anti-Soviet creation of the class enemy, and Vasil Bilak, the secretary of the Czechoslovak CP Central Committee, said, "Its content is traitorous. It is a deliberate effort to split the international Communist movement according to geographical zones and various regions, to incite all that breaks the unity of our movement." * These sentiments mirror Moscow's real feelings. Nonetheless, the Kremlin continues to work with the Eurocommunists, and the reasons go to the heart of the relationship between Soviet foreign policy and the world Communist movement.

To begin with, in the absence of the Red Army, Moscow knows that there is nothing it can do to prevent foreign Communists from speaking out, short of excommunicating them or breaking up the entire movement, which is probably what would happen if it tried the tactics of 1948 in the 1980s. Its authority is no longer sufficient to intimidate a maverick into silent submission to Moscow's views on the promotion of world revolu-

---

* Kevin Devlin, "Comrade Bilak and the Eurocommunists," RFE Research, RAD Background Report/119 (June 22, 1977), p. 3.

tion. Lacking Lenin's moral stature or Stalin's coercive apparatus, Brezhnev and his successors must rely on persuasion and consensus — time-consuming, untidy, and often frustrating procedures.

Furthermore, Moscow finds the support given by the West European Communist parties to Soviet foreign-policy positions more than ample recompense for the ideological and political difficulties those parties cause. Soviet proposals usually (though not always — witness the PCI's support for the Common Market and criticism of the USSR's 1968 invasion of Czechoslovakia) meet with their unqualified approval on a wide and significant range of issues, varying from disarmament to the Middle East, from opposition to the neutron bomb to the establishment of nuclear-free zones, from opposition to enlargement of existing alliances (that is, to keep Spain out of NATO) to détente. The net effect is reinforcement for Moscow's general foreign-policy line. If not exactly a Trojan horse, the Communists and their affiliated, manipulated, Communist-front organizations help mold public opinion in ways congenial to the promotion of Soviet foreign-policy aims in Europe, and this is what matters most to Moscow. If the Communists were to come to power, they would most probably not become Soviet puppets, but their success would undoubtedly weaken U.S. influence, which would suit Moscow just fine.

Next, for all the attention given in the West to the Eurocommunist challenge to the Soviet Union, Moscow senses that it is an even more immediate problem for the United States and its NATO allies. NATO's southern flank is beset with rivalries and serious internal difficulties, and leftist revolutions or parliamentary triumphs are not impossible. A sizable Communist component in the government of Greece, Portugal, Italy, or France could destabilize NATO (the entry of Communists into the coalition government of Iceland in 1978 did not produce any changes in foreign policy, but Iceland's homogeneous, democratic society is quite different from those of NATO's Mediterranean members).

In addition, Moscow temporizes with the would-be Eurocommunists because it realizes that they need Moscow as much as Moscow needs them. However much they may criticize Moscow on this doctrinal point or that foreign-policy issue, they will not — they dare not — split with Moscow, because without affiliation with the Soviet Union they are just another political party, which the faithful would quit in disillusionment and find a substitute for elsewhere.

The West European Communists may criticize Moscow to display their independence to their countrymen and enhance their internal prestige for electoral contests, but they will not reject the mythology of the Bolshevik Revolution and the Soviet role in building socialism. Nor have they so far been willing to democratize their party organizations. Every Communist party remains totalitarian, a state within a state. Each is hierarchically structured to prevent grass-roots revolts and is led by a small elite of tough, shrewd, pragmatic leaders, whose first commandment is "Thou shalt stay in power." Their followers follow for a number of reasons, an essential one being the umbilical tie to the Soviet Union. Party leaderships have tiffs with Moscow and temporarily remain aloof from intraparty gatherings, but they invariably return to the fold, as did the Norwegian CP in 1975, the Dutch CP in 1977, and the Belgian CP in 1979. Indeed, by early 1980, under the pressure of sagging domestic fortunes, even Carrillo had muted some of his criticisms of Moscow and moved the PCE closer to a pro-Soviet position, criticizing NATO's decision to deploy new missiles and accusing the CIA of fomenting Basque terrorist activity, but also condemning the Soviet invasion of Afghanistan.

Soviet leaders know it is important for West European Communist leaders to present an independent and democratic image, but they are not always certain how to react to a Carrillo or a Berlinguer. Aware that human rights are one of the most sensitive issues for Western parties, they continue to harass and imprison dissidents and to refuse visas to those wishing to emigrate. They persevere because of their confidence that in any showdown their foreign constituencies would be reluctant to leave the fold.

Finally, Eurocommunism is a pill that Moscow swallows to keep alive its pretensions to ecumenism. Moscow needs the international movement not only to justify the legitimacy of its ideology and of one-party rule in the USSR, but also because "a total break with major Communist parties could possibly prove even more harmful to the internal legitimacy of the Soviet-bloc regimes than proclamation of even serious heresies by those nonruling parties while still in communion with the ruling ones."[21] Its belief in the utility of the world Communist movement for the promotion of Soviet foreign-policy interests helps explain the Kremlin's readiness "not only to grant the nonruling parties an almost complete autonomy with regard to strategy and tactics [which cannot in any event be proscribed], but also to react to deviations from the Soviet interpretations of Communist doctrine and to public critiques of Soviet and Soviet-bloc actions with comparative moderation, and to confine attempts to exert pressure in cases they consider extreme chiefly to nonpublic channels."[22] After all, if Moscow has been shaken by Eurocommunism, imagine how the Eurocommunists had been shaken by de-Stalinization and détente.

From the foregoing analysis, we may hazard a number of propositions concerning the *present* relationship between Soviet foreign policy and the world Communist movement, to help fix the areas and limits of its importance to Moscow.

First, the significance of international communism as a tool of Soviet foreign policy is greatly exaggerated. The core of the Soviet threat, whether to the West, China, Japan, or the Third World, is military and political, not ideological or subversive, though these occasionally are effective, as in the coup in Afghanistan in April 1978. Nonruling Communist parties are rarely in a position to deliver — when and where Soviet policymakers want it — the kind of assistance that would make a difference in the promotion of concrete policy objectives.

Second, Western observers tend to overrate the extent of Soviet influence over nonruling Communist parties because of a persisting propensity to view all of them as compliant and effective proxies of Moscow and to attribute to these parties a capacity for influencing policy that few of them possess.

Third, the authority that Soviet leaders wield within the world Communist movement is constrained by Moscow's need to accommodate to divergent interests and outlooks, by ingrained opposition of nonruling Communist parties to Moscow's ever again acquiring the kind of authority it held prior to 1953, and by the evolutionary assertiveness of the independent Communist parties (for instance, Yugoslavia and Vietnam), as well as by the very range and increasing complexity of the foreign-policy issues that Moscow must deal with.

Fourth, the diversity and disunity of the movement is no charade intended to lull the West into inactivity. It is a real and permanent development, as momentous in its own way as the schism in the Christian church in the sixteenth century.

Finally, Soviet leaders continue to use the movement as best they can in their ongoing global rivalry with the United States.

## Notes

1. For a particularly thoughtful discussion and application of these generalizations to the relationship between the Comintern and Soviet foreign policy, see Bernard S. Morris, *International Communism and American Policy* (New York: Atherton Press, 1966), 3–25.

2. Ibid., 11.

3. Ibid., 14–15.

4. Benjamin Schwartz, "Sino-Soviet Relations — The Question of Authority," *The Annals of the American Academy of Political and Social Science,* vol. 349 (September 1963), 42.

5. Ibid., 44.

6. Donald S. Zagoria, *The Sino-Soviet Conflict 1956–1961* (Princeton: Princeton University Press, 1962), 367–368.

7. William E. Griffith, "The November 1960 Moscow Meeting: A Preliminary Reconstruction," *The China Quarterly*, no. 11 (July-September 1962), 55.

8. *New York Times*, September 5, 1964.

9. For the best account of the background and significance of the East Berlin Conference of European Communist and Workers' Parties, see Kevin Devlin, "The Challenge of Eurocommunism," *Problems of Communism*, vol. 26, no. 1 (January-February 1977), 1–18.

10. Ibid., 3.

11. Ibid., 5.

12. U.S. Information Agency, Office of Research, *The European Communist Media Debate on the Santiago Carrillo–NOVOE VREMYA Controversy: Search for or Avoidance of a Definition of Eurocommunism* (R-25-77) (Washington, D. C.) (November 15, 1977).

13. As in most intra-Communist–world doctrinal quarrels, the polemics turn up some choice morsels. Carrillo's initial reaction to the attacks in *Novoe vremya* compared the Kremlin with the Spanish Inquisition: Soviet leaders have forgotten that "the world communist movement is no longer a church and Moscow is no longer Rome. We cannot accept the existence of a 'Holy Office' within the Central Committee of the Soviet Communist Party with the power of dispensing excommunications or blessings." *The Guardian*, June 30, 1977.

14. Rodger Swearingen, "Japanese Communism and the Moscow-Peking Axis," *The Annals of the American Academy of Social and Political Science*, vol. 308 (November 1956), 63–75.

15. Sheldon W. Simon, "New Soviet Approaches to the Japanese Left," *Asian Survey*, vol. 6, no. 6 (June 1966), 319–326.

16. Joseph Kun, Radio Liberty Dispatch, "Communism with a Human Face: The JCP's Stand on Freedom, Democracy, and Independence" (June 21, 1976), 2.

17. *Pravda*, June 12, 1977.

18. Charles Gati, "The 'Europeanization' of Communism?" *Foreign Affairs*, vol. 55, no. 3 (April 1977), 546.

19. Heinz Timmermann, "Eurocommunism: Moscow's Reaction and the Implications for Eastern Europe," *The World Today*, vol. 33, no. 10 (October 1977), 379.

20. For a richly textured analysis of Soviet views of the evolving revolutionary situation in Portugal in 1974–1975, see Joan Barth Urban, "Contemporary Soviet Perspectives on Revolution in the West," *Orbis*, vol. 19, no. 4 (Winter 1976), 1360; 1391–1396.

21. Richard Lowenthal, "Moscow and the 'Eurocommunists,'" *Problems of Communism*, vol. 27, no. 4 (July–August 1978), 47.

22. Ibid., 48.

## Selected Bibliography

ALBRIGHT, DAVID E. *Communism and Political Systems in Western Europe*. Boulder, Col.: Westview Press, 1979.

BLACK, CYRIL E., and THOMAS P. THORTON (eds). *Communism and Revolution: The Strategic Uses of Political Violence*. Princeton: Princeton University Press, 1964.

BLACKMER, DONALD. *Italian Communism and the International Communist Movement*. Cambridge: MIT Press, 1968.

BORKENAU, FRANZ. *The Communist International*. London: Faber and Faber, 1938.

————. *World Communism*. Ann Arbor: University of Michigan Press. 1962.

CARRILLO, SANTIAGO. *Eurocommunism and the State*. Westport, Conn.: Lawrence Hill, 1978.

CLAUDIN, FERNANDO. *The Communist Movement: From Comintern to Cominform*. 2 vols. New York: Monthly Review Press, 1976.

DEGRAS, JANE (ed.). *The Communist International 1919–1943: Documents*. vol. I: 1919–1922; Vol. II: 1923–1928; Vol. III: 1929–1943. London: Oxford University Press, 1956, 1960, 1965, respectively.

FEJTO, FRANCOIS. *The French Communist Party and the Crisis of International Communism*. Cambridge: MIT Press, 1967.

GODSON, ROY, and STEPHEN HASELER. *"Eurocommunism": Implications for East and West*. London: Macmillan, 1978.

GRIFFITH, WILLIAM E. *Albania and the Sino-Soviet Rift*. Cambridge: MIT Press, 1963.

GRUBER, HELMUT. *International Communism in the Era of Lenin*. Garden City: Anchor Books, 1967.

————. *Soviet Russia Masters the Comintern: International Communism in the Era of Stalin's Ascendancy*. Garden City, N. Y.: Anchor Books, 1974.

HAMRIN, HARALD. *Between Bolshevism and Revisionism: The Italian Communist Party, 1944–1947*. Stockholm: Scandinavian University Books, 1975.

HERMAN, DONALD L. *The Comintern in Mexico*. Washington: Public Affairs Press, 1974.

HODGSON, JOHN H. *Communism in Finland*. Princeton: Princeton University Press, 1967.

JACOBS, DAN N. (ed.). *The New Communisms*. New York: Harper and Row, 1969.

LABEDZ, LEOPOLD (ed.). *International Communism After Khrushchev.* Cambridge: MIT Press, 1965.

LANGER, PAUL F. *Communism in Japan: A Case of Political Naturalization.* Stanford: Hoover Institution Press, 1972.

LAZITCH, BRANKO, and MILORAD DRACHKOVITCH. *Lenin and the Comintern.* Stanford: Hoover Institution Press, 1972.

LINDEMANN, ALBERT S. *The "Red Years": European Socialism Versus Bolshevism, 1919–1921.* Berkeley: University of California Press, 1974.

MCKENZIE, KERMIT E. *Comintern and World Revolution, 1928–1943.* New York: Columbia University Press, 1964.

MORRIS, BERNARD S. *International Communism and American Policy.* New York: Atherton, 1966.

OVERSTREET, GENE D., and MARSHALL WINDMILLER. *Communism in India.* Berkeley: University of California Press, 1959.

SCALAPINO, ROBERT A. *The Japanese Communist Movement, 1920–1966.* Berkeley: University of California Press, 1967.

SETON-WATSON, HUGH. *The Imperialist Revolutionaries: Trends in World Communism in the 1960s and 1970s.* Stanford: Hoover Institution Press, 1978.

STAROBIN, JOSEPH R. *American Communism in Crisis, 1943–1957.* Cambridge: Harvard University Press, 1972.

STARR, RICHARD F. (ed.). *1978 Yearbook on International Communist Affairs.* Stanford: Hoover Institution Press, 1978. (A valuable compilation on foreign Communist parties and front groups; published annually since 1966.)

STIEFBOLD, ANNETTE EISENBERG. *The French Communist Party in Transition: PCF-CPSU Relations and the Challenge to Soviet Authority.* New York: Praeger, 1977.

SWEARINGEN, RODGER, and PAUL LANGER. *Red Flag in Japan: International Communism in Action, 1919–1951.* Cambridge: Harvard University Press, 1952.

SZAJKOWSKI, BOGDAN (ed.). *Documents in Communist Affairs.* Swansea, Wales: University College Cardiff Press, 1978.

TÖKES, RUDOLF L. (ed.). *Eurocommunism and Détente.* New York: New York University Press, 1979.

URBAN, G. R. (ed.). *Communist Reformation: Nationalism, Internationalism and Change in the World Communist Movement.* New York: St. Martin's, 1979.

ZAGLADIN, Z. *Europe and the Communists.* Moscow: Progress Publishers, 1977.

# 8

# The Military Dimensions
# of Soviet Foreign Policy

Military power has brought a new dimension to Soviet foreign policy: for the first time in its history, the USSR is truly a global power. Not only can it intervene effectively to preserve its imperial system in Eastern Europe and the Far East, but its nuclear weapons can shower enormous destruction on the United States, and it can project conventional military power beyond its continental confines into the Third World. This overall military capability has reinforced the basic world outlook and ambitions of Soviet rulers, strengthened their confidence, and provided them with a wider range of options for dealing with adversaries. Militarily, the Soviet Union can hold up its end of the global balance of power with the United States. Moreover, it may be far less hesitant in the future about utilizing military power for political ends, judging by the comment the Soviet chief of staff, Marshal Nikolai V. Ogarkov, made to a visiting congressman in 1979: "The Soviet Union has military superiority over the United States and henceforth the United States will be threatened. You had better get used to it."

The aims of Soviet military policy have evolved since 1917 from preservation of the Soviet state and defense against external threat to expansion of the Soviet empire and promotion of global objectives. The basic aim is still to defend the Soviet homeland, a theme that dominated Soviet thinking during the 1917-to-1945 period, but following the annexations and expansion after World War II, the military was assigned the additional task of defending the entire Communist camp. As a result of the direct assistance rendered by the Red Army, the People's Republic of China and North Korea consolidated their power in the Far East. Through the deployment of its units in occupied Germany and Austria, and then on the basis of bilateral agreements in Poland, Hungary, and Romania, the Soviet Army on the one hand improved the security of the Soviet Union, and on the other hand helped the weak communist parties in East Germany, Poland, Czechoslovakia, Hungary, Romania, and Bulgaria to take power and initiate a gradual social transformation . . . . In this way, and with full use of the Soviet armed forces, the basic goals of Soviet foreign policy in World War II were realized: the capitalist encirclement of the USSR and its isolation were broken, a belt of socialist states along Soviet borders was created, and the Soviet Union acquired the position of a world power.[1]

Discouraging intrasystemic efforts to break away from Moscow's hegemony or a Marxist-Leninist political system, the Soviet armed forces suppressed rebellions in Eastern Europe in 1953, 1956, and 1968, and, by demonstrating overwhelming military force and determination, dissuaded the Western powers from any intervention. In addition to their deterrent function, they have enabled Soviet diplomats to negotiate with NATO countries from a position of strength.

Finally, the Soviet military has been an indispensable adjunct of Moscow's "forward policy" in the Third World. In country after country in the Middle East, southern Asia, Africa, and Latin America (thus far, primarily only in Cuba), Soviet arms, advisers, and sheltering shields have aided client states and undermined Western positions. In a number of instances, Soviet combat forces have actually participated in engagements to defend and promote the interests of beleaguered clients (see chapters 10 and 11). This international outreach signifies the metamorphosis of Soviet foreign policy from a continental-based strategy to a global strategy.

## From Strategic Inferiority to SALT I

After 1945 Soviet foreign policy was geared to the consolidation of the empire in Eastern Europe. In view of the American nuclear monopoly, Moscow placed a premium on maintaining a commanding conventional capability in the area. Implicit in Stalin's strategy of neutralizing the U.S. nuclear advantage, by which the United States could strike targets in the Soviet Union without fear of retaliation, was the belief that the United States could be deterred by the USSR's deployment of substantial conventional forces in the European theater and by the impression that those forces would be used "for a rapid advance to the Atlantic" if America tried nuclear blackmail; moreover, these same forces "also provided insurance against defections in East Europe."[2]

The Soviet strategy of deploying strong forces in Central Europe heightened Western fears, prompting the establishment of NATO and the West's rearmament, responses that Stalin had hoped to forestall. Essentially, however, this has remained the centerpiece of Moscow's approach, though by the late 1960s the USSR had developed a credible nuclear capability of its own, thanks to the investment and impetus given to nuclear programs during the Stalin years.

The Soviet Union was the first to test an intercontinental ballistic missile (ICBM) successfully, in late August 1957, and it placed the first space satellite, Sputnik I, in orbit on October 4, 1957. These scientific achievements emboldened Khrushchev to seek political advantages — prematurely, as it turned out. Convinced that the balance of world forces was shifting to the Soviet camp, he precipitated a new crisis over Berlin in November 1958, hoping to wrest concessions from the West — at a minimum, its recognition of East Germany. Nineteen fifty-nine proved to be an inconclusive year, notwithstanding Khrushchev's visit to the United States. Then on May 1, 1960, a U.S. spy plane was shot down while on a routine mission over the Soviet Union, an event that aborted the summit meeting that had been scheduled for mid-May in Paris. The incident revealed the hollowness of Khrushchev's strategic claims, which the Soviet military had known all along because this was the first of the U-2's they had been able to shoot down ever since the U.S. intelligence missions had started in 1955, and because they knew how few ICBMs were available (for technical and economic reasons) in the Soviet arsenal. In fact, the undeniable Soviet strategic (that is, nuclear) inferiority to the United States was one of the considerations that had led Khrushchev to shy away from supporting Mao Zedong during the 1958 Quemoy crisis and to resist his pressure for a tougher stance toward the United States.

In January 1960 Khrushchev proposed a far-reaching reform of the Soviet military establishment which called for reliance on nuclear-armed missiles to deter any would-be attacker and for a sharp reduction in military manpower to ease the severe labor shortage in Soviet industry. Elements in the military pressed for acceleration of the buildup of strategic forces beyond what Khrushchev thought necessary, as part of the revolution in Soviet military doctrine being formulated by the high command. With other domestic priorities attracting his support, Khrushchev sought an alternative that would minimize defense expenditures on strategic weapons systems and still satisfy the military. Accordingly, to strengthen the credibility of the USSR's nuclear deterrent, Khrushchev agreed in the spring of 1962 to implant short- and intermediate-range ballistic missiles (IRBMs) in Cuba. Not only would the success of this stratagem have enhanced Soviet prestige, punctured Chinese criticisms that Khrushchev was behaving timidly vis-à-vis U.S. imperialism, and demonstrated Moscow's credibility as a patron, but "the force of some forty MRBM and IRBM launchers dispatched to Cuba would have narrowed in one quick stroke the actual margin of the U.S. advantage in strategic forces, for it would have had the effect, as Raymond Garthoff has pointed out, of transforming readily available missiles of 1,100 to 2,200-mile range into 'ersatz' intercontinental missiles. In terms of the Soviet Union's then-existing first-strike salvo capability against targets in the United States, this would have meant an increase of almost 50 percent." [3]

Khrushchev's failure in Cuba strengthened his opponents in Moscow. An ever-larger percentage of Soviet defense expenditures was committed to an accelerated buildup of strategic forces, while Soviet diplomacy worked to slow down the U.S. program through a combination of disarmament proposals and extensive antiwar propaganda. When the Kremlin

mined — as the Soviet UN delegate, Vasily Kuznetzov, warned his American counterpart — that this would be the last time the Soviet Union would bow to America's nuclear superiority.

Between late 1953 and 1960, as the leadership sought to adapt to the nuclear age, Soviet military doctrine and the composition of the military forces that were to serve as the instruments of Soviet foreign policy underwent a searching review. The debate was started in November 1953 in the journal of the general staff, *Voennaia mysl'* (Military Thought), by its editor, Major-General Nikolai A. Talenskii. His arguments, which were bitterly fought but eventually accepted by the traditionalists, implicitly challenged Stalin's dogma that the Soviet Union was inherently superior to its opponents because it was a socialist state and that it was destined to win any future war by virtue of the advantage of "permanently operating factors," such as a stable, loyal home front, high morale of the army, quality of leadership, and so forth. He tried to convince the leadership that the principles of military science needed revision and that they operated with equal validity for both sides; he also pointed out that the introduction of nuclear weapons required a far-reaching modification of the laws governing the strategy and conduct of war. [4]

By January 1960, when Khrushchev unveiled the essentials of a new military doctrine, the Soviet high command had embraced Talenskii's basic argument and moved far beyond it, in what came to be called "the revolution in military affairs," the term used to describe the enormous changes wrought in warfare by nuclear weapons and missiles. Henceforth Soviet military writings made it clear that since nuclear war was possible, it had to be analyzed and prepared for like any other war. The USSR's military doctrine and strategic concepts have been constantly modified and refined, in keeping with the development of a burgeoning arsenal of sophisticated and varied delivery systems and nuclear weapons.

Starting in 1960 (before the 1962 Cuban missile crisis), the Soviet leadership embarked on a buildup of its Strategic Rocket Forces, which were established as a separate arm of the Soviet armed forces; on the development of theater nuclear weapons, in accordance with a general program of modernizing and upgrading all weapons systems; and on the strengthening of anti-air defense and civil defense. The aims were to improve the country's ability to absorb a possible nuclear attack and to enhance deterrence. In the late 1950s, the Kremlin had decided to give priority to IRBMs and MRBMs (just as earlier it had concentrated on medium- rather than long-range bombers) because most NATO military bases were located in Western Europe, and the early ICBM (SS-6) "was too ungainly a beast, and much too expensive, to deploy widely;" the SS-6 was a good rocket for Khrushchev to rattle when the West did not know how few he had, but after the Cuban crisis, Moscow realized that it had a significant missile gap to overcome and acted accordingly.[5]

There were other shifts of emphasis as well. Whereas Khrushchev wanted to rely primarily on the Strategic Rocket Forces, essentially emulating U.S. reliance on massive retaliation to ensure deterrence, his successors opted for across-the-board investment, building up not only nuclear but conventional force capabilities so as to obtain maximum flexibility in foreign policy. This policy was to pay off handsomely in the 1970s, when the Soviet capability to project military power greatly enhanced its prestige and attractiveness among Third World clients and contributed to the globalization of its rivalry with the United States.

Moscow's determination to redress its inferiority to the United States in strategic weapons brought impressive results. During the 1965-to-1969 period, the USSR tripled the number of ICBMs (in 1967 alone it more than doubled its force, from 340 to 720) and greatly expanded the number of submarine-launched ballistic missiles (SLBMs). By the end of the 1960s, it exceeded the U.S. force (which has not been increased up till now) of 1054 land-based ICBMs, 656 Polaris SLBMs, and approximately 400 to 600 long-range bombers that were deemed sufficient by Washington for an assured destruction capability. Having developed what President Richard Nixon and Secretary of Defense James Schlesinger were later to term "essential equivalance," Moscow agreed to enter into the Strategic Arms Limitation Talks (SALT) with Washington.

As far back as 1964, President Lyndon Johnson had proposed a freeze on strategic weapons, but he had been rebuffed by Soviet leaders, who wanted a stronger hand for the next nuclear facedown. His next invitation to discuss limitations on offensive and defensive delivery systems, on January 27, 1967, was accepted in principle by the Soviet government in March 1967, but not until June 27, 1968, did Moscow formally agree to open talks. The reasons for the prolonged delay are obscure; we can only surmise that they were due to the combination of sharp differences within the Politburo over how to deal with the United States, the calculation that a delayed response would aggravate political cleavages in the United States and postpone deployment of a thin anti-ballistic missile system (ABM), and the determination to overcome the U.S. advantage in strategic weapons before commencing the talks.[6] The Soviet invasion of Czechoslovakia then intervened, leading Washington to postpone the start of SALT. Another year passed before the new Nixon administration was ready to start negotiations in Helsinki on November 17, 1969.

The talks dragged on into 1970 and 1971, in an international environment of high U.S.-Soviet tension in the Arab-Israeli sector (until late 1970), Soviet border troubles with China, the USSR's military assistance to North Vietnam in support of its war against the United States, and the Indo-Pakistani war and resulting emergence of East Pakistan as the new, independent nation of Bangladesh. In the spring of 1972, even though the United States was bombing and mining North Vietnamese ports, the Kremlin decided to conclude the SALT I agreement, for reasons of its own — whether from satisfaction at having completed its planned expansion of strategic forces, from a desire to give impetus to its policy of détente with the United States and garner the long-term economic credits that were a likely part of the package, from concern that further delay might jeopardize the entire process, or from uneasiness over the Sino-American reconciliation, epitomized by Nixon's visit to China in February, is not clear.

## The Payoff in SALT

SALT I was signed by President Nixon and CPSU Secretary Brezhnev on May 26, 1972. It consisted of three agreements. The first is a treaty of unlimited duration on the limitation of anti-ballistic missile systems, entered into force on October 3, 1972. The treaty prohibits the development of an ABM system, but originally permitted each side to protect its national capital and one ICBM silo launcher area with 100 ABM launchers and interceptors per area; a protocol was signed in 1974 restricting each side to only one ABM deployment. The second agreement was a five-year interim agreement that entered into force on October 3, 1972 (and formally expired on October 3, 1977). It fixed Soviet ICBM and SLBM launchers at 2350 and American launchers at 1710, thus marking the first time in the nuclear era that the USSR and the United States had agreed to set quantitative limits on their strategic delivery systems (that is, missiles capable of striking the other's homeland). Bombers were not covered by the agreement. The third set of documents dealt with interpretations of technical issues such as radars, testing, and so on. The two parties agreed to rely on national technical means of verification to ensure compliance, and not to interfere with the other side's space satellites.

There were several immediate advantages to SALT I for the USSR, each presumably interested constituency in the Soviet political-military establishment realizing some preferred objective, however imperfectly. Politically, the Soviet Union was recognized by the United States as a full-fledged and equal nuclear superpower. In the decade since the Cuban crisis, it had moved from strategic equivalence. Militarily, through the ban on ABM development, the USSR nipped in the bud the American deployment of a more technologically advanced ABM system, and it negotiated a quantitative edge in offensive delivery systems. This included provision for 313 heavy missiles, compared to none for the United States — a quantitative advantage that became qualitative with the deployment of MIRVed missiles, that is, those capable of carrying more than one nuclear warhead. Economically, the USSR avoided the strains that an ABM race would have brought and was able to concentrate on upgrading its offensive capability. SALT also enabled Moscow to invest heavily in reasearch and development, looking ahead to the upgrading of existing weapons systems and the development of new ones. Finally, Moscow's policy of promoting détente, one aim of which was to slacken U.S. defense efforts, was greatly enhanced.

The 1972 Moscow summit also helped Soviet diplomacy in Europe, by making possible CSCE and accompanying Western recognition of the territorial status quo in Europe and Moscow's sphere of influence in Eastern Europe — prime postwar Sovict objectives. However, the budding Soviet-American détente went awry in October 1973 over the Arab-Israeli war, in 1974–1975 over competition in Angola, and in 1977–1978 in the horn of Africa. These regional quarrels, coupled with mounting congressional criticisms of SALT I and the Watergate affair which forced Nixon to resign in August 1974, made a new agreement limiting offensive weapons more difficult to negotiate.

At Vladivostok in November 1974, President Gerald Ford and Brezhnev agreed to guidelines that established quantitative equality in strategic delivery vehicles; each side was to be permitted a limit of 2400 ICBMs, SLBMs, and heavy bombers as well as a ceiling of 1320 MIRVed missiles. Secretary of State Henry Kissinger exultantly reported that the Vladivostok accord (which was never ratified) put "a cap on the arms race," but closer examination revealed that it had considerably raised the threshold of the number of deliverable nuclear weapons. There were other criticisms, too. Critics alleged that Soviet technological advances and larger throw-weight capacity on newly developed MIRVed missiles could give the USSR a capacity by the mid-1980s to destroy the U.S. land-based ICBM force in a first-strike attack. Further complicating the negotiation of a follow-up SALT agreement was the intrusion of technology in the form of cruise missiles (a guided missile remaining within the Earth's atmosphere, capable of being launched from the ground, aircraft, or ships and delivering nuclear warheads with great accuracy in large numbers, but thus far with much smaller ranges than an ICBM or IRBM); mobile missiles of increasing range and accuracy; and MIRVed missiles that could not be distinguished from non-MIRVed missiles (as someone observed, we can detect the make of a car from space satellites, but there is no way of knowing what its engine power is). The verification problem, the issue of forward base systems (of which mobile missiles are a part), and the political aspects of arms control versus force reduction, to mention but a few of the complicating variables, placed formidable obstacles in the path of a new SALT agreement.[7]

The Soviet government was prepared to sign an accord on offensive missiles based on the Vladivostok formula, but in March 1977 the new Carter administration offered its own proposals for a sharp reduction in the quantitative limits, which would have affected Soviet production schedules and imposed qualitative constraints on the Vladivostok ceilings. For substantive as well as procedural reasons (Soviet leaders do not like surprises sprung on them in negotiations, least of all with public fanfare), Moscow demurred, and the 1972 interim agreement on offensive missiles lapsed in October 1977. However, a month before, the two governments had stated their willingness not to take any action inconsistent with the provisions of the interim agreement, pending negotiation of SALT II.

After two years of protracted negotiations in an environment of deteriorating Soviet-American relations, the USSR and the United States reached an agreement that was closer to the Vladivostok proposals than the Carter administration's original counterproposals. SALT II produced none of the euphoria of SALT I. On June 18, 1979, at a summit meeting in Vienna, Brezhnev and Carter signed an agreement stipulating that it would "remain in force through December 31, 1985, unless replaced earlier by an agreement further limiting strategic offensive arms." In its essentials, SALT II sets a ceiling of 2250 strategic delivery systems, effective January 1, 1981 (prior to this, each party had been permitted 2400). It places a limit of 1320 on the number of such delivery systems that can be MIRVed. The Soviet Union was permitted to retain a 308-to-0 advantage in heavy silo-based ICBMs (SS-18) — it successfully resisted U.S. pressure to reduce the number of heavy missiles to 150 — in return for agreeing to equal aggregate force levels. The Backfire bomber, which it insisted is a medium bomber, was not included in the formal agreement, but Brezhnev gave assurances that the USSR "does not intend to give this airplane the capability of operating at intercontinental distances," nor does it plan "to increase the Backfire's capability in any other manner, including in-flight refueling," or increase the aircraft's present production rate. SALT II also placed limitations on the development of cruise missiles with a range in excess of 600 kilometers. Compliance with the treaty shall be by national technical means of verification.

Though the Soviet government was ready to ratify the agreement promptly, the U.S. government was not able to do so. Carter wanted quick ratification but encountered increasing opposition from the Senate. First, critics of SALT argued that the treaty gave the Soviets too many advantages, including the already-mentioned capability possibly to destroy the entire U.S. land-based ICBM force in a first-strike attack by the mid-1980s. Second, in the summer and early fall of 1979, Carter himself fed the anti-SALT forces by initially magnifying the significance of the Soviet military presence in Cuba and then accepting the status quo when Moscow refused to make even token concessions to help him sell SALT domestically. Third, the anti-Soviet mood in the United States spread in the wake of Moscow's unhelpful position on the seizure of American embassy personnel in Tehran in early November 1979 by Iranian radicals demanding extradition of the shah. The final blow to early ratification was the Soviet invasion of Afghanistan in December, as Moscow decided to extirpate Afghani nationalist opposition to the Communist regime that it had helped to bring to power in April 1978. On January 2, 1980, President Carter formally requested the Senate to postpone consideration of the SALT II treaty indefinitely. The chill in Soviet-American relations put the SALT process into deep freeze.

SALT II, even if eventually ratified, is a minor station stop on the infinitely more difficult track to SALT III, if only because the relatively easily defined 1960s notion of strategic forces has broken down as a result of the development of theater nuclear forces. The Soviet Union enjoys a lead in these "Eurostrategic" weapons, which do not have an intercontinental capability but can strike targets anywhere in Western Europe. Moreover, the Soviet SS-20, an intermediate-range mobile missile, can be transformed into an ICBM by adding a third stage to the rocket, thus achieving a breakout in the number of deployed strategic delivery systems limited by SALT II; and it can be used as a first-strike weapon against Western Europe. If the Soviet Union achieves unquestioned dominance in theater nuclear forces and if it can check the U.S. strategic capability, it will be advantageously situated, in nuclear terms, to play on West European fears and intra-alliance divisions and to advance Soviet political objectives in Europe.

The Soviet Union would like to perpetuate Western Europe's inferiority in theater nuclear weapons and delivery systems. Faced with a U.S. proposal to provide NATO with new nuclear-tipped medium-range missiles (Pershing-2s which would be deployed in the mid-1980s) capable of hitting targets in the Soviet Union from Western Europe, Brezhnev proposed on October 6, 1979, to withdraw up to 20,000 troops and 1000 tanks from East Germany and also to reduce the number of Soviet medium-range missiles aimed at Western Europe, provided the U.S. missiles are not deployed. Whether it was a shrewd diplomatic ploy to intensify differences within NATO or a serious offer to negotiate, or both, Brezhnev's proposal did not prevent NATO from voting at its December 1979 meeting in favor of the deployment of the Pershing-2s and cruise missiles. The development highlights the need for the active participation of the West European countries in the SALT III negotiations, which promise to be far more difficult than their predecessors.

Moscow's interest in SALT is as much political as military; it wishes to perpetuate the general diplomatic environment and stretegic balance that it has nurtured in Europe. In the process of negotiating a SALT III agreement, Moscow will seek to upgrade the quality of its programs while trying to dissuade the United States and Western Europe from taking steps that would significantly alter the current relationship. Like the United States, the Soviet Union wants to avoid an unconstrained strategic arms race because its own economic resources are already invested heavily in military expenditures. An all-out race would seriously strain the Soviet economy. The present Soviet leadership also has a stake in maintaining its relationship with the United States within the parameters established by the treaty, the collapse of which would force momentous policy reappraisals and possibly reverse the tortoiselike progress made by the Soviet Union against the U.S. hare.

## The Buildup of Conventional Forces

Another dimension of Soviet military policy with far-reaching foreign-policy implications has been the sustained buildup of Soviet conventional force levels. Ever since 1945 the USSR has maintained large military forces in Central and Eastern Europe. Originally designed to deter Western interference with the imposition of the Soviet imperium in Eastern Europe and to ensure internal security in the bloc, by the 1970s Soviet forces could, if required, assume an offensive role capable of overrunning key sectors of NATO. The aim of making the USSR the dominant military power in Europe has been achieved; the preservation of this preeminence is what drives Soviet policy and has given it impressive momentum in acquiring new weapons systems and deploying combat-ready divisions in Europe. Most reliable estimates of the military balance assign the Soviet-dominated Warsaw Pact a margin of at least two to one over NATO forces.[8] This military might is both a type of insurance and a threat to the West. Given the present nuclear stalemate between the superpowers, in the event of a crisis or an opportunity in Europe, Moscow will not lack the wherewithal for influencing a preferred political outcome with its army, widely accepted in the West as the most powerful in the world. What is particularly notable about the Soviet army is its high state of battle readiness, its offensive capability for a massive breakthrough on several fronts, and its ability to carry on sustained operations for several weeks without reinforcements from the Soviet Union proper. Moreover, there is strong evidence that the USSR intends to maintain and even increase defense expenditures in the 1980s, notwithstanding difficult domestic economic and social problems.

Apart from the influence that the forward deployment of powerful Soviet conventional forces has on diplomacy in Europe — for example, in discouraging challenges to Moscow's rule in Eastern Europe and in prompting the MFR talks which began in Vienna in 1973 as an outgrowth of SALT I — and in relations with China, the consequences for Soviet policy in the Third World have been incalculable. Military power is the arm of Soviet diplomacy that has made the USSR a real rival of the United States in the Middle East, Africa, and southern Asia. In the mid-1950s Moscow could frustrate the Western powers and their diplomacy by sending arms to anti-Western Third World leaders; in the 1960s it could enable prized clients to engage in overseas adventures (for example, Nasser's intervention in Yemen from 1962 to 1967) and avoid lasting defeats (for example, by rearming the Egyptian and Syrian armies after their trouncing by Israel in June 1967). But in the 1970s it could intervene directly to protect clients from defeat and provide decisive assistance to produce political and military outcomes regarded as congenial to the spread of Soviet influence — for example, in Angola in 1975, in Ethiopia in 1977–1978, and in the People's Democratic Republic of Yemen in 1978, and in Afghanistan in 1979–1980.

Until the early 1970s the Soviet Union lacked the military capability to project military power in a decisive fashion outside of the Eurasian land mass, a shortcoming that hampered the conduct of a forward policy in the Third World. This has changed. The development of a long-range air transport capability, the construction of a blue-water fleet and a large, versatile merchant marine, and the availability of huge stockpiles of surplus weapons have provided the Kremlin with the military clout it needed for interventions in Africa, the Middle East, and Vietnam. In late 1977–early 1978, the USSR poured more tha $2 billion in weapons, ammunition, and supplies, with essential personnel, into Ethiopia, changing the entire complexion of regional affairs in the Horn without in any way diminishing its military capability in Europe.[9] Thus, the Soviet military has become an indispensable adjunct of Soviet overseas policy, and many features of its most modern force additions bespeak an intention to play an increasingly active role in the Third World (see chapters 10 and 11).

## Arms Control Measures

Disarmament has been a subordinate but nonetheless useful component of Soviet military and diplomatic strategy. Linked to the traditional imperial and Soviet Russian policy of maintaining a large standing army, it has been a political tool for trying to redress adverse military balances. It was Czar Nicholas II who was instrumental in convening the first world disarmament conference in 1899. Throughout the 1920s and 1930s, when threats loomed from Japan and Germany and when Britain and France were seriously regarded as advocates of another capitalist coalition to destroy the Soviet state, the Soviet government was in the forefront of campaigns for universal disarmament — for example, Litvinov's proposal in 1927 to the League of Nations' Preparatory Commission on Disarmament. At the same time it did everything possible to build up the Red Army. By the mid-1930s, Soviet policy in Europe changed for a few years, and diplomacy shifted from disarmament to collective security.

What is important to keep in mind is that Russian leaders have never regarded disarmament as a panacea for ensuring peace; they have always used the appeal of disarmament for political ends. Thus, any detailed examination of Soviet disarmament policy reveals that Moscow has exploited the theme as a means of compensating for military and technological inferiority, trying to induce a rival to offer unilateral concessions and limit its military programs, and gaining support internationally and among pacifist-minded groups whose domestic lobbying might affect their own government's policies.

The disarmament issue became prominent in the United Nations at a very early stage. At the first meeting of the UN Atomic Energy Commission in June 1946, the United States made a comprehensive proposal for controlling the atom. The Baruch Plan called for the establishment of an international agency to control, own, and operate all nuclear facilities "from the mine to the finished product" and provided for the *eventual* destruction of existing nuclear weapons, but only after an adequate international inspection system had been set up. Molotov attacked the proposal as intended to guarantee the United States monopoly possession of the atomic bomb, warning that "no single country can count on retaining a complete monopoly. Science and its exponents cannot be shut up in a box and kept under lock and key . . . . It must not be forgotten that atomic bombs on one side may draw a reply in atomic bombs, and perhaps something else to boot, from the other side." (The USSR was then intensely engaged in its own effort to build a bomb.)

By 1947 the Cold War took over and disarmament had become a dead issue. To block Western rearmament programs, the Soviet government regularly condemned NATO and launched a global propaganda campaign calling "for the unconditional abolition of atomic weapons and the branding of any government which first used such weapons against another as guilty of war crimes against humanity." In March 1950, the World Peace Congress, a Soviet-front organization, met in Stockholm and initiated the Stockholm Peace Campaign, which gathered millions of signatures throughout the world in an attempt to mobilize international public opinion against the United States and its deterrent policy based on nuclear weapons. (Moscow's detonation of an atomic bomb in September 1949 was conveniently ignored.) The campaign ran afoul at the outbreak of the Korean War, but it demonstrated the enormous potential of antinuclear campaigns and resistance to rearmament that could be exploited by Soviet propaganda.

After Stalin's death, the Soviet leadership decided on a more conciliatory approach toward the West. This thaw in the Cold War raised expectations in the West for disarmament, though the inadequacy of provisions for international inspection was an insuperable hurdle to agreement. At the fall 1954 session of the UN General Assembly, the Soviet delegate called for the reduction of conventional arms by 50 percent, the establishment of a temporary commission under the Security Council to study methods of controlling nuclear weapons, and an end to their manufacture. These proposals provided a basis for negotiation because they avoided previous Soviet insistence that talks be preceded by the immediate prohibition of nuclear weapons.

On May 10, 1955, the Soviet government presented concrete and detailed proposals calling for a gradual reduction of conventional forces to fixed levels, the destruction of nuclear stockpiles after these levels had been reached, and the establishment of measures to prevent surprise attack. Though recommending the creation of "control posts at the big ports, railway junctions, motor roads, and in airfields . . . to see that no dangerous concentrations of land, air, or naval forces are effected," the Soviet proposals failed to provide for an actual inspection system. Nevertheless, they were important for two reasons. First, they recognized the need to limit nuclear stockpiles and safeguard against surprise attack. Second, they encouraged further discussions. At the Big Four summit conference in Geneva two months later, President Eisenhower responded with his "open skies" proposal, under which each country would carry out aerial photography of the other to detect and thereby to discourage any concentration of military forces that might be used to launch a surprise attack. Moscow was not about to expose the Soviet Union to such detailed intelligence reconnaissance (though within a decade or so the development of space satellites was to provide each superpower with exactly this type of information-gathering capability). During the Suez and Hungarian crises of October–November 1956, the Soviet offer to consider the use of aerial photography in Europe "to a depth of 800 kilometers" on both sides of the NATO–Warsaw Pact line of demarcation was a gambit to discourage Western aggravation of the USSR's troubles in Eastern Europe, since it came at a time when no groundwork had been laid for meaningful negotiations on very complicated security issues.

At the 1957 meetings of the UN Disarmament Subcommittee, the serious participation of Soviet delegates in discussions on arms control raised speculation that Khrushchev needed a respite from the onerous arms burden, that Soviet leaders genuinely feared a nuclear war through inadvertence, and that they wanted to limit the number of powers possessing nuclear weapons, though they could not say this openly for fear of antagonizing China. On the other hand, many Western analysts argued that the Soviet motivation was merely to sow dissension among NATO powers and promote Soviet objectives in Europe.

Speaking to the UN General Assembly in 1959, Premier Khrushchev unveiled his proposal for general and complete disarmament (GCD) — a policy the Soviet government has propounded ever since. While GCD was a chimerical notion that no nation, least of all the Soviet Union, really took seriously, it ushered in a period in which Moscow devoted more attention to partial measures in order to improve its military position and relationship with the United States. In the decade or so preceding the milestone SALT I agreement, Soviet diplomacy in the general field of disarmament sought to narrow the areas of Soviet-American competition in strategic weapons, reduce the danger of accidental war, and ensure the best possible bargaining environment for the USSR by giving particular attention to four broad issues: (1) limiting nuclear testing; (2) protecting against surprise attack; (3) restricting outer space to peaceful purposes; and (4) confining the proliferation of nuclear weapons.

*Limiting nuclear testing.* The Soviet government has been an advocate of a nuclear test ban since it was first proposed by Indian Prime Minister Nehru in 1954. In March 1958, having completed a series of A-bomb explosions, Moscow announced its unilateral renunciation of further tests. (It was aware at the time of the West's intention to do testing during the summer.) However, by October, the Soviet government resumed testing, as military and strategic considerations outweighed the propaganda advantage accruing from advocacy of the ban.

Before March 1958, the United States had rejected proposals calling for a cessation of nuclear tests unless they included a ban on the production of nuclear weapons. Moscow countered with the demand that the *use* of nuclear weapons be outlawed. It also argued that linking a test ban with an end to bomb production was not practical, for while a cessation of tests could be verified, a production cutoff could not. The United States modified its position and agreed to a moratorium on nuclear testing for one year, effective October 31, 1958; this agreement lasted almost three years.

On August 31, 1961, amid mounting tensions over Berlin, Laos, and the Congo, the Soviet government abrogated the informal moratorium without warning and resumed testing in the atmosphere the next day. This was done despite Khrushchev's statement to the Supreme Soviet on January 14, 1960, that the "Soviet Government, prompted by the desire to provide the most favorable conditions for the earliest possible drafting of a treaty on the discontinuance of tests, will abide by its commitment not to resume experimental nuclear blasts in the Soviet Union unless the Western Powers begin testing atomic and hydrogen weapons" (at the time, Khrushchev had found it convenient to ignore France's continued testing). It was also done despite the gathering in Belgrade of the first summit meeting of nonaligned Afro-Asian countries, a group opposed to all testing and the target of intensive Soviet diplomatic attention since the mid-1950s. Khrushchev justified breaking the moratorium on several grounds: the requirements of Soviet security, the inability to agree on a treaty, and the testing by France during the time of the moratorium, allegedly with NATO's blessing. What Khrushchev did not mention was the intense pressure of the Soviet military to test new weapons and catch up to the United States.

After the Cuban missile crisis, the Soviets redoubled their efforts to improve relations with the United States, at the same time that they gave top priority to overcoming their glaring inferiority in strategic weapons. The Treaty Banning Nuclear Weapons Tests in the Atmosphere, in Outer Space, and Under Water was signed in Moscow on August 5, 1963. This was the first concrete result to emerge from post-1945 disarmament negotiations. The treaty does not cover underground testing, ostensibly because of the inability to agree on an acceptable system of on-site inspections but more likely because of the possiblity that seismic instruments would not detect all possible violations and because of the resistance from each country's military establishment, which wants to continue testing of low-yield weapons. The treaty is self-executory: it continues to be operative for as long as each signatory observes it. In the event of a putative violation, "each Party shall in exercising its national sovereignty have the right to withdraw from the treaty."

Why did the Soviet Union sign the limited test ban treaty? Khrushchev said that these considerations were controlling: to end the radioactive contamination of the atmosphere (since 1964 the French and the Chinese have been the gross pollutors), to decrease international tension and pave the way for a settlement of the German problem, to slow down the arms race, to allow greater attention to domestic problems, and to ease the negotiation of an agreement on measures to prevent surprise attack. Four other factors may have been equally important. First was the urgency of improving relations with the United States, dramatized by the Cuban crisis, in order to enable Moscow to concentrate on narrowing the gap in strategic delivery systems. Second, the Soviets realized that further atmospheric testing was not necessary for national security, which could be assured with existing weapons and with expanded underground testing of smaller-yield weapons. Third, the growing rift with Beijing was absorbing Soviet energies. Fourth, the Kremlin hoped that the treaty might help forestall the proliferation of nuclear weapons to other countries, especially to West Germany.

Improved seismological techniques and interest in détente brought significant progress toward a comprehensive nuclear test ban treaty. In 1974, the Soviet Union and the United States signed a treaty (not yet ratified) restricting underground nuclear weapons tests to a maximum of 150 kilotons (the equivalent of 150,000 tons of TNT). Verification is to be by national technical means. The increasingly reliable ways of distinguishing between natural seismic phenomena and weapons testing has nudged the two sides toward a total ban on all nuclear testing, but thus far they have not been willing to bite the bullet, in part because Moscow wants to use nuclear explosions for peaceful purposes and the United States suspects that these would be used to provide data for nuclear warheads.

*Protection against surprise attack.* As the military capability of the superpowers increases, fear of a crippling first strike becomes more intense and justifiable. Safeguards against surprise attack are difficult to build into a treaty. Advances in military technology inevitably give rise to conflicting national assessments of areas of possible compromise; in some instances they make agreement less imperative, in others, even more so. Thus, on the one hand, fear of surprise attack has been allayed by the development of space satellites and high-altitude photography, which enable each superpower to gather reliable information about troop movements, missile placements, and the military testing of the other. These national technical means of verification reduce the need for international inspection. On the other hand, each side fears that the other may make a major technological breakthrough that could abruptly shift the strategic balance of power.

For example, FOBS, MOLs, and laser beams are among the weapons systems with the potential to change the balance. FOBS (fractional orbital bombardment system) refers to a missile with an ICBM capability that can be placed in a very low orbit and release its warhead without leaving the Earth's atmosphere. FOBS allow for even less warning time than ICBMs, are more difficult to detect, and are not technically in violation of the treaty forbidding weapons of mass destruction in outer space. MOLs (manned orbiting laboratories) would give the country able to establish a network of space stations decided military advantages in the event that it decided to stock them with nuclear weapons. Technically this is possible, but that is not to say that it is practical or militarily significant at this time. If one side were to place a large number of weapons in orbit, the other side would probably know, thereby lowering the threshold for preemption or rapid escalation. The development of laser beams for military uses would, of course, usher in the age of Buck Rogers and *Star Wars.*

At the heart of concern over surprise attack is the attention given to preventing misunderstandings in moments of crisis. A pioneering agreement establishing a direct communications link between Moscow and Washington was signed in Geneva on June 20, 1963, and became operational on August 30, 1963. This hot-line teletype link is intended for use only in extreme situations requiring immediate and direct communication between the top political leaders of the two countries. It was used for the first time on June 5, 1967, when the Soviet government wanted to ascertain American intentions in the Arab-Israeli war that had started earlier that day.

Two other agreements designed to lessen the fear of surprise attack and the danger of nuclear war through inadvertence were signed on September 30, 1971. One is intended to prevent overreaction in the case of an accidental launch of a nuclear weapon; it calls on each party to notify the other immediately "in the event of an accidental, unauthorized or any other unexplained incident involving a possible detonation of a nuclear weapon" and for advance notification of planned missile launches "if such launches will extend beyond its national territory in the direction of the other party." The second agreement improves the hot-line service by providing for a direct communications connection via satellite.

*Restricting outer space to peaceful purposes.* In an age when man has walked on the moon, lived in space for months at a time, and launched unmanned probes to Venus, Mars, and Saturn, the military implications of peaceful explorations of outer space are ever present. A decided military advantage would accrue to the nation that constructed missile-mounted space platforms, thus reducing to less than six minutes the time required to hit a target on earth. Through the UN in December 1966, the superpowers joined in signing a treaty prohibiting weapons in outer space, but the space age is still in its infancy, and this kind of agreement is only a preliminary.

The Soviet space program is active, broadly gauged, and heavily supportive of military missions. All Soviet space launches, many with civilian-type missions having military relevance (weather reporting, navigation, communications, geodesy, and mapping), are conducted by the Strategic Rocket Forces branch of the ministry of defense.[10] The development of orbiting space stations is well advanced, as is the ability to man them — in 1979, two Soviet astronauts spent six months, a record, in one. More ominously, in the late 1970s, Soviet experiments seemed directed toward development of an antisatellite interceptor capability: a hunter-killer satellite that would paralyze an adversary's "strategic nervous system" by

destroying its communication and early-warning satellites.[11] If such pred-
ators were outfitted with laser beams, they could destroy satellites thousands of miles away. An accord limiting such antisatellite systems is being
considered.

*Confining the proliferation of nuclear weapons.* Moscow's interest in
limiting the proliferation of nuclear weapons goes back to 1957 and rearmament of the Federal Republic of Germany. In the early 1960s the USSR
assailed the U.S. proposal to provide NATO with a multilateral nuclear
force, which was intended to satisfy Bonn without actually permitting it to
acquire an independent nuclear capability. The entry of China into the
nuclear club in October 1964 and the growing number of countries on the
threshold of acquiring a nuclear capability (India, Israel, Pakistan, Sweden,
and Japan) raised the importance of nonproliferation in Moscow's overall
disarmament policy.

In general, Soviet opposition to the diffusion of nuclear weapons
stemmed from a number of pragmatic considerations involving its perception of national security and strategic interests, such as "a) concern that
further nuclear spread might eventually add Nth-power threats to the
physical security of the Soviet Union; b) concern that proliferation would
undermine the stability of the prevailing U.S.-Soviet nuclear dominance
over the international arena by introducing less nuclear principalities led
by men of questionable responsibility and rationality; c) fears that local use
of nuclear weapons in regional crises might generate enormous escalatory
pressures threatening to enbroil the superpowers in an unwanted nuclear
confrontation."[12]

In 1968 the Soviet Union and the United States cosponsored a UN
resolution that resulted in the 1970 Non-Proliferation Treaty (NPT). The
USSR has looked favorably on the establishment of nuclear-free zones in
regions now lacking nuclear weapons and where regional members agree
not to manufacture, stockpile, or use nuclear weapons (Latin America has
such a treaty). Its ultimate aim, of course, is to see such nuclear abnegation
extend to Western Europe, and especially to West Germany. Its strong
condemnation of certain nonsigners of NPT (notably Israel and Japan) but
not of others (India, for one) indicates that Soviet leaders view the issue
as much in its political as its military context. Though Moscow has "sol-
emnly" promised to assist "any nonnuclear signatory of the treaty who
becomes the victim of aggression or threatened aggression with the use of
nuclear weapons," the treaty remains vague on who decides when and how
to implement the "guarantee" of assistance. In light of Bonn's commitment
to nonproliferation, the issue has for the time being lost some of its former
salience for the USSR.

Another step to curtail nuclear proliferation centered on barring the
"emplanting or emplacing" of nuclear weapons on the ocean floor more

than twelve miles offshore. The issue was originally raised in 1967 by Ambassador Arvid Pardo of Malta, who urged the United Nations to demilitarize the seabed "beyond the limits of present national jurisdiction and to internationalize its resources in the interest of mankind." The superpowers pushed the military aspect but showed little interest in the economic one. On February 11, 1971, the USSR, the United States, and Great Britain signed a treaty prohibiting "any nuclear weapons and launching installations or any other facilities specifically designed for storing, testing, or using such weapons" from the ocean seabed beyond a twelve-mile coastal zone. The treaty does not ban nuclear-armed submarines or the emplacement of submarine detection devices, items that the Soviet Union tried to include but that the United States forestalled because of the difficulties of verification and the military's interest in perfecting anti-submarine defenses.

As adduced from proposals in the UN and official speeches, Soviet priorities in the disarmament field in the coming decade will stress a halt to the manufacture of all nuclear weapons; a comprehensive nuclear test ban treaty; opposition to the development and deployment of the neutron bomb; a treaty to prohibit the stationing of nuclear weapons on the territories where they are not now present; reduction in military budgets; the curbing of nuclear weapons proliferation by tightening existing treaty obligations; the prohibition of chemical and bacteriological weapons; the prohibition of the creation of new types and systems of weapons of mass destruction, such as radiation or infrasonic weapons; reduction of conventional force levels; the creation of zones of peace in the Indian Ocean and other regions; and curbing the arms race.

During the 1970s, while negotiating SALT and the aforementioned varied arms control-related measures, the Soviet Union is estimated to have spent upwards of $100 billion more than the United States on strategic nuclear weapons and delivery systems alone. It now has the strategic parity with the United States and the "equal security" that Brezhnev postulated in June 1971 as a Soviet foreign-policy objective. Yet there is no evidence of any greater readiness to negotiate meaningful arms limitation agreements, though these will be the subject of SALT III talks. The CIA estimates that Soviet military expenditures take approximately 13 percent of Soviet GNP and increase by 4 to 5 percent annually in real terms; other analysts insist these figures are too low. Is the Soviet Union striking for strategic superiority? Does it intend to build a conventional force capability suited to the advancement of global aims, irrespective of possible damage to détente and notwithstanding severe domestic economic difficulties? Moscow proclaims that it is committed to stability and arms limitation, but its behavior bespeaks the opposite; and its military seems to be exerting a disproportionate influence on foreign policy. Despite the statement by

Soviet Chief of the General Staff Marshal Ogarkov in an article in *Pravda* on August 2, 1979, at the time of the U.S. Senate hearings on the SALT II treaty, that the Soviet Union was not building a first-strike capability to destroy U.S. land-based ICBMs, that it was not aiming for strategic superiority, and that Soviet forces were not a "military menace" to the West, Western uneasiness over Soviet intentions remains.

## Trends

Soviet military (and by transference, foreign) policy has been consistently misperceived and misunderstood because it has not conformed to what the West expects it to be. Soviet leaders have acted on a set of assumptions very different from the West's, concerning the meaning of nuclear weapons for foreign policy, the centrality of political aims in military policy, and the kinds of uses to which military power can be harnessed in the pursuit of foreign policy. At least part of the continuing U.S. perplexity over Soviet policy is due to a stubborn unwillingness to draw the necessary implications from the direction that military doctrine and strategic thinking has taken in the Soviet Union and to accept the asymmetries in Soviet and American thinking and policy as intrinsic to the countinuing superpower rivalry.[13]

First, the Soviet Union surprised the United States by its unrelenting drive to overcome strategic inferiority, irrespective of cost, and by the speed with which this was accomplished. In the early 1960s, the U.S. civilian leadership thought that Moscow wanted its own assured destruction capability and would settle for a credible force of 400 to 500 ICBMs and symbolic parity, if only to free resources for the civilian sector of the economy. Consequently, Washington failed to appreciate the Kremlin's profound determination never again to be in the position it was during the Cuban missile crisis and its complete rejection of the political implications that would follow its acceptance of institutionalized inferiority. Undaunted by this misassessment, Washington thought that if it exercised restraint, the USSR would automatically follow suit once it caught up to the United States. Instead, the USSR has kept the momentum of its military buildup, bargaining hard and making concessions only if it has something to gain, that is, if it can effect a trade-off between an incipient U.S. technological advantage and an obsolescing Soviet system.

Second, whereas U.S. strategic and military policy has been formulated by civilian strategists and arms control specialists who have believed that limiting the arms race is essentially a technical, not a political, problem and who have sought strategic stability, not superiority — in 1974, Kissinger expostulated: "What in God's name is the meaning of strategic superiority? What do you do with it?" — the Soviet counterpart developed with the full participation of and significant contributions from professional military officers and with a more conscious effort to tailor military policy to political goals. Inevitably, this resulted in the greater influence of historical factors on Soviet decision-makers — the traditional Russian stress on mass, bigness, and numbers to compensate for weakness and insecurity. Nowhere is this more apparent than in the differing Soviet and American attitudes toward nuclear war.

Soviet military doctrine regards nuclear war as a war that has to be won, like any other. The U.S. position that nuclear war would be a catastrophe for both sides, with no winners and no losers, helps explain its lack of interest in civil defense programs and its willingness to bargain away the ABM chip. The Soviet approach does not mean that Moscow wants a nuclear showdown or expects a nuclear war. But it is frighteningly pragmatic. It assumes that nuclear war is possible and that such a war, if it should come, however horrible to contemplate, "must be survivable and some kind of meaningful victory attainable . . . . Not so to believe would mean that the most basic processes of history, on which Soviet ideology and political legitimacy are founded, could be derailed by the technological works of man and the caprice of an historically doomed opponent." [14] Accordingly, Soviet leaders have invested heavily in civil defense organization and structurally reinforced factories designed to withstand any but direct or near-direct hits, and they have trained the Red Army to cope with nuclear attack. They have also consciously tried to anticipate the problems of preserving the existing social system after a nuclear holocaust.

Third, when SALT began, the United States assumed that the guiding principle would be the preservation of stability through mutual assured destruction (the ability to destroy an "unacceptable" percentage of the adversary's population and industry) and that the aim of the negotiations was strategic stability. That was never the Soviet goal. Soviet leaders have been indifferent to the static, illusory, apolitical concept of stability. They have regarded destabilizing technologies with greater equanimity than the West and sought to exploit them for political ends. They "worry less about the destabilizing effects of rendering land-based ICBM forces vulnerable. Particularly when it is only the American ICBM force that faces the danger, they will take the short view. Better that their ability to take out the largest part possible of American ICBMs remain unimpaired . . . than that the unsettling effects of a counterforce race be precluded . . . . Only when the issue becomes the very survival of the Soviet ICBM force are they likely to accept this [stability] as a pressing matter in SALT." [15]

Fourth, the USSR's overall military buildup has been consistently underestimated. Soviet technological and industrial expertise in the military sphere — whether in developing an atomic or hydrogen bomb, an

ICBM force, land-based silos with a reload capability, MIRVs, enormous quantities of diverse and high-quality conventional weapons from tanks to SAMs, long-range air transport, or the navy's helicopter carriers, missile-firing ships, and roll-off, roll-on merchant vessels — has always surprised Western analysts. Soviet military expenditures as a percentage of GNP have also been consistently underestimated.[16]

Fifth, American leaders have all too often approached negotiations with the Soviets in an intellectually patronizing way, as if they have been assigned the mission of educating Soviet leaders to the dangers of nuclear war and strategic instability. With a far richer experience in safeguarding vital national interests than the civilian strategists who dominated the U.S. establishment in the 1960s and 1970s, the Soviet leadership and general staff was quite able to determine its national interests without an assist from Washington. Throughout the postwar period, Soviet propaganda has denounced the U.S. policy of negotiating from "positions of strength," probably because Moscow fully appreciated just how important it was to be in such a position when negotiating. Soviet leaders know how essential military power has been in preserving their East European empire, discouraging outside interference, obtaining Western acceptance of the division of Europe, and enabling them to compete with the United States in the Third World.

Finally, lacking a grand strategy, the United States has projected onto the Kremlin its own ambivalence and confusion over the relationship between military policy and foreign policy. But there has never been any mirror image in this realm. Moscow has fashioned a functional nexus between the political and military components of its foreign policy, and it is a firm believer in the ability of military power to provide additional foreign-policy options and political advantages. Understanding this central theme of Soviet policy is crucial for future assessments and actions pertaining to the Soviet-U.S. strategic interaction.

# Notes

1. Anton Bebler, "The Armed Forces' Role in Soviet Foreign Policy," *Delo*, March 20, 1976; translated by Zdenko Antic in *Radio Free Europe Research Paper*, RAD Background Report, no. 70 (Yugoslavia), March 25, 1976.

2. Thomas W. Wolfe, *Soviet Power and Europe 1945–1970* (Baltimore: Johns Hopkins University Press, 1970), 33–34.

3. Ibid., 98.

4. Herbert S. Dinerstein, "The Revolution in Soviet Strategic Thinking," *Foreign Affairs*, vol. 36, no. 2 (January 1958), 244–245. See also Harriet Fast Scott

and William F. Scott, *The Armed Forces of the USSR* (Boulder, Colo.: Westview Press, 1979), 39–47. The far-ranging debate on military doctrine drew on many sources, including Henry Kissinger's seminal book, *Nuclear Weapons and Foreign Policy* (New York: Harper and Row, 1957), which was translated into Russian the following year.

5. William T. Lee, "Soviet Military Policy: Objectives and Capabilities," *Air Force Magazine* (March 1979), 55.

6. A fuller discussion is found in Raymond L. Garthoff, "SALT and the Soviet Military," *Problems of Communism,* vol. 24, no. 1 (January-February 1975), 21–24.

7. The literature on this entire complex of problems and their implications for Soviet-American relations is enormous. Those interested in probing these issues in greater depth will have no difficulty finding abundant and readily available material.

8. There is no dearth of literature on Soviet and Warsaw Pact conventional forces. Of particular value in tracing the steady increase in Soviet weaponry is *The Military Balance,* published annually by the highly-respected International Institute of Strategic Studies in London.

9. By contrast, after three weeks of supplying Israel with antitank and surface-to-air missiles and other types of ammunition, the chairman of the U.S. Joint Chiefs of Staff reported that U.S. reserves had been seriously depleted.

10. See Committee on Aeronautical and Space Sciences, U.S. Senate, *Soviet Space Programs, 1971–75,* vol. 1 (Washington, D.C.: USGPO, 1976), 375–402.

11. Herbert Scoville, Jr., and Kosta Tsipis. *Can Space Remain a Peaceful Environment?* (Muscatine, Iowa: Stanley Foundation, 1978). According to American officials, the Soviets tested an antisatellite weapon, apparently unsuccessfully, in early April 1980. *New York Times,* April 19, 1980.

12. Benjamin S. Lambeth, "Nuclear Proliferation and Soviet Arms Control Policy," *Orbis,* vol. 14, no. 2 (Summer 1970), 308.

13. Some recent insightful analyses on which I have drawn are Fritz Ermarth, "Contrasts in American and Soviet Strategic Thought," *International Security,* vol. 3, no. 2 (Fall 1978), 138-155; Colin S. Gray, *The Soviet-American Arms Race* (Lexington, Mass.: Lexington Books, 1976), and "Détente, Arms Control and Strategy: Perspectives on SALT," *American Political Science Review,* vol. 70 (1976), 1242–1256; Robert Legvold, "Strategic 'Doctrine' and SALT: Soviet and American Views," *Survival* (January-February 1979), 8–10; Edward Luttwak, "Why Arms Control Has Failed," *Commentary,* vol. 65, no. 1 (January 1978), 19–28; and Stanley Sienkiewicz, "SALT and Soviet Nuclear Doctrine," *International Security,* vol. 2, no. 4 (Spring 1978), 84–100. For a Soviet perspective, see Radomir Bogdanov and Lev Semeiko, "Soviet Military Might: A Soviet View," *Fortune,* vol. 99, no. 4 (February 26, 1979), 46–47.

14. Ermarth, "Contrasts in American and Soviet Strategic Thought," 144.

15. Legvold, "Strategic 'Doctrine' and SALT," 9.

16. For a detailed treatment, see William T. Lee, *The Estimation of Soviet Defense Expenditures 1955–75: An Unconventional Approach* (New York: Praeger, 1977).

## Selected Bibliography

BERMAN, ROBERT P. *Soviet Air Power in Transition*. Washington, D.C.: Brookings Institution, 1978.

BLOOMFIELD, LINCOLN, WALTER C. CLEMENS, JR., and FRANKLYN GRIFFITHS. *Khrushchev and the Arms Race: Soviet Interests in Arms Control and Disarmament, 1954–1964*. Cambridge: MIT Press, 1966.

BOOTH, KEN. *The Military Instrument in Soviet Foreign Policy 1917–1972*. London: Royal United Services Institute, 1973.

CLEMENS, WALTER C., JR. *The Arms Race and Sino-Soviet Relations*. Stanford: Hoover Institution Press, 1968.

COLLINS, JOHN M. *American and Soviet Military Trends Since the Cuban Missile Crisis*. Washington, D.C.: Center for Strategic and International Studies, Georgetown University, 1978.

——, and ANTHONY H. CORDESMAN. *Imbalance of Power: Shifting U.S.-Soviet Military Strengths*. San Rafael, Calif.: Presidio Press, 1978.

DALLIN, ALEXANDER (ed.). *The Soviet Union and Disarmament: An Appraisal of Soviet Attitudes and Intentions*. New York: Praeger, 1965.

DINERSTEIN, HERBERT S. *War and the Soviet Union*. Rev. ed. New York: Praeger, 1962.

DOUGLASS, JR., JOSEPH D. *Soviet Military Strategy in Europe*. New York: Pergamon Press, 1980.

——, and AMORETTA M. HOEBER. *Soviet Strategy for Nuclear War*. Stanford: Hoover Institution Press, 1979.

ERICKSON, JOHN. *Soviet Military Power*. London: Royal United Services Institute, 1971.

GALLAGHER, MATTHEW, and KARL SPIELMANN. *Soviet Decision-Making for Defense: A Critique of U.S. Perspectives on the Arms Race*. New York: Praeger Publishers, 1975.

GARTHOFF, RAYMOND L. *Soviet Strategy in the Nuclear Age*. New York: Praeger, 1958.

——. *Soviet Military Policy: A Historical Analysis*. New York: Praeger, 1966.

GORSHKOV, ADMIRAL SERGEI G. *Sea Power of the State*. Annapolis, Md.: United States Naval Institute, 1978.

GOURE, LEON, FOY KOHLER, and MOSE HARVEY. *The Role of Nuclear Forces in Current Soviet Strategy*. Coral Gables, Fl.: University of Miami Press, 1974.

HERRICK, ROBERT W. *Soviet Naval Strategy: Fifty Years of Theory and Practice*. Annapolis, Md.: United States Naval Institute, 1968.

HORELICK, ARNOLD L., and MYRON RUSH. *Strategic Power and Soviet Foreign Policy*. Chicago: University of Chicago Press, 1966.

GRAY, COLIN S. *The Soviet-American Arms Race*. Lexington, Mass.: Lexington Books, 1976.

JACOBSEN, C. G. *Soviet Strategy — Soviet Foreign Policy*. Glasgow: Robert Maclehose, 1972.

———. *Soviet Strategic Initiatives: Challenge and Response* New York: Praeger, 1979.

JÖNSSON, CHRISTER. *Soviet Bargaining Behavior: The Nuclear Test Ban Case*. New York: Columbia University Press, 1979.

KINTNER, WILLIAM R., and HARRIET FAST SCOTT (eds.). *The Nuclear Revolution in Soviet Military Affairs*. Norman: University of Oklahoma Press, 1968.

KOLKOWICZ, ROMAN, et al. *The Soviet Union and Arms Control: A Superpower Dilemma*. Baltimore: Johns Hopkins University Press, 1970.

KULISH, V. M. *Military Force and International Relations*. Translated from Russian. Washington, D.C.: Joint Publications Research Service, 1973.

LARSON, THOMAS B. *Disarmament and Soviet Policy, 1964–1968*. Englewood Cliffs, N.J.: Prentice-Hall, 1969.

LEEBAERT, D. (ed.). *Soviet Military Thinking*. London: Allen and Unwin, 1980.

MACKINTOSH, MALCOLM. *Juggernaut: The Russian Forces, 1918–1966*. New York: Macmillan, 1967.

MCCGWIRE, MICHAEL, KEN BOOTH, and JAMES MCDONNELL (eds.). *Soviet Naval Policy: Objectives and Constraints*. New York: Praeger, 1975.

MCCGWIRE, MICHAEL, and JOHN MCDONNELL (eds.). *Soviet Naval Influence: Domestic and Foreign Dimensions*. New York: Praeger, 1977.

NEWHOUSE, JOHN. *Cold Dawn: The Story of SALT*. New York: Holt, Rinehart and Winston, 1973.

NITZE, PAUL H., LEONARD SULLIVAN, JR. and the ATLANTIC COUNCIL WORKING GROUP ON SECURING THE SEAS. *Securing the Seas: The Soviet Naval Challenge and Western Alliance Options*. Boulder, Colo.: Westview Press, 1979.

SCOTT, HARRIET FAST, and WILLIAM F. SCOTT. *The Armed Forces of the USSR*. Boulder, Colo.: Westview Press, 1979.

SOKOLOVSKIY, MARSHAL V. D. (ed.). *Soviet Military Strategy*. 3rd ed. (1968). Translated, annotated, and edited by Harriet Fast Scott. New York: Crane, Russak, 1975.

TALBOTT, STROBE. *Endgame: The Inside Story of SALT II*. New York: Harper and Row, 1979.

WHETTEN, LAWRENCE (ed.). *The Future of Soviet Military Power*. New    ork: Crane, Russak, 1976.

WILLRICH, MASON, and JOHN RHINELANDER (eds.). *SALT: The Moscow Agreements and Beyond*. New York: Free Press, 1974.

WOLFE, THOMAS W. *Soviet Strategy at the Crossroads*. Cambridge: Harvard University Press, 1964.

————. *The SALT Experience*. Boston: Balinger, 1979.

# 9

# Soviet Diplomacy
## in the United Nations

The antecedents of the Soviet attitude toward the United Nations are to be found in the Kremlin's ideological perceptions and diplomatic experience with the League of Nations. The League was created after World War I to preserve an international system based on capitalism and colonialism and epitomized the antithesis of the world revolution and anticolonialism propagated by Soviet and Comintern leaders. Dominated by Britain and France and their visceral fear of communism, it barred the USSR from membership. During the 1920-to-1934 period, Moscow saw it as an instrument of "imperialism" designed to promote the encirclement and eventual destruction of the Soviet state. Lenin called it "a League of bandits." Maxim Litvinov, then deputy foreign minister, termed it "a masked league" engaged in anti-Soviet intrigues. He said the Soviet Union had no desire to be a member, knowing that "it would then be confronted, in the form of partners, or even judges, with states, many of which have not even recognized it, and [which] consequently do not conceal their enmity toward it, and with others, even among those which have recognized it, which even now behaved toward it with ill-concealed hostility."[1]

Expediency, however, dictated accommodation. Global realignments of power prompted the Soviet Union and the Western powers to draw closer together in the face of the common threat from Hitler. When Hitler discarded Rapallo, Stalin could no longer rely on the special relationship with Germany. He turned to France, which was interested in reviving a variation of the pre-1914 Franco-Russian alliance against the threat of a strong and expansionist Germany. To ease the way for the Franco-Soviet rapprochement, which the French believed would be facilitated by Soviet membership, Stalin — who was increasingly concerned also over Japan's military threat in Manchuria and Korea — joined the League of Nations.

On September 18, 1934, in his maiden speech, Foreign Minister Litvinov sought to allay the League's anxieties over the presence of a Marxist-Leninist member in a bourgeois political organization:

> I should like further to state that the idea in itself of an association of nations contains nothing theoretically inacceptable for the Soviet state and its ideology .... The Soviet state has ... never excluded the possibility of some form or other of association with states having a different political and social system, so long as there is no mutual hostility and if it is for the attainment of common aims.*

For the next few years, Litvinov championed the concept of collective security and tried to fashion an effective security arrangement with Britain and France. However, the Western sellout at Munich and Hitler's subsequent readiness (in contrast to Britain and France) to meet Stalin's stiff terms for friendship set in motion the chain of events that resulted in the Nazi-Soviet pact and the outbreak of World War II. The denouement of the Soviet Union's experience in the League came after its invasion of Finland; the League, already an anachronism in a dying era, denounced the USSR's aggression and expelled it from the organization on December 14, 1939.

As World War II drew to a close, the enthusiasm of the Western powers for a new international organization was not shared in Moscow, but Stalin obliged Roosevelt and Churchill once he had secure guarantees for safeguarding Soviet interests. The Soviet Union joined the United Nations as an act of accommodation, not out of conviction. Its aim was to ensure that the League's successor would not become an anti-Soviet alliance; and its participation was predicated on the assumptions that the United Nations would function primarily to handle political and security problems, and that the ultimate responsibility for the maintenance of international peace and security would devolve upon the permanent members of the Security Council, the five great powers: the USSR, the United States, Britain, France, and China. In essence, Stalin envisaged an extension in peacetime of the wartime condominium of the United States, Britain, and the Soviet Union, which would preserve the peace, determine and respect spheres of influence, and settle disputes among themselves at clubby summit meetings. The USSR approved the UN Charter, but only after the inclusion of the veto power in the Security Council and the provision that amendments to the charter would be subject to the approval of the five permanent members.

---

* League of Nations, *Official Journal,* Special Supplement No. 125 (September 1934), p. 67.

Unlike influential private circles in the United States, Soviet leaders never had any illusions about what the UN was and what it was not. They considered the UN *"an inter-state organization, an organization of sovereign independent states":*

> As an inter-state organization, the United Nations does not, and cannot, stand above states; it is not and cannot be a self-sufficient body, independent of states . . . . It is for this reason that no United Nations body, except the Security Council, can take any decisions, binding on all member states of the Organization, on any question except administrative matters and procedural questions.[2]

There was no visionary interest in integration or supranational institutions. Soviet writers denounced all proposals to transform the UN into a world parliament, emphasizing that this would undermine the concept of national sovereignty.

## The Early Years

The Cold War and the polarization of political alignments dominated the period from 1945 to 1953. From the very first session of the Security Council in January 1946, when the USSR was severely criticized for its failure to withdraw Soviet troops from Iran in accordance with the 1942 treaty between Iran, Britain, and the USSR, Moscow felt its isolated minority position in the UN. Its attention was riveted on issues directly affecting Soviet interests. To offset Western "mechanistic voting" majorities, the Soviet government used the veto, which Molotov strongly justified in a speech at the UN on September 14, 1946. He noted that the veto prevents one group of powers from organizing themselves to act against one or another of the five permanent members and that its very existence encourages frank discussions on disputed issues and provides an incentive for concessions and eventual agreement; and he pointed out that unlike the League, which in theory was built on the principle of equality of large and small states, the United Nations institutionalizes a process of ensuring that the interests of the great powers in matters of international peace and security are not ignored.

During the first postwar decade, the USSR exercised the veto eighty times, usually to keep out new members pending a deal with the United States on quid pro quos. The USSR has also used the veto to prevent attempts to interfere in any way with its hegemonial position in Eastern Europe and to assist client states. For example, in December 1971, during the Indo-Pakistani war, it vetoed a resolution calling for a cease-fire and troop withdrawals, because the Indian government, which was favored by Moscow, was not yet interested in halting military operations; and in July 1979, the mere threat of a veto was sufficient to terminate the UN Emergency Force (UNEF) operation in Sinai, a move favored by the anti-Sadat Arab states that Moscow courts. In 1960 Khrushchev himself warned the General Assembly (which at the time was discussing possible revisions of the charter) that "if there is no veto, there will be no international organization; it will fall to pieces."

Stalin's only interest in the United Nations was to ensure that it would not serve an anti-Soviet function or interfere with the realization of Soviet objectives in Eastern Europe. Moscow thwarted all UN efforts to function in that region; it denounced UN reports implicating the Communist governments of Albania, Bulgaria, and Yugoslavia for their role in fueling the Greek civil war, and it refused entry to economic survey missions and investigators of human rights violations. The USSR also tried to keep the UN's authority as circumscribed as possible. It interpreted the concept of national sovereignty to mean the exclusion of any outside interference in the domestic affairs of Soviet-bloc countries.

But consistency is not a strong card in the ongoing international game of weakening the enemy. When the target of interference was non-Communist countries, especially Western-dominated colonial areas, adherence to a narrow interpretation of the charter's provisions on sovereignty and nonintervention in the domestic affairs of member states was supplanted by espousal of the principles of national self-determination and the need to act against "threats to international peace." These principles were given a very broad interpretation by Soviet officials, who wished to align themselves with Third World countries and undermine the overseas empires of the Western powers.

During the Stalin period, the USSR was slow to perceive the advantages of active participation in the UN. Wedded to the two-camp conception of international alignments, Moscow made tactical errors on colonial questions, alienating Indonesia, India, and the Philippines, among others; and its support for the creation of Israel in 1948 alienated the Arabs. A miscalculation with far-reaching consequences occurred in January 1950 when the USSR abruptly walked out of the Security Council, the General Assembly, and the other UN bodies over the question of Chinese representation; Moscow argued that the People's Republic of China, proclaimed on October 1, 1949, and not the Kuomintang regime of Chiang Kai-shek, was the legitimate government of China and should be seated in the Security Council. The USSR announced a boycott of all UN organizations and activities until the PRC's admission was procured. The resultant absence of the Soviet Union at the time of the North Korean aggression on June 25, 1950, enabled the Security Council to pass resolutions calling for the cessation of hostilities, the withdrawal of North Korean forces from South Korea, and the rendering of all possible assistance to South Korea by UN members. No doubt Moscow assumed that the UN, like the League, would take no effective action to repel the aggression; hence its absence from the council. It returned on August 1, 1950, but too late to block the UN's authorization of a police action to "restore international security in the area."

The Western powers, realizing that the Security Council's decisiveness had been possible only because of the absence of the Soviet delegate, used their commanding voting majority in the General Assembly to pass the Uniting for Peace Resolution on November 3, 1950. This stipulates that if, because of the lack of unanimity of its five permanent members, the Security Council fails to act in a situation threatening international peace and security, the General Assembly itself may discuss the problem and recommend appropriate measures, including the use of armed forces. The effect of the American-engineered resolution was a de facto amendment of the charter and an enhanced role for the General Assembly in the sphere of security affairs. The Soviet Union condemned the resolution on the grounds that the Security Council is the sole body responsible under the charter for initiating and implementing measures to preserve the peace, and that the assumption of such authority by the General Assembly was illegal; and that the procedures for amending the charter had been violated. (Ironically, by the 1970s, it was the United States that bitterly criticized the General Assembly's arrogation of powers as unwarranted and contrary to the charter and that objected to interpretations of the charter as too flexible.)

It was during the Korean War that the Soviet leadership came to the realization that participation in the United Nations was important, not just to prevent the UN's being used by the United States as an anti-Soviet instrument, but to establish closer relations with the emerging Afro-Asian group of nonaligned countries, which were neither Western puppets nor necessarily opposed to policies advantageous to Moscow. Moscow perceived that it could actively exploit, not merely thwart, the UN to keep the West on the defensive and strengthen the international position of the Soviet Union.

There were hints of these changed perceptions — and a foreshadowing of the Khrushchev courtship of developing countries — at the nineteenth congress of the CPSU in October 1952. At that time Stalin propounded a sophisticated variant of the two-camp thesis by declaring that war between the Communist and capitalist worlds was less likely than intercapitalist wars, a corollary that paved the way ideologically for Khrushchev's recognition of the importance of the Third World at the twentieth congress in

February 1956. The death of the tyrant brought a new flexibility and activism to Soviet policy in the UN.[3]

## Decolonization

The process of decolonization has now been virtually completed, but in the early postwar years the issue of independence for colonial areas occupied a central place in UN deliberations. From the beginning Moscow staked out a position in the UN debates that placed it in the vanguard of anticolonialism. The USSR did not face any agonizing dilemmas; its imperial system did not include Asian or African territories agitating for independence. Moscow generally applauded the mushrooming national liberation movements, including peoples' wars waged against colonial regimes. But though aware that such struggles weakened its Western rivals, Moscow offered only moral support and rhetorical encouragement during the first postwar decade. That it did not offer tangible assistance can perhaps be explained in part by its absorption with internal reconstruction, consolidation of Soviet rule in Eastern Europe, and an unwillingness to confront American power in areas lying outside the Soviet imperium, and in part by a lack of capability for projecting military power.

Such ambitions as the USSR had in 1945 to become the administering authority for one of the trusteeships that were to be established for former Italian colonies, that is, Libya and Somaliland, were blocked by the United States. But the Soviet Union did join the call in the United Nations for the dismantling of the British, French, Dutch, and Portuguese overseas empires. As India, Burma, Ceylon, Indonesia, and the Philippines became independent, Moscow was ideologically supportive but otherwise passive, precluded by geographical distance, ignorance of local conditions, isolation in the UN, the absence of meaningful contacts with Asian national liberation leaders, and military inferiority from any active role.

By the mid-1950s, when the anticolonial movement assumed an increasingly radical bent, Moscow moved into the Third World, with a view toward hastening the end of Western domination and establishing a permanent Soviet presence. In rapid succession it extended aid to Afghanistan, India, Burma, Egypt, Indonesia, Iraq, and Guinea. In 1960, seventeen new nations — sixteen of them African — became independent and members of the UN. Premier Khrushchev shrewdly seized the moment to propose a declaration (subsequently adopted in modified form as General Assembly Resolution 1514 [XV]) embodying the most radical denunciation of colonialism in all of its aspects and calling for the independence of all colonial countries and peoples. The abstention by the Western powers enhanced the political impact of the Soviet proposal among the African and Asian leaders.

The following year the Soviet Union again laid claim to a bold initiative, proposing the establishment of the Special Committee on the Situation with Regard to the Implementation of the Declaration on the Granting of Independence to Colonial Countries and Peoples (known informally as the Special Committee of Twenty-four) to ensure that Resolution 1514 (XV) was implemented and decolonization brought to a successful completion. Under the weight of its African membership, the committee militantly pressed for independence of the Portuguese colonies (Angola, Mozambique, Guinea-Bissau); and since the mid-1970s, it has zeroed in on South Africa and urged independence for Zimbabwe (Rhodesia) and Namibia, the former German colony of Southwest Africa which was taken over by South Africa after World War I and administered as a possession until the late 1970s, when Pretoria grudgingly acquiesced to Namibia's independence (though the transition is still to be worked out). To the annoyance of the United States and the satisfaction of the Soviet Union, the committee classified Puerto Rico as a colony and condemned the United States, prompting Washington's withdrawal from the committee in January 1971.

The Soviet Union has supported radical Afro-Asian resolutions in the General Assembly (regarding them as recommendations only, albeit ones requiring careful attention, and not as legally binding obligations under international law); but in the Security Council, it shies away from the demands of the militants for military action under the Uniting for Peace Resolution. Thus, in the General Assembly, it cultivates its image as a concerned anticolonialist power, while in the Security Council, it opposes any broadening of UN operational responsibilities or financial levies on member states. Because it had no direct links with Afro-Asian colonial areas and could not bring influence to bear on Britain, France, or Portugal outside the framework of the UN, the USSR used the UN as the forum in which it could directly address itself to the decolonization issue and hope to exert some leverage, if only by exhortation and escalatory, declaratory initiatives. For Moscow, the colonial issue has gone a long way politically.

## Peacekeeping

UN peacekeeping operations have become useful adjuncts of the USSR's efforts on behalf of Third World clients and exploitation of tensions between the Western powers and developing countries. After the combined British, French, and Israeli attack on Egypt at the end of October 1956 and the paralysis of the Security Council because of the British and

French veto, Moscow saw a chance for prospective benefit. Though in principle deploring the General Assembly's allegedly unconstitutional assumption of authority for international security under the Uniting for Peace Resolution, the Soviet Union in practice was not averse to the resolution's application to the 1956 Middle East crisis, and merely abstained when the assembly created the United Nations Emergency Force (though it formally objected to financing the operation by levies assessed on all member states, insisting that the aggressors should bear the costs). UNEF suited Soviet aims: to bring about a withdrawal of British, French, and Israeli forces; to preserve Nasser in power; to weaken the position of Britain and France in the Middle East; and to sow discord in NATO.

At the same time, however, Moscow bitterly opposed the General Assembly's attempted intercession in the Hungarian crisis of November 1956, arguing that the "unrest" was purely an internal matter and came under the domestic jurisdiction of the Hungarian government — despite the presence of 5000 Soviet tanks and 250,000 Soviet troops. In this instance, it invoked Article 2, paragraph 7 of the UN Charter, which says that the United Nations shall not "intervene in matters which are essentially within the domestic jurisdiction of any state" nor shall it "require members to submit such matters to settlement." Eastern Europe was off limits to the United Nations.

In the Congo crisis of mid-1960, the USSR approved the United Nations Peacekeeping Operation in the Congo (ONUC) in order "to ensure the immediate and unconditional withdrawal of the Belgian troops," but soon reversed itself when the possibility of acquiring a foothold in the Congo disappeared. It has not opposed the United Nations Force in Cyprus (UNFICYP), created in March 1964 to keep Greek and Turkish Cypriots separated, in part because the operation has been financed by voluntary contributions, in part because the nonaligned government of Cyprus has favored the peacekeeping operation, and in part because Moscow considers that festering tensions are useful in its attempt to improve relations with Greece and Turkey and weaken NATO's southern flank.

The Soviet position on the financing of peacekeeping operations precipitated a major crisis in the UN in 1964–1965. At issue was the Soviet conception of what should be the outer limits to political and economic commitments by UN organizations. The USSR (as well as France) refused to pay its assessed share of the UNEF and ONUC operations on the ground that they were not legal, having been authorized by the General Assembly and not the Security Council. As mentioned, it maintained that the charter invests the Security Council with the sole responsibility for defining the terms, including the financial terms, under which armed forces may be employed by the UN to maintain international peace and security. To substitute the General Assembly or the UN Secretariat for the

Security Council (and its Military Staff Committee) is to undermine the principle of great-power unanimity that is embodied in the charter and that must be controlling in situations involving the use of armed forces under UN auspices. Moscow dismissed the July 1962 advisory opinion of the International Court of Justice, which ruled that the UNEF and ONUC operations were legitimate expenses of the United Nations and thus subject to the budgetary authority of the General Assembly, as devoid of legal value, since advisory opinions are not binding on the parties. Also, in company with such other countries as France and the Arab nations, the USSR insisted that full responsibility for these operations must be borne by the countries most directly responsible for their having been undertaken by the United Nations.

The financial crisis erupted in late 1964, at the nineteenth session of the General Assembly, when the United States' delegation contended that Article 19 of the charter should be invoked against delinquent countries. Under this article, a nation that falls two years behind in paying its assessments "shall have no vote in the General Assembly." With Moscow threatening to withdraw from the UN — having refused to pay its assessment in the regular UN budget for activities it considered illegal — the General Assembly adjourned in February 1965 without debating the issue. The crisis passed soon thereafter, only because the United States, sensing the reluctance of the membership to implement Article 19, decided not to press the issue. From time to time, Moscow has indicated that it will make a "voluntary contribution" to help ease the UN deficit caused by peacekeeping expenditures, but it has yet to do so. A Special Committee of Thirty-Three nations has been at work since 1964 trying to devise guidelines for organizing, financing, and supervising peacekeeping operations. The Soviets insist on "the principle of the unanimity of the permanent members of the Security Council in taking decisions concerning the preservation of international peace"; moreover, the control of armed forces deployed on the UN's behalf must rest with the Security Council and not with the Secretariat.

Political considerations have determined the USSR's policy on peacekeeping, as developments in the Middle East have shown. In the aftermath of the Suez War of October 1956, UNEF contingents were stationed in Gaza and Sinai and for one decade helped create a situation that allowed the uneasy truce between the Egyptians and the Israelis; but Nasser's summary termination of the UNEF presence on May 18, 1967, set in motion the chain of events that triggered the Arab-Israeli war of June 5–10, 1967. In the wake of the Egyptian defeat and with the approval of the Security Council, the secretary-general assigned UN observers to the Suez Canal zone, but they played a minor role.

After the 1973 October War, the Security Council, with Soviet approval, established two peacekeeping forces to preserve the peace and uphold the interim agreements reached between Israel and Egypt and Israel and Syria: UNEF in Sinai, and the United Nations Disengagement Observer Force (UNDOF) on the Golan Heights. During the 1974-to-1978 period, the USSR went along with a series of six-month extensions because the Arab states wanted them. However, Egyptian President Anwar Sadat's decision to sign a separate peace treaty with Israel on March 26, 1979, polarized the Arab world and precipitated Soviet opposition to a renewal of UNEF, that is, the UN units supervising the gradual Israeli withdrawal from Sinai and safeguarding the peace in that sector. Rather than incur a Soviet veto, Washington accepted the withdrawal of the 4000-man armed force on July 24, 1979, and the substitution of the unarmed United Nations Truce Supervisory Organization (UNTSO), which has operated in different parts of the world since 1949 and which is directly responsible to the Security Council, unlike UNEF.

Just as the USSR's opposition to UNEF's continuation was in deference to the wishes of Arab states which are against Sadat's treaty with Israel, so its support for UNDOF's renewals has been conditioned by the desires of Syria, a prime Soviet client. When the United Nations Force in Lebanon (UNIFIL) was established in March 1978, Moscow went along because Syria favored it as a way of containing Israeli intervention in strife-torn southern Lebanon. Increasingly, the USSR has favored UNIFIL, if only because it restrains the Syrians and lessens the likelihood of a direct confrontation between them and Israel, a situation that would inevitably draw in the USSR.

The Soviet Union's criticisms of peacekeeping operations have been tempered by its objectives in its broader struggle with the United States and its courtship of African and Asian countries. The Soviets oppose any strengthening of UN authority but are adroit in exploiting UN activities that can advance their interests, and they have come to appreciate the advantages inherent in the peacekeeping operations in Cyprus, the Golan Heights, and in Lebanon — none of which they assist financially or materially.

## Global Issues

The growing politicization of the less developed countries (LDCs) and the escalation of their demands for a New International Economic Order (NIEO) have been applauded by the Soviet Union, which sees these pressures weakening the international system long dominated by the Western powers. Yet Moscow's actions on behalf of the LDCs bear little resemblance to its principled declarations. On issue after issue, when push comes to shove, its approach is to safeguard Soviet state interests and refuse to contribute in any significant fashion, arguing that the problems are a legacy of colonialism and imperialism and hence the responsibility of the Western countries. The USSR's approach is best exemplified in its record on the issues of economic development, the law of the sea, environmental protection, and food to the needy.

During the Stalinist period, the Soviet Union did not contribute "one Red ruble" to UN programs designed to promote the development of the new nations. Soviet delegates criticized the West's emphasis on agriculture and light industry and, oblivious of the resource base and immediate needs of developing countries, insisted that only heavy industry could make the countries truly independent. They opposed any kind of direct investment, saying that it led inevitably to political interference, but refused to assist in the creation of a fund that would instead disburse loans and credits, allegedly because the amounts contemplated were inadequate to the task. Nonparticipation in any of the UN economic and technical assistance programs was the policy.

When Stalin died this damaging legacy was ended, and the USSR began to contribute to UN technical assistance programs. It sought thereby to make its bilateral assistance, which it was then dangling before developing countries, respectable and desirable. The Soviet courtship of the LDCs in turn induced Soviet participation in UN activities, though Moscow was more interested in image-building than in nation-building. It opposed the view that aid should be given primarily in the form of grants and insisted that the problem "could not be solved by the creation of a charitable society." Neither the establishment of the Special Fund in 1959 nor the UN Capital Development Fund in 1966 brought forth any generous Soviet response. Moscow's niggardliness reinforced the impression that its small contributions to UN programs was the price it paid to play power politics in the United Nations.

In the 1950s and 1960s, Soviet delegates argued to often sympathetic delegates that "the principal sources of means for the economic development of underdeveloped countries should be their own exploitation of their natural resources and natural wealth." The elites of these countries found the Soviet diagnosis of their economic backwardness plausible, sufficiently familiar in essentials to be readily accepted, and comforting to believe, as it relieved them of any responsibility for their present malaise and instead blamed foreign rule, exploitation of national wealth by foreign monopolies, forced dependence upon a single crop, and lack of industry. However, after two decades of racing on a treadmill, few LDCs today can uncritically accept Soviet exhortations to concentrate on heavy industry, nationalize the multinational corporations, and introduce Soviet-style central planning and control over the economy in order to attain the desired economic takeoff.

In the 1970s, especially after the dazzling success of the OPEC nations in revolutionizing their economic situation, the Group of 77 (as the huge bloc of LDCs in the UN calls itself) hoped to do the same for the less richly endowed Third World countries by pressuring the industrialized nations for more assistance and concessions. It flooded the General Assembly with resolutions for redistributing the world's wealth. In particular, at the United Nations Conference on Trade and Development (UNCTAD), first convened in 1964 and then in 1968, 1972, 1976, and 1979, the LDCs pressed for higher commodity prices, lower tariffs, concessionary loans, more favorable terms of trade, and debt remissions. For all its oft-proclaimed sympathy for their dire plight, the Soviet Union offered little and played an insignificant part in the deliberations. It consistently opposes recommendations for new international funds to be provided by the developed countries, of which it is one.

Nor has Moscow altered its commercial practices. Soviet foreign-trade organizations exact high prices for their products (unless political considerations are controlling, as in dealings with Cuba); they buy primary products at the lowest possible prices and will not increase their purchases — for example, of cocoa, beans, coffee, or fresh produce — to assist the producing countries in disposing of surpluses (and, incidentally, to give Soviet consumers a better choice of food); and Soviet terms of trade are rarely more favorable than those offered by the Western countries. Indeed, as a practitioner of the double standard, the USSR is notorious. For example, in the mid-1970s, it began requiring Western firms to purchase some of the finished goods produced in the factories built by them in the Soviet Union; however, when Moscow helps LDCs (India is a case in point), it resists such "industry-branch" or cooperative arrangements and does not wish to link its production needs to the supplies from Soviet-built factories in Third World countries. In the international economic arena, the Soviet Union is very much the tight-fisted state power vis-à-vis the LDCs, looking out for its own interests; in UN meetings, it throws out the same old line of discussing the problems of LDCs without attaching any new bait.

Examination of another global issue shows that the emergence of the Soviet Union as a major naval and maritime power has had the curious effect of aligning it with the United States against the LDCs on many issues affecting the regulation of the high seas. The necessity of clarifying and modifying traditional practices on such issues as the establishment of the limits of the territorial seas, innocent right of passage, fishing rights, and exploitation of the mineral resources to be found on the seabed prompted the 1958 convening of the United Nations Conference on the Law of the Sea (UNCLOS I); a second conference was held in 1960, and a third, started in 1973, will be reconvened periodically until the major problems are hammered out. All these conferences have put new nails in the coffin of the long-dominant sixteenth- and seventeenth-century notion of freedom of the seas.

At first a vigorous advocate of retaining the traditional freedom of the seas, the Soviet Union has tried unsuccessfully to confine the agenda to narrowly conceived issues. Though claiming twelve miles for its territorial sea since 1927, in opposition to the Western-preferred norm of three miles, it favored the traditional limiting of national jurisdiction over fishing zones. However, as many countries unilaterally extended their territorial waters and claims to exclusive fishing rights in these waters, the USSR followed suit. Thus, on December 10, 1976, the Supreme Soviet extended to two hundred miles the coastal waters limit over which the USSR was prepared to exercise control on all fishing, most likely in response to similar actions by other states, including the United States, which were unwilling to await the final results of UNCLOS III. The move was taken reluctantly, because the Soviet fishing fleet is enormous and ranges from the English Channel to the waters off the Arabian Peninsula to Antarctica, and Moscow would have preferred to avoid the complications of impinging on national jurisdictions. Like the United States, the Soviet Union is adapting to the restraints imposed by increasingly nationalistic governments on previously unfettered fishing rights.

An issue of particular strategic significance on which the superpowers find themselves aligned against radical Third World countries is the right of innocent passage through international straits where the extension of sovereignty to twelve miles offshore (from the present generally practiced three-mile limit) would restrict the free movement of naval ships. However, whereas the USSR advocates a twelve-mile limit for territorial waters, it disputes the extension of the present right of innocent passage through international straits to straits that are situated wholly within the territorial waters of one country — for example in Soviet territorial waters. (The United States favors this extension.) Thus, when "in 1967, the United States sent two coastguard ice-breakers, the *Edisto* and the *Eastwind*, along the Northern Sea Route, outside a line 12 nautical miles from the Soviet Arctic coast, intending them to pass through the Vilkitskogo Straits,"[4] they were turned back at the straits by the Soviets, who contended that these waters are "Historic Bays and Straits" for which no right of innocent passage is held to exist under Soviet law. Though "Soviet law in fact refrains from defining Soviet historic or internal waters — either theoretically or geographically" — Soviet jurists include all the Arctic Seas "in the category of what are called 'historic internal waters.'"[5] The effect is to deny other countries access to the vast Arctic areas north of the Soviet Union and innocent passage through straits located in Soviet waters.

One global issue on which the USSR is sharply at odds with LDCs relates to their proposals for exploitation of the minerals of the seabed lying in international waters. Moscow opposes LDC proposals for creating a supranational authority, under the aegis of the General Assembly, that would be responsible for mining the polymetallic nodules found on the ocean floor and distributing the earnings to needy countries; it has repeatedly cautioned against turning the United Nations into "some kind of philanthropic society."

However, the Soviet government does recognize the need for international cooperation to control pollution of the environment. The oil and industrial wastes in the Caspian and Baltic seas, the depletion of marine life in foreign and international waters that could affect the Soviet diet, which relies heavily on fish it catches there, and the growing toxicity of the atmosphere are but three of the spheres that it acknowledges need attention. Although the USSR had been active in the preparatory meeting of the UN Conference on the Human Environment, it saw fit not to attend the 1972 conference for the political reason that East Germany, not then a member of the UN, had been excluded as a voting member. However, Moscow did go along with the creation of the UN Environment Program in 1973 and contributes to its activities. But the fact is that Soviet officialdom is both skeptical and suspicious of multilateral negotiations for solving problems that do not immediately threaten Soviet interests; Moscow prefers bilateralism.

Though the literature is still relatively scanty, Soviet analysts increasingly write about the emergence of new and complex global problems ranging from energy and raw-materials scarcity to eradication of diseases, from developing the resources of the oceans to regulating communications. They attribute this vast network of problems to the profound political changes in international alignments and attitudes and the multifaceted phenomenon they call the scientific and technological revolution (STR). As they see it, the STR arose out of military needs but now compels qualitative changes in international economic relations and socioeconomic patterns; "a correct grasp of the main features and trends in contemporary economic relations is impossible without due consideration of the powerful impulses flowing from the revolutionary changes in science and technology in the second half of the century."[6] Moscow explains the STR's adverse effects in terms of capitalist cupidity, swollen arms budgets, and waste, and the Soviet leadership has shown little inclination to involve the USSR actively in the UN programs designed to tackle global problems related to them.

The Soviet Union is also indifferent to the global food problem, though in the 1970s it became a major importer of grain. (Whether this is a new development or a temporary phenomenon resulting from unfavorable weather conditions remains to be seen.) Moscow refuses to participate in multilateral efforts to assure food assistance to needy countries; it declined "to participate within the International Wheat Council in negotiations for a new international Food Aid Convention," or to work with the UN Food and Agriculture Organization; and, while a participant in the 1974 World Food Conference in Rome, it "refused to contribute to the single most tangible result of that conference, the $1 billion International Fund for Agricultural Development, which had received pledges of support from both the OECD and the OPEC nations."[7]

## Organizational Issues

With the exception of its expressed hostility to Secretary-General Trygve Lie during the early stages of the Korean War, the USSR paid little attention to the UN Secretariat during the Stalinist period. Until 1960 Moscow assigned few Soviet nationals to the secretariats of international organizations, a reflection of its general depreciation and lack of understanding of the value of such groups in shaping the implementation of policy and gathering intelligence. Not until Khrushchev's troika proposal at the 1960 session of the General Assembly did Moscow begin to assign more of its nationals to a wide range of posts in international organizations.

The failure of the Soviet Union to gain a foothold in the Congo turned Khrushchev against Secretary-General Dag Hammarskjöld, because of his allegedly partisan handling of the ONUC peacekeeping mission. Speaking before the General Assembly on September 23, 1960, the Soviet premier attacked the office of the secretary-general and the entire concept of an impartial international civil service. He proposed replacement of the secretary-general by a three-man directorate representing the three political blocs — Western, Communist, and nonaligned — and justified it on the ground that the UN should reflect the changed alignment of political forces in the world. On another occasion, Khrushchev declared that "while there are neutral countries, there are no neutral men. You would not accept a Communist administrator and I cannot accept a non-Communist administrator. I will never entrust the security of the Soviet Union to any foreigner. We cannot have another Hammarskjöld, no matter where he comes from among the neutral countries."[8] The troika proposal was rejected, because the African and Asian countries saw that it would give the USSR a veto over Secretariat activities with which it disagreed.

Moscow's use of its nationals as intelligence agents in international organizations was confirmed by Arkady N. Shevchenko, the Soviet citizen who was under secretary-general for political and security affairs, when he defected to the West in April 1978. He said that because of the UN, New York had become "the most important base of all Soviet intelligence operations in the world . . . . Soviet intelligence officers have become a Trojan horse behind the wall of the United Nations."[9]

The Soviet Union has usually tailored its position on organizational issues such as membership and accreditation of nongovernmental groups, including national liberation movements such as the Palestine Liberation Organization (PLO), to the sentiments prevailing among its Third World constituents. But exceptions have clearly occurred, as in differences between the USSR and Third World nations over restructuring the composition of international secretariats; Soviet reluctance to expand the membership of the Security Council (from eleven to fifteen) and the Economic and Social Council (from eighteen to twenty-seven) during the decade from 1955 to 1965; and Soviet opposition to increasing the UN budget or expanding the UN's authority in the economic, social, and humanitarian realms.

## Sino-Soviet Interaction

Since the PRC took its place in the United Nations in 1971 — a development Moscow had advocated since 1950, albeit with less conviction after 1961 — the most caustic criticisms of USSR policies have come from its erstwhile ally and Communist neighbor. These attacks are particularly troublesome since as a Communist country, China cannot be dismissed like the Western powers as representative of a socioideological outlook whose demise is foreshadowed by the "correlation of forces" that Moscow sees shifting toward the Communist world. Being both non-Western and underdeveloped, China in addition enjoys a natural link to the Afro-Asian bloc that Moscow courts and seeks to influence, and can in this relationship place a mirror to distinctly unflattering Soviet warts.

Sino-Soviet wrangling in the UN provides a glimpse into the depth of the two countries' differing perceptions, policies, and objectives. How much is tactical and how much is substantive is difficult to say. Whereas the USSR opposes revision of the charter, China insists on the need for fundamental changes that would give the Third World more authority and eliminate superpower domination, especially of the Security Council — though one wonders whether Beijing would really agree to dispense with the veto. Furthermore, Brezhnev's proposal for an Asian collective security system is denounced by Chinese delegates as intended "to control and divide Asian countries and incorporate them gradually into [the Soviet Union's] sphere of influence."* Every Soviet move in Asia is invariably interpreted by the Chinese in the worst and most threatening light.

In addition, China mocks Soviet professions of interest in international cooperation, calling what Moscow actually practices "not internationalism, but great-power chauvinism, national egoism and territorial expansionism." It states that the USSR's aims are imperial and selfish. In its courtship of Third World countries, China seeks to set itself apart from the Soviet Union and the United States, arguing that the two superpowers are not practicing peaceful coexistence, "only a travesty of peaceful coexistence; the substance is coexisting in rivalry." Though castigating both superpowers as obstinate obstacles to the prohibition and destruction of the nuclear weapons that they are "feverishly developing," Beijing increasingly singled out the Soviet Union for the harsher attacks by the end of the 1970s, when Beijing sought better relations with the United States. For example, at the General Assembly's special session on disarmament in May 1978, Foreign Minister Huang Hua averred that "facts show that this superpower flaunting the label of socialism is more aggressive and adventurous than the other superpower; it is the most dangerous source of a new world war and is sure to be its chief instigator."[10] He labeled Soviet proposals for disarmament "illusory bubbles."

China also belittles the USSR's aid to less developed countries and lumps the USSR with the United States as developed, industrialized, rich, selfish. It regards the superpowers as constituting the First World, the Second World being a motley combination of Western Europe and Japan, and the Third World made up of everyone else. This Chinese "three-camp" variation on the Soviet thesis is designed to weaken the Soviet position with the Afro-Asian countries and to broaden the base of its own constituency in the Third World.

Finally, in the initial maneuvering in 1979 over which Kampuchean regime the UN ought to recognize — the ousted, genocidal Pol Pot regime, supported by Beijing, or the Heng Samrin government, brought to office by invading Vietnamese troops and upheld by Moscow — the Chinese demonstrated considerable skill in lobbying support for the unpopular Pol Pot. They mobilized the rebuff to the Soviet-Vietnamese puppet by hammering at a principle widely accepted in the Third World, namely, that there can be no justification for a military invasion to change the political character of a government, no matter how gross the violations of human rights that are to be set right.

The nations of Southeast Asia fear Vietnam more than China. As a result, Moscow's special relationship with Vietnam is held at the expense

---

* *New York Times,* April 15, 1973.

of improved ties with the other countries of the region. For the moment, China is the defender of noninterference in the domestic affairs of member states — the position Moscow had heretofore championed in the Third World. Southeast Asia is not a region of high priority for the Soviet Union, yet China is forcing greater Soviet involvement on conditions that at best have little to offer politically. The discussion in the UN rivets world attention on a complex and political dilemma, in a manner not apt to enhance Soviet prestige abroad. (The full impact on the nonaligned countries of the USSR's invasion of Afghanistan in December 1979 has yet to show its political consequences.)

## Persisting Motifs

Soviet interest in the UN is an outgrowth of the changed environment within the UN in the 1960s, when the membership more than doubled, America's reliable voting majority came to an end, the LDCs developed a heightened radicalism and anti-Western attitudes on a growing number of political and economic issues, and the Soviet bloc's isolation within the organization drew to a close. One Soviet commentator summed up the UN's usefulness for advancing Soviet aims in this way:

> It facilitates to a certain extent the establishment and development of ties and intercourse between states and in this way provides some prerequisites for an extension of international cooperation in various fields — political, economic, social, and others. The consideration of numerous international problems by UN bodies contributes to the clarification of the views of various states on this or that issue, brings the most important international questions to the notice of a broad public and helps to mobilize the progressive forces of various social groups for the preservation and consolidation of peace and for the peaceful settlement of international issues. In certain instances, UN consideration of international disputes has facilitated their settlement in the interests of world peace and security.[11]

The UN is a forum that enables the USSR to present its views and support nonaligned countries in ways that weaken their links to the West and strengthen their ties to the Soviet bloc. In it, anti-Western sentiments are crystallized, and the United States is kept almost continually on the defensive by the barrage of ever-escalating demands for NIEO, disarmament, and so on.

The USSR participates minimally in the developmental and nation-building programs of the UN. It sees the UN primarily as an arena for political struggle, a place where Soviet leaders can proclaim their commitment to peaceful coexistence of different social and political systems, encourage the demands of the LDCs on the capitalist world, and offer their support on issues that polarize alignments or promote Soviet objectives. Courtship of the nonaligned countries, to detach them from the Western camp and offset Chinese inroads, has high priority. Though Moscow makes and upholds proposals that find favor with the LDCs and seeks to place itself in the forefront of movements for change, however, it seldom provides substantive support for any of these proposals. It assuredly is unwilling to relinquish the veto or permit any revision of the charter that might give the UN the status of an incipient world parliament. Khrushchev made the Kremlin's views on this sentiment abundantly clear:

> Suppose the delegates of UN member countries suddenly hit on the 'grand' idea of resolving to abolish the socialist system in the Soviet Union. What would happen if everybody voted for it except ourselves, the representatives of the socialist countries? What would we say to this? We would say what we Russians usually say in such cases: 'Get out!' You took the decision, so live with it; as for us, we will live under our socialist system as we have lived so far. And whoever pokes in his nose — excuse me for the coarse but rather lucid expression — will get a punch in the face! [12]

Conflict, not cooperation, is the dynamic that impels Soviet behavior in international organizations. No issue is too insignificant, no problem too trivial to be exploited if it holds out the promise of a shred of political advantage. The Soviet government is attentive, active, and insistent in safeguarding its national interests and urging on its clients, whether the issue is advocacy of the non-use of force in international relations and the permanent prohibition of the use of nuclear weapons, exclusion of Israel from UNESCO's activities, support for restrictions on the dissemination of news by Western press services — or expulsion of a student UN Assembly from UN buildings because of a mock resolution calling for the ouster of the Ukraine and Byelorussia from the United Nations on the ground that these two republics are an integral part of the USSR and the USSR, like other countries, should have only one vote.

The extensive Soviet politicization of UN proceedings is clearly tactical, not principled, in character. Thus the USSR encourages militant proposals on anticolonialism, but refuses to facilitate their implementation with increased authority, money, or arms for relevant UN bodies (as is evident, for example, in its unwillingness to contribute to the cost of a proposed UN peacekeeping operation that would supervise the peaceful transition of Namibia from South African control to independence). In 1966, when it sought to mobilize world public opinion against United States involvement in Vietnam, it urged the General Assembly's adoption of a Declaration of the Inadmissibility of Intervention in the Domestic Affairs of States; but in August 1968 and December 1979, indifferent to foreign criticism, it militarily intervened in Czechoslovakia and Afghanistan, respectively. Long an advocate for a definition of aggression, in 1953 and 1956 it proposed that the establishment of a blockade (among other things) should be deemed an act of aggression on the part of the initiator of the blockade; but when Nasser announced Egypt's imposition of a blockade of the Straits of Tiran on May 21, 1967, and thereby helped to precipitate the Israeli response of June 5, 1967, the USSR ignored its own criterion and condemned Israel as the aggressor. Moreover, in February 1969 at the UN Special Committee on the Question of Defining Aggression, with cynical disdain for the legal norms it professes to wish to see established, it tabled a new draft definition of aggression that omitted provisions contained in previous Soviet drafts. (For example, dropped was the provision in the 1956 draft that an act of aggression was the sending of military forces "inside the boundaries of another State without the permission of the government of the latter, or the violation of the conditions of such permission, particularly as regards the length of their stay or the extent of the area in which they stay."[13]

In working tirelessly to undermine the Western conception of what the UN should be, the Soviet Union finds a large and receptive constituency among the authoritarian, antidemocratic governments that increasingly dominate the plenary sessions of international organizations. Moscow's constrictive interpretations of Western proposals are not unwelcome among Third World countries, where the U.S. and West European penchant for human rights does not strike a responsive chord, except on a very selective and politically partisan basis. The USSR proclaims the need for safeguarding human rights but pressures the secretary-general to order UN information centers abroad (specifically, the one in Moscow) to stop accepting individual petitions to the United Nations for redress of discriminatory treatment. While a party to international conventions against terrorism, Moscow wants hijacking left to the present discretionary authority of individual governments; furthermore, it shied away from a U.S. proposal for a new convention requiring signatory nations to suspend air services with any country that did not extradite or punish hijackers or terrorists, ostensibly because the imposition of sanctions is the responsibility of the Security Council, but in fact because the LDCs it courts favor making distinctions between terrorism and acts committed by national liberation movements such as the PLO. On the charged issue of regulating direct broadcasting from space satellites, Moscow has sided with many Third World countries in pressing for regulations that prohibit radio and television transmissions via satellite to foreign audiences unless permission is specifically granted by the respective foreign government.

All of these are segments of an overarching Soviet effort to restructure international law and the norms regulating behavior among states. In conjunction with the LDCs, the USSR seems eager to use international organizations to adopt — through consensus of the Soviet-LDC majority and under the banner of "peaceful coexistence" — a body of "progressive" law that would strengthen "socialism" in the world.[14]

Eschewing the negativism of the Stalin period, the USSR has taken to bloc politics in the UN with a vengeance, exploiting voting majorities (as the United States did in the 1945-to-1960 period) to weaken the West and advance Soviet proposals and preferred resolutions. International organizations are battlefields for competing ideas and approaches to concrete issues, and Moscow has decided that the game is worth the effort.

## Notes

1. A statement made to the press, as quoted in Jane Degras, *Soviet Documents on Foreign Policy* vol. II (New York: Oxford University Press, 1952), 66.

2. M. Lvov, "United Nations: Results and Prospects," *International Affairs,* no. 9 (September 1965), 4.

3. Alvin Z. Rubinstein, *The Soviets in International Organizations: Changing Policy Toward Developing Countries, 1953–1963* (Princeton: Princeton University Press, 1964), 31.

4. Elizabeth Young and Viktor Sebek, "Red Seas and Blue Seas: Soviet Uses of Ocean Law," *Survival,* vol. 20, no. 6 (November/December 1978), 256.

5. Ibid.

6. A. Bykov, "The STR and International Relations," *International Affairs,* no. 5 (May 1979), 73.

7. Robert L. Paarlberg, "The Soviet Union and the World Food System" (Paper presented at the annual meeting of the American Association for the Advancement of Slavic Studies, New Haven, Conn., October 1979), 12.

8. Khrushchev's interview with Walter Lippmann, *New York Herald Tribune,* April 17, 1961.

9. *New York Times,* September 25, 1979.

10. *New York Times,* May 30, 1978.

11. A. Vorobyov, "The Tenth Anniversary of the United Nations Organization," *International Affairs,* no. 6 (June 1955), 44.

12. N. S. Khrushchev, *On Peaceful Coexistence* (Moscow: Foreign Languages Publishing House, 1961), 286.

13. Radio Liberty Dispatch, "The New Soviet Definition of Aggression," April 9, 1969.

14. John N. Hazard, review of *Soviet Yearbook of International Law 1975,* in *American Journal of International Law,* vol. 73, no. 2 (April 1979), 319–320.

## Selected Bibliography

BUTLER, WILLIAM E. *The Soviet Union and the Law of the Sea.* Baltimore: Johns Hopkins University Press, 1971.

DALLIN, ALEXANDER. *The Soviet Union at the United Nations.* New York: Praeger, 1962.

GRZYBOWSKI, KAZIMIERZ. *Soviet Public International Law: Doctrines and Diplomatic Practice.* Leyden: Sijthoff, 1970.

HIGGINS, ROSLYN (ed.). *United Nations Peacekeeping, 1946–1967: Documents and Commentary.* Vol. I: *The Middle East.* London: Oxford University Press, 1969.

JACOBSON, HAROLD K. *The USSR and the UN's Economic and Social Activities.* Notre Dame, Ind.: University of Notre Dame Press, 1963.

JAMES, ALAN. *The Politics of Peacekeeping.* New York: Praeger, 1969.

LALL, ARTHUR. *The UN and the Middle East Crisis, 1967.* New York: Columbia University Press, 1968.

LIE, TRYGVE. *In the Cause of Peace.* New York: Macmillan, 1954.

MOROZOV, G. *International Organization: Some Theoretical Problems.* Moscow: Mysl, 1969.

NOGEE, JOSEPH L. *Soviet Policy Towards International Control of Atomic Energy.* Notre Dame, Ind.: University of Notre Dame Press, 1961.

PIRADOV, A. S. *International Space Law.* Moscow: Progress, 1976.

RAMUNDO, BERNARD A. *Peaceful Coexistence: International Law in the Building of Communism.* Baltimore: Johns Hopkins University Press, 1967.

RUBINSTEIN, ALVIN Z. *The Soviets in International Organizations: Changing Policy Toward Developing Countries, 1953–1963.* Princeton, N.J.: Princeton University Press, 1964.

———, and GEORGE GINSBURGS (eds.). *Soviet and American Policies in the United Nations.* New York: New York University Press, 1971.

SLUSSER, ROBERT M., and JAN F. TRISKA. *A Calendar of Soviet Treaties, 1917–1957.* Stanford: Stanford University Press, 1959.

STOESSINGER, JOHN C. *The United Nations and the Superpowers.* 2nd ed. New York: Random House, 1970.

TARACOUZIO, T. A. *The Soviet Union and International Law.* New York: Macmillan, 1935.

WALTERS, F. P. *A History of the League of Nations.* New York: Oxford University Press, 1960.

# 10
# Moscow's Forward Policy in the Third World

The emergence of the Soviet Union as a superpower was marked by its shift from a continental-based strategy to a global one. This development, a function as much of military capability as of diplomatic opportunity, is most evident in the USSR's penetration of the Third World. It is in this arena, made up of two-thirds of the world's nations, that the Soviet Union engages the United States in a low-cost, relatively low-risk, highly intensive pattern of classical imperial competition.

For reasons that have become more rather than less compelling in an age of nuclear stalemate, the regions of the Third World have taken on special importance for Soviet strategists. Whereas Europe and the Far East have relatively stable political and military constellations that coincide generally with established territorial boundaries and spheres of influence shielded by security agreements, Southern Asia, the Middle East, and sub-Saharan Africa are characterized by transient alliances and systemic instability and so have attracted superpower attention and rivalry. Gains or setbacks in these areas of contention are not likely to have a significant effect on the fundamental balance of power in the short run. Yet the implications for the long term are enormous; and for ideological and strategic reasons, Moscow considers the prizes worth the effort and the possible jeopardy to the Soviet-American relationship.

## Lenin's Theory of Imperialism Lives On

Third World countries have long occupied an important place in Soviet ideological formulations and long-term projections. The essentials upon which Soviet strategy is predicated were set forth first by Lenin in his

214

theory of imperialism: a belief that capitalist countries, impelled by their economic and government systems to seek cheap sources of raw materials and labor as well as outlets for their surplus production and capital, expanded into Africa, Asia, the Middle East, and Latin America in order to stave off their own decay and disintegration; and that this expansionistic compulsion bred wars among capitalist countries which were competing for choice colonies and markets. Originally published in Switzerland in 1916, Lenin's *Imperialism: The Highest Stage of Capitalism* attempted to extend Marx's concept of the class struggle from the domestic to the international arena and to show thereby that World War I had stemmed from the avarice of monopoly capital and the big financial interests. Whereas Marx predicted that the downfall of capitalism would be brought about by the proletariat of the industrialized nations, Lenin's thesis was that this process could be hastened and the capitalist countries could be undermined and eventually toppled by detaching the colonies from the control of the capitalist rulers — that "the road to Paris and London lies through Calcutta and Bombay," as an apt phrase erroneously attributed to Lenin says.

Lenin, the revolutionary, advocated national self-determination. As a concept meaning the political freedom of a people to establish and to function as an independent nation, national self-determination had but a brief and almost exclusively tactical significance in Russia during the period of War Communism, when some non-Russian peoples took advantage of the Bolsheviks' weakness to gain their independence. Once secure in power, the Bolsheviks interpreted national self-determination in such a way as to preclude any further secessions from the Soviet Union. However, *outside* of the Soviet Union, the concept has been used to portray the Soviet Union as a champion of the liberation of all peoples from colonial rule and as an opponent of imperialism.

In the early years, the Soviets were engrossed with survival in European Russia, but as the situation stabilized, Lenin shrewdly perceived that the East could be used to improve Russia's military and political situation. Accordingly, he assigned colonial areas a more significant role in Soviet strategy. In July 1920, at the second Comintern congress, Lenin's "Preliminary Draft of Theses on the National and Colonial Questions" stressed the division of the world into oppressing and oppressed nations and enjoined the Comintern to promote the alliance between the proletariat of the advanced industrialized countries and the peoples of the economically backward colonial areas. As natural allies, the two would work toward the defeat of capitalism, the proletariat by weakening imperialist power at its home base and the colonial peoples by driving out the European rulers and thereby creating social and economic unrest in their home bases. Lenin acknowledged that nationalist movements in colonial areas would usually have a bourgeois character initially. Nevertheless, he endorsed temporary cooperation with them, provided that the Communist movement, however rudimentary, maintained its sense of identity and independence of action. (The first Soviet experiment with such a coalition was in China in the 1923-to-1927 period and had disastrous results.) Lenin also stressed the need "to fight against the clergy" and against "Pan-Islamism and similar tendencies which strive to combine the liberation movement against European and American imperialism with the strengthening of the positions of the Khans, the landlords, the mullahs, etc." *

During the period from 1931 to 1945, Stalin had little time for the colonial question. Because of growing threats from Japan and Germany, he needed to cultivate closer relations with the colonial countries and was hence quite circumspect about Comintern activities in the British and French colonies. Moreover, except for flurries of attention to Turkey, Afghanistan, India, and Indonesia, the Kremlin was in no position to engage in any independent foreign policy beyond the immediate confines of its security sphere. Even after 1945, when the Cold War chilled the relations of the former allies, Stalin's priorities — the reconstruction of a nation devastated by war, the consolidation of Soviet rule over Eastern Europe, the rivalry with the United States over Germany, the challenge of the Titoist heresy, the adaptation required by the triumph of the Communists on the Chinese mainland, and the Korean War — still kept the Soviet purview localized.

Whether it was through ineptitude or inadvertence, Moscow's application of the Zhdanov line (the unremitting hostility to the West and capitalism proclaimed at the founding conference of the Cominform in September 1947) to newly independent India, Burma, Indonesia, and the Philippines spelled disaster for almost a decade. It resulted in the decimation of local Communist parties, whose abortive coups against the infant bourgeois nationalist governments isolated them from the mainstream of indigenous national liberation movements, and in the increased suspicion of the Soviet Union among Third World countries and elites. After 1945, Stalin's policy made the Middle East also a wasteland for Soviet diplomacy. Relations with Iran and Turkey were severely strained as a consequence of his attempt to force Iran to accept puppet status and to blackmail Turkey into granting concessions on the straits that would have preluded its becoming a Soviet satellite. In addition, Moscow's support for the partition of Palestine and the creation of the state of Israel alienated the Arab world.

Stalin's death came at a time when a series of imperatives demanded

---

* V. I. Lenin, *Sochinenia,* Vol. XXXI (Institute of Marx-Engels-Lenin, 1950, 4th ed.), pp. 123–27, excerpts.

far-reaching changes in Soviet society and foreign policy. Had Stalin lived for another decade he might well have implemented some of the innovations introduced by his successors; at the 1952 party congress, for example, hints that war between capitalism and communism was not inevitable and that war between capitalist countries was more probable were already discernible. However, there is no gainsaying that Stalin's demise enabled the new Soviet leaders to move more rapidly at home and abroad.

The Leninist legacy of exploiting the Third World to advance Soviet security and strategic interests found a kindred heir in the ideological revisions of Khrushchev. Starting from the fundamental Leninist assumptions concerning the vulnerability of the Western capitalist countries to pressure from colonial and developing areas, the universal urge of national liberation movements toward independence from their colonial rulers, the irresistible attraction to capitalists of the markets and resources of the Third World, and the inevitability of competition among capitalist countries and groups, Khrushchev modernized Marxist-Leninist thought on Third World developments and gave it an optimism characteristic of his own nature. He substantially modified Stalin's two-camp thesis and, at the twentieth congress of the CPSU in February 1956, proclaimed the existence and growing role of a "zone of peace," which gave ideological recognition to the independent role in world affairs of the former African and Asian colonies that Moscow had already begun to appreciate. Khrushchev also revised Lenin's thesis that the contradictions arising out of the rivalry for the spoils of colonial expansion would drive the capitalist nations to war, maintaining instead that decolonization and the disintegration of Western overseas empires had gone too far to be reversed and that the "camp of socialism" acted as a restraint on old-fashioned imperialism. Therefore, he said, in order to preserve their foothold in the Third World, the Western powers now cooperate through multinational corporations and various associations whose intent is to disguise neocolonialism, that is, the preservation of Western influence through economic leverage. On February 26, 1960, during a visit to Indonesia, Khrushchev coined the phrase "collective colonialism" to describe the process.

Khrushchev also devised an ideological justification for differentiating among developing countries and for offering assistance to some non-Communist developing countries but not to others. The concept of the national democratic state was originally advanced at the November 1960 Moscow Conference of Communist and Workers' Parties and later modified in the party program adopted at the twenty-second congress of the CPSU in late 1961. It referred to radically oriented non-Communist developing countries that adhere to nonalignment in world affairs, adopt anti-Western foreign policies, and pursue domestic programs aimed at building socialism through a "noncapitalist path of development." These national democracies are promising candidates for eventual transition to the status of people's democracies. The "national democratic state" is seen as a stage in the consolidation of the anti-imperialist, antifeudal, democratic revolution, as a temporary, transitional form for developing countries desiring to move toward socialism. In 1963, a refinement, the "revolutionary democratic state," was added — apparently to distinguish the radical Third World regimes that implemented many of the programmatic demands of the local Communist party and tolerated its active functioning from the ones that persecuted Communists.

Khrushchev's effort to devise ideological typologies for categorizing developing countries according to their pro-Soviet affinities was not continued by Brezhnev, who is generally less interested in doctrinal exegesis. But if Soviet writings and offical pronouncements contain any clue at all to understanding the leadership's perception of Third World developments, it is the bedrock belief in Lenin's theory of imperialism. This, coupled with the pervasive optimism that says that world trends favor the advance of socialism, is evident in Soviet explanations of Third World alignments, policies, and developments. It may not be the entire truth behind Moscow's way of seeing and responding to reality, but it provides the Soviets with an outlook, a way of organizing and weighing the importance of events, and a useful road map for traversing the changing international system. Whether it be the Congo in 1960, Cuba and the Bay of Pigs in 1961, Chile in 1973, Zimbabwe/Rhodesia and southern Africa or the Persian Gulf currently, Soviet assessments of key Third World developments are Leninism made modern. In recent decades, firsthand experience with the Third World has dictated modifications of Lenin's theory of imperialism, in conformity with the historical forces at work there, but always within its overall framework.

## Strategic Impetus for the Forward Policy

A combination of strategic, political, ideological, and marginally economic considerations ushered in Moscow's "forward policy" in the Third World. Ironically, it was Washington's deterrent policy during the pre-missile age when U.S. nuclear superiority was paramount that facilitated the USSR's entry into and courtship of Third World countries. The Soviet leadership perceived the U.S. defense strategy of ringing the Soviet Union with military and refueling bases in neighboring states in order to enhance the nuclear strike effectiveness of the Strategic Air Command's long-range bomber force as a threat to their national security; even more important, the polarization this engendered ran counter to the thrust of the forces of nationalism and nonalignment in the Third World, which aimed at discard-

The USSR and the Afro-Asian World

ing all traces of former Western overlordship and at steering an independent course in world affairs.

It was in the interest of Soviet leaders to eliminate, or at least neutralize, the U.S. military presence in the countries lying south of the USSR and to end the intelligence flights over the Soviet heartland. Accordingly, starting in 1954 with Afghanistan, they gave varying degrees of encouragement to the policies of Third World elites who found military alliance with Western countries difficult to sustain domestically and who therefore opted for foreign policies ranging from coolness to outright hostility toward the West. Politically, these overtures were intended to dispel the suspicion of the Kremlin that was inherent in the attitudes of many of the ruling elites in less developed countries. Some of this anti-Communist sentiment derived from the Western European education of the elites, but a deep animus against communism also existed in Muslim countries, and Southern Asia clearly remembered Communist attempts at armed revolution in the late 1940s.

Notwithstanding this legacy from the Stalinist period, Moscow's proclaimed anticolonialism, its expert application of olive branch and checkbook, and its shrewd diplomatic maneuvering began to show results; in 1955 readiness to build a major steel-producing plant in India and the arms deal with Egypt heralded a stunning diplomatic breakthrough. In UN forums and through bilateral relationships, Moscow encouraged the nationalization of key industries and resources, heavy public-sector investment, and central economic planning, stressing the relevance for developing countries of its own experience with modernization and economic development. All of this had a favorable impact upon socialistically inclined elites, at least during the early years of courtship by the "new" Soviet Union.

Proceeding on the age-old dictum "The enemy of my enemy is my friend," Moscow courted those regional actors who were most opposed to the U.S. policy of global containment, which led to the pressing of military pacts everywhere in the Third World, often in countries that were not directly threatened by Soviet attack and that agreed only in order to obtain U.S. weapons for possible use against local rivals. In 1955 India and Egypt were the two most likely targets of Soviet attention: India opposed the U.S.-organized SEATO (Southeast Asia Treaty Organization) pact, which provided military assistance to Pakistan, India's regional archrival; and Egypt opposed the Baghdad pact, whose only Arab member was Iraq, Egypt's principal competitor for leadership in the Arab world. The result of the U.S. "pactitis" was to polarize regional conflicts and give Moscow an incentive for discarding its outmoded ideological baggage from the Stalin era.

Two purposes initially underlay the emerging Soviet courtship of key Third World countries: to undermine the Western system of alliances and international economic order, and to establish a political and economic presence in areas that had previously been outside the realm of Soviet capabilities. In the 1960s two other broad purposes emerged: to offset the Chinese challenge for leadership in the Communist world; and to acquire naval and air bases that would provision the USSR's blue-water fleet, keep close tabs on and counteract U.S. forces operating in strategically important areas, protect clients threatened by their pro-Western rivals, and enable Moscow to project military power more expeditiously into politically promising situations.

## Southern Asia

The shift in Soviet policy toward India may be dated from September 1953, when the Kremlin appointed a personable ambassador who immediately initiated discussions aimed at closer economic relations. The first success was a dramatic agreement, signed on February 2, 1955, under which the Soviet government undertook to finance and construct a million-ton steel plant in the public sector in the Bhilai region of central India. By the time of the visit of Party Secretary Khrushchev and Premier Nikolai Bulganin in December 1955, Soviet-Indian friendship had become important for both countries. For the Soviet Union, it meant a link with the region's leading power and nonaligned country and a safeguard against India's membership in any anti-Soviet military alliance; it offered a showcase for Soviet assistance — a demonstration to the new nations of the tangible benefits to be derived from improved relations with the USSR; it brought the USSR respectability right at the takeoff stage of its courtship of African and Asian nations; and it served as a marked contrast to the military-minded, Cold War-oriented policy of the United States. For India, the relationship served as a potentially significant counterpart to U.S. support for Pakistan. It brought much-needed investment for public-sector industries, which the United States was ideologically leery of supporting, and it led quickly to Moscow's support in the United Nations for India's position on Kashmir. Furthermore, it enhanced India's prestige in the Third World. Moscow's penetration of the "zone of peace" was off to an impressive start. Similar agreements with other nonaligned countries were concluded in the decades that followed.

Under Khrushchev, the USSR sided with India in its dispute with Pakistan. It upheld India's policy of nonalignment and opposition to U.S. military alliances in the area, to Western colonialism in Africa, and to U.S. involvement in Vietnam. During the Goa affair of December 1961, the Soviet Union alone among the great powers fully upheld India's use of force to liquidate the Portuguese enclave on its west coast. Moscow's judicious neutrality on the Sino-Indian border dispute was especially appreciated.

However, when China attacked India in October 1962, Moscow uncomfortably straddled the fence; it was unwilling to condemn its Communist ally and thereby foreclose all possibility of a reconciliation, yet it wanted to retain its expensively cultivated stake in Asia's leading nonaligned nation. Luckily for the Soviets, the Chinese did not press their advantage, and the Western powers came to India's defense with military assistance. The crisis passed, and Moscow reingratiated itself with offers of MiG fighter aircraft, SAMs (surface-to-air missiles), warships, and other military equipment. In 1964 Khrushchev agreed to sell India a factory for producing MiGs, on license; Brezhnev reaffirmed this commitment with ancillary agreements. Though most of the MiG-21 is manufactured and assembled in Indian plants — the engines are produced at Korapur in Orissa state, the electronic components in Hyderabad, and air frames at Nasik, a hundred miles northeast of Bombay — Moscow provides some crucial equipment, no doubt to enhance its political leverage. The first MiGs built in India were delivered to the air force in the early 1970s.

During the undeclared war that erupted between India and Pakistan in September 1965, Moscow was instrumental in persuading the two disputants to cease hostilities and sign the Tashkent declaration of January 1966. This was the first time that the USSR had played the role of peacemaker in a Third World conflict. Its aims were to prevent China's involvement in the region and to improve relations with Pakistan as well as with India. The Soviets' longer-range goal in drawing closer to Pakistan and encouraging a gradual normalization of relations between India and Pakistan was to realize their dream of a land route that would link Soviet Central Asia to India via Afghanistan and the Khyber Pass and enormously expand their economic penetration of the subcontinent. A more prominent Soviet role on the subcontinent would thwart China and provide greater support for Soviet naval activities in the Indian Ocean and Arabian Sea. Coincidentally, between June 1967 and June 1975, the land route to India partially offset the inconveniences and expenses incurred by the closure of the Suez Canal.

Soviet prestige in India soared on August 9, 1971, with the signing of a twenty-year Soviet-Indian treaty of friendship and cooperation, which India wanted as a deterrent to possible Chinese intervention on behalf of Pakistan. India's need for the treaty had arisen five months earlier out of the Pakistani government's suppression of the separatist movement in East Pakistan. As millions of refugees fled to India, tensions built up, exploding into war in December 1971. The treaty proved its worth: China stayed out, limiting itself to diplomatic support of Pakistan, while India, well supplied with Soviet weapons, crushed Pakistani forces. In the UN Security Council, the Soviet Union vetoed all resolutions calling for an immediate cease-fire, thus enabling India to complete its military campaign in East Pakistan and help create the independent nation of Bangladesh in its stead.

But prestige is not tantamount to influence; nor can it necessarily be translated into secure military advantage, as Moscow discovered again in its relations with Egypt and Iraq, both of which also signed friendship treaties with Moscow, in May 1971 and April 1972, respectively. These treaties which loom so prominently in Western assessments of the putative Soviet stranglehold on Third World countries *must* be analyzed in the context of the domestic political situation of the courted countries. Otherwise, it is impossible to appreciate the extent to which the Soviets, far from ensnaring the client, were themselves ensnared by the native leadership for internal or regional political reasons. The answer to the question, "Who is influencing whom?" does not lie in the uncritical assumption that the USSR is always, or even usually, in command of events when it is dealing with a Third World country. India's use of its treaty with the USSR to humble and partition Pakistan and become the undisputed dominant power on the subcontinent was a development Moscow had not foreseen. Neither had Moscow anticipated that lessened military dependence on the Soviet Union would result in New Delhi's feeling no compulsion to respond to repeated Soviet allusions to desired naval privileges at Visakhapatnam, a major port on India's southeastern coast.

The Soviet Union did everything to foster intimate ties. For example, in 1973 it signed a fifteen-year economic accord on terms advantageous to India and lent India two million tons of wheat; it put two scientific space satellites in orbit for India and agreed to make the countries' five-year economic plans complementary. In late 1976, when oil was difficult to obtain at prices India could afford, Moscow proposed a barter deal on favorable conditions, and it offered a $450 million credit in September 1976 to enable India to expand steel-making capacity in the public sector. Soviet-Indian relations remained close under Prime Minister Indira Gandhi (1966 to March 1977), but Moscow did not receive what it really wanted: naval facilities for its Indian Ocean flotilla; support for Brezhnev's plan, floated in June 1969, for an Asian collective security system; and a special relationship that would keep India at a distance from China. Brezhnev had to settle for Mrs. Gandhi's understanding attitude toward the Soviet invasion of Czechoslovakia, criticism of U.S. policy in Vietnam and the Middle East, and general support on issues that were of little direct interest to India, such as SALT, Berlin, and CSCE. The USSR did not obtain the privileged strategic foothold it coveted.

Under the Janata coalition government, which took office after defeating Mrs. Gandhi in March 1977, India looked increasingly to the West for economic assistance. (By the late 1970s, taking into account debt repayments, Soviet net economic aid to India was less than $50 million a year; the Western aid consortium provided ten to twenty times more assistance.) New Delhi normalized its relations with Beijing in 1977 and was unwilling to condemn China's attack against Vietnam in February 1979. In January 1980, Mrs. Gandhi returned to power in a stunning electoral triumph. Moscow moved to strengthen Soviet-Indian ties, exploiting Mrs. Gandhi's coolness toward the United States and negotiating a huge $1.6 billion arms deal on terms extremely favorable to India. The USSR clearly seeks to nurture friendly relations with India and the other nations of the subcontinent, but it has no illusions about the difficulties it may encounter in its quest for military bases or political influence.

A different set of priorities shaped Moscow's policy toward Vietnam. America's major intervention after 1964 prompted extensive Soviet economic and military assistance to enable Hanoi to prosecute its war: aid rose from approximately $40 million in 1964 to almost $1 billion annually from 1967 to 1972. At stake was not only Soviet credibility as an ally and Soviet rivalry with China for influence among Asian Communists, but a desire to embroil the United States in a quagmire that would reduce its capacity for decisive action in areas of greater concern to the USSR.

Soviet aims in Vietnam were ambivalent in the years after 1945, when Stalin refused to support Ho Chi Minh's bid for Vietnamese independence in order to avoid antagonizing France and compromising the strong position of the French Communist party. Moscow established diplomatic relations with Ho Chi Minh's Democratic Republic of Vietnam (DRV) on January 30, 1950, soon after the Communist triumph in China, but gave Hanoi little attention or aid. It served as cochairman of the 1954 Geneva Conference, which formally ended French rule in Indochina and recognized the two Vietnams, but despite a limited involvement in the 1961 Laotian crisis, Moscow did not urge intensification of "wars of national liberation" by Vietnam; it regarded Vietnam as a sideshow and did not want a Communist insurgency in Laos or Cambodia to hamper its efforts to improve relations with Indonesia, Burma, India, Malaysia, Thailand, and Ceylon. However, Ho Chi Minh had his own ambitions, which inexorably drew Moscow into the Vietnam conflict, as much because of its rivalry with China as because of that with the United States.

In the early stages of the American military escalation in 1965, Soviet leaders may have been concerned over the United States' intentions, the DRV's capability, and China's response. But the ineffectiveness and cost of American policy soon revealed unanticipated benefits for Moscow. Nurtured by Soviet propaganda, anti-Americanism rose sharply in the Third World and Western Europe. Domestic strife intensified in the United States and bred an incipient neoisolationism. America's economy was beset by serious inflation and a growing deficit in the international balance of payments, leading to a de facto devaluation of the dollar in August 1971. All of this exacerbated strains in the Western alliance and reinforced American domestic pressures for a retrenchment of foreign-policy commitments. U.S. military power was squandered in a war that the United States could not win and that was strategically peripheral to the global superpower rivalry.

During the late 1960s and early 1970s, both Moscow and Beijing, though increasingly at odds on a wide range of issues, lent support to Vietnam. For its part, Hanoi sought to preserve an essential neutrality on the Sino-Soviet dispute. It benefited from the rivalry that impelled each party to accede to Hanoi's requests lest it be labeled defeatist and seem overly concerned about the United States. In 1972, when both Moscow and Beijing were courting Washington — the USSR in order to reach an agreement on SALT I and promote détente in Europe, and China in order to have the Nixon visit lead to diplomatic normalization — they still met the DRV's economic and military needs. Neither Communist power was willing to pressure Hanoi to agree to a negotiated settlement, even in the interests of better relations with the United States.

Hanoi's victory in 1975 brought Moscow new problems. Now a unified nation of more than fifty million people, Vietnam has expanded into Laos and Kampuchea. Moscow's support of this expansionism has made the other nations of Southeast Asia leery of Soviet overtures for closer ties, which are intended to offset China's diplomatic efforts in the region.

Vietnam's economic and military reliance on the Soviet Union has become even more pronounced since 1975 because of Vietnam's deteriorating relationship with China and erratic progress toward normalization with the United States: in December 1975, Le Duan, the general secretary of the Vietnamese Communist party (Ho Chi Minh died in 1969) signed a long-term economic agreement with the USSR; in June 1978, Vietnam joined Comecon as a full member; and on November 3, 1978, the USSR and Vietnam signed a twenty-five-year treaty of friendship and cooperation. Although not a formal military alliance, the treaty calls for mutual consultations in the event of a military threat — an obvious allusion to China. For Moscow, the treaty represented a step toward the containment of China and possible military privileges at the Cam Ranh Bay naval base. When Vietnam overthrew the pro-Beijing Pol Pot regime in Kampuchea in January 1979, it could count on the USSR's support. During the Chinese attack against Vietnam the following month, Moscow warned

Beijing not to press its incursions to the breaking point; Chinese troops pulled back, with the Moscow-Hanoi treaty still untested. The Sino-Soviet rivalry seems likely to intensify in Southeast Asia in the years ahead.

## The Middle East: Iran and Turkey

The importance of the Middle East needs no elaboration. Geographically, it is the land bridge linking Europe to Africa and Asia; strategically, it commands key air routes and maritime communications and lies south of the soft underbelly of the USSR; economically, it possesses vast amounts of oil, the critical energy resource of the next generation; and politically, as a region experiencing simultaneous political, social, and economic change and rivalry, it suffers from the systemic instability that attracts superpower involvement.

Russian interest in the non-Arab Muslim areas of the Middle East goes back several centuries to czarist wars and expansion at the expense of the former Ottoman and Persian empires. In this century, during the 1917-to-1945 period, the Soviet Union lacked the strength or opportunity to play an important role in the Middle East, and after World War II, Stalin failed in his efforts to wrest strategic concessions from Turkey and Iran or to acquire a UN trusteeship over Tripolitania (Libya). He did indirectly affect developments in the Arab east, however, by supporting the United Nations' partition of Palestine in November 1947 and by recognizing Israel in 1948 in order to weaken the British position in the area. Indeed, even though 1948–1949 was a period of virulent anti-Semitism in the Soviet Union, Stalin's sanction for the sale of Czech arms to Israel at that critical time was a crucial factor in the survival of the infant Israeli nation. But aside from this, during the Stalinist period, Moscow was a sideline observer of the political controversies plaguing the Middle East.

In 1953 the change of leadership in the Kremlin brought with it a readiness to chart new approaches to improve the USSR's security and strategic position in the Middle East. Geographical contiguity mandated special attention to improving relations with Muslim Turkey, Iran, and Afghanistan. This courtship started slowly but was pursued consistently. By promoting economic ties and avoiding rocket-rattling, Moscow sought to induce Turkey and Iran, both military allies of the United States, to diminish their military commitments to the U.S. policy of containing the USSR.

Soviet-Iranian relations, poor between 1945 and 1961, improved gradually after 1962, when the shah announced that no United States military bases or missile sites would be permitted on Iranian territory. Although Iran was a member of the pro-Western CENTO military pact, she did not keep a large military force along the Soviet-Iranian border, a fact that made her participation in CENTO tolerable to Moscow and played an important role in the Soviet-Iranian rapprochement. Economic ties expanded significantly. The USSR built a major steel plant and various industrial projects; in return, it received natural gas and oil. Increasingly the government-to-government relationship improved, to the point that the shah even returned Soviet defectors.

Iran has experienced periodic social unrest and political protests, the frustrated responses of different groups to rampant inflation, urban blight, agrarian dislocation, extensive corruption, and modernization on the one hand, and dictatorial rule, repressive policies, and rising expectations on the other. For complex reasons, the disparate groups in opposition to the shah found a unifying symbol in the late spring of 1978: Ayatollah Ruhollah Khomeini, the octogenarian religious leader who had been exiled by the shah in 1962. Events moved with tumultous rapidity, so that by mid-January 1979, the shah was forced into exile; within a month, Khomeini had returned and established an Islamic republic.

The Soviet role in these momentous and unexpected developments remains a subject of speculation. In the early stages of the antishah protests — from late spring to early fall 1978 — Soviet commentators generally restricted themselves essentially to reporting what was happening in the cities and oil fields. They did not turn against the shah or proclaim his imminent demise. Moscow, like Washington, was surprised by the shah's ineptness. Only gradually did Soviet broadcasts begin to criticize the shah's government, attack United States involvement in Iran, and demand that U.S. imperialism be kicked out of the country.

A turning point in the Kremlin's attitude came on November 19, 1978, when Brezhnev issued a statement noting Moscow's opposition to any outside interference in Iran. In effect, he warned the United States that if it attempted to act directly to keep the shah in power, the Soviet Union might undertake an intervention of its own in accordance with a 1921 Soviet-Iranian treaty concerning threats to the territorial integrity of the country. By January 1979 Moscow had decided that the shah would not hold. Soviet anti-American agitation acquired an incendiary dimension, and Communist agents played an important (but as yet only imperfectly understood) role in aggravating labor unrest in the oil fields (where the Communists were influential among the minority Arab and Kurdish workers), thereby contributing to the general economic paralysis that finally undermined the shah's position.

The fall of the shah was in general a boon to Moscow and, of course, a grievous blow to the United States. Soviet benefits are considerable and primarily strategic. The American-manned intelligence-gathering stations situated along the Soviet border have been shut down; Iranian arms purchases from the United States have been abruptly terminated, and Iran has withdrawn from the role of policeman for the West in the Persian Gulf (thus, should there be another rebellion against the sultan of Oman, Iran would not send troops to save this pro-Western leader, as it did in 1974–1975). The alignment of Iran with the Arab confrontation states weakens not only Israel but Egypt as well. CENTO collapsed after Iran's withdrawal, and Moscow obtained information about some of the most advanced military hardware in the United States arsenal. Economically, however, Moscow has been hit by the disruption of Iranian natural-gas deliveries and the Khomeini government's decision not to go ahead with the completion of a second, much larger pipeline, known as IGAT-2. Soviet industrial projects in Iran are also being curtailed. Moreover, in the long term, Moscow may find Iran's Islamic fundamentalism troublesome, especially if there is a spillover into other areas of its potentially disruptive religious and ethnic militancy.

Even more than Iran, Turkey has developed good relations with the Soviet Union since the mid-1960s. The Turks remain wary — five hundred years of suspicion, hostility, war, a common frontier, and Moscow's burning ambition to control the Turkish straits are all givens in Turkish thinking — but the bear has been almost benign. The frontier has been quiet, though Moscow occasionally protests the presence of U.S. monitoring stations on Turkish territory. No threatening Soviet military buildups or maneuvers and no serious incidents have taken place. Since 1965 economic relations have greatly expanded and government-to-government ties improved. Extensive Soviet economic commitments have resulted in the construction of important industrial projects, including an iron and steel complex, an oil refinery, and an aluminum plant, and Soviet loans to Turkey for economic projects have been larger than those extended to any LDC in recent years. In 1975 Kosygin's suggestion of a nonaggression pact was politely rejected, but during Turkish Premier Bulent Ecevit's visit to Moscow in June 1978, the two governments signed a political document on the principles of good neighborly and friendly cooperation, similar to a 1972 communiqué issued from Ankara during a visit by Soviet President Nikolai Podgorny.

All of this helps explain the ease with which Moscow was able to carry out its military deployments and overflights of Turkish (and Greek) airspace during the 1973 October War and the 1977–1978 Somali-Ethiopian war. Turkey looked the other way. In July 1976, at the height of Turkey's anger at the U.S. arms embargo over Cyprus, the Turks interpreted the 1936 Montreux Convention flexibly and, by designating the USSR's Kiev-class carrier an antisubmarine cruiser, permitted it to be the first carrier ever to transit the Turkish straits.

Relations with Turkey epitomize the progress Moscow has made toward promoting the dealignment of the entire rimland region from Greece to Afghanistan and toward assuring an easy access to the Arab east.

## Sub-Saharan Africa

Soviet interest in Africa, though low-keyed in the early years of Moscow's policy in the Third World, nonetheless has been persistent. The Soviet interventions of 1975–1976 in Angola and 1977–1978 in Ethiopia suggest that the past constraints of limited capability and political priorities elsewhere are no longer operative. As the Chinese ideograph for *crisis* combines the symbols for opportunity and danger, so the term *détente*, referring to the foreign policy between the USSR and the United States under Presidents Richard Nixon, Gerald Ford, and Jimmy Carter, has combined for Moscow the quest for coexistence in Europe and stabilization of the superpower nuclear relationship with the intense competition in the gray areas lying outside each superpower's core security community — and Africa is a vast, promising, uncommitted political preserve.

By the 1960s Moscow recognized the significance of sub-Saharan Africa's emergence upon the international stage. At first the Soviet operations were heavy-handed and they were bungled egregiously: in the Congo in the early 1960s, in Guinea in late 1961, and in Kenya in 1965. Soviet diatribes against Western power and declarations of support for decolonization and for African development were seldom followed up by meaningful deeds, and preoccupation with tactics to outmaneuver the Chinese Communists often left the Africans confused and with unfulfilled needs. Initially, too, an unsophisticated tenor was apparent in most Soviet writing on Africa, which rigidly applied a Marxian class analysis to tribal and cultural animosities and mistook economic dependency for political subservience. Nevertheless, the Soviet Union did in time demonstrate a sound appreciation of political realities and strategic possibilities, and its policy in Africa has been relatively effective.

A few generalizations about Soviet behavior between 1957 and 1974 — before the takeoff stage — may help to keep in focus the scope and character of the USSR's aims and policies in Africa. With the surge of decolonization seemingly capable of shaking the foundations of the Western international system, the anticolonialism and radical nationalist outlook of Kwame Nkrumah and Sekou Touré drew Moscow to Ghana and Guinea and boosted Khrushchev's doctrinally inspired expectations. A key objective was the normalization of diplomatic ties. Though most African governments of the time were innately conservative and suspicious of communism and kept the USSR at a distance, Moscow persisted and eventually did establish diplomatic ties with most of black Africa. Its network is now very active.

These ties were partly made effective through an economic program applied with erratic success; its incremental nature suffered because of the encumbrance of experts who could communicate only with difficulty, because of faulty equipment and tardy delivery schedules, and because of a Soviet inability to offer adequate assistance where it was needed most, in agriculture and in light industry. The principal recipients of economic assistance were Guinea, Ghana, Ethiopia, Mali, Somalia, Nigeria, and Sierra Leone; commitments were made mostly during the Soviet-African honeymoon of the late 1950s when, expecting to acquire prestige, Moscow complied willingly with sometimes vainglorious requests from indigenous elites for showpiece projects and instead wasted resources and reaped disenchantment. It has since preferred small-scale practical investments in which development loans are supplemented by trade credits to promote imports of Soviet equipment. In the late 1960s, the USSR began to concentrate on Nigeria, where it has been aiding in the development of the petroleum and the iron and steel industries. Although Soviet-built projects now dot Africa — an oil refinery in Ethiopia, a dairy farm in Guinea, a hydroelectric power station in Ghana, a cannery in Kenya, a spinning mill in Uganda — Soviet impact on the economies of courted African countries has been marginal, mainly because of an unwillingness to transfer substantial economic resources to the continent. In fact, until the Angolan episode, the Soviet Union had been almost niggardly: from 1957 to 1974, it provided more economic credits (approximately $850 million) to Afghanistan than to all of sub-Saharan Africa, which received about $780 million.

In the military sphere, the record is quite different. Arms helped widen and ease Soviet political access to Africa. Realizing that no African proletariat, no well-organized Communist parties, and no divisive class antagonisms existed, and that African states were heavily rural, often rent by tribal and ethnic feuds and as often dissatisfied with colonial territorial divisions, the Soviet Union has been ever ready over the years to exploit local rivalries, secessionist impulses, and national liberation movements seeking the end of European colonialism and, more latterly, of white supremacist regimes, by assuming a major role as supplier of weapons and advisers. Though it spreads its stake thinly over a number of actors on the African stage, the USSR has usually gravitated toward those elites who are particularly receptive to Soviet ideas and who are anti-Western not because of Cold War preferences, but for reasons relating to inter-African rivalries — for example, to tensions between Somalia and Ethiopia or Congo-Brazzaville and Zaire (formerly the Belgian Congo). As in the economic sphere, these efforts to influence the outcome of internal struggles for power have met with mixed fortunes. The Soviet government was stymied in the Congo in 1960, and again in 1964–1965 when it backed an attempt by Algeria and Egypt to maintain a rebel group in Stanleyville (now Kisangani). But its support for the central government in the Biafran civil war vastly improved its relations with Nigeria (that is, until 1979, when the Lagos government expelled Soviet military advisers). Arms supplies have also been helpful in establishing closer ties at various times with Guinea, Ghana, Mali, Benin (formerly Dahomey), Upper Volta, Burundi, and Uganda (until Idi Amin was toppled in 1979).

The attention of Soviet strategic planners has been focused increasingly upon the Horn of Africa and southern Africa. In both cases, the impetus is strategic and political rather than ideological or economic. Moscow's interest in the Horn is an outgrowth of its Middle East policy and its ambitious contruction of a blue-water fleet.

The prospect of a foothold in Somalia, which dominates the entrance to the Red Sea and the northwest littoral of the Indian Ocean, led in 1969 to a significant flow of military and economic aid and in 1974 to a multifaceted treaty of friendship and cooperation. In a gesture unprecedented in Soviet diplomacy, Moscow cancelled Somalia's foreign aid debt, which amounted to about $45 million (or 16 percent of Somalia's gross national product for one year). In return, the Somali connection brought Moscow naval and communications facilities at Berbera on the Red Sea and at Mogadishu, and access to the Soviet-modernized airfields at Berbera and Uanle Uen. By virtue of the ample missile storage as well as port-handling and repair facilities that it acquired in Somalia, Moscow greatly extended the range of Soviet air reconnaissance and strengthened the support structure for Soviet antisubmarine warfare capabilities in the Arabian Sea–Indian Ocean region. Somalia became the most important Soviet client in sub-Saharan Africa.

But privileges and a major presence do not make a satellite. What led to the toppling of the infrastructure that Moscow had built in Somalia was Soviet strategic covetousness and political myopia. Tempted by the revolution that followed the overthrow of Emperor Haile Selassie and the anti-Western policies of the self-proclaimed "Marxist-Leninist" military leadership in Addis Ababa, the Soviet Union agreed after two years of hesitation to Ethiopia's requests for arms. In December 1976, against the backdrop of deteriorating Somalian-Ethiopian relations, the Soviets started to supply small arms, and by April 1977, they raised their ante, furnishing Ethiopia with heavy weapons including tanks and aircraft, Soviet military advisers, and Cuban myrmidons. Moscow tried to keep a foot in both warring camps, hoping to mediate the conflict and emerge with its Somalian facilities more or less intact and with a vastly improved position in populous, large, politically radical (for the moment), and potentially important Ethiopia.

Soviet leaders fully expected Somalia's complete dependency on Soviet weapons to constrain President Mohammed Siad Barre's independence of action. Instead, Barre chose to foreclose the Soviet option. In November 1977, he renounced the 1974 treaty of friendship, expelled Soviet military personnel, and withdrew the use of all facilities enjoyed by the USSR in Somalia. The situation in the Horn of Africa remains in flux, but understandable Western concern over the USSR's escalating involvement in the area should not obscure the very real limitations under which the Soviets operate.

By contrast, the scale and character of Soviet commitments to southern Africa suggest that until 1974 the region was considered relatively unimportant. It was dominated by South Africa, Portugal, and Rhodesia (Zimbabwe); the independent black African states were weak, and the prospects of the various liberation movements based in Zambia, Tanzania, and Zaire were unpromising. Moscow kept its economic assistance to a minimum, although from the early 1960s, the Soviet Union and its eastern-bloc associates helped to train (and presumably to indoctrinate) guerrillas and to channel a trickle of weapons to favored national liberation groups, often through second parties such as Algeria and Egypt and occasionally through the Liberation Committee of the Organization of African Unity, which was created shortly after the OAU's establishment in 1963.

However, Moscow preferred bilateral contacts. In the Portuguese colonies, its matériel went to Marxist-oriented movements — the Popular Movement for the Liberation of Angola (MPLA) and the Front for the Liberation of Mozambique; and in Zimbabwe, after its unilateral declaration of independence from Britain in 1965, assistance went to the ideologically more congenial Zimbabwe African People's Union, which proved to be far weaker than its rival, the Zimbabwe African National Union. Except for the MPLA, however, whose Communist antecedents and pro-Moscow orientation date back to 1955, most of the liberation movements in southern Africa seemed able to work better with the Chinese, so Moscow did not press its affiliations with them and until 1974 wielded little clout in the region. Since southern Africa was not a centerpiece of Soviet global strategy, the main Soviet objectives there were to use the simmering situation to exacerbate the West's relations with African countries by polarizing alignments and issues, and to counter the challenge of China's activism.

The overthrow of the decades-old military dictatorship in Portugal on April 25, 1974, transformed the political situation in the region with dramatic suddenness and led Moscow to intensify arms shipments, especially to the MPLA. Portugal's decision to pull out of Africa after more than five hundred years of colonial rule accelerated the decolonization

process. In Guinea-Bissau, the Cape Verde Islands, and Mozambique, power was transferred smoothly. Only in Angola did the absence of an undisputed indigenous leadership result in civil war and a superpower contest of wills. The massive influx of Soviet arms and Cuban troops in mid-1975 and 1976 brought victory to the MPLA and demonstrated the readiness of Moscow to take bolder risks in promoting strategic goals. (The MPLA controlled the capital of Luanda when independence was formally proclaimed on November 11, 1975. In the civil war that followed, the overwhelming Soviet military hardware — armored cars, tanks, jeeps, small arms, and batteries of 122mm ground-to-ground rockets — manned by approximately 20,000 Cuban troops proved decisive. This same mix of Soviet and Cuban aid was also to prove effective in Ethiopia in 1977–1978.)

The success of the MPLA in Angola was a welcome antidote to the Kremlin's setbacks in the Middle East. In exercising its greatest show yet of resoluteness in sub-Saharan Africa, Moscow calculated that there were few risks and many prospective gains, not the least of which was exposure of China's inability to act in critical periods on behalf of liberation movements and its backing of groups that were also the protégés of Western countries. Soviet intervention also highlighted the United States' unwillingness to use force to help its clients, and demonstrated to friendly states what Moscow could do in Africa on behalf of prospective clients. In the words of *Pravda,* the MPLA's success would prove "a stimulus for the development of the liberation struggle of the peoples of Namibia [South-West Africa], the South African Republic, and Zimbabwe."

Admittedly, Angola is a tempting plum. Abundantly endowed with oil, untapped mineral resources, and fertile land, it is potentially one of the wealthiest countries in Africa. Moreover, air and naval facilities there would position the Soviets to interdict the sea route around the Cape of Good Hope. But a scenario in which Angola becomes a Soviet satellite and the Soviets build a naval base to rival the South African base at Simonstown, though theoretically possible, is most improbable in the foreseeable future. To press now for military privileges would lend credence to China's charges of Soviet imperialist designs, which could prove embarrassing to the USSR and to the MPLA (still in a politically precarious position and subject to harassment by the rival UNITA guerrilla group operating in southern Angola) and which in the long term could prove counterproductive to Soviet aims of undermining the West.

The Soviet courtship of Angola is being handled in a way intended to assure the USSR of a cordial welcome elsewhere in southern Africa, especially among the front-line states (Botswana, Mozambique, Tanzania, and Zambia) bordering Zimbabwe and pressing independence for Namibia and an end to apartheid in South Africa. In October 1976, Angolan President

Agostinho Neto (who died in September 1979) journeyed to Moscow to sign a treaty of friendship and cooperation, which serves as a guarantee of Soviet protection against threats to the survival of the Marxist-Leninist regime. Cuban troops are stationed in Angola and the country's links to the Soviet bloc have been strengthened, but it does seek expanded trade relations and diplomatic contact with the West as well.

On the issues of Zimbabwe and Namibia, the USSR has played a waiting game and contented itself for the time being with making propaganda, instructing cadres, and supplying some arms to different groups. It seeems prepared to follow the line laid down by the front-line states. A festering crisis in southern Africa would serve Soviet long-term interests much better than a quick solution.

The manifestations of Soviet interest in sub-Saharan Africa are widespread and unambiguous. What remains very much a subject of speculation and disagreement, however, are the motives that prompted this imperial outreach and what it has achieved. Here I offer some tentative observations on the impact of Soviet policy in the African milieu and the way in which developments on the African continent are in turn shaping that policy. These observations may be pertinent also to Soviet policy in southern Asia, the Middle East, and Latin America, and thus in a sense serve as a set of capsule assessments of the achievements and disappointments of Moscow's forward policy.

First, there are still no Soviet satellites in Africa. Moscow has not succeeded in drawing any African state into the kind of relationship that it has with the East European members of the Warsaw Pact. During the past two decades, it has found that the African countries that have sought Soviet aid are not so weak that they cannot determine their own policies. Some countries may be beholden for military and economic favors, as in the cases of Angola and Ethiopia, and they may even grant Moscow air and naval privileges, as did Somalia and Guinea; but as has been seen in Ghana, Mali, and Somalia, the evanescence of privileges makes reliance upon these countries for the conduct of an imperial policy difficult.

Obviously, Moscow gives in expectation of a return. It covets special favors, and when they are proffered, accepts them with the clear realization that they may be abruptly withdrawn. These unpredictable hazards are a new feature of the changing international order, but in terms of its philosophy of incrementalism, the USSR is prepared to take the risks; in its view, the main advantages it stands to gain from aiding African countries and movements are those that place it in an improved strategic and military position vis-à-vis the United States. Any improvement in the strategic context within which the Soviet Union regionally and globally operates justifies the outlay. The USSR is less impelled by the uncertain increments in leverage that it may acquire over developments within a recipient country, but if local advantages also accrue, so much the better.

Second, there is little evidence that in pursuing their forward policy, Soviet leaders have been concerned about the growing financial and military costs of involvement in Africa, or that the Kremlin has made any agonizing reappraisal over any damage that may have been done to the U.S.-Soviet détente by its intervention in Angola and Ethiopia. Still, Soviet activism does not necessarily foreshadow the adoption of an adventurist or high-risk policy. The Soviet and Cuban involvement in Angola and Ethiopia rested on political principles that evoked a sympathetic African reaction: defense of regimes recognized by most African states; upholding of the territorial inviolability of an existing nation (Ethiopia); and cooperation in response to specific requests for military assistance. While Moscow demonstrated an impressive military capability and a willingness to project its power on behalf of prospective clients, it depended for its efficacy upon landing and staging facilities from sympathetic governments whose immediate aims were congruent with its own.

A politically congenial set of circumstances is prerequisite for the projection of military power in the Third World. For this reason alone, Moscow may be expected to tread gingerly in its behavior toward African states. Despite the varied Soviet military privileges in Guinea, Angola, Ethiopia, and Mozambique, the threat posed by the Soviet naval presence in southern Africa and the Indian Ocean has been exaggerated. Moscow does not possess the fully controlled land-based support facilities so vital for a politically significant projection of military power; it lacks even an equivalent of the United States' military installation on the Indian Ocean island of Diego Garcia. Therefore, its naval forces must rely on local goodwill, which is an ephemeral phenomenon in Third World politics.

Third, Moscow responds to local initiatives in its pursuit of limited objectives. Whatever the strategic rationale and objective for its far-ranging policy may be, each particular move is a result of an African need and an invitation to cooperate and not of Soviet pressure (though the Soviet hand may well be involved in local intrigues that result in the coming to power of elites predisposed to Moscow, as in Angola). The application of infinitely malleable ideological criteria (exemplified by Soviet support for such bloody tyrants as Idi Amin of Uganda and Bokassa of the Central African Republic), the downgrading of expectations for a rapid transformation of African economic and social institutions, and the readiness to absorb setbacks (witness the acceptance of the deposals of Kwame Nkrumah in Ghana and Modibo Keita in Mali) show that Moscow puts a premium on pragmatism and prompt adaptation to political realities and is demonstrably able to find its way in the labile African political environment.

Fourth, while the USSR has reason to be concerned over its poor relations with China, Sino-Soviet rivalry is not the prime catalyst of Moscow's African policy. Western analysts have made too much of this as a policy determinant, with the consequent tendency to underestimate the centrality of the global rivalry with the United States in Soviet thinking. Moscow knows that China lacks the resources, military capability, or political urgency to intervene effectively on behalf of vulnerable clients and that in the unfolding struggle for southern Africa, Moscow — not Beijing — holds most of the trumps. Only in Southeast Asia is China a credible competitor.

Finally, Africa's resentment of the West provides Moscow with its greatest asset. Residual regional and ethnic rivalries, economic dislocation and dissatisfaction, and black Africa's shared animosity toward South Africa are the stuff on which the Soviet future in Africa is predicated. Resolution of the Namibian crisis and an evolution acceptable to the outside world in South Africa's policy toward its black people could cut the ground from underneath the USSR's policies, leaving Moscow the odd capital out in southern Africa. Moscow can contribute relatively little to the tasks of nation-building, modernization, socioeconomic transformation, and integration into the world economy; the Soviet Union is no model for Africa, though there are those who persist in arguing that it is.

The Soviet Union came to Africa with clean hands — without the taint of a colonial legacy. It experienced an intoxicating initial accumulation of prestige. But Moscow is no longer unknown or umblemished, and in the coming decades Soviet diplomacy will be forced to adapt to an environment more complex and demanding than the one into which it adroitly moved in the 1960s and 1970s. The next stage — the preservation and extension of influence and the transference of economic and military assistance into political advantage — is a more trying, uncertain enterprise, as Moscow has already learned.

## Selected Bibliography

ALBRIGHT, DAVID E. (ed.). *Communism in Africa*. Bloomington, Ind.: Indiana University Press, 1980.

BARNDS, WILLIAM J. *India, Pakistan, and the Great Powers*. New York: Praeger, 1972.

BRUTENTS, K. N. *National Liberation Revolutions Today*. Moscow: Progress, 1977.

BRZEZINSKI, ZBIGNIEW K. (ed.). *Africa and the Communist World*. Stanford: Stanford University Press, 1963.

CAROE, OLAF. *Soviet Empire*. London: Macmillan, 1953.

CARR, EDWARD HALLETT. *The Bolshevik Revolution, 1917–1923*. Vols. 1, 2, 3. New York: Macmillan, 1951, 1952, 1953.

COHN, HELEN DESFOSSES. *Soviet Policy Toward Black Africa: The Focus on National Integration.* New York: Praeger, 1972.

DATAR, ASHA L. *India's Economic Relations with the USSR and Eastern Europe, 1953–1969.* London: Cambridge University Press, 1972.

DINERSTEIN, HERBERT S. *The Making of a Missile Crisis: October 1962.* Baltimore: Johns Hopkins University Press, 1976.

DISMUKES, BRADFORD, and JAMES M. MCCONNELL (eds.). *Soviet Naval Diplomacy.* Elmsford, N.Y.: Pergamon Press, 1979.

DONALDSON, ROBERT H. *Soviet Policy Toward India: Ideology and Strategy.* Cambridge: Harvard University Press, 1974.

———— (ed.). *The Soviet Union in the Third World: Success or Failure.* Boulder, Colo.: Westview Press, 1980.

DUNCAN, W. RAYMOND (ed.). *Soviet Policy in Developing Countries.* Waltham, Mass.: Ginn-Blaisdell, 1970.

FARER, TOM J. *War Clouds on the Horn of Africa: The Widening Storm.* 2nd ed., rev. Washington, D.C.: Carnegie Endowment for International Peace, 1979.

GOLDMAN, MARSHALL I. *Soviet Foreign Aid.* New York: Praeger, 1967.

GUPTA, BHABANI SEN. *The Fulcrum of Asia: Relations Among China, India, Pakistan and the USSR.* New York: Pegasus, 1970.

————. *Soviet-Asian Relations in the 1970s and Beyond.* New York: Praeger, 1976.

HASELKORN, AVIGDOR. *The Evolution of Soviet Security Strategy 1965–1975.* New York: Crane, Russak, 1978.

JACKSON, D. BRUCE. *Castro, the Kremlin, and Communism in Latin America.* Baltimore: Johns Hopkins University Press, 1969.

JOSHUA, WYNFRED, and STEPHEN P. GILBERT. *Arms for the Third World: Soviet Military Aid Diplomacy.* Baltimore: Johns Hopkins University Press, 1969.

JUKES, GEOFFREY. *The Soviet Union in Asia.* Berkeley: University of California Press, 1973.

KANET, ROGER (ed.). *The Soviet Union and the Developing Nations.* Baltimore: Johns Hopkins University Press, 1974.

KAUTSKY, JOHN H. *Moscow and the Communist Party of India.* New York: Wiley, 1956.

KAZNACHEEV, ALEKSANDR. *Inside a Soviet Embassy.* Philadelphia: Lippincott, 1962.

KLINGHOFFER, ARTHUR JAY. *Soviet Perspectives on African Socialism.* Rutherford, N.J.: Fairleigh Dickinson University Press, 1969.

KUNIHOLM, BRUCE R. *The Origins of the Cold War in the Near East: Great Power Conflict and Diplomacy in Iran, Turkey, and Greece.* Princeton: Princeton University Press, 1979.

LEGVOLD, ROBERT. *Soviet Policy in West Africa.* Cambridge: Harvard University Press, 1970.

LEVESQUE, JACQUES. *The USSR and the Cuban Revolution: Soviet Ideological and Strategical Perspectives, 1959–77.* New York: Praeger, 1978.

LICHTHEIM, GEORGE. *Imperialism.* New York: Praeger, 1971.

LOWENTHAL, RICHARD. *Model or Ally? The Communist Powers and the Developing Countries.* New York: Oxford, 1977.

MCLANE, CHARLES B. *Soviet Strategies in Southeast Asia.* Princeton: Princeton University Press, 1966.

MEYER, ALFRED C. *Leninism.* Cambridge: Harvard University Press, 1957.

MÜLLER, KURT. *The Foreign Aid Programs of the Soviet Bloc and Communist China: An Anlysis.* New York: Walker, 1969.

OVERSTREET, GENE, and MARSHALL WINDMILLER. *Communism in India.* Berkeley: University of California Press, 1959.

POPPINO, ROLLIE E. *International Communism in Latin America, 1917–1963.* New York: Free Press, 1964.

RAMAZANI, ROUHOLLAH K. *Iran's Foreign Policy 1941–1973.* Charlottesville: University of Virginia Press, 1975.

REMNEK, RICHARD B. *Soviet Scholars and Soviet Foreign Policy: A Case Study in Soviet Policy Towards India.* Durham, N.C.: Academic Press, 1975.

RUBINSTEIN, ALVIN Z. (ed.). *Yugoslavia and the Nonaligned World.* Princeton: Princeton University Press, 1970.

———. *Soviet and Chinese Influence in the Third World.* New York: Praeger, 1975.

STEIN, ARTHUR. *India and the Soviet Union: The Nehru Era.* Chicago: University of Chicago Press, 1969.

STEVENS, CHRISTOPHER. *The Soviet Union and Black Africa.* New York: Holmes and Meier, 1976.

SUÁREZ, ANDRÉS. *Cuba: Castroism and Communism 1959–1966.* Cambridge: MIT Press, 1967.

TABORSKY, EDWARD. *Communist Penetration of the Third World.* New York: Robert Speller, 1973.

THORNTON, THOMAS P. (ed.). *The Third World in Soviet Perspective.* Princeton: Princeton University Press, 1964.

WEINSTEIN, WARREN (ed). *Chinese and Soviet Aid to African Nations.* New York: Praeger, 1980.

WILSON, EDWARD T. *Russia and Black Africa Before World War II.* New York: Holmes and Meier, 1974.

ZABIH, SEPEHR. *The Communist Movement in Iran.* Berkeley: University of California Press, 1966.

ZAGORIA, DONALD S. *Vietnam Triangle: Moscow, Peking, Hanoi.* New York: Pegasus, 1967.

# 11

# The Soviet Union
## and the Arab World

In the Third World it is the Arab East that has drawn most of the Soviet attention; and it is there that the Soviet Union and the United States have consistently had their most serious crises. Tension between them in the decades ahead seems inevitable, because of the region's intrinsic strategic and economic significance.

By concluding an arms deal with Nasser in August 1955, the USSR discovered that arms were the key to access to the Arab world and erased the diplomatic debits of the Stalin era. Moscow's aims were unmistakably strategic: to undermine the American policy of containment, establish a Soviet presence, and encourage anti-Western manifestations of Arab nationalism. The initial targets were Egypt and Syria, both of whom opposed Western military pacts in the area and sought alternative sources of weapons with which to counter their Western-armed regional rivals. Moscow seemed fully in tune with the anticolonialist and anti-imperialist sentiment cresting in the Arab world. Soon afterward, the Arab-Israeli conflict provided Moscow with a convenient issue for exploiting Arab ties with the West and enhancing its status with radical states. In time, Moscow's goals expanded to include the quest for military privileges and manipulation of Arab oil to weaken the Western world.

Soviet policy in the Arab world may for convenience be divided into first, the USSR's focus on Egypt, which quickly entailed partisanship in the Arab-Israeli conflict and the wars of 1967, 1969–1970, and 1973, and second, the penetration of the Persian Gulf and Arabian Peninsula. We shall trace these two aspects separately, though by the late 1970s they had become increasingly enmeshed, as oil spread its influence across every issue and actor.

240

## The Egyptian Connection

Moscow sold Egypt arms with several purposes in mind, primarily to establish firm ties with a key Arab country and to encourage its opposition to the Baghdad pact (established in the spring of 1955 and reorganized as CENTO in 1959, following the revolution in Iraq that brought in an anti-Western regime). When Washington's precipitate withdrawal of its offer to assist Egypt in building the Aswan High Dam provoked Nasser to nationalize the Suez Canal Company in July 1956, the Soviet government upheld the Egyptian action. Moscow also championed Nasser's cause during the Israeli-Anglo-French invasion of Egypt in October 1956; and though it was American rather than Soviet pressure on the invaders that forced their withdrawal and saved Nasser, the Soviet Union's prestige nonetheless rose spectacularly in the Arab world as it replaced Egyptian arms lost to the Israelis in Sinai, lent Egypt and Syria several hundred million dollars for economic development, and supported Arab positions in the UN. However, Moscow was careful to avoid any military actions that might occasion a strong response from the United States, still the preeminent military power in the area.

Arab nationalism posed dilemmas for the Soviet Union in the years immediately after the merger of Egypt and Syria created the United Arab Republic (UAR) and the military made an anti-Western coup in Iraq, in March and July 1958, respectively. Though unhappy over the establishment of the UAR because this "nullfied some of the gains made in Syria by both the USSR and the indigenous Communist Party" and also served to strengthen Nasser's bargaining position, "making him less amenable to Moscow's wishes and more immune to Soviet pressure," Moscow reconciled itself to the newest manifestation of Arab nationalism and "chose to continue to protect Soviet interests in the Middle East through cooperation with, not opposition to, Cairo."[1] Pleasantly surprised by the overthrow of the pro-Western Iraqi regime on July 14, 1958, the USSR saw in the emergence of the Qasim government a sharp blow to the Western position in the Middle East (Nasser also considered it a move toward Arab unity). An early and unexpected falling-out between Cairo and Baghdad, however, confronted Moscow with difficult choices. How was it to differentiate between two "progressive" Arab regimes without alienating either? How was it to nourish anti-imperialism without arousing Arab suspicions of communism by pressing for better conditions for indigenous Arab Communists? How was it to strengthen the progressive component of Arab nationalism and at the same time minimize its bourgeois component?

For a time, Moscow backed Abd al-Karim Qasim against Nasser because in contrast to Nasser, who repeatedly expressed interest in improving relations with the Western countries, Qasim was militantly critical. Also in contrast to Nasser, who cracked down on local Communists and asserted that communism was incompatible with Arab nationalism and unity, Qasim brought Communists into the government and relied on their support against his Nasserite opponents; and where Nasser had ambitions to unify the Arab world under his leadership, Qasim represented a force for retaining the existing nation-state system in the Arab world, thus affording Moscow more room for diplomatic maneuver and lessening the likelihood that Arab nationalism would take on a bourgeois complexion that might impede the move toward socialism. Furthermore, Moscow could not fail to regard with utmost concern the possibility, however remote, of a unitary Arab nationalist state, which might exert a strong attraction for Soviet Muslims.

Shrewdly, Khrushchev kept this mini-Cold War with Cairo over strategy, outlook, and issues from interfering with the expansion of economic ties, as exemplified by the USSR's commitment in October 1958 and January 1959 to help build the Aswan High Dam. Aware of Nasser's enormously enhanced position as the standard-bearer of Arab nationalism, Moscow tolerated his anti-Communist outbursts and sporadic moves toward improved relations with the West. Moreover, by 1961–1962, disenchantment with Qasim had set in because of his suppression of Iraqi Communists.

Military considerations were even more important motivations for Moscow's careful courtship of Nasser. In May 1961, Albania evicted the Soviet Union from the naval base it had enjoyed at Vlone on the Adriatic Sea since 1945, and U.S. deployment of Polaris submarines in the Mediterranean was impending. These events prompted friendlier relations with Nasser and serious Soviet efforts to obtain naval facilities in Egyptian ports.[2] This quest for tangible military privileges increasingly absorbed Moscow and muted political differences with Egypt. The collapse of the Egyptian-Syrian federation in September 1961 also helped; and, buttressed by the growing interest of Soviet strategic planners in Aden, the USSR subsidized Egyptian intervention in the Yemeni civil war after 1962.

Once again, in the mid-1960s as in the mid-1950s, Egypt emerged as the key Arab target of Soviet attention, and Moscow grudgingly acquiesced to its espousal of Arab unity, subordinating ideological and political dilemmas to strategic and military objectives. Although Moscow failed to obtain the coveted naval facilities until Nasser's crushing defeat in June 1967, it benefited enormously in its broader aim of penetrating the Arab world, by heeding a formula devised by Khrushchev.

This formula had simple elements: first, the delivery of arms to Arab states, to break their dependence on the West and create a new dependence; second, the building of a political and economic relationship with those states based on the calculated self-interest of each party and the willingness of each to pay something in the coin of the interest of the other; and third, a rather vague ideological solidarity grounded in anticolonialism, anti-imperialism, anti-Zionism, national liberation, revolutionary change, and 'socialism' in a sense broad enough to evade definition, for precision in that respect could undermine and destroy the cooperation.[3]

Egypt's disastrous showing in the Arab-Israeli war of June 1967 proved a boon for Moscow, paving the way for the extensive privileges that the Soviet military had sought. The political and strategic consequences of the June War concern us here only insofar as they relate to Soviet policy. Briefly, the background was this: In the spring of 1967, Moscow feared for the future of the pro-Soviet government in Syria. To rally support behind its Syrian client, it spread false reports of an impending Israeli attack against Syria. (To prove that there was no military buildup, the Israeli prime minister even offered to tour the Israeli-Syrian border with the Soviet ambassador, who refused.) Nasser, who had been persuaded by the Soviet Union to sign a defense pact with Syria in November 1966, did not check on Soviet intelligence reports; he mobilized his army in Sinai and ousted UNEF, which had kept the Egyptians and Israelis apart since 1957. At this point, Nasser went beyond Soviet expectations. Instead of settling for the tactical political triumph of liquidating UNEF — the last vestige of Israel's advantage from the 1956 war — and thus diverting the supposed threat away from Syria, he announced the closing of the Straits of Tiran, blocking Israel's outlet to the Red Sea and Indian Ocean, and moved the mass of his army into position for invasion of Israel. However, the combination of Israeli air superiority and surprise was decisive, and in a lightning campaign from June 5 to June 10, the Israelis defeated the Egyptians in Gaza and Sinai, the Jordanians in Jerusalem and on the West Bank, and the Syrians on the Golan Heights.

Soviet leaders, unwilling to abandon their ambitions in the Arab world, poured new weapons and Soviet advisers into Egypt and Syria. Cairo's dependence was total; the army and air force had to be reequipped and retrained to handle advanced weaponry, and the economy required imports of food, industrial materials, and machinery, much of which Moscow bank-rolled. Between 1967 and 1969 alone, the Soviet investment into Egypt was in the range of $3 to $4 billion. Nevertheless, against Soviet wishes, Nasser started a "war of attrition" against Israel along the length of the Suez Canal in March 1969; but this effort backfired. In early 1970, Moscow was forced to up its ante to the point of committing 20,000 combat troops to man missile sites and the air defense of Egypt's heart-land.[4] In its complete dependence on the Soviet Union, Egypt granted significant concessions: naval facilities at Alexandria and Port Said, the assignment of airfields for the almost exclusive use of Soviet forces, and approval for the transformation of Mersa Matrûh into a naval "facility" (the term preferred by Third World countries, since it does not imply surrender of sovereignty or smack of colonial rule) to be used by the Soviet Mediterranean fleet. These privileges marked the high point of Soviet presence in an Arab country.

When Nasser died in late September 1970, Moscow expected continuity in leadership but instead watched a struggle for power that resulted in the virtual elimination in May 1971 of Nasser's entire entourage, on which it had predicated its aim of consolidating and preserving the privileged Soviet position in Egypt. Seeking to stabilize relations with Anwar Sadat, the victor in the succession struggle, and to institutionalize its political and military presence, Moscow pressed for the Soviet-Egyptian treaty of friendship and cooperation of May 27, 1971. Article 7 of the treaty held that "in the event of development of situations creating, in the opinion of both sides, a danger to peace or violation of peace, they will contact each other without delay in order to concert their positions with a view to removing the threat that has arisen or reestablishing peace." For the first time, the USSR bound itself to a military commitment in the Third World — a measure of Egypt's importance to Moscow and of the USSR's growing military confidence. Moscow hoped that the treaty would assure its position in Egypt and serve as a model for cementing ties with other Third World countries. (And indeed, similar treaties were signed with India in August 1971, Iraq in April 1972, Somalia in 1974, Angola in October 1976, Ethiopia in November 1978, Afghanistan in December 1978, and the PDRY in October 1979, to mention a few of the most important ones for the Soviet Union.)

Despite the treaty, the Soviet leadership found Sadat difficult. Cairo wanted more weaponry than Moscow, influenced by its developing détente with the United States, was prepared to deliver; the Egyptian military was restive over the patronizing attitude of Soviet advisers; and the completion of the Aswan Dam in January 1971 brought new requests for major economic commitments. Also, Sadat helped to suppress a Communist-inspired coup in the Sudan in July 1971, subsequently cracked down on Egyptian Communists, and made independent efforts to deal with the United States and diminish its support of Israel. On July 18, 1972, he publicly announced the expulsion from Egypt of Soviet military personnel (between 15,000 and 20,000), including all Soviet pilots; the removal of Soviet units included "120 MiG-21Js, 20 Sukhoi-11s, about four MiG-23s, up to 260 SAM-3s at about 65 Soviet-controlled sites, some SAM-4s and SAM-6s, and a squadron of TU-16 maritime reconnaissance aircraft" disguised in Egyptian colors but flown by Soviet personnel.[5] Of the once extensive

Soviet military presence in Egypt, only the naval facilities were permitted to remain more or less as before. This stunning turn of events demonstrated that neither a major presence nor heavy dependency would necessarily bring influence to the patron, and that a superpower unable or unwilling to project its military power directly into the domestic politics of a client state was vulnerable to the vagaries of a client's change of attitude or policy.

By January 1973, Moscow and Cairo had effected a reconciliation, Sadat unilaterally extending Soviet naval facilities beyond the April 1973 expiration date and Brezhnev again turning on the arms tap, in part for strategic reasons and in part for Arab oil money. In the summer of 1973, Soviet leaders — perplexed by the contradictions arising out of their interest in détente, their ambitions in the Arab world, and their rivalry with the United States — sought to accentuate the positive and minimize the negative. It remained for Sadat to influence the pattern not only of Soviet-Egyptian but also of Soviet-American relations.

When Sadat and Syrian President Hafez Assad launched the fifth Arab-Israeli war on October 6, 1973, they started a conflict that Moscow did not want but did nothing to stop.[6] The Soviet leadership risked the budding détente with the United States in order to back its Arab clients, going nearer to the brink of a confrontation with the United States than ever before, even during the 1962 Cuban missile crisis. By 1973, the Soviet Union had achieved strategic equivalence with the United States, and both sides had sizable conventional forces deployed in proximity, so that a small incident might easily have triggered a chain reaction. Moscow acted very much the generous and protective patron, saving Egypt and Syria from another military disaster and enabling both to emerge from the war with significant strategic and political gains.

But Sadat, far from being grateful, repaid Soviet help with contumely and a political rebuff. For a combination of personal, strategic, political, and economic reasons, Sadat turned sharply to Washington, openly alienating the Soviet Union.[7] Acrimony and increasing friction characterized Soviet-Egyptian relations for the next two-and-a-half years, as Sadat looked increasingly to Washington for economic assistance and for political solutions to the Arab-Israeli conflict. On March 15, 1976, Sadat unilaterally abrogated the 1971 treaty; a month later, he announced the cancellation of facilities for the Soviet navy. In less than five years, the formerly impressive Soviet military presence in Egypt had turned to sand.

The end of the Egyptian connection forced Moscow to search anew for a secure foothold in that part of the Arab world directly involved in the Arab-Israeli conflict. Thus, while the United States was fashioning two disengagement agreements on the Egyptian-Israeli front and a first-stage pullback in the Syrian-Israeli sector, the Soviet Union was looking elsewhere for an active role and a constituency for itself. It built up Syria's military capability, reluctantly supporting Assad's intervention in Lebanon in 1976; it sold massive amounts of arms to Iraq and Libya; and it followed the lead of the Arab rejectionist front in espousing the maximalist demands of the Palestine Liberation Organization.

President Jimmy Carter took office in January 1977 determined to press for a comprehensive Middle East settlement. Deteriorating relations with the Soviet Union prompted by the president's abrasive emphasis on the human rights issue and introduction of sudden changes in the SALT negotiations led Secretary of State Cyrus Vance to seek Soviet cooperation on the Arab-Israeli problem, in the hope that progress on a Middle East settlement would have a salutary effect on negotiations in other sectors. On October 1, 1977, the Soviet Union and the United States issued a joint statement that would have moved the Middle East negotiations to a Geneva venue and included all the parties. However, Israeli objections and congressional opposition rendered the statement ineffective within a week. This led Sadat to take matters into his own hands. The result was his historic trip to Jerusalem on November 19, 1977, and the pursuit of a separate Egyptian-Israeli accord. Once again the Soviet Union was left outside the bargaining process.

Moscow denounced Sadat's initiative as "an act of capitulation" and strongly supported the position of the hard-line Arab states — Syria, Iraq, Libya, and Algeria — who sought to prevent any Egyptian-Israeli agreement. It also bitterly criticized the United States for reneging on the joint statement and encouraging a separate accord, allegedly at the expense of Arab unity and the interests of the Palestinians. During the months that followed, Moscow watched the ups and downs of the Egyptian-Israeli talks and Washington's inability to bring matters to a conclusion. By the end of July 1978, the Soviet Union had reason to expect an American failure — then came the August 8 announcement in Washington of a meeting to be convened on September 5, 1978, at Camp David, Maryland. President Carter's personal commitment and involvement made the difference. The Egyptian-Israeli-American negotiations bore fruit in the signing of a formal treaty between Egypt and Israel on March 26, 1979.

Moscow regards any agreement on the Middle East made without its participation as anti-Soviet and devoid of political realism. Time and again, Soviet officials have insisted that a conflict as extensive and explosive as that between the Arab states and Israel cannot be settled without the cooperation of the Soviet Union. They claim that what happens in the Middle East is a matter of vital national interest to the USSR and that Soviet strategic concerns encompass the entire region and not merely the areas bordering on the USSR. Moreover, some Soviet officials make the point in private that they will not be "pushed around" by the United

States. However, though the Soviet Union wants to be treated as an equal of the United States, it is hamstrung by its tactical blunder in having broken diplomatic relations with Israel in June 1967, by the residual suspicion with which it is viewed by all Arab parties, and by Sadat's deep personal conviction that Moscow is out to get him.

Though opposed to the Egyptian-Israeli treaty, the Soviet Union was a beneficiary in terms of its position in the Arab world. The treaty crystallizes Arab opposition to Sadat, whose anti-Soviet attitude cost Moscow its previous commanding position in Egypt and creates a new polarization in the Arab world, with the United States seen as Egypt's patron and the Soviet Union as siding with most Arab states; it intensifies Arab militancy and reinforces the importance of the Soviet connection for the Arab rejectionist group; it may help break down some of the residual suspicion of Moscow held by countries such as Saudi Arabia, the gulf states, and Jordan; and it puts U.S. policy under great pressure everywhere in the area.

There is little evidence that the Soviet Union has any genuine interest in a comprehensive Arab-Israeli settlement, which would severely diminish its attractiveness to Arab states as a supplier of weapons and a shield against military defeat. It is obvious that Moscow has its own interests whether or not it participates in the settlement process. Some American officials reported that the Soviets were trying to be helpful during the Arab-Israeli crises of 1967, 1969–1970, 1973, 1974–1975, and 1977, yet when one probes to find out precisely how Moscow was helping, one is left with ambiguity. This was evident, for example, during the flareup of the Lebanese civil war in early October 1978, when Carter used the hot line to enlist Brezhnev's assistance in preserving the precarious cease-fire. Moscow apparently counseled the Syrians, who occupied Lebanon north of the Litani River, to exercise restraint. But the decisive element was Syrian President Hafez Assad, who did not require any Soviet reminder of the critical nature of the crisis or of Israel's vital interest in seeing that the Lebanese Christian forces were not destroyed and that no Syrian or Palestinian attempt would be made to eliminate the Lebanese Christian enclaves south of the Litani River.

Would Assad have behaved differently if Moscow had remained silent? Not likely. In this instance, Moscow could afford to be helpful because it was urging a policy that paralleled Syria's. But if by "helpful" one means a readiness to pressure a client in a direction that it prefers not to go, or a willingness to resist a client's major initiative, then since 1967 Moscow has not been helpful in any effort to settle the Arab-Israeli conflict. (This view, it should be noted, is not held by all analysts of Soviet policy.) The reason for Soviet reluctance is simple: continued close relations with its Arab clients, whoever they may be, are more important to Moscow's long-term aims in the area than is an end to the Arab-Israeli conflict. Moreover, Moscow does not believe that its opposition to United States policy in the Arab-Israeli sector will have any adverse effect on two of its important objectives, the SALT II treaty and expanding U.S.-Soviet economic ties.

## The Gulf and the Arabian Peninsula

The differentiated policy Moscow has pursued in the Third World — the adaptability, persistence, and pragmatism as well as the opportunistic and low-risk character of that policy — is very apparent in the USSR's drive to penetrate the Arabian Peninsula. In recent years, particularly since the oil and energy crises roared onto the international scene in the wake of the October War, the area has assumed greatly increased importance in Soviet calculations. A geographically strategic land mass lying to the south of the USSR's Muslim, non-Slavic union-republics and flanked by busy sea routes whose choke points at the Strait of Hormuz and the Strait of Bab al-Mandab expose Western economic vulnerability to any cutoff of oil, the peninsula is an obvious target for U.S.-Soviet rivalry in the Middle East.

The Soviet Union's interest in the Arabian Peninsula started in the late 1920s and early 1930s, when Moscow established relations with Yemen and Saudi Arabia. However, the essentially marginal commercial ties of that time never took hold. Moscow's attempts to establish firm footholds on the peninsula lagged far behind its efforts in other regions, in part for want of opportunity but also because the less explosive political tensions offered few quick rewards. Post-Stalin Soviet diplomacy made its first inroad on the peninsula with the treaty of friendship signed with Yemen in Cairo on October 31, 1955, though not until 1968 did the USSR become directly and intimately involved in the Yemeni sector.

Moscow's readiness to assume extensive economic and military commitments in pursuit of strategic interests in the Arabian Peninsula was first demonstrated in Iraq. The military coup that overthrew the pro-Western Hashemite monarchy in Baghdad on July 14, 1958, brought the Soviet Union into an important tributary of Middle East developments quite independent of its growing involvement with Egypt and the Arab-Israeli conflict. After an initial halcyon period, Soviet-Iraqi relations went through a trying ten-year phase, primarily as a result of the changing fortunes of the Iraqi Communist party. But this did not prevent the steady expansion of government-to-government ties, because regardless of the group in power, Baghdad pursued an anti-Western policy, which Moscow found congenial.

By the late 1960s, with the Baath party in power in Iraq, Soviet-Iraqi relations improved. Moscow looked favorably on the Baath's anti-Western and radical orientation, its determination to settle the Kurdish issue, its greater tolerance of local Communists, and its growing reliance on Soviet assistance and arms. Not only did Moscow's concern over its southern tier ease as a consequence of Iraq's nonalignment and the shah's decision in 1962 to bar U.S. military bases or missiles from Iranian territory, but its intrusive activities in the gulf and Arabian Peninsula region were aided by changes in the strategic environment: the end of the British imperial presence in the gulf; the creation of independent ministates along the eastern littoral of the Arabian Peninsula, which fueled residual Iraqi-Iranian-Saudi rivalry; and the growth of Soviet military capability.

Symptomatic of the improving Soviet-Iraqi relationship was the fifteen-year treaty of friendship and cooperation signed on April 9, 1972, which strengthened the expanding cooperation and gave Moscow regular access to the port of Umm Qasr. The treaty helped convince Baghdad of Moscow's readiness to back the Baath's decision to settle the Kurdish problem, nationalize Western oil holdings, and oppose the threat from Iran. When the Kurds rejected the Baath's offer of limited autonomy in March 1974 and the civil war gradually resumed, Moscow sided with Baghdad. The Soviet leadership's desertion of the Kurds and of support for the Baath furthermore dissuaded the shah from interference.

Moscow's aim was to consolidate relations with Iraq, but also to prevent an Iraqi-Iranian conflict that could have scuttled the Soviet-Iranian rapprochement. The effort succeeded well, and the Soviets used a limited display of military force (overt shipments of sophisticated weapons and occasional strafing runs by Soviet-piloted MiG-25s along the Iraqi-Iranian border) without alienating either party. The Iraqi-Iranian agreement of March 1975 sealed the fate of the Kurds and exempted the USSR from having to take sides in a regional conflict whose outbreak would have jeopardized its quest for better relations with both countries. In this instance, the USSR proved to be a force for stability and the territorial status quo. Yet Soviet influence did not increase appreciably.

In recent years Soviet-Iraqi relations have been far from intimate. Moscow remains Iraq's principal source of arms (for cash), but the Baath has begun to diversify its suppliers. Soviet-Iraqi economic ties are extensive, but Baghdad looks increasingly to the West for technology and equipment, much to Moscow's annoyance. The relationship has been further strained by far-ranging differences over the Arab-Israeli problem (Iraq refuses even to accept UN Security Council Resolutions 242 and 338 as a basis for a possible settlement); over clients in the Horn of Africa, where Iraq supports Eritrean separatists against the Moscow-backed Ethiopian regime; over Iraqi Communists, who are represented in the Baath government but are periodically executed for organizing party cells in army units; and over Moscow's quest for privileged treatment, which the Baath has generally refused (even to the extent of forcing the Soviet embassy in Baghdad to move house because of Iraqi suspicions that the Russians were monitoring discussions in nearby government buildings).

These disagreements have been kept under control because of shared opposition to U.S. policy, Sadat's opening to the West, and the Egyptian-Israeli treaty of March 26, 1979. However, the erratic course of revolutionary changes in Iran could disturb Soviet-Iraqi relations. For example, should there be a spillover of religious unrest from the Iranian revolution (the Iranians are predominantly Shiite Muslims) to the Shiite "silent majority" in Iraq, now ruled by Sunni Muslims, the consequent strains in Iraqi-Iranian relations might force the Soviet Union to take sides. Certainly Moscow is going to find it more and more difficult to play the honest broker between Iraq's radical Arabism and Iran's Islamic fundamentalism.

The Yemeni sector of the Arabian Peninsula, stretching in a northerly direction along the Red Sea and eastward along the Gulf of Aden, has received attention second only to Iraq in Moscow's quest for footholds on the peninsula. Soon after the 1955 treaty of friendship, Moscow gave Yemen small amounts of economic and military assistance to encourage its opposition to British rule in the Aden–South Yemen region. For a short time after Yemen's accession to the union formed by Egypt and Syria in February 1958, Nasser was uneasy over the influx of Soviet technicians and advisers into Yemen, fearing that the country might come under Soviet domination and that Imam Ahmad might provoke a war with the British in Aden. A military coup in September 1962 and the proclamation of the Yemen Arab Republic (YAR) led Nasser to commit Egyptian forces in order to prop up the pro-Egyptian putschist Brigadier Abdullah al-Sallal, whose forces were no match for the Zaidi tribes supporting Imam al-Badr (who had succeeded to office on the death of his father a week before Sallal's coup). Thus began Nasser's Soviet-subsidized Vietnam: the 60,000 to 80,000 troops were Egyptian; the weapons and supplies were Soviet. Moscow funneled most of its aid through Cairo, avoiding direct involvement in the civil war that pitted the Egyptian-backed republicans and Shafeite tribes against the Saudi-backed royalists and long-dominant Zaidis.

In contrast to its behavior in Iraq, Moscow tried in Yemen to upset the status quo and exploit regional instability. Soviet objectives included deepening Nasser's dependence, with the hope of obtaining naval facilities that would replace the loss of the Soviet base in Albania; intensifying pressure on the British in Aden and on Saudi Arabia; and establishing close ties with a new progressive force and preventing its overthrow by reactionary, Western-supported forces. Without the Soviet wherewithal, Nasser could not have sustained his overseas adventure. Indeed, it is difficult to imagine that he would have gotten so enmeshed in the first instance but for Soviet assurances and encouragement. Certainly he would not have been able to sustain five years of demanding, inconclusive conflict.

Nasser's defeat in the June War forced him to withdraw and leave the field to the Saudis. Consequently Soviet prospects in Yemen declined. At the same time, the British crown colony of Aden and the associated surrounding miniprotectorates were emerging to independence under the name of the South Arabian Federation. Instead of fostering the nationalist coalition of the pro-Egyptian Front for the Liberation of Occupied Southern Yemen (FLOSY), the British shortsightedly allowed power to gravitate toward the National Liberation Front (NLF), an umbrella organization for a motley mixture of Marxist-Leninists and Maoists, out of hostility towards Nasser after their humiliation in 1956. When the British left in November 1967, the NLF seized power in Aden and soon extended its control over the entire country, whose population of approximately 1.8 million is about one-third that of the neighboring Yemen Arab Republic (YAR). In June 1969, the more radical faction of the NLF gained control; it changed the country's name in November 1970 to the People's Democratic Republic of Yemen (PDRY) and rammed through drastic institutional arrangements designed to secure its base of power.[8] A marked radicalization and militancy, including a proclaimed policy of spreading revolution to the entire Arabian Peninsula, triggered Saudi enmity and attracted additional Soviet-bloc aid.

From the start, the PDRY cultivated close relations with the Soviet Union. Military assistance, economic aid, and Soviet, Cuban, and East German advisers and technicians poured in, the first shipment of Soviet arms arriving in August 1968.[9] By early 1978, the number of military personnel had risen to about 2000.[10] Moscow's assistance has been essential not only for the internal retention of power, but also for waging an ongoing fight with the YAR and sustaining the Dhofari rebellion which started in western Oman in 1965 (the Dhofaris have been using PDRY territory since 1968 as training and staging areas and have been seeking with PDRY assistance to overthrow the pro-Western regime in Oman).[11] By the mid-1970s, the Dhofaris had been defeated militarily by a combination of Iranian troops and British advisers, and they were stripped politically of leverage when the financially sorely pressed PDRY leadership decided to accept Saudi financial assistance in return for normalization of relations in March 1976. This meant an end to support for the Dhofari insurgency, though it shows signs of being revived as the 1980s begin.

Once again, as in the YAR in 1967–1968, Moscow had to adapt to a client's shift in policy,[12] all the while continuing its aid in competition with Saudi attempts to woo the PDRY leadership away from close ties with the Soviet Union. The USSR's concern that the PDRY-Saudi reconciliation could threaten its position in Ethiopia was evident in criticisms of "the imperialists and their agents" who seek to make the Red Sea an "Arab lake" — a reference to Saudi efforts to promote PDRY-YAR cooperation and Arab support for Somalia and to limit the Soviet role in the region.[13]

Moscow also expanded supplies to the PDRY to offset Sadat's peremptory abrogation of the Soviet-Egyptian treaty in March 1976; it could ill afford to lose the few footholds it had in the Arab world. Its policy was a classic example of great-power maneuvering: low cost, small outlay, minimum risk; mischievous, with little to show in the short run, but potentially capable of generating important tactical advantages.

The PDRY-Saudi rapprochement was short-lived, and very possibly the coup de grace was administered by Soviet agents. A series of bizarre and complex events in June 1978 resulted in the assassinations of the top leaders in Sana and Aden in the course of a factional struggle in which personal animosities underlay differing ideological and political outlooks. The previous murders in October 1977 of President Ibrahim al-Hamdi, of the Yemen Arab Republic, and his brother had strengthened the faction of Ahmad al-Ghashmi, who then became president. Al-Ghashmi, who favored better relations with Saudi Arabia and the PDRY, was murdered in June 1978. Within a matter of days it appeared that the deed had been planned in Aden to frame the PDRY's president, Salim Rubayyi Ali, a pragmatist who reciprocated al-Ghashmi's desire for accommodation. Behind the plot was his rival, the more ideological and militantly pro-Soviet Abd al-Fatah Ismail al-Jawfi. One week later, in the struggle for power at the top that broke out between Ismail's Soviet and East German-trained People's Militia and Rubayyi Ali's army units, Ismail triumphed and his opponent was killed. The Soviet role in these events is impossible to document, but Moscow's preference for the outcome is not.

First, Moscow stood to lose from Rubayyi Ali's opening to the YAR and Saudi Arabia, so its support for Fatah Ismail was understandable. The sharp increase in Soviet arms shipments after July 1978 suggests a desire to buttress Ismail's position and demonstrate the USSR's reliability in the face of Arab criticism of the PDRY. Second, the Soviet Union has further consolidated its presence in the PDRY since the assassination of Rubayyi Ali; Fatah Ismail seems more receptive to Soviet requests. Third, by the end of 1978, Fatah Ismail had remodeled the party and government structures on the lines of East Germany's, and he had assumed the posts of secretary-general of the Yemeni Socialist party and chairman of the governmental Supreme People's Council.* If Aden is a strategic prize, Moscow appears to be holding strong chips in a complicated political game.

---

* On April 20, 1980, an abrupt change of leadership resulted in Fatah Ismail's replacement as President by his prime minister, Ali Nasir Muhammad, who took over as secretary-general of the party. Fatah Ismail was appointed to the new post of president of the party, a position of dubious importance.

Soviet-PDRY relations remain close, so the foreign policy consequences of the internal struggle for power are still not clear. *Mid-East Intelligence Survey,* Vol. 8, No. 2 (April 16–30, 1980), 12.

On the other side of the peninsula, the Soviet Union's inroads are far more marginal. Only Iraq and Kuwait have diplomatic ties with the USSR. Notwithstanding the growth of Soviet military capability, Bahrain, Qatar, the United Arab Emirates (Abu Dhabi, Dubai, Ajman, Sharjah, Fujayrah, Umm al-Qaywayn, and Ra's al-Khaymah), Oman, and Saudi Arabia have kept the Soviets at a distance and settled their disputes without recourse to a Soviet connection. The constraints on Soviet penetration of the lower gulf stem from fundamentalist Islamic propensities, an intrinsic traditionalism, stable oligarchies, and strong prevailing ties to British and American expertise and technology, as well as suspicion of the USSR's military buildup of Iraq and military intervention in Afghanistan, Saudi influence, and the absence of politically destabilizing regional rivalries.

Tiny Kuwait established diplomatic ties with the Soviet Union in March 1963, after Qasim was overthrown and Moscow showed itself unwilling to uphold Baghdad's territorial claims against Kuwait. It is, in addition to Iraq, the only one among the Arab states of the gulf to have taken a token plunge, and it has done so for reasons pertaining more to intra-Arab relationships in the region than to the Arab-Israeli conflict. Its motives have been to signal to the Saudis not to take it for granted; to buy some Soviet goodwill as a form of protection against a possible renewal of Iraqi pressure; and to put Washington on notice that the oil-rich Arabs might turn to Moscow for weapons if the United States stops pressuring Israel to relinquish Arab lands.

All Moscow can do is bide its time and await disruptive developments. Lack of opportunity limits Soviet options; without clients eager to exploit the Soviet connection for their own ends, Moscow lacks the entanglement essential for political maneuver and influence. Its repeated feelers for normalization of relations with Saudi Arabia and the lower-gulf states have thus far been checked by the substantial consensual outlook that is shared by the gulf actors. All the regimes except Iraq are monarchical, oligarchical, and anti-Communist. In such a setting, Moscow has trouble finding suitable levers for an initial penetration. Whereas elsewhere in the Arab world Moscow has found militancy against Israel to go hand-in-hand with a general policy of anti-imperialism and an invariable readiness to improve relations with the Soviet Union, in the gulf the local rivalries are not limited to attitudes on the Arab-Israeli conflict. Thus Moscow is deprived of a position to which it could fall back on this old standby issue.

The Soviet willingness to make a virtue out of patience and wait for a major upheaval to alter the domestic outlook of one or more gulf countries may also be a function of the very limited and steadily diminishing U.S. military influence in the area. However much Moscow may denounce the presence of foreign military bases in the region and the arms buildup of the Saudis (and of the Iranians under the shah), it has little cause for concern over the minuscule American presence in Bahrain or Oman or the periodic showings of the flag.

The Soviet approach to the Arabian Peninsula has been pragmatic and low-key. Moscow has adapted to regional upheavals with flexibility and shrewdness, in the main tempering its activism to political circumstances. Opportunism, not ideology, impels Soviet policy. The USSR has been quick to establish diplomatic ties and a presence, assist prospective client states, and prove its reliability as a provisioner and superpower protector. The inhibitions on greater activism come primarily from the preferences and domestic pressure of the clients themselves and not from considerations relating to prospects for the Soviet-American relationship or to the power of the United States, whose capacity for affecting developments on the peninsula has diminished considerably. The USSR has been a generally accommodating patron; its ups and downs with Yemen, the PDRY, and Iraq have turned more often on their political variability than on its own mistakes. With the exception of possible complicity in the Yemeni assassinations, the Soviets have not been well placed to meddle effectively in leadership quarrels and have wisely concentrated on maintaining good government-to-government relations, reinforcing convergent policy goals, and providing such assistance as is necessary to keep a client in power.

The level and character of Soviet involvement have been determined by each Third World country. Though understandably reluctant to accede to all requests for aid, Moscow has nonetheless given what support has been necessary to assure a client's security, without (it must be noted) always being able to obtain comparably significant returns — witness the limited nature of Soviet naval privileges in Umm Qasr. In rendering military assistance, the USSR has avoided mindless polarization of regional conflicts. Initially it benefited from the feuds between Iraq and Iran, Iraq and Kuwait, the YAR and the PDRY, the PDRY and Oman, and Iraq and Saudi Arabia by developing a close working relationship with one party to the dispute; but having once forged a connection, it prefers generally to dampen regional conflicts and, as in the Iraqi-Iranian and Iraqi-Kuwaiti cases, to improve its relations with both parties and help mediate their disputes. Moreover, Moscow's commitment of military power has been prudent, designed to achieve limited and specific military and political ends and to satisfy the prime client without unnecessarily alarming the United States.

Moscow accepts the dilemmas that result from courting opposing sides in regional disputes and the periodic frustration with unmanageable clients as the lot of a superpower pursuing a multiplicity of goals in an age of complexity and change. Thus, it knows that the 1972 treaty with Iraq aroused suspicions among the Arabs of the lower gulf and temporarily scuttled Soviet efforts to effect a diplomatic breakthrough, and that the

Dhofari revolt fed the shah's fears and stimulated his military buildup, which was a bulwark against the emergence of pro-Soviet regimes in the gulf as long as Iran was stable. Even the replacement of the shah by a revolutionary, anti-Western regime has not been an unmixed blessing for the Soviet Union, if only because of the uncertainties that such a development entails for Iraqi-Iranian relations. The more Moscow builds up the PDRY (and the treaty of friendship and cooperation signed on October 25, 1979, presages closer ties), the more resistance it may encounter from Yemen, Saudi Arabia, Sudan, and Egypt. In case after case, its efforts to exercise influence arouse nationalist resentment and resistance; and to the extent that Moscow tries to mediate local disputes, it confronts divergent tugs that set limits to the influence it can wield over either party.

Recent developments on both sides of the Bab al-Mandab Strait, in Afghanistan, and in Iran raise inevitable questions about Soviet involvement, and specifically about the extent to which Moscow has benefited from its patient courtship of key countries of the Persian Gulf–Arabian Peninsula area. The regional opportunities to which Moscow has responded have been internally generated. What Moscow has done — and done with alacrity — is to cater to clients, some of whom have sought protection against external threats (as in the case of Iraq in 1974–1975), or to reinforce regimes with strong anti-Western biases (the PDRY, for instance). All of this has been intended to demonstrate the Soviet Union's credibility as a patron-protector. Moscow has also helped mediate some regional disputes, in the process improving its standing with the adversaries (for example, India and Pakistan in 1966, Iraq and Iran in 1975, and for limited periods the two Yemens). Even when it has failed in its attempt to fashion a settlement between regional rivals, as in the Horn of Africa, Moscow has shown a keen appreciation of local realities and U.S. interests; it has projected military power in a way that differentiates between preserving a client's position and upsetting local, regional, and superpower balances and relationships. Above all, when presented with a combination of opportunity and invitation, Moscow has repeatedly not been constrained by considerations of its relations with the United States, a phenomenon that puzzles Washington.

Moscow's tangible benefits in the Arabian Peninsula have on the average been modest. Its position in the PDRY is better now than at any time since the British withdrawal in late 1967 opened the way for the Soviet Union to engage the new Arab state. Privileged access to Aden, the best port in that part of the world, facilitates the Soviet navy's forward deployment; unlike Berbera (in Somalia), Aden has ample supplies of fresh water (which may be more important than fuel oil). It is also cooler by ten degrees and has better docking, storage, and repair facilities; it lacks only Berbera's isolation from heavy traffic. The huge floating drydock that had to be removed from Berbera when the Somalis evicted the Soviets is apparently still moored off the Dahlac Islands (belonging to the PDRY), though it could presumably be shifted to Aden if the PDRY leadership gave the go-ahead. The Soviet navy has also made use of the island of Socotra, but more as an anchorage to escape the monsoon swells and heat than as a significant facility.

Aden is certainly satisfactory for Soviet naval needs, though Moscow has yet to test the extent to which it can exploit the port in time of tension. Far more valuable to the Soviet military have been the air privileges accorded it. Since late 1978, Ilyushin-38 reconnaissance patrol aircraft have been flying on anti-submarine warfare (ASW) and intelligence missions. Moreover, the ability to give Aden as a destination made it easier for the Soviets to obtain overflight permission from Turkey, Iraq, and Iran for airlifting supplies and personnel to Ethiopia during the intensive resupply effort in late 1977–early 1978. In other words, access to PDRY airfields expedited Soviet intervention in the Horn — certainly a handsome short-time return on Moscow's investment.

In Iraq, the Russians have less to show. Their planes may refuel en route to Aden and the Horn, but since Iraq supports one faction of the Eritrean separatist movement against the Soviet-backed Ethiopian regime, Moscow's access has not been automatic or unimpeded; and though the Soviet navy can show the flag regularly at Umm Qasr, it must request official permission for each visit. Besides, despite alarm in Western quarters concerning the Soviet navy's operations in the gulf, Umm Qasr is poorly situated for military (as opposed to political) operations. At the closed end of the gulf and on a narrow, windy, shallow channel, it is hardly an unequivocal strategic asset.

It is too soon to know whether the past is a prologue to the Soviet future on the Arabian Peninsula. Moscow's presence has assisted in but not determined the setbacks to Western interests. It has complicated U.S. diplomacy and contributed to a diminution of the West's military presence without significantly affecting the peninsula's politics. The radical Arab impulse arising out of the lurch toward modernity occasionally redounds to Moscow's benefit. But the emergence of anti-Western regimes does not necessarily presage the establishment of a Soviet imperium.

## Looking Ahead

Moscow has sensed that the Yemenis are a key to the future of the peninsula. Forming the most numerous single Arabic-speaking group and dispersed throughout Arabia, they are a multiplying, energetic, economically backward, and socially depressed people, whom the Saudis view with great suspicion. Yemeni unity is as much an anathema to Saudi Arabia as Yemeni radicalism.

Of the two superpowers, the USSR has been the one sedulously courting both Yemens. Not only did Moscow arm the PDRY and support its guerrilla war against Oman — the first time that the Soviet Union openly encouraged a client to upset the existing territorial status quo — but it also intrigued to bring regimes more congenial to its political aims to power in Aden and Sana. Though it could not prevent a limited PDRY-Saudi reconciliation in 1976, the USSR may have been instrumental in arresting that development. It has shipped enormous quantities of arms to the PDRY, and at the same time has held out tantalizing offers of quick arms deliveries to Sana, with assurances that Soviet leaders will use their good offices to restrain the PDRY. Nowhere has the Soviet attempt to use arms transfers as an instrument of diplomacy, or Moscow's unwillingness to aggravate regional arms races for the promotion of political ends, been more blatant. If its present close relationship with the PDRY could be extended to the YAR as well, the Soviet Union's psychopolitical impact would be felt far beyond the Yemens.

In addition to polarizing the peninsula as a result of direct superpower interventions, a militant Yemeni nationalism could, by politicizing the Yemeni work force — now the most important in Saudi Arabia — undermine Saudi rule. If the Saudis become afflicted by an Iranian-type modernization virus, their Yemeni workers could be an aggravating catalyst; the way would be open for the Balkanization of the Arabian Peninsula and with it, a surge in Soviet prospects. So far the Saudis have kept the USSR at a distance, but fear of Yemeni nationalism, compounded by an untoward dangerous twist to the Iranian revolution and perceptions of the United States as indecisive, unreliable, and excessively military-minded in groping for ways to meet the Soviet challenge in the Arab world, could lead them to normalize relations with the Soviet Union, on the assumption that Moscow would be prepared to play a restraining role in the PDRY and Iraq in return for diplomatic normalization.

Prior to the Soviet military invasion of Afghanistan in December 1979, there were signs of an incipient Soviet courtship of Saudi Arabia. In late January 1979, O. A. Grinevskii, the head of the Near Eastern department of the USSR Ministry of Foreign Affairs, made a special visit to Kuwait to reassure Arab leaders in the gulf about the USSR's interest in maintaining friendly relations and about its lack of responsibility for the turbulence in Iran. At the same time, Igor Beliaev, a leading Soviet specialist on the Middle East, published an article suggesting that the time might be ripe for a Soviet-Saudi rapprochement.[14] Noting that "the Soviet Union and Saudi Arabia have never been at war with each other and they have never had any implacable conflicts," he opined that different social systems were no reason for mutual enmity, especially since both countries shared many important foreign-policy objectives, namely, opposition to Israel's occupation of Arab lands and recognition of "the right of the Arab people of Palestine to self-determination and the creation of their own independent state and also the return of East Jerusalem to the Arabs." He suggested that Saudi Arabia's anti-Sovietism was deliberately fostered by Western circles seeking to keep the two countries apart and alienated. Beliaev also implied that the special relationship that Washington was trying to nurture with Riyadh — witness the sale of F-15 fight bombers and other advanced weaponry — was vitiated by the "anti-Arab essence" of the Camp David agreements, which the United States was desirous of imposing on the Arabs. Overall, Beliaev struck a tune he hoped would arouse Saudi interest.

A little more than a month later, in an interview with the Beirut magazine *Al Hawadith,* Prince Saud al-Faisal, the Saudi foreign minister, acknowledged the importance of the Soviet Union in world affairs and said that his country often appreciated "the positive policy adopted by the Soviet Union towards Arab issues." A resumption of Soviet-Saudi diplomatic relations would be an enormous achievement for Soviet leaders.[15] But the Afghan crisis has chilled Saudi interest.

The renewed PDRY militancy against Yemen and Oman and indications of a possible Soviet-Saudi rapprochement are the first signs on the peninsula of the ripple effect from the Iranian revolution. Western uneasiness over its vital interests in the area is understandable, but there is no cause for excessive pessimism. A few observations may be appropriate.

First, Soviet influence is thus far very limited. With the possible exception of its relations with the PDRY, Moscow is not in a position to shape the domestic or foreign policies of the countries of the Arabian Peninsula. What it seeks is a presence which could act as a springboard for the future.

Second, again with the possible exception of the PDRY, none of the countries of the area wants to see a consolidated Soviet presence. Each of them would like to use the Soviet Union for its own purposes, just as Moscow seeks to exploit, and not be exploited by, its Arab clients. A convergence of some goals often gives the impression that the Russians are achieving more than they are — for instance, note the limited dividends that Moscow has realized from its Iraqi connection. The confining of Soviet influence is a theme running through the policies of all the countries in the region.

Third, though developments on the Arabian Peninsula can no longer be isolated from changing power-political relationships in the Arab East, the Horn of Africa, or the peninsula's northern tier (Turkey, Iran, Afghanistan, and Pakistan), they are likely to continue to be determined primarily by factors indigenous to the peninsula itself. Assuming that each super-power will not go beyond prudent support for its clients in order to effect a sudden shift in the peninsula's military and political alignments, the prognosis is for residual tensions fueled by personal and ideological anti-pathies that will generate low-grade, limited conflicts between the regional adversaries. However, the Soviet military intervention in Afghanistan in December 1979 to prop up a beleaguered Communist puppet regime may herald a change in the USSR's Third World policy.

Fourth, the USSR's primary aim in the Arab world is to weaken the strategic and economic positions of the United States. Strategic advantage, not oil or the spread of communism, impels current Soviet policy; hence Moscow's readiness to absorb setbacks and bide its time. Proceeding on assumptions derived from Lenin's theory of imperialism, the Soviet leadership sees a weakening of the West in the Arab world as a key to strengthening its bargaining position in Europe, which remains strategically the pivot of Soviet aspirations.

Finally, the Soviet threat in the Arabian Peninsula is not a military one, though large-scale Soviet arms transfers and assignments of Cuban and East German personnel do provide the Soviet-subsidized PDRY with considerable clout. Basically, Moscow seeks influence, not instability, though it will not be above exploiting and aggravating the latter in the quest for the former. As the area enters a period of political and diplomatic fluidity, the Soviet Union is well situated to take advantage of the opportunities that are bound to emerge. The bar to the Soviet quest for the mantle of Britain's former role as imperial mediator of regional disputes should not be underestimated, but neither should the imperial impetus that drives Moscow's forward policy in the Third World and places it in increasing competition with the United States.

## Notes

1. Oles M. Smolansky, *The Soviet Union and the Arab East Under Khrushchev* (Lewisburg, Pa.: Bucknell University Press, 1974), 80.

2. George S. Dragnich, "The Soviet Union's Quest for Access to Naval Facilities in Egypt Prior to the June War of 1967," in Michael MccGwire, Ken Booth, and John McDonnell (eds.), *Soviet Naval Policy: Objectives and Constraints* (New York: Praeger, 1975), 252-269.

3. John C. Campbell, "Communist Strategies in the Mediterranean," *Problems of Communism,* vol. 28, no. 3 (May-June 1979), 5.

4. Alvin Z. Rubinstein, *Red Star on the Nile: The Soviet-Egyptian Influence Relationship Since the June War* (Princeton: Princeton University Press, 1977), 79-126.

5. *Strategic Survey 1971* (London: International Institute for Strategic Studies, 1971), 31.

6. The literature on the October War is voluminous. For a detailed examination, see some of the major sources listed in the reference list at the end of the chapter.

7. Rubinstein, *Red Star on the Nile,* 288–291.

8. Haim Shaked and Tamar Yegness, "Continuity and Change in Saudi Arabia, Yemen and South Yemen, 1967–1973," in Itamar Rabinovich and Haim Shaked (eds.), *From June to October: The Middle East Between 1967 and 1973* (New Brunswick, N.J.: Transaction Books, 1978), 299–301.

9. R. B. Serjeant, "The Republic of South Yemen," in Michael Adams (ed.), *The Middle East: A Handbook* (New York: Praeger, 1971), 269.

10. *Washington Post,* January 25, 1978.

11. R. P. Owen, "The Rebellion in Dhofar — A Threat to Western Interests in the Gulf," *The World Today* (June 1973) pp. 266–272.

12. Richard E. Bissell, "Soviet Use of Proxies in the Third World: The Case of Yemen," *Soviet Studies,* vol. 30, no. 1 (January 1978), 87–106.

13. *Izvestiia,* April 16, 1977.

14. Igor Beliaev, "Saudi Arabia: What Next?," *Literaturnaya gazeta,* no. 5 (January 31, 1979), 14.

15. The advantages of a Soviet link may, however, have palled on the Saudi leadership since late November 1979, when approximately 500 heavily armed and well-trained guerrillas attempted to undermine the Saudi regime by seizing the Grand Mosque in Mecca. Preliminary reports indicate that they were trained in Aden, very likely under Soviet sponsorship. See *New York Times,* December 17, 1979.

## Selected Bibliography

ABIR, MORDECHAI. *Oil, Power and Politics: Conflict in Arabia, the Red Sea and the Gulf.* London: Frank Cass, 1974.

———— and ARYEH YODFAT. *In the Direction of the Gulf: The Soviet Union and the Persian Gulf.* London: Frank Cass, 1977.

AGWANI, M. S. *Communism in the Arab East.* London: Asian Publishing House, 1969.

BAR-ZOHAR, MICHAEL. *Embassies in Crisis.* Englewood Cliffs, N.J.: Prentice-Hall, 1970.

CONFINO, M., and S. SHAMIR (eds.). *The U.S.S.R. and the Middle East.* New York: Wiley, 1973.

DAWISHA, KAREN. *Soviet Foreign Policy Towards Egypt.* London: Macmillan, 1979.

FREEDMAN, ROBERT O. *Soviet Policy Towards the Middle East Since 1970.* 2nd ed. New York: Praeger, 1978.

GLASSMAN, JON. *Arms for the Arabs: The Soviet Union and War in the Middle East.* Baltimore: Johns Hopkins University Press, 1976.

GOLAND, GALIA. *Yom Kippur and After: The Soviet Union and the Middle East Crisis.* Cambridge: Cambridge University Press, 1977.

————. *The Soviet Union and the Palestine Liberation Organization.* New York: Praeger, 1980.

HAZEN, BARUCH. *Soviet Propaganda: A Case Study of the Middle East Conflict.* New Brunswick, N.J.: Transaction Books, 1976.

HEIKAL, MOHAMED. *The Road to Ramadan.* London: Collins, 1975.

————. *The Sphinx and the Commissar: The Rise and Fall of Soviet Influence in the Middle East.* New York: Harper & Row, 1978.

HUREWITZ, J. C. (ed.). *Soviet-American Rivalry in the Middle East.* New York: Praeger, 1969.

KAPLAN, STEPHEN S. (ed.). *Mailed Fist, Velvet Glove: Soviet Armed Forces As A Political Instrument.* Washington, D.C.: The Brookings Institution, 1980.

KASS, ILANA. *Soviet Involvement in the Middle East: Policy Formulation, 1966– 1973.* Boulder, Colo.: Westview Press, 1978.

KLIEMAN, AARON S. *Soviet Russia and the Middle East.* Baltimore: Johns Hopkins University Press, 1970.

KLINGHOFFER, ARTHUR JAY. *The Soviet Union and International Oil Politics.* New York: Columbia University Press, 1977.

KOHLER, FOY D., LEON GOURE, and MOSE L. HARVEY. *The Soviet Union and the October 1973 Middle East War: The Implications for Détente.* Washington, D.C.: Center for Advanced Studies, University of Miami, 1974.

KRAMNER, ARNOLD. *The Forgotten Friendship: Israel and the Soviet Bloc 1947– 1953.* Urbana: University of Illinois Press, 1974.

LAQUEUR, WALTER Z. *Nationalism and Communism in the Middle East.* New York: Praeger, 1956.

————. *The Soviet Union and the Middle East.* New York: Praeger, 1959.

————. *The Struggle for the Middle East: The Soviet Union in the Mediterranean, 1958–1968.* New York: Macmillan, 1969.

MANGOLD, PETER. *Superpower Intervention in the Middle East.* New York: St. Martin's, 1978.

McCGwire, Michael (ed.). *Soviet Naval Developments: Capability and Context.* New York: Praeger, 1973.

McCGwire, Michael, Ken Booth, and John McDonnell (eds.). *Soviet Naval Policy: Objectives and Constraints.* New York: Praeger, 1975.

Page, Stephen. *The USSR and Arabia.* London: Central Asian Research Centre, 1971.

Pennar, Jaan. *The USSR and the Arabs: The Ideological Dimension.* New York: Crane, Russak, 1973.

Ra'anan, Uri. *The USSR Arms the Third World.* Cambridge: MIT Press, 1969.

Ro'i, Yaacov (ed.). *From Enroachment to Involvement: A Documentary Study of Soviet Policy in the Middle East, 1945–1973.* New York: John Wiley, 1974.

———. (ed.). *The Limits to Power: Soviet Policy in the Middle East.* New York: St. Martin's, 1979.

———. *Soviet Decision Making in Practice: The USSR and Israel, 1947–1954.* New Brunswick, N.J.: Transaction Books, 1980.

Rubinstein, Alvin Z. *Red Star on the Nile: The Soviet-Egyptian Influence Relationship Since the June War.* Princeton: Princeton University Press, 1977.

Smolansky, Oles. *The Soviet Union and the Arab East Under Khrushchev.* Bucknell, Pa.: Bucknell University Press, 1974.

Whetten, Lawrence L. *The Canal War: Four Power Conflict in the Middle East.* Cambridge: MIT Press, 1974.

Yodfat, Aryeh. *Arab Politics in the Soviet Mirror.* New York: John Wiley, 1973.

# 12
# Soviet-American Relations: The Elusive Accommodation

The Soviet Union has been locked in struggle with the United States ever since the end of World War II, when its expansion in Europe and the Far East placed it astride areas that were vital to the United States. An imperial-minded Stalin pursued policies that exacerbated Western insecurity and residual ideological antipathies and that polarized East-West relations. His obsession with security — an understandable reaction to a war that had brought the USSR to the brink of disaster — became more acute as the United States gained obvious superiority in strategic weapons and developed its policy of containment. Tension was endemic.

By the mid-1950s, however, relations between the two blocs had stabilized, and the fear of war in Europe had receded. Soviet possession of nuclear weapons ensured the effectiveness of deterrence. The new leadership inched toward a limited accommodation with the West, based on the preservation of the territorial status quo. But the essentially competitive character of Soviet-American relations did not significantly diminish; indeed, it grew as Moscow's might expanded and assertiveness in the Third World took form. In the consequent globalization of the rivalry, the Soviet-American relationship assumed an adversarial nature in which competition overshadowed cooperation; the latter is served by a mutual desire to avoid nuclear war and direct confrontation of Soviet and American forces, but the former seems destined to persist for the foreseeable future in a wide number of areas.

Our interest here is in the dynamics of the current situation and the troublesome issues that lie ahead, yet in assessing the Soviet-American relationship, we should not ignore certain shared characteristics that hold out a promise — in the long run — of limited détente and attenuation of the impetus to war.

First, the Soviet Union and the United States have never fought a war against one another. This is a remarkable fact of more than two hundred years of modern history. Notwithstanding tense crises and local wars, the two superpowers did not go to war with each other over Berlin in 1948–1949, Korea in 1950–1953, Hungary in 1956, Cuba in 1962, Czechoslovakia in 1968, Vietnam in the late 1960s–early 1970s, or the Middle East in 1970 or 1973. Both refrained from taking steps that might have precipitated a direct confrontation between them.

Second, neither covets the territory of the other. There are no outstanding irredentist claims. Real estate is not at the heart of their difficulties. A rivalry that is imperial rather than nationalist in character does not generate volatile emotional passions and thus is far easier for the elites in power to manage domestically and is less likely to get out of hand. Each side can more easily accept limited gains by the other.

Third, as peoples, the Russians and Americans have many positive images of one another. (While the Russians constitute only 52 percent of the total population of the Soviet Union, they are the politically dominant group and their culture pervades the society.) Russians and Americans appreciate each others' literature, music, theater, and sports, as is evident in the general popularity of the visiting artists and cultural troupes of both countries.

Fourth, Soviet and American societies share the admirable but quixotic belief of the eighteenth-century Enlightenment that through science, education, and man's reason, society can be transformed. This fundamental outlook predominates despite mushrooming ecological, social, and economic problems. For both, gleaming technology still stands at the center of the societies that their elites seek to build; for both, technological "fixes" are seen as the cure for man's ills.

Fifth, both the United States and the Soviet Union are disliked and mistrusted by their immediate neighbors. Both have alliance problems. Concerns over maintaining intra-alliance cohesion help to limit each superpower's temptation to interfere directly in the other's primary sphere of influence.

Sixth, as urban, industrialized societies, the two countries face common problems such as alienation, resource depletion, environmental deterioration, and so on. Their racial and nationality problems cause political unrest and absorb an increasing amount of the attention of the leaderships.

Finally, both face the supreme paradox of the nuclear age: Despite ever-increasing military power, their influence over allies and clients is progressively more difficult to manage and maintain. Small nations have found a new lease on autonomy and independence in this nuclear age, and their initiatives often confound the best-laid plans of their patrons and putative masters.

## Moscow's Quest for Peaceful Coexistence and Détente

Since the death of Stalin in March 1953, the Soviet leadership has sought to improve relations with the United States and the Western countries for combinations of reasons which have varied over time. The origin of this policy can be pinpointed to the 1954–1955 period and Khrushchev's withdrawal of Soviet military power from Austria and Finland. Whatever the other considerations, Moscow's pullback from forward positions in Europe signified its readiness to pare its territorial ambitions somewhat and to seek an accommodation with the West, even at the expense of Soviet relations with China. The Geneva summit conference in July 1955 marked Khrushchev's entry onto the international stage and the beginning of a more open and active Soviet diplomacy.

The process of negotiating with the West however, was erratic and periodically disrupted by intra–Soviet-bloc crises, such as the 1956 upheavals in Eastern Europe, and by tensions with the West, such as the Berlin crisis between 1958 and 1961 (when the wall surrounding West Berlin was erected), the U-2 affair of May 1960 (when the shooting down of a U.S. spy plane over the USSR reminded the Soviet military of their vulnerability to a U.S. nuclear attack), and the Cuban missile crisis of October 1962. The Cuban missile crisis was the most dangerous Soviet challenge to the United States during the Khrushchev period. It had a profound effect on Soviet-U.S. relations and on the acceleration of the USSR's buildup of strategic forces in the 1960s and 1970s.

After Fidel Castro came to power in January 1959, his commitment to revolution elsewhere in Latin America prevented a normalization of Cuba's relations with the United States. Moscow was slow to court Castro, but it denounced the Monroe Doctrine, the better to uphold Cuba's increasingly anti-American policy and revolutionary outlook. In July 1960, Khrushchev said the Monroe Doctrine was dead: it "has outlived its time, has outlived itself, has died, so to say, a natural death. Now the remains of this doctrine should best be buried as every dead body is so that it should not poison the air by its decay."* After the abortive CIA-engineered effort to overthrow Castro at the Bay of Pigs in April 1961, Moscow undertook a program of economic and military assistance to Cuba. In the spring of 1962, the Kremlin decided to install intermediate-range missiles and bombers in Cuba, ostensibly to protect Castro (who proclaimed himself a Marxist-Leninist) from another U.S.-organized invasion, but primarily to attempt a sweeping shift in the balance of power.

---

* *Pravda,* July 13, 1960.

According to Khrushchev, it was during his visit to Bulgaria in mid-May 1962 that he conceived the idea of installing nuclear-tipped missiles in Cuba without allowing Washington to find out about them until it was too late for anything to be done.[1] In late July, after obtaining Castro's permission, Moscow began pouring in men and matériel. On September 2, it announced an expanded program of arms deliveries and the sending of unspecified "technical specialists" to help Cuba meet the "threats" from "aggressive imperialist quarters." On September 11, in a major policy statement, the Soviet government gave assurances of peaceful intent, asserting that "the armaments and military equipment sent to Cuba are designed exclusively for defensive purposes" but warning that "if war is unleashed," the Soviet Union will render assistance to Cuba "just as it was ready in 1956 to render military assistance to Egypt at the time of the Anglo-French-Israeli aggression in the Suez Canal region." During the next few weeks, the Kremlin carried on an intensive program of disinformation and deception, issuing placatory statements and sending diplomats to assure officials in the Kennedy administration, including the president, of the defensive nature of the weapons being introduced into Cuba.

The dramatic account of the "eyeball-to-eyeball" Soviet-American confrontation in the Caribbean is well known. On October 22, President John F. Kennedy told the American people that the United States had "unmistakable evidence" that the USSR was constructing a series of offensive missile sites in Cuba and that the United States aimed "to prevent the use of these missiles against this or any other country and to secure their withdrawal or elimination from the western hemisphere." By the end of October the crisis was over.

Though forced to remove the missiles and disappointed at his failure to redress the strategic imbalance between the Soviet Union and the United States, Khrushchev did ensure the security of his Cuban protégé, having extracted a U.S. pledge not to invade Cuba in return for the removal of the missiles. Domestically, his failure to implant the missiles in Cuba and obtain U.S. acceptance of the USSR as an equal in the strategic equation meant that the Soviet military would have its way; a massive and accelerated buildup of strategic forces was undertaken, reflecting the determination of the Soviet leadership never again to have to back down to the United States because of military inferiority.

In the realm of foreign policy, the crisis led to renewed efforts to reach an accommodation through negotiation, "but within a mutually acceptable balance of strategic power." It gave new impetus to the quest for an improvement in Soviet-American relations, leading to the conclusion of the limited nuclear test ban treaty in the summer of 1963 and the establishment "of the so-called hot-line of instant communications between Washington and Moscow. In general, these ameliorating measures were intended to lower the level of tension, facilitate the management of future crises, and clear the way for greater accommodation."[2]

After Khrushchev's deposal in October 1964, the Brezhnev-Kosygin team continued the policy of trying to improve relations with the United States, but headway was slow. Complicating the process were the Soviets' decisions to help North Vietnam, to rearm the Arabs after the June War, to invade Czechoslovakia, and to strengthen Soviet forces in Europe. But West German Chancellor Willy Brandt's *Ostpolitik* and readiness to accept the division of Germany, and the momentum of Moscow's buildup of strategic weapons, made the United States receptive to an improvement of Soviet-American relations.

By the early 1970s, the Soviet Union's interest in détente derived from a series of compelling policy objectives which are still operative. First is the desire for Western, especially American, technology and credits to increase industrial and managerial efficiency and modernization in the non-military sectors of the economy. In March 1971, at the twenty-fourth congress of the CPSU, the Politburo made the decision — which had been deferred in late 1969 and frequently discussed in 1970 — to seek better relations with the United States in order to assure the importation from that country of large amounts of advanced technology and equipment. It did so after five years of futile efforts to overcome lagging productivity and technological advances in the nonmilitary sectors of the Soviet economy. In September 1965, the Brezhnev-Kosygin leadership had introduced a series of major economic reforms to overcome the shortcomings that had allegedly resulted from Khrushchev's "hare-brained" policies; but like the fabled monkey who tried to organize the barnyard animals into a symphony orchestra by continually reassigning instruments, they realized that domestic realignments were not sufficient to stimulate innovation and efficiency. For this they would have to turn to the West and Japan.

The importation of technology and machinery is a fundamental reason for the USSR's interest in détente. Some argue that it is the *only* reason. By importing on an enormous scale, the leadership seeks to offset the deleterious combination of party and bureaucratic interference in the operation of industry and the imbalances between the military and nonmilitary branches of the economy that account for shortages and shoddy goods and that plague planners and decimate production targets. Western technology has been in vogue before, both under Stalin and Lenin and under the czars. But the scale of the present need is enormous, and meeting it is crucial for overcoming the critical bottlenecks in important economic sectors: "(1) petroleum and natural gas extraction, processing, and transmission; (2) computer-related systems in planning and management; (3) mass industrial production processes, such as those of the automotive industry; and (4) agribusiness activities, such as animal husbandry."[3]

A second factor in the Soviet interest in détente is Moscow's China problem. Despite their preponderance of military power, the Soviets are uneasy over the Chinese almost to the point of paranoia. Long-dormant cultural stereotypes of the "inscrutable" Chinese have been revived in the wake of the Sino-Soviet quarrel. The fear of a Chinese threat is aggravated by periodic outbreaks along the thousands of miles of exposed border; by Beijing's vestigial territorial grievances, its growing nuclear capability, and its formal termination of the 1950 treaty of alliance; and by the evolving Sino-U.S. rapprochement. In recent years, Moscow has tried to normalize relations with Beijing, but with little success. Meanwhile, unhappy over the need to maintain large conventional forces along the Chinese border and disturbed as much by China's active challenge to Soviet interests and clients in the Far East as by its potential as a superpower, Moscow seeks détente in the West in order to acquire maximum latitude for dealing with China in the East.

A third important consideration — certainly one that has been a constant in Soviet thinking after 1945 — was the desire to obtain formal Western recognition of the territorial status quo in Europe. What gained momentum with Chancellor Willy Brandt's policy of accommodation with the Soviet Union in 1969 was completed at the Conference on Security and Cooperation in Europe in Helsinki in July 1975: the final legitimation of the division of Germany and the Soviet imperial system in Eastern Europe.

Fourth, the Soviets have an interest in stabilizing the strategic arms race and limiting the escalation of defense expenditures. Though Western analysts are now more prone to question the validity of this proposition, Moscow's campaign for SALT II suggests that the Soviets do want stabilization of strategic delivery systems, if only to keep their own swollen arms budget within tolerable economic limits, and also to avoid an open, all-out arms race with the United States. Moscow's keen interest was evident in the SALT I agreement in 1972 and the Ford-Brezhnev accord at Vladivostok in November 1974, when "essential equivalence" or parity was determined (though at a much higher threshold than had been expected by Western proponents of arms control). Nevertheless, the Carter administration's attempt in March 1977 to lower the quantitative ceilings that had been agreed to at Vladivostok occasioned bitter Soviet opposition, which led to the lapsing of SALT I and inordinate difficulty in obtaining the U.S. Senate's approval for SALT II. Moscow believes that SALT II should not be linked to the ongoing Soviet-American rivalry in the Third World.

Finally, Moscow views détente as a form of political struggle that is compatible with avoidance of nuclear war. It sees no essential contradiction between seeking much-needed economic and technological supplements to its industrial network and simultaneously maneuvering for strategic and political advantages to improve its overall global position vis-à-vis the United States. For Moscow, this is the competitive aspect of peaceful coexistence.

## Ideological Struggle: Systemic or Sideshow?

Prior to 1945, a weak, isolated Soviet Union resorted to the idea of peaceful coexistence to buttress its essentially defensive strategy. Peaceful coexistence was a policy dictated by weakness; but by the end of the Stalin period and particularly under Khrushchev and Brezhnev, it was refashioned for a strong, internationally vigorous, imperial Soviet Union.

Attempts to understand Soviet foreign policy frequently founder on differences of interpretation concerning the Soviet meaning of "peaceful coexistence." To many in the West, the term signifies the maintenance of status quo in the international arena, with any changes to take place gradually and in accordance with some generally accepted code of conduct that preserves stability and a balance of power between the two rival security systems. To the Soviets, on the other hand, it implies a strategy of conflict, short of nuclear war, in which the Soviet camp is strengthened and extended to encompass new members. An authoritative Soviet publication explains:

> Peaceful coexistence is a specific form of class struggle between socialism and capitalism. In peaceful competition with capitalism, the socialist system will win, that is, the socialist method of production has decisive advantages over the capitalist system .... Peaceful coexistence concerns relations between states. It does not touch upon relations within states; it does not touch upon the revolutionary struggle for the transformation of society.
>
> Peaceful coexistence among the states of the two [different] systems does not mean compromise in ideological questions. The bourgeois and communist world outlooks cannot be reconciled; moreover, this is not necessary for peaceful coexistence among states. Each can maintain its own position on ideological questions without having this serve as a roadblock preventing cooperation in economic questions and in questions concerning international peace and security.
>
> Naturally, the concept of peaceful coexistence as a condition of relations among states is inapplicable to the internal relations of a state. Therefore, the attempts of the revisionists to extend the concept of peaceful coexistence to class relations within a state are absurd. The recognition of the necessity and possibility of peaceful coexistence does not signify rejection of the class struggle, of the idea of the inevitability of the victory of communism over capitalism.[4]

What often confuses Westerners is the way the term can be variously used, at some times to convey a spirit of conciliation and at others, conflict. Thus, speaking before the United Nations General Assembly on September 28, 1960, Khrushchev stated that

> . . . we do not want to impose our order by force upon other countries. Let those who determine the policy of states with a social order differing from ours also renounce futile and dangerous efforts at dictating their will. It is time for them also to recognize that the choice of one way of life or another is a domestic matter for each people. Let us build up our relations, taking into consideration the hard facts of reality. And this will be peaceful coexistence.

A few months later, speaking in Moscow to Communist officials, he declared: "The policy of peaceful coexistence, as regards its social content, is a form of intense economic, political, and ideological struggle of the proletariat against the aggressive forces of imperialism in the international arena."

Perhaps nothing illustrates the ambiguity of the term better than Khrushchev's attempt to explain away the implied threat in the ominous words "We will bury you." For example, on one occasion, at a reception at the Polish Embassy in Moscow on September 4, 1959, he went out of his way to reaffirm the USSR's belief in the peaceful competition implied in peaceful coexistence and to calm Western uneasiness:

> Some representatives of the capitalist countries reproach me for having allegedly said that we shall bury capitalism. I have already said that I want only one thing — that they should understand me correctly. The imperialists are digging their own grave. Such is their nature. Karl Marx long ago explained how this is being done, but they still do not understand it.
>
> I want to say only one thing: You must know that physically we shall not dig a grave for you. If you like the capitalist system so much, live under capitalism to your heart's content as long as you can, but how long you will be able to do so I cannot tell.[5]

In general, to the Soviets, peaceful coexistence means competition and incessant struggle in all spheres short of total war. "Imperialist" wars will be resisted, just as all national liberation movements will be aided, irrespective of the effect on Soviet-U.S. relations. His successors share Khrushchev's firm belief that the balance of world power is shifting inexorably toward the Soviet camp and that capitalism is no more capable of preventing the triumph of communism than feudalism was of forestalling the advent of capitalism. Implicit in peaceful coexistence are continued rivalry, endemic suspicion, and unrelenting effort to weaken the adversary in order to alter the correlation of world forces through a combination of political, economic, cultural, and ideological means.

When relations between the Soviet Union and the West began to improve in the early 1970s, the word *détente* — the French word for a relaxation of international tension — was widely used in the West. In the English language, it connotes not only easing tensions but also developing extensive, friendly relations in all areas of national interaction. During the heady days after the signing of SALT I in May 1972, the Soviets too began to use the word *détente* in conjunction with calls for peaceful coexistence. But the crucial term for the Soviets is peaceful coexistence, not détente. It is important that we understand their usage of *détente* and not extrapolate Soviet interpretations from our own. There is nothing to suggest that the Soviet interpretation foresees a time or a situation in which the USSR and the United States will end up as friends, settling their differences congenially around the bargaining table.

In the United States, as in Western Europe, there were many who behaved as if the mere use of the term had suddenly transmuted the essence of the conflictual Soviet-American relationship. Events since 1974 have battered at sanguine views of interdependency and the cooperation it is supposed to foster. Détente was oversold, and there is good reason for a cautious approach to evaluations that anticipate a significant improvement in Soviet-American relations.

In the past, Soviet ideology has been highly malleable. Policy shifts occasioned by changes in the correlation of forces were incorporated in refurbished ideological formulations. Thus Khrushchev, recognizing in 1956 that nuclear weapons had made war between great powers unthinkable as a means of acquiring tactical political and strategic advantages, announced in a sweeping doctrinal change that war between capitalism (that is, the United States) and communism (the Soviet Union) was no longer "fatalistically inevitable." But though Khrushchev dropped the inevitability-of-war thesis from Moscow's doctrinal baggage, he did not cease in his efforts to undermine his adversaries and extend Soviet influence; nor did he cooperate with other powers to alleviate global ills. Brezhnev has followed in Khrushchev's footsteps, without the bluster and doctrinal pretentiousness but with comparable determination, skill, and readiness to exploit regional tensions and U.S. weakness.

## The New Cold War

An examination of Soviet-American relations reveals the persistence of basic asymmetries that preclude significant progress toward a better relationship and that foreshadow a time of continuing troubles. These asymmetries arise from the different values, perceptions, interests, and ambitions of their respective leaderships. They need not lead to war, for reasons mentioned earlier, but they assuredly hold out little prospect for cooperation and friendship.

The first asymmetry relates to the general posture of the United States and the Soviet Union in world affairs today. Whereas the United States is pruning its commitments and policy to what might be described as a status quo orientation in the face of serious setbacks in different parts of the world, the Soviet Union is riding the crest of an imperial-minded phase of its foreign policy. It seeks influence in the major areas of the world, especially in the regions lying south of the USSR; Afghanistan, Iran, and the Arab states of the gulf and Arabian Peninsula became targets of opportunity in the late 1970s. Soviet ambitions in black Africa, a low-priority area until the mid-1970s, have been whetted by the ascendancy in Angola, Mozambique, and Ethiopia of leaderships professing a belief in Marxism-Leninism, and Soviet involvement is increasing, notwithstanding the additional strains this has imposed on the relationship with the United States. Readiness to commit economic and military resources to Third World clients shows no signs of flagging. Underlying Soviet willingness to accept the higher costs of an imperial policy is a belief in what might be called incrementalism: the view that modest gains, systematically garnered, can undermine the geopolitical foundations of an adversary and bring benefits, which over time can produce qualitative changes in the diplomatic environment within which the USSR operates and in the balance of power itself. To Soviet leaders, the nuclear age has not rendered obsolete the time-honored principle of strengthening one's position by undermining the alliances and alignments of an adversary.

A second asymmetry inheres in the growing disparity between the conventional force levels and capabilities of the Soviet Union and the United States, and between the Warsaw Pact and NATO. The ratio of two to one has been bandied about for many important categories of weapons. However, the Soviets enjoy greater — and growing — advantages in such crucial categories of conventional weapons as tanks, artillery, motorized armored personnel carriers, and attack helicopters.[6] The Soviet program of modernizing its armed forces shows no signs of abating.

Third, a fundamental asymmetry lies in the way in which each superpower relates to the members of its respective alliance system. There is no need to detail here how little control the United States exercises over the behavior of its NATO allies. Furthermore, NATO's southern flank is going through a period of grave internal troubles that calls into question the very viability of the alliance in the Mediterranean. In the short run, at least, there is little that the United States can do to set the alliance in order. Certainly it cannot impose the kind of outward discipline on its allies that the Soviet Union can within the Warsaw Pact. The Romanians may behave like mavericks; but Bucharest remembers Prague in August 1968. It is careful to stay within the narrow limits of assertive autonomy allowed by Moscow. The Brezhnev Doctrine is a writ no national Communist regime in Eastern Europe can afford to forget or ignore. Moscow's mailed fist keeps its reluctant allies in line.

A fourth asymmetry, adversely affecting the ability of the two superpowers to reach meaningful political-military accords, is the differing approach and attitude toward China. Moscow is uneasy over the kind of relationship that Washington seeks to establish with Beijing. Ever since Nixon's 1972 visit to China, the USSR has warily watched U.S. overtures, fearing that they presage a military buildup of China. In a remarkably candid interview, Dr. Georgii Arbatov, a member of the CPSU Central Committee and director of the Institute for the USA and Canada (an important Soviet think tank), noted that any effort to reequip the Chinese army "cannot be considered a step that can be reconciled with good intentions" toward the Soviet Union. The United States has to make a crucial decision, he continued: Does it want to build the bridge across the river or along the river? What kind of international situation does it want to create "in this dangerous nuclear age? . . . If you do want détente in Europe, let us say, if you want arms reduction, you would be very unwise and inconsistent and even self-defeating if at the same time you tried to fan up dangerous situations in another part of the world."[7]

The Soviets tell the fable of two hunters who are stalking tigers. They separate, and then one shouts, "I found a tiger!" The other cries, "Why don't you bring him back?" "He won't let go of me" is the answer. The moral is for the United States to be careful not to let the Chinese drag it too far away from better relations with the USSR. The Kremlin blamed Carter for encouraging the anti-Soviet statements (the attacks on "hegemonism") of Deng Xiaoping, the deputy premier and vice-chairman of the CCP, during his visit to the United States in February 1979. It also believed that China's invasion of Vietnam a month later was made possible only because of tacit support from Washington. The United States' backing of China in its quarrel with Vietnam, its preferential treatment of China economically, and the fear that it may seek to modernize China's military machine all heighten Soviet uneasiness about American policy.

A fifth asymmetry is the difference between the open society of the United States and the closed society of the Soviet Union. In the United States, public opinion and lobbying can influence official policy (as they did on the issues of Vietnam, Cyprus, and Angola, for example); in the Soviet Union, they cannot. There are no tugs in the USSR between the executive and legislative branches of government to complicate the conduct of foreign policy or exasperate allies. If there are détentists or antidétentists in the Kremlin, we have no sure way of identifying them and little likelihood of directly influencing the outcome of whatever Soviet internal debate on foreign policy may be going on at any given time. The Soviet public assuredly has no voice in foreign-policy making, a matter of considerable advantage to Soviet leaders in their dealings with the outside world.

More serious in its implications for day-to-day relations between Moscow and Washington is the apparent ignorance of the American political system that pervades the top Soviet leadership. American officials who visit Moscow to discuss policy differences with Soviet leaders are invariably shocked by their lack of understanding of the dynamics of American politics. Moreover, visiting congressional representatives are often appalled by the experience — witness Senator Henry Bellmon's (R-Oklahoma) comment: "They were abrasive, arrogant. I was kind of turned off by the whole experience."[8]

The differences in the two political systems reinforce the suspicions harbored by top leaders and complicate the tasks not just of negotiation but also of the communication of strongly held attitudes. Thus, Moscow's insensitivity to the political difficulties that its military presence in Cuba creates for a U.S. administration that would like to stabilize the arms race, expand trade, and improve relations derives partially from its erroneously attributing to the United States the mode of decision-making that operates in the Soviet Union. For example, Soviet leaders appear not to appreciate fully the independent and powerful role that the Congress plays in shaping U.S. foreign policy.

Finally, there is a profound asymmetry in the way in which each country tends to view the other. U.S. leaders often think that they and Soviet leaders see the world similarly; the Soviets know better! The American perception of the Soviet-American strategic relationship differs markedly from the Soviet perception. Paul Nitze, an influential critic of SALT, has argued that the Soviets may well hold a significantly different conception of "strategic parity": Whereas in the SALT negotiations U.S. officials have "consistently argued for the acceptance by both sides of the concept of 'essential equivalence,'" the Soviets have never agreed to this concept, "but have argued instead for the concept of 'equal security taking into account geographic and other considerations.' . . . They never went so far as to say that this really amounts to a requirement for Soviet superiority in capabilities over the United States, the U.K., France and China simultaneously, but watching the way they added things up and how they justified their position, this is what it boiled down to."[9] The Nitze position, which goes against two decades of American efforts to persuade the Soviets of the mutual benefits of arms control, may more accurately reflect the prevailing mood in the Soviet military and political establishment, namely, that the way to security is through a preponderance of military power vis-à-vis one's adversary. That such a conception of security serves only to heighten the insecurity of the adversary and thereby gives renewed impetus to the arms race goes to the heart of the fundamental asymmetry between Soviet and American perceptions of security, stability, and survival in an increasingly dangerous world.

## Dilemmas of an Imperial Policy

By the second half of the 1970s, Moscow's ambitions in the Third World had seriously compromised its efforts to improve relations with the United States. The optimistic expectations for détente raised by the signing of SALT I and the subsequent roundrobin of summit visits had begun to wane by the convening of the Conference on Security and Cooperation in Europe in July 1975. A number of developments adversely affected the Soviet-American relationship: the near confrontation during the Arab-Israeli war in October 1973; the resignation of Richard Nixon in August 1974; the uncertainty that followed the military coup in Portugal in April 1974 and led to the Portuguese Communist party's coming close to gaining effective control of the country; and the passage of the Jackson-Vanik amendment restricting U.S. credits to the USSR and denying most-favored-nation treatment in tariffs until Moscow eased restrictions on the emigration of dissidents, and the USSR's consequent abrogation of the economic agreement reached with Nixon for the repayment of World War II lend-lease debts. The Soviet-Cuban intervention in Angola in late 1975, which successfully brought to power a pro-Soviet regime, and the USSR's intervention in Ethiopia in 1976–1977 also contributed to the growing difficulties.

The list could be extended without difficulty, because everywhere one looked in the Third World in the late 1970s, the USSR and the United States stood essentially in an adversarial relationship. From the start of the Carter administration in January 1977, Soviet leaders went from uncertainty to disappointment to uneasiness over their relations with the United States. In their view, the principal responsibility for the steady deterioration in Soviet-American relations rests with Washington. They were annoyed by Carter's stress on human rights, which was viewed as a move toward intensification of ideological struggle. His letter, written soon after taking office, to the dissident nuclear physicist Andrei Sakharov, and his support for Anatoly Shcharansky, the Jewish refusnik (that is, one who seeks to emigrate from the USSR) when the latter was arrested by Soviet authorities in 1977 and accused of working for U.S. intelligence, were especially irritating to the Soviets. More important, Kremlin officials sharply criticized the Carter administration in March 1977, after a visit to

Moscow by Secretary of State Cyrus Vance, for seeking to undermine the essentials of the SALT II agreement which Moscow had regarded as all but sealed by negotiations with the Ford administration. According to Gromyko:

> At every meeting in Moscow we emphasized the main idea that the foundation for a new agreement that had been built before should not be destroyed but should be preserved at all cost. Indeed, what will come about if each time a new leadership takes office in some country everything positive that has been achieved in relations with other states is crossed out? What stability of relations with other countries can one talk about in such circumstances? What talk can there be about the stability of relations between the USA and the USSR in this case? . . .
>
> Further, at the talks with Cyrus Vance it was proposed that we revise the right of both sides to modernize the existing missiles which is laid down in the agreement now in force and in the Vladivostok accord [reached between Brezhnev and Ford in November 1974]. This has never been questioned. . . . Now, however, it is urged that this part of the agreement be scrapped too, in a way that would be advantageous to the United States and to the disadvantage of the Soviet Union.[10]

In Geneva in May 1977, Vance suggested cooperation on the Arab-Israeli problem as an indication of Washington's desire to put relations back on track. After some very secret discussions (only Carter, Vance, and National Security Council Adviser Zbigniew Brzezinski were involved on the American side), a U.S.-Soviet statement on the Middle East was issued on October 1, 1977, calling for a return to the Geneva venue and agreement on bringing the PLO into the negotiating process. However, within a week the Carter administration was forced by Israeli and congressional objections to renege on the agreement, to the ire of Moscow. Sadat's dramatic initiative and trip to Jerusalem and Carter's subsequent efforts on behalf of a separate Egyptian-Israeli agreement reinforced Moscow's view that divergence rather than convergence characterized Soviet-U.S. aims in the Middle East. Moscow questioned Washington's seriousness about détente. It criticized Carter's tough speech on March 17, 1978, at Wake Forest College, in which he warned the Soviet Union that its continued military activity in the Third World would result in an increased U.S. defense effort; and *Pravda* described his Annapolis speech on June 7, 1978, though it contained some conciliatory parts, as "fraught with serious dangers, dangers for the United States, for all countries interested in peace, for the entire course of development of international relations."

During the following year the relationship continued to be troubled. Moscow resented the Camp David process that brought an Egyptian-Israeli treaty on March 26, 1979, without Soviet participation; the encumbrances that Washington placed in the way of greater trade and technological imports from the United States; U.S. attention to the normalization of Sino-American relations, at the expense, Moscow thought, of Soviet-American relations; and the fracas in August-September 1979 over the Soviet "combat brigade" in Cuba. Developments in Afghanistan and Iran further aggravated the Soviet-American relationship: a Soviet-backed Communist coup in Kabul in April 1978 triggered an anti-Communist nationalist guerrilla war that brought increasingly blatant Soviet involvement, culminating in December 1979 in a formal Soviet military invasion to prop up its Afghan puppets; and the toppling of the pro-Western regime of the shah in February 1979 ushered in a time of turmoil in Iran, highlighted by the seizure of U.S. embassy personnel in Tehran in early November 1979 and Moscow's unhelpful attitude throughout.

Symptomatic of the soured state of Soviet relations with the United States was the imbroglio over Cuba — it was hardly a crisis — that erupted in July 1979. Soon after President Carter returned from his Vienna meeting with Brezhnev, reports surfaced in Washington of a Soviet military buildup in Cuba. The administration's mishandling of the issue led to an escalation of tensions with Moscow out of all proportion to any substantive threat. Terming the Soviet combat brigade of 2600 men, 40 tanks, 60 armored personnel carriers, and other equipment an "unacceptable" military presence, Carter apparently expected the Kremlin to make some token concessions or conciliatory statements assuring the United States of the nonthreatening character of these troops, if only in the interest of strengthening his hand against the opponents of SALT II in the U.S. Senate. But Moscow obdurately denied that any buildup had taken place, insisting that the Soviet military presence in Cuba had not significantly changed since the 1962 Khrushchev-Kennedy understanding that settled the Cuban missile crisis.

An editorial in *Pravda* set the Soviet tone:

> A hostile campaign with regard to Cuba, the latest of a whole number, has recently been started in Washington again. This time it is being built up around allegations about the appearance in Cuba of 'Soviet combat units.'
>
> Aggravating the situation and trying to give a semblance of truth to these contentions, the American propaganda media are making great play with all kinds of 'details' which they themselves have invented . . . . Alarmist statements on this matter have also been made by a number of members of the U.S. Congress . . . .
>
> In this connection the need arises to recall the true state of affairs concerning Soviet military personnel in Cuba. For seventeen years now, a training center has existed in Cuba at which Soviet military personnel have helped Cuban servicemen to master Soviet military equipment used by the Cuban armed forces. Neither the number nor the functions of the said Soviet

personnel have changed throughout all these years. All contentions about
the arrival in Cuba of 'organized Soviet combat units' are totally groundless . . . .

It is also perfectly clear that the Soviet military personnel in Cuba do
not and cannot pose any threat, either as regards their size or their functions,
to the United States or any other country.[11]


Moscow refused to budge and successfully faced down Washington's efforts
to pressure a change in the size and character of the Soviet military presence
in Cuba. Only the advent of a more serious crisis in Iran brought a
temporary end to the issue.

During the 1970s, however, all was not tension and disagreement.
After Nixon's 1972 visit to Moscow, the two countries concluded a series
of agreements covering such diverse fields as science, public health, culture,
space, housing, agriculture, oceanography, and nuclear energy. A particularly notable agreement was the U.S.-Soviet grain agreement of October
20, 1975.

In the early years of the decade, Soviet grain production fell far below
expected levels and necessitated large-scale imports, mainly from the
United States. In 1972–1973, thanks to shrewd Soviet business tactics and
inefficient U.S. government accounting procedures, the Soviet government
bought cheaply in the American market, and the U.S. government inad-
vertently subsidized Soviet grain purchases. The resulting public furor
greatly embarrassed Washington. To preclude a recurrence of the great
Soviet "grain robbery," regularize commercial arrangements, and stabilize
prices with a minimum dislocation of the American domestic market,
Washington insisted on a more controlled contractual arrangement. The
two governments concluded a five-year agreement in October 1975, covering the period from October 1, 1976, to September 30, 1981. Under
this agreement, the Soviet government accepted to "purchase from private
commercial sources, for shipment in each twelve-month period beginning
October 1, 1976, six million metric tons of wheat and corn, in approximately equal proportions, grown in the United States." The USSR may
buy an additional quantity of up to two million metric tons in any twelve-
month period without consultation (in 1979 it purchased about twenty-five
million tons). All purchases and sales are made at the market price prevailing at the time of purchase or sale and in accordance with normal
commercial terms. In addition, the USSR agreed to have a certain percentage of the grains transported in American ships.

Commercially, the agreement was profitable for the United States.
Advocates of a tougher line toward the USSR repeatedly urged that grain
purchases be linked to Soviet behavior that is consonant with détente, but
not until the Afghan crisis did Carter resort to the food weapon. On

January 4, 1980, in response to the Soviet military intervention in Afghanistan, he announced the cancellation of shipments of seventeen million metric tons of grain beyond the normal eight-million-ton Soviet allotment, a halt of sales of high-technology computers and sophisticated oil-drilling equipment, and the curtailment of Soviet fishing quotas in U.S. waters.

At the end of the 1970s, the Soviet leadership found its relationship with the United States jarred by tension and beset by uncertainty. Compared to the optimistic outlook for forging a special relationship with the United States that characterized the Politburo's mood in March 1971, at the time of the twenty-fourth congress of the CPSU, the perception at the end of the decade was one of foreboding about the future of SALT, arms reduction in Europe, trade, and rivalry in the Third World. In James Reston's words: "At the beginning of the 70's, the United States and the Soviet Union were talking with each other about their common interests. At the beginning of the 80's, they are talking again as they did in the 40's and 50's about their differences."[12]

The prospects for Soviet-American relations are perhaps best captured in a joke. It seems that Hua Gofeng, Carter, and Brezhnev were talking to God. Hua Gofeng asked, "When will China become a modern industrial nation, a superpower the equal of the Soviet Union and the United States?" "In fifty years," God said, and Hua started to cry, because he would not be alive to see that glorious day. "When," asked Carter, "will the United States become independent in energy and again recognized as the undisputed leader of the Western world?" "In fifty years," said God, and Carter started to cry, because he knew he would not live to see that day. Then Brezhnev asked God, "When will the Soviet Union and the United States be friends, working together in a spirit of friendly cooperation and mutual recognition of each other's vital interests and in a way designed to strengthen international peace and stability?"

And God started to cry.

## Notes

1. *Khrushchev Remembers* (Boston: Little, Brown, 1970), 546–547.

2. Joseph G. Whelan, *Soviet Diplomacy and Negotiating Behavior: Emerging New Context for U.S. Diplomacy* (Washington, D.C.: Committee on Foreign Affairs, 1979), 360–361.

3. John P. Hardt, "Soviet Commercial Relations and Political Change," in Robert A. Bauer (ed.), *The Interaction of Economics and Foreign Policy* (Charlottesville: University of Virginia Press, 1975), 57.

4. "Mirnoe sosushchestvovanie" [Peaceful Coexistence], *Diplomaticheskii slovar'* [*Diplomatic Dictionary*], Vol. II (Moscow: Politizdat, 1961), 299.

5. *Soviet News,* no. 4107 (September 8, 1959), 142.

6. *The Military Balance 1979–1980* (London: International Institute for Strategic Studies, 1979), 5.

7. *London Observer,* November 12, 1978.

8. *Washington Post,* December 24, 1978.

9. Paul H. Nitze, "Assuring Strategic Stability in an Era of Detente," *Foreign Affairs,* vol. 54, no. 2 (January 1976), 217–218.

10. Statement at a press conference on March 31, 1977.

11. *Pravda,* September 11, 1979.

12. *New York Times,* December 30, 1979.

## Selected Bibliography

ARBATOV, GEORGII. *The War of Ideas in Contemporary International Relations.* Moscow: Progress Publishers, 1973.

BARNET, RICHARD J. *The Giants: Russia and America.* New York: Simon and Schuster, 1977.

BELL, CORAL. *The Diplomacy of Detente: The Kissinger Era.* New York: St. Martin's Press, 1977.

BYRNES, ROBERT F. *Soviet-American Academic Exchanges 1958–1975.* Bloomington: Indiana University Press, 1976.

GADDIS, JOHN LEWIS. *Russia, the Soviet Union and The United States: An Interpretive History.* New York: John Wiley, 1978.

GAMSON, WILLIAM A., and ANDRE MODIGLIANI. *Untangling the Cold War: A Strategy for Testing Rival Theories.* Boston: Little, Brown, 1971.

GIBERT, STEPHEN P. *Soviet Images of America.* New York: Crane, Russak, 1977.

GOODMAN, ELLIOT R. *The Soviet Design for a World State.* New York: Columbia University Press, 1960.

HALLE, LOUIS J. *The Cold War as History.* New York: Harper & Row, 1967.

KISSINGER, HENRY. *White House Years.* Boston: Little, Brown, 1979.

LARSON, THOMAS B. *Soviet-American Rivalry.* New York: Norton, 1978.

ROCK, VINCENT P. *A Strategy of Interdependence: A Program for Control of Conflict Between the U.S. and the Soviet Union.* New York: Scribner's, 1964.

RUMMEL, R. J. *Peace Endangered: The Reality of Detente.* Beverly Hills, Calif.: Sage, 1976.

RUSSELL, JEREMY. *Energy as a Factor in Soviet Foreign Policy.* Farnborough, Hants: Saxon House, 1976.

SCHWARTZ, MORTON. *Soviet Perceptions of the United States.* Berkeley: University of California Press, 1978.

SHULMAN, MARSHALL D. *Beyond the Cold War.* New Haven: Yale University Press, 1966.

SIVACHEV, NIKOLAI, and NIKOLAI N. YAKOVLEV. *Russia and the United States: U.S.-Soviet Relations from the Soviet Point of View.* Chicago: University of Chicago Press, 1979.

ULAM, ADAM B. *The Rivals: America and Russia Since World War II.* New York: Viking, 1971.

U.S. CONGRESS. SENATE. COMMITTEE ON FOREIGN RELATIONS. *Perceptions: Relations Between the United States and the Soviet Union.* Washington, D. C.: Government Printing Office, 1979.

WEEKS, ALBERT L. *The Troubled Detente.* New York: New York University Press, 1977.

WELCH, WILLIAM. *American Images of Soviet Foreign Policy.* New Haven: Yale University Press, 1970.

WHELAN, JOSEPH G. *Soviet Diplomacy and Negotiating Behavior: Emerging New Context for U.S. Diplomacy.* Washington, D.C.: Congressional Research Service, Library of Congress, 1979.

WILSON, JOAN HOFF. *Ideology and Economics: U.S. Relations with the Soviet Union, 1918–1933.* Columbia: University of Missouri Press, 1974.

YANOV, ALEXANDER. *Detente After Brezhnev: The Domestic Roots of Soviet Foreign Policy.* Berkeley, Calif.: Institute of International Studies, 1977.

————. *The Russian New Right: Right-Wing Ideologies in the Contemporary USSR.* Berkeley, Calif.: Institute of International Studies, 1978.

# 13

# Soviet Policy in the 1980s

      The Soviet Union is a global power whose central geostrategic position on the Eurasian land mass, growing capability to project military power, relentless probing of Western vulnerabilities, and readiness to exploit regional conflicts has made its policies crucial determinants of war and peace. It has achieved strategic equivalence with the United States and essential security in Europe, though perhaps not in the Far East. With the Third World ripe for imperial intrusion and increasingly important economically to the Western countries and Japan, the United States no longer asks itself whether Moscow intends to develop a comparable military capability and seek a presence in all parts of the globe; now it debates whether the Soviet Union is striving for military superiority and to what lengths the Soviet leadership is prepared to go to realize global ambitions.

      Western analysts offer various speculations about the roots of Soviet behavior. Some claim that it arises from Moscow's compulsive concern for security; others, from its ideologically engendered drive for "Pax Sovietica." There are those who accuse the Soviet Union of ruthless opportunism; others see a stubborn insistence on condominium with the United States in the evolving international system. Analysts have studied such themes as Soviet perceptions of the military balance and the future of Soviet-American relations; the Kremlin's view on multipolarity, interdependence, the energy crisis, and intra-NATO tensions; and Soviet conceptions of the relative strengths of the détentist and antidétentist forces in American political life. Though based on careful examinations of Soviet writings, these analyses cannot tell us how key decisions are made in the Kremlin, who stands with whom on what issue, and what values or priorities prompt the adoption of alternative A rather than B, C, or D. The wellspring of Kremlin policy remains as much a riddle as ever.

In many ways, the Brezhnev era has been the most successful in Soviet history. The average citizen enjoys the highest standard of living ever achieved under Soviet rule. The USSR has achieved strategic parity with the United States and recognition as a global power; it has strengthened its position in Eastern Europe, normalized relations with the Federal Republic of Germany, and enormously expanded economic relations with Western Europe and Japan, in the process obtaining much-needed technology and equipment; and it has become a central actor in the politics of the Third World. Only in the Far East — with China — has Soviet diplomacy been a failure, although the relationship with the United States must also be viewed as a keen disappointment, judged by the expectations of the early 1970s.

Notwithstanding the inability of the Brezhnev oligarchy to agree on measures for reforming Soviet society, in foreign policy its overall record is impressive. Brezhnev carried forward Khrushchev's policies and accommodated seemingly incompatible policies: repression in Czechoslovakia and rapprochement with Western Europe; significant strides in nuclear and missile capability and SALT talks with the United States; imperial expansion in the Middle East, Africa, and Southern Asia and dexterous maneuvering to avoid direct confrontation with the United States; pressure on China and attempts to restore unity in the world Communist movement; neo-Stalinism at home and greater receptivity to Western technology and cultural and scientific exchanges. To see only indecisiveness and weakness in such behavior is to undervalue the short-term dividends of a policy of chameleonlike adaptation to regional opportunities with little concern for the niceties of a coherent global design. Far from being indecisive, Brezhnev has realized or come within reach of a number of long-standing aims, such as the stabilization of the Soviet imperial system in Eastern Europe, the recognition by the Western powers of the territorial status quo, the exclusion of the Federal Republic of Germany from any access to nuclear weapons, the expansion of ties with Western Europe, the projection of Soviet power in the Third World, and the USSR's emergence to the status of a genuine global power.

But at the end of the 1970s, in the waning moments of his era, Brezhnev found Soviet relations with the United States strained as they had not been for almost a decade. Détente was in limbo, and the growing uneasiness of many Muslim countries was increased by the Soviet move into Afghanistan.

What of the 1980s and beyond? Any attempt to speculate about probable Soviet foreign policy would require a lengthy examination of all the options and their underlying assumptions regarding the domestic and external environment, which is beyond the scope of the present study. Soviet policy is not formulated in a vacuum. It is a result not only of capabilities but also of opportunities, and of the political costs inherent in them. How many Communist coups such as the one in Afghanistan in April 1978 will tempt the Kremlin to intervene militarily to ensure their survival and, while improving the USSR's geostrategic position, seriously exacerbate relations with the United States and increase international tensions? How far will Moscow go in exploiting instability in Iran and Pakistan? Or in subsidizing groups whose aim is the overthrow of the pro-Western regimes on the Arabian Peninsula? Soviet policymakers must calculate the probable response of the United States to any initiative to further imperial aspirations that they might contemplate. To Moscow, Washington has been highly unpredictable and inconsistent in recent years, a situation that, if likely to continue for the foreseeable future, must inevitably color Soviet behavior.

One crucial determinant of Soviet policy will be the internal condition of the USSR. We know as a general proposition that foreign policy is a function of domestic politics — of the outlook and stability of the ruling elite, the dilemmas arising from economic, social, and ethnic problems, the contradictions between the political pressures for repression and the economic requirements for relaxation, and so forth. How will these constrain the leadership in the 1980s?

There is sound basis for the assumption that Soviet domestic problems will be more numerous and difficult to resolve in the future than in earlier periods. Whereas under Lenin and Stalin the quest for the internal transformation of Soviet society and the absorption with national security loomed large in Kremlin thinking, under Brezhnev neither has had the particular importance it once held because both have basically been achieved. The Soviet Union is a modern industrial state with strategically secure borders. Another invasion is most improbable. Soviet institutions are solidly entrenched and stable, and the Soviet leadership is able to produce guns and potatoes.

But agriculture is a perennial problem which is readily manageable only as long as huge imports of grain from the United States, Canada, and Australia are possible. The rate of economic growth is slowly declining in the fields of both energy and industry, prompting the government in late 1979 to issue stern decrees calling for increased production of oil, coal, natural gas, and nuclear energy. Although the USSR is the world's largest producer of petroleum (and the possessor of enormous reserves of oil and valuable minerals), according to CIA estimates its export surplus is declining, and it may become a net importer of oil by the mid-1980s, competing with the West for available supplies and further inflating energy costs. Industry is experiencing shortages of power, transportation bottlenecks, labor shortages, declines in productivity, and costly inefficiency. The technological gap between the West and the Soviet Union is as great in many areas (though not in sectors affecting military capability) as it was a generation ago. Demographically speaking, a decline in the birthrate of the Slavic portion of the Soviet population, coupled with an increase in that of the non-Slavic components (about 25 percent of the total) and a concomitant increase of their societal expectations, may intensify discord among nationality groups. Some Western experts believe this to be the tinder that could cause the regime much trouble.

Will these problems inhibit activism abroad? Will they severely limit the ability of the leadership to pursue an ambitious global policy? To these portentous and unanswerable questions must be added that of the succession. Who is going to rule in the Soviet Union? Brezhnev and his cohorts came of political age during the Stalinist era; they survived the great purges, World War II, and the traumas of de-Stalinization, desatellitization, and polycentrism. They brought stability to Soviet institutions and a slowly rising standard of living to the Soviet people. The next generation of leaders, now entrenched in the lower and middle echelons of the party and government, is waiting expectantly in the wings. Its attitudes, its ambitions, its priorities are unknown. One can devise scenarios for the liberalization and reform of Soviet society and a moderate foreign policy designed to improve relations with the United States; but just as easily and perhaps with greater realism, one can make the case for the obverse — namely, that the next generation will resort to repression rather than relaxation to cope with the myriad problems, that bureaucratic autocracy will favor the party, the KGB, and the military and preserve the Brezhnev legacy intact. No leadership deliberately courts the unanticipated consequences of extensive change.

The next generation of Soviet leaders will be better educated than those currently in power, but no technocratic determinism necessarily predisposes a highly trained elite toward greater prudence and humility in foreign affairs. (After all, it was "the best and the brightest," not the professional military, who tragically mired the United States in a wasteful and debilitating war in Vietnam.) Indeed, well-trained, self-confident leaders may be more assertive in competing with the United States; they may be even more chauvinistic — and Russian nationalism is a powerful sentiment, one that is not likely to foster greater cooperation with the outside world. At its best, Russian nationalism is egocentric, exclusivist, intolerant. The controversy between Westernizer and Slavophile (a group of nineteenth-century writers and philosophers who believed in orthodoxy, the czar, and Russia and who shared a profound distrust of Western ideas and institutions) lives on in the Soviet establishment.

For example, one analyst suggests that the kind of thinking characteristic of Andrei Zhdanov, Stalin's lieutenant and chief spokesman for hardline policies, is making a comeback and gaining adherents in the upper echelons of the CPSU. At the twenty-fifth congress in March 1976, the rehabilitation of Zhdanov was evidence "of the presence within the Party of individuals to whom a Zhdanovite, and hence Stalinist, outlook and approach to foreign and domestic policy are congenial. These people share Zhdanov's view of the aggressive intentions of and ideological threat posed by the capitalist world. They would like to revive many of the policies associated with Zhdanov and Stalin."[1] They view détente with the United States as illusory and the emergent Eurocommunism as a subversive threat to the Soviet position in Eastern Europe. The implications for Soviet foreign policy of such a group coming to power could lead to a revived Cold War. This does not mean that nuclear war is closer or more probable, but if such is indeed the shape of Soviet politics to come, it does foreshadow a time of tension between Moscow and the rest of the world.

The notion of an internally troubled Soviet Union gradually democratizing its society and softening its foreign policy seems as chimerical as that of the convergence of capitalist and Communist systems. What most scenarios presume is essential continuation of Brezhnev's foreign policy — an amalgam of caution and low-level risk-taking, of interest in détente but not to the extent of resisting temptations to expand influence and weaken the United States.

In speculating about what the most likely Soviet policy in the 1980s will be, Western analysts tend to impute their mentality and reasoning to Soviet leaders. However, there is no convincing evidence that the Kremlin's policy of seeking a general relaxation of tensions with the West in the 1960s and 1970s was due to the ascendancy of a détentist faction over an antidétentist one. Such toying with typologies is standard fare in Western circles, where political analysis is often blurred by political preference. Charles Yost (a former U.S. diplomat), for one, marshals no evidence for his contention that when Washington toughens its positions, it strengthens the hard-liners in the Kremlin — "a particularly unfortunate effect at this moment when the succession to Brezhnev is being contested."[2] The implication is clearly that American leaders can affect the outcome of the struggle for power in the Soviet hierarchy. Attempts to impute to a new generation of Soviet leaders a reformist bent which is necessarily linked to a propensity toward détente in foreign policy must be seen as mere speculations, not as the result of serious research or empirical evidence.

In general, Western analyses of Soviet policy and intentions suffer from numerous fallacies, described by Raymond L. Garthoff, a senior fellow at the Brookings Institution, former Foreign Service officer, and longtime specialist on Soviet affairs as follows: (1) when in doubt, assume the worst; (2) never estimate intentions, only capabilities; (3) assume that Soviet leaders always (or never) have the same perceptions and aims as their Western counterparts; (4) assume that the Soviets never (or always) mean what they say; (5) consider Soviet capabilities to be larger than are needed — or than they believe are needed — for deterrence; (6) assert a Soviet intention to seek military superiority; and (7) believe that the "facts" speak for themselves, ignoring selection and definition of data.[3]

If it is important to avoid preconceived conceptual traps, it is equally essential to learn from the Soviet record. A few propositions may be gleaned from the Kremlin's behavior in foreign affairs.

First, the Soviet leadership believes in the utility of force as a means of preserving or promoting strategic interests. The Kremlin is not embarrassed by its power, nor unduly worried about international public opinion. It is, of course, willing to utilize diplomacy and negotiation to achieve its goals, but Moscow has demonstrated — in Eastern Europe in 1953, 1956, and 1968 and increasingly in the Third World — an equal readiness to use the powerful force that it has built up. Its military intervention in Afghanistan in December 1979, when for the first time it used force in a Third World country in order to effect a change of leadership and secure the Soviet position within the country, is but the most recent evidence of this readiness.

Second, the Kremlin leadership is wedded to the preservation of its imperial system; it has little interest in interdependence or involvement with the outside world beyond what it sees as necessary for strengthening its own society. Moscow may not be isolationist, but neither is it internationalist in the Western sense of the word.

Third, Soviet leaders respect power and correlate power with diplomatic moves; they disdain weakness and equivocation. They are not captivated by appeals to friendship and humanitarian ideals. What motivates Moscow is a restless search for strategic advantages — an imperial ambition that is the other side of the obsessiveness with security. To the extent that Soviet leaders perceive a weak, vacillating, and musclebound United States which is stymied by domestic bickering, unsure of its priorities, and unwilling or unable to project military power in defense of clients or allies, they will exploit existing opportunities. According to James Reston, "from the Sea of Japan to the Indian Ocean to the oilfields of the Persian Gulf, the Soviets have been slowly but carefully trying to change the balance of power in their favor, and this is a strategic decision of considerable world importance."[4] Moscow will be influenced not by what Washington wants, but by what it can do.

Finally, the Soviets have a different set of values which feeds the all-pervasive political and strategic rivalry. Brezhnev told the 1976 party congress: "Détente does not in the slightest abolish, nor can it abolish or change, the laws of the class struggle . . . we do not conceal the fact that we see détente as a way of creating more favorable conditions for the peaceful building of socialism and communism." As long as the reality they see offers corroborative evidence for the continuation of ideological struggle and all that it implies, the Soviet leaders will be encouraged to use their relationship with the West to secure an increasing imbalance of forces in their favor in the military, economic, and political spheres so as to advance the "profound revolutionary changes" that they believe to be characteristic of the present epoch. There is no writ for a relaxation of tension and an agreement to live and let live.

Under Khrushchev and Brezhnev, foreign policy toward the non-Soviet world became more important, and this should continue in the 1980s. There are no isolationists in the Kremlin. Step by step, Brezhnev has advanced Soviet interests: preservation of hegemony in Eastern Europe; avoidance of nuclear war; expansion and modernization of the USSR's nuclear and conventional military capability; perpetuation of a favorable balance of power in Europe; uneasy coexistence with China; the search for a special relationship with the United States; and a forward policy in the Third World. Confident of its power but aware of the problems, the next generation of Soviet leaders will most likely continue along this line. Its choices, however, will depend both on the external environment that it finds and on the severity of the domestic difficulties that demand attention.

Moscow pursues peaceful engagement in Europe and competitive rivalry in the Third World. It sees the world as a basically hostile, uncertain place in which strategic aims often conflict with economic needs. Its approach to the various and complex forces that it perceives as shaping the evolution of the international system derives from assumptions and aims that are different from Washington's, and in this are contained the seeds of struggle and crisis. In dealing with the West, Soviet leaders seem able to keep their options open while keeping their strategic objectives clear. The West can do no less.

# Notes

1. Dina Spechler, *Zhdanovism, Eurocommunism, and Cultural Reaction in the USSR.* Research Paper no. 34 (Jerusalem: Soviet and East European Research Centre, March 1979), 6, 35.

2. *Christian Science Monitor,* June 27, 1978.

3. Raymond L. Garthoff, "On Estimating and Imputing Intentions," *International Security,* vol. 2, no. 3 (Winter 1978), 22–32.

4. *New York Times,* December 30, 1979.

## Selected Bibliography

ADOMEIT, HANNES, and ROBERT BOARDMAN (eds.). *Foreign Policymaking in Communist Countries.* Farnborough, Hants: Saxon House, 1979.

AZRAEL, JEREMY R. (ed.). *Soviet Nationality Policies and Practices.* New York: Praeger, 1978.

CALDWELL, LAWRENCE T., and WILLIAM DIEBOLD. *Soviet-American Relations in the 1980s: Superpower Politics and East-West Trade.* New York: McGraw-Hill, 1980.

ERAN, ODED. *Mezhdunarodniki: An Assessment of Professional Experties in the Making of Soviet Foreign Policy.* Tel Aviv: Turtledove Press, 1979.

HUNTER, HOLLAND (ed.). *The Future of the Soviet Economy: 1978–1985.* Boulder, Colo.: Westview Press, 1978.

INTERNATIONAL INSTITUTE FOR STRATEGIC STUDIES. *Prospects of Soviet Power in the 1980s.* Adelphi Papers nos. 151 and 152: London: International Institute for Strategic Studies, 1979.

NITZE, PAUL H, et al. *Securing the Seas: The Soviet Naval Challenge and Western Alliance Options.* Boulder, Colo.: Westview Press, 1979.

RUSSELL, JEREMY. *Energy as a Factor in Soviet Foreign Policy.* Lexington, Mass.: Saxon House, 1976.

THOMAS, JOHN R., and URSULA M. KRUSE-VAUCIENNE (eds.). *Soviet Science and Technology: Domestic and Foreign Perspectives.* Washington: George Washington University, 1977.

U.S. CONGRESS. HOUSE COMMITTEE ON INTERNATIONAL RELATIONS. *The Soviet Union: Internal Dynamics of Foreign Policy, Present and Future.* Hearings before the Subcommittee on Europe and the Middle East. 95th Cong., 1st session, September-October 1977 (Washington, D.C.: Government Printing Office, 1978).

# Index

Other books by Alvin Z. Rubinstein

SOVIET FOREIGN POLICY TOWARD WESTERN EUROPE (co-editor)

RED STAR ON THE NILE: THE SOVIET–EGYPTIAN INFLUENCE
  RELATIONSHIP SINCE THE JUNE WAR

SOVIET AND CHINESE INFLUENCE IN THE THIRD WORLD (editor)

THE FOREIGN POLICY OF THE SOVIET UNION

SOVIET AND AMERICAN POLICIES IN THE UNITED NATIONS:
  A TWENTY-FIVE YEAR PERSPECTIVE (co-editor)

YUGOSLAVIA AND THE NONALIGNED WORLD

THE CHALLENGE OF POLITICS (co-editor)

SOVIET WRITINGS ON SOUTHEAST ASIA (co-editor)

COMMUNIST POLITICAL SYSTEMS

THE SOVIETS IN INTERNATIONAL ORGANIZATIONS: CHANGING POLICY
  TOWARD DEVELOPING COUNTRIES, 1953–1963